Professional JSP Tag Libraries

Simon Brown

Wrox Press Ltd. ®

Professional JSP Tag Libraries

Published by Wrox Press Ltd,
Arden House, 1102 Warwick Road, Acocks Green,
Birmingham, B27 6BH, UK
Printed in USA
ISBN 1861006-21-7

Trademark Acknowledgements

Wrox has endeavored to provide trademark information about all the companies and products mentioned in this book by the appropriate use of capitals. However, Wrox cannot guarantee the accuracy of this information.

Credits

Author
Simon Brown

Managing Editor
Adam MacLean

Commissioning Editor
Chanoch Wiggers

Technical Editors
Dipali Chittar
Kalpana Garde
Kedar Kamat
Matthew Moodie
Nilesh Parmar

Project Manager
Emma Batch

Author Agent
Nicola Phillips

Production Coordinator
Abbie Forletta

Indexing
Andrew Criddle

Technical Reviewers
Phil Powers De George
Kapil Apshankar
Sachin Khanna
Matt Staples
Sam Dalton
Sue Spielman
Don Reamey
Ramesh Mani
Steve Baker
Ersin Eser
Tony Loton
Jim Macintosh

Proof Reader
Dev Lunsford

Illustrations
Santosh Haware

Cover
Chris Morris

About the Author

Simon is a Technical Architect with Concise, a J2EE solutions provider based in London. He has been using Java since 1996, during which time he has been involved with many Java developments having acted as technical lead, mentor and trainer. Outside of work he has spoken at several Java events including JavaOne, has been published in JavaWorld magazine and co-authored the 2nd edition of Professional JSP and more recently, Professional Java Servlets 2.3.

Simon graduated from the University of Reading in 1996 with a First Class BSc (Hons) degree in Computer Science. He has also attained many Sun Certifications, including the Enterprise Architect for J2EE, Web Component Developer for J2EE and Developer for the Java 2 Platform.

Feel free to e-mail any questions or comments to projsptags@simongbrown.com.

There are many people that I would like to thank for their help in writing this book over the past few months. First of all a huge thank you to everybody at Wrox, especially Chanoch and Matt for all of their input and inspiration. In addition to this, I would like to thank all of the technical review team, Sam for looking at some of the (very) early drafts and also Nicola who speaks much better French than I do.

Last, but by no means least, is my loving fiancée Kirstie – this is dedicated to you.

LONDON

Table of Contents

LONDON

Introduction

Welcome to *Professional JSP Tag Libraries.* This book is designed to help newcomers and experienced JSP developers alike learn about and get the most from this exciting technology that has the power to revolutionize the way that you'll write JSP based applications.

Since its inception, **Java Servlets** has been an important server-side technology for the development of scalable and secure web-based applications and components. With the introduction of **JavaServer Pages** (JSP), these two very complementary technologies are now viewed as one of the most important and widely used server-side technology sets for building web-based applications that are not only secure and scalable, but also well designed, flexible and maintainable.

JSP Tag Extensions, or **custom tags**, are a powerful addition to the JSP specification that allow sophisticated actions to be encapsulated into simple XML-like tags that can be used on any JSP page. These tags can then be bundled up into **tag libraries** for use and reuse on other pages, other web applications and in other organizations. Up until recently, such actions have typically been written using Java code in scriptlets on the page. While this achieves the end-goal, embedding Java code (and therefore logic) in the page does present issues around maintainability, reusability, extensibility, and readability.

Custom tags are a mechanism for moving this code away from the page and into reusable components, therefore providing gains in maintainability and reusability of the code, and also readability of the page.

This book covers all features of the tag API, including:

- Simple tags and the use of attributes to further customize functionality
- Tags that can programmatically evaluate their body content
- Tags that can introduce scripting variables into the page
- Tags that can be used to evaluate their body content many times to provide iteration
- Tags that can manipulate and transform their body content
- Tags that can cooperate on the page

An underlying theme throughout all of the chapters in this book are those of maintainability and reusability, showing you how to best use custom tags to achieve the most benefit on your JSP projects. In addition to this, however, are chapters that are specifically dedicated to discussing some of the more theoretical facets of tag development, including:

- When to use custom tags and when to use JavaBeans to encapsulate functionality for use on JSP pages
- How OO and component-based development relate to designing custom tags
- How the intended audience can affect the design and development of tags and tag libraries
- Best practices associated with the tag lifecycle
- How validation can be used to provide more robust tag libraries
- A look at the deployment options available and some of the common errors that occur at deployment time

Throughout this book, and to underpin all of the discussions and techniques, real-world code examples are used to demonstrate the principles in practice. By the end of the book, you'll be in a position to use custom tags to help write more maintainable, readable JSP pages with less effort, while at the same time building up a library of useful, reusable components.

What This Book Covers

The book begins with a discussion of the introduction of JSP as a technology. This discussion includes the benefits and drawbacks in terms of readability, maintainability, power, and ease of development. We will look at why we need **JSP Tags** and where we would choose tags over other mechanisms for dynamic generation of data such as JavaBeans and scriptlets.

The section assumes some knowledge of Servlets and JSP. We will put in reminders as we go along but the pace will be fast.

In chapter 2, we will write our first tag. We will learn the lifecycle of tags, the interfaces that define those lifecycles, and the environment that tags live in. This includes a look at the resources that are available to tags, including scoped variables and the implicit JSP variables.

We will then look at how to define **Tag Libraries**, collections of tags that are linked in functionality, and how to deploy our first tag. We'll finish by discussing **Tag Attributes**, one mechanism for passing information to tags, in order to customize the way they work to the situation at hand, thus making them more flexible.

In Chapter 3, we will discuss how a tag can interact with its **Body Content**; a tag's body content may have special meaning to the tag, or be otherwise manipulated by the tag to create dynamic content in the resulting page. This can be used to secure sections of the site, repeat or iterate through values, and otherwise programmatically include and exclude page content.

Chapter 4 covers **Scripting Variables**. If you are familiar with JSP, you will know that scripting variables are pieces of data that are available in the JSP page. JSP Tags can introduce scripting variables into the page, and can be customized by having scripting variables passed to them as attribute values. This chapter covers the way in which JSP Tags can interact with local data on the page.

Chapter 5 covers **Iteration** using variables. Iterating through collections of data is a technique that without JSP Tags introduces the most confusion into the page. Tags can be used to iterate through data keeping the JSP Page cleaner, so that page designers can modify the look of the site without danger of breaking important functionality.

Body Tags are the mechanism for conditionally including body content and iterating over tag body content. In Chapter 6 we will see where this mechanism should be used over its simpler, but ultimately less powerful brother, iteration.

Chapter 7 will cover **cooperation** between tags. Up until this point, the book only covers how tags can interact with the page they are in. When tags are also allowed to interact with each other, the possibilities are endless and we will discuss when to best apply this technique.

Chapter 8 covers **Tag Patterns**. The power of tags means that a given problem may have several solutions. Choosing between them is a matter of experience and so we will try and outline best use scenarios of using tags, how to best design cooperation between tags, generation of formatted data and what problems to avoid, naming conventions, using resource bundles, how to approach the replacement of standard HTML tags with JSP Tags, and finally accessing Enterprise Resources on the page including a look at accessing EJBs and messaging infrastructures.

Chapter 9 will continue this theme with a look at the **design principles** of tags. We will look at OO design principles, and Component Based Development. We will investigate what makes a good tag, and how to handle exceptional conditions from a tag. We will also cover in more detail how to best use attributes to maximize customization, reusability, and performance. The chapter finishes with a look at the tradeoffs in performance in Tags and discusses the performance implications of using tags vs the more traditional scriptlet-based JSP development.

Chapter 10 discusses **Validation** of tag usage on the page, and tag deployment. We will investigate how to make our tags usable to those who are not familiar with programming concepts by looking at the granularity of functionality offered by tags, the names we call them, and the ways that we can limit misuse of tags on the page. The second half of the chapter will discuss deployment; this will include how to reduce dependencies, and how to customize tags post-deployment using properties files and servlet context initialization. We will finish with some information on testing on multiple containers and troubleshooting tips.

Chapter 11 puts all of the parts learned so far in the book together to create a **case study** like chapter. This will show a fully functional web site designed entirely with tags.

Finally, in Chapter 12, we will discuss some **third party libraries**. Using third party libraries can be very useful as they can save much work, and may sometimes be ultimately more stable and trustworthy. We will look specifically at three: the Struts library, Jakarta Tag libs, and JSPTL – the proposed standard tag library.

Conventions

We have used a number of different styles of text and layout in the book to help differentiate between the different kinds of information. Here are examples of the styles we use and an explanation of what they mean:

Bullets appear indented, with each new bullet marked as follows:

- **Important Words** are in a bold type font
- Words that appear on the screen in menus like the File or Window are in a similar font to the one that you see on screen
- Keys that you press on the keyboard, like *Ctrl* and *Enter*, are in italics

Code has several fonts. If it's a word that we're talking about in the text, for example, when discussing the `if...else` loop, it's in `this font`. If it's a block of code that you can type in as a program and run, then it's also in a gray box:

```
public void someFunction() {
  return someValue;
}
```

Sometimes you'll see code in a mixture of styles, like this:

```
// If we haven't reached the end, return true, otherwise
// set the position to invalid, and return false.
pos++;
if (pos < 4)
   return true;
else {
   pos = -1;
   return false;
}
```

The code with a white background is code we've already looked at and that we don't wish to examine further.

Advice, hints, and background information come in an italicized, indented font like this.

Important pieces of information come in boxes like this.

We demonstrate the syntactical usage of methods, properties (and so on) using the following format:

```
javac [-classpath .] MyTag.java
```

Here square braces indicate optional parameters.

Technical Support

If you wish to directly query a problem in the book with an expert who knows it in detail then e-mail support@wrox.com with the title of the book and the last four numbers of the ISBN in the subject field. A typical e-mail should include the following things:

- The **name**, **last four digits of the ISBN**, and **page number** of the problem in the Subject field.
- Your **name**, **contact information**, and the **problem** in the body of the message.

We *won't* send you junk mail. We need the details to save your time and ours. When you send an e-mail message, it will go through the following chain of support:

- **Customer Support** – Your message is delivered to one of our customer support staff, who are the first people to read it. They have files on most frequently asked questions and will answer anything general about the book or the web site immediately.
- **Editorial** – Deeper queries are forwarded to the technical editor responsible for that book. They have experience with the programming language or particular product, and are able to answer detailed technical questions on the subject. Once an issue has been resolved, the editor can post the errata to the web site.
- **The Authors** – Finally, in the unlikely event that the editor cannot answer your problem, he or she will forward the request to the author. We do try to protect the author from any distractions to their writing, however, we are quite happy to forward specific requests to them. All Wrox authors help with the support on their books. They will mail the customer and the editor with their response, and again all readers should benefit.

The Wrox support process can only offer support to issues that are directly pertinent to the content of our published title. Support for questions that fall outside the scope of normal book support is provided via the community lists of our http://p2p.wrox.com/ forum.

p2p.wrox.com

For author and peer discussion join, the **P2P mailing lists**. Our unique system provides **programmer to programmer™** contact on mailing lists, forums, and newsgroups, all *in addition* to our one-to-one e-mail support system. Be confident that your query is being examined by the many Wrox authors, and other industry experts, who are present on our mailing lists. At p2p.wrox.com you will find a number of different lists that will help you, not only while you read this book, but also as you develop your own applications.

To subscribe to a mailing list just follow this these steps:

1. Go to http://p2p.wrox.com/.
2. Choose the appropriate category from the left menu bar.
3. Click on the mailing list you wish to join.

4. Follow the instructions to subscribe and fill in your e-mail address and password.
5. Reply to the confirmation e-mail you receive.
6. Use the subscription manager to join more lists and set your mail preferences.

LONDON

1

JSP and Tag Extensions

From a presentation perspective, the Java 2 Platform, Enterprise Edition (J2EE) consists of two different technologies for generating dynamic web content – **Java servlets** and **JavaServer Pages** (JSP). Servlets was the first of these technologies to appear, and with the introduction of the JSP technology, both are capable of generating the same results. What is different between the two is the paradigm used for building components – whether they build dynamic web pages, perform business processing, or provide web services. Servlets embed content into logic and carry out server side processing of logic, and JSP pages embed logic into content.

JSP pages are written using a syntax that is very similar to HTML, and therefore lend themselves well to generating dynamic web pages. Servlets-on the other hand-are built by writing a Java class and the Java code is ideally suited for creating highly programmatic content. Although it's the development perspective that we're interested in here, both JSP pages and servlets are proven techniques for generating dynamic content. However, the maintainability and readability can easily be compromised through mixing application level code with the content that is to be displayed.

This book will introduce **JSP tag extensions**, a powerful mechanism for encapsulating reusable functionality in JSP pages and a great way for writing more maintainable and readable pages. We'll start with a step-by-step guide that takes us through building our first tag before moving on to more advanced topics such as sharing information between tags and pages, controlling the page, accessing enterprise resources, and finally covering some design guidelines and considerations.

Let's first get ourselves acquainted with some JSP terminology:

- **Custom Tag**
  Refers to a single tag (defined and built by a JSP developer) which is used on the JSP page and the associated code that drives the logic behind the scenes

- **Tag Library**
  A collection of custom tags packaged together

Before we delve into building our first tag, let's take a look at what tags are and why we need them.

In this chapter we'll look at the two paradigms for generating dynamic content by showing how a simple dynamic web page can be generated with a Java servlet and a JSP page. In presenting these examples, we'll also look at some of the design and implementation issues surrounding both these approaches. Finally, we'll see how we can tackle some of these issues with the use of **JavaBeans** before introducing JSP tag extensions.

JSP tag extensions are generally considered an advanced JSP topic, and as such, a basic familiarity with Java servlets and JavaServer Pages is assumed. As we progress through the book, we will reiterate those servlet and JSP topics that are required from a tag perspective; however, further in-depth information can be found in other books in the Wrox Press Professional series:

- *Professional JavaServer Pages, 2nd edition (ISBN 1-861004-95-8)*
- *Professional Java Servlets 2.3 (ISBN 1-861005-61-X)*

Java Servlets

Java servlets are Java's answer to the Common Gateway Interface (CGI), for which the development is traditionally written in languages such as Perl, C, C++, and UNIX shell scripts. These CGI programs service HTTP requests usually in a process external to the web server, and generate content to send back to the client web browser. Typically, every request spawns a new process and this requires a large amount of resources in terms of processing power and memory. As a result, there is almost certainly a reduction in performance and scalability.

To address this, Java servlets run inside the web container, and use multiple threads to service many requests simultaneously. As the web container manages the threads that service the requests, the risk of a high load taking down the machine on which the container is running is greatly reduced.

Content, Presentation, and Business Logic

No matter which language is chosen, CGI programs and Java servlets are both typically written in a procedural way with one long method (or function) to generate the entire response. Of course other functions, methods, or objects may be used, but there is usually a single method that co-ordinates them and generates the response. This means that when writing a program where a web browser is used as the presentation medium, the following characteristics might be included in the source code:

- **Static content**
  For example HTML, including markup for formatting and layout
- **Presentation logic**
  Code affecting the presentation in some way, for example transformational or formatting information
- **Business logic**
  Code that looks up information or performs processing, for example validation

A Simple Java Servlet

To demonstrate what this means, let's look at an example Java servlet that finds the locale of the client and generates an HTML page that contains the current date in a format appropriate for that locale. The servlet is deliberately simple so that the complexity of the solution does not get in the way of the illustration.

When a user sends a request to this servlet, the resulting HTML page might look something like the following:

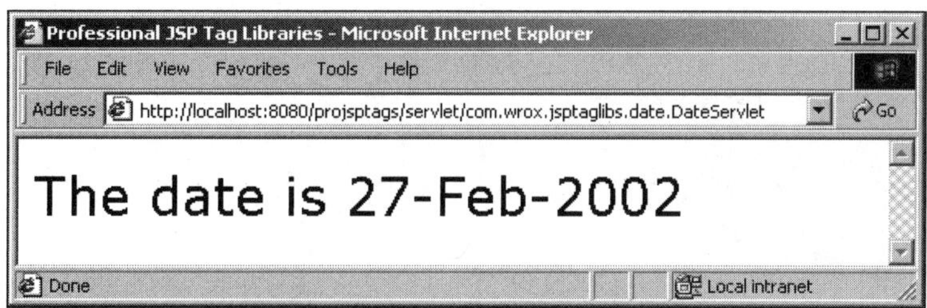

To show how this could be implemented as a servlet, consider the following Java code:

```
package com.wrox.jsptaglibs.date;

import java.io.IOException;
import java.io.PrintWriter;
import java.text.DateFormat;
import java.util.Date;
import java.util.Locale;

import javax.servlet.http.HttpServlet;
import javax.servlet.http.HttpServletRequest;
import javax.servlet.http.HttpServletResponse;
import javax.servlet.ServletException;

public class DateServlet extends HttpServlet {

  protected void doGet(HttpServletRequest req, HttpServletResponse res)
    throws ServletException, IOException {

    PrintWriter out = res.getWriter();
```

First we find the client's locale from the HTTP request, and create an appropriate `java.text.DateFormat` instance using the factory method `getDateInstance()` on the `DateFormat` class itself. Since we're making use of the client's locale, the output from this servlet will vary depending on where the user is based:

```
    // get the locale of the client and create an appropriate date format
    Locale loc = req.getLocale();
    DateFormat df = DateFormat.getDateInstance(DateFormat.MEDIUM, loc);
```

Following this we have both the static and dynamic content, which is embedded within `println()` statements. The markup, such as `<h1></h1>`, that provides the formatting and layout is also contained within these statements:

```
        out.println("<html>");

        out.println("<head>");
        out.println("<title>Professional JSP Tag Libraries</title>");
        out.println("<link rel=\"stylesheet\" href=\"../page.css\">");
        out.println("</head>");

        out.println("<body>");
        out.println("<h1>The date is ");
        out.println(df.format(new Date()));
        out.println("</h1>");
        out.println("</body>");

        out.println("</html>");

        out.flush();
        out.close();
    }
}
```

As we can see from this simple example, there is a single method that coordinates the generation of the response, and in which the various types of content and logic are embedded and intermingled.

> *Before we continue, you will notice that there is a reference to* `page.css` *in the servlet code above. This file is available with the code download for this book from* www.wrox.com*. It has merely been provided for its pleasing visual effect over the output in the many examples given here and in the remainder of the book, and so will not be discussed in the text; feel free to omit this and consequent references as has been done in the text, or include it, as has been done in the download code.*
>
> *To find out more about CSS (Cascading Style Sheets) please refer to the many online and dead tree documents on the subject.*

Maintainability

While the above servlet works and achieves the aim of outputting the date in the required format, there are some questions that arise:

- What happens if we need to change the content?
- What happens if we need to change the style and layout?
- What happens if we need to change the format of the date?

The answer to all of these questions is the same: any change to the generated code requires us to modify, recompile, and redeploy the servlet. Although it wouldn't take long with this simple example, the effort required for modifying any of the above-mentioned properties (or similar properties) of a larger and ultimately more complex page is greatly increased. In other words, the difficulty in maintaining our web application has greatly increased.

Add to this a requirement to modify a visual element of a web site and you can imagine the work involved in amending every single servlet in order to update the site.

Readability

This is not the end of the story, however, as embedding content within the source code (inside the `println()` statements in this case) affects another important factor – readability. Although not a large problem with our simple example, a larger servlet generating a much more complex response will usually consist of many lines of code to generate, format, and write out the generated HTML page. With lines and lines of appending, concatenating, and writing strings, the resulting Java code will become messy and eventually unreadable.

This is not a new problem and typically CGI programs have suffered in the same way. Java servlets address the issues around performance and scalability but not, it seems, around maintainability and readability. This is not to say that servlets aren't suited for building web applications, in fact it is quite the opposite. They are well suited to tasks such as controllers in a **Model-View-Controller** (MVC) architecture, as units of processing, or as single points of entry to filter out unauthenticated requests.

So what about the issues of maintainability and readability? We shall address these in the next section.

JavaServer Pages

As discussed at the onset of this chapter, Java servlets embed content into the logic, while JSP pages do the opposite – they embed logic into content. JSP is also a technology for generating dynamic content, although it is written as markup (for example HTML, XML, and so on) containing one or more of the following elements:

- Scriptlets
- Expressions
- Declarations
- Directives
- Actions (or tags)

Let's take a look at each of these in turn.

Scriptlets

Scriptlets are small blocks of sourcecode contained within the `<%` and `%>` delimiters:

```
<%
  String name = request.getParameter("name");
%>
```

Although the JSP specification currently requires that compliant JSP engines only provide support for scriptlets written in Java, there is potential for other languages to be supported in the future.

Expressions

Expressions are similar to scriptlets but return a value. Embedding a short Java expression between <%= and %> delimiters has the effect of writing the result of the expression back to the page, and hence the client:

```
<%= name %>
```

They are also used for providing request-time values to other actions on the page, but we'll leave this for the next chapter.

Declarations

In the same way that methods and variables can be declared on a class, methods and variables can also be declared on a JSP page. For example, we might want to declare a method in our JSP page that we can use in several places to save copying and pasting scriptlets. Declarations are made between <%! and %> delimiters:

```
<%!
  private int calculate(int a, int b) {
    ...
  }
%>
```

Directives

While expressions, scriptlets, and declarations are used to define the logic to be executed at run-time, directives are used to provide pages with information at translation time – when the JSP page is converted to a servlet. Directives can be used to specify the classes that are imported, to specify the error page used for catching exceptions, and, as we'll see later on, for importing tag libraries and making them available to use on the page. Although there are various types of directives, they are all written between <%@ and %> delimiters:

```
<%@ page import="java.util.Date" %>
```

Actions (or Tags)

The last type of elements that can be included in a JSP page are actions or tags, which further break down into standard and custom tags. The JSP specification currently defines several standard actions that must be provided by JSP compliant containers. These are simply a way of wrapping up reusable functionality and making it available to developers as tags on the page. These standard tags are identified by the use of the `jsp` prefix, examples of which include `<jsp:include/>` and `<jsp:useBean/>`. Soon we'll be seeing some examples of how these can be used.

Custom tags-on the other hand-are JSP tags that we write ourselves or are supplied by a third party.

The JSP Lifecycle

JSP technology is actually an extension of the Java servlets technology and although JSP pages are written as markup with all of these elements embedded within them, they are converted into the equivalent servlet to handle the request. Once a JSP page has been written and deployed onto a web server, the first request initiates the JSP lifecycle as shown in the following diagram:

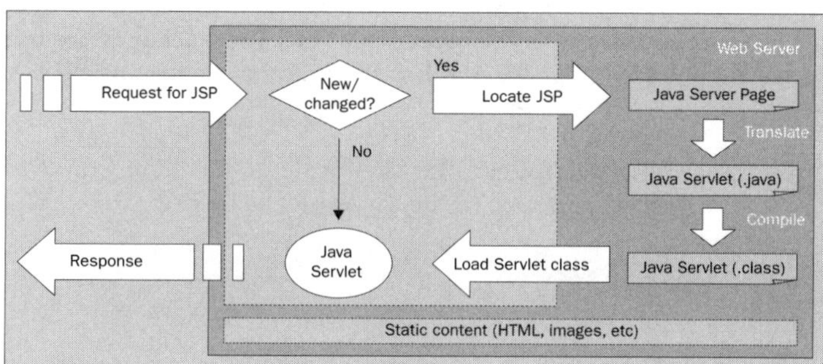

As we can see from the diagram, a request for a new or modified JSP page causes the web server to translate it into Java code representing the equivalent Java servlet. This can be a fairly complex step, but essentially what happens is that the entire JSP page is translated into a single method in the resulting servlet called `_jspService()`. Static content is wrapped up in `out.println()` calls while the sourcecode, which is contained within scriptlets and expressions, is inserted as is.

Once the Java code has been generated, it is compiled into a standard class file. The web server then loads this class, services the request, and finally returns the response to the client.

> *Although not shown in the diagram, some vendors of JSP compatible servers supply tools for pre-compiling JSP pages into their respective Java servlets. Here, the resulting servlet classes are packaged up and deployed rather than the JSP pages themselves. This is useful in those situations dealing with issues around licensing or intellectual property rights.*
>
> *Also, Java compilers are often deemed a security risk in a production environment because malicious code could be compiled and executed on the server. Finally, delivering the compiled servlets is useful where we wish to remove the initial performance hit of translating and compiling the JSP pages.*

A Simple JSP

Let's now take a look at the JSP equivalent of the Java servlet that we saw earlier on in the chapter. This JSP page generates the same response as the Java servlet, but this time the formatting code, the logic to find the client's locale, and the date format creation are embedded inside the HTML:

```
<%@ page language="java" isErrorPage="false" %>
<html>

  <head>
    <title>Professional JSP Tag Libraries</title>
  </head>
```

As we are using classes outside of the `java.lang` package, we must first import them using the page directive as follows:

```
<%@ page import="java.text.DateFormat" %>
<%@ page import="java.util.Date" %>
<%@ page import="java.util.Locale" %>
```

> **Classes in the `javax.servlet` and `javax.servlet.jsp` packages are imported by the resulting servlet and therefore we don't need to import them explicitly.**

Once this is done we can use a Java scriptlet to get the locale of the client from the HTTP request and create an appropriate `DateFormat` instance in the same way as before:

```
<body>

  <%
    // get the locale of the client and create an appropriate date format
    Locale loc = request.getLocale();
    DateFormat df = DateFormat.getDateInstance(DateFormat.MEDIUM, loc);
  %>
```

Finally, to generate the dynamic part of the page we use a short expression to format and output the date:

```
    <h1>The date is <%= df.format(new Date()) %></h1>

  </body>

</html>
```

When we request this JSP page from our web server, once again the resulting HTML page should look something like this:

As we can see, the end result is the same. However, the JSP code version is not only shorter but also easily readable.

Easy to Write, Easy to Break

One of the benefits of JSP is that pages are fairly easy to write. You just have to create an HTML file with a `.jsp` extension, import the required Java classes, and write some Java code. On the flip side, however, we can say that JSP pages are fairly easy to break too. All it takes is a person or tool (for example a page authoring or web design tool) that doesn't know Java to remove a small snippet of Java code and some essential business processing or presentation logic could be lost. In addition to this, what about some of the other design and implementation issues that we looked at earlier, such as maintainability and reusability?

Maintainability

JSP pages require less effort than servlets to modify the content and the presentation for two reasons – first, the content is in a much more appropriate form (for example HTML), and second, JSP pages can easily be modified and recompiled because of their lifecycle. However, saying that JSP pages require less effort to modify than servlets doesn't immediately imply that JSP pages are more maintainable or more readable.

For example, a complex JSP page with a large quantity of embedded Java code could easily reduce both the maintainability and readability of the page, ultimately leading us back to the same maintainability issues as Java servlets where application code and content are mixed together.

Reusability

Should we wish to display the current date on other pages within our web application, we could copy the appropriate elements from our JSP page and paste them into other pages. Although the code is reusable on a sourcecode level, this method is not efficient because modifying the functionality that it provides means finding and changing each and every occurrence within the web application. This in turn can lead to maintainability issues further down the line when the same code has to be extended or fixed in multiple places. With object-oriented practices in mind, ideally we are looking for reuse at the class or component level.

JSP and JavaBeans

Fortunately (and for the reasons just highlighted), JSP has a built-in mechanism for utilizing JavaBeans through a family of standard actions (or tags) that must be provided by all JSP containers.

What is a JavaBean?

A JavaBean is simply a Java class that adheres to a particular set of standards, the main ones from a JSP viewpoint are:

- A default, no arguments constructor must be defined
- Any properties should be declared as private and accessed/modified through methods complying with the JavaBeans naming conventions

This naming standard states that, a property, for example `name`, should be named with a lowercase starting character, and have an accessor called `getName()` and a mutator called `setName()`.

In addition to these, it is also good practice (and in fact mandated by the JavaBeans specification) for the class to be declared as `Serializable` or `Externalizable`. While this isn't necessarily required in reality, making JavaBeans serializable from a JSP perspective means that the state of the beans can easily be transferred from server to server in a fail-safe, multi-server (clustered) environment. This is useful because, should a server go down for any reason, another server in the cluster will have access to the state stored by the JavaBeans and start to service the requests without the user being aware that something has gone wrong.

JavaBean Support in JSP

There are three standard JSP actions that are available to us and they are as follows:

- `<jsp:useBean/>`
  Allows us to bind an instance of a JavaBean to a particular name and a particular scope, one of `request`, `page`, `session`, and `application`
- `<jsp:getProperty/>`
  Allows us to get a named property from a named JavaBean instance and display it on the page
- `<jsp:setProperty/>`
  Allows us to set a named property on a named JavaBean instance to an arbitrary value

Building the JavaBean

To demonstrate these features, let us once again look at the date example. To generate a page that displays the current date, we could create a JavaBean that has a property representing the current date, which is defined as follows:

```
package com.wrox.jsptaglibs.date;

import java.io.Serializable;
import java.util.Date;

public class DateBean implements Serializable {

  private Date date;
```

To ensure that our `DateBean` class is compatible with the standard JSP mechanisms mentioned previously, it has a no arguments constructor and an accessor/mutator for its `date` property. On instantiation, the default constructor is called and the `date` property is set to the current date:

```
  public DateBean() {
    // set the date property to the current date
    this.date = new Date();
  }

  public Date getDate() {
    return this.date;
  }
```

```
   public void setDate(Date newDate) {
      this.date = newDate;
   }
}
```

Using the JavaBean

To display the current date, a JSP page only needs to create an instance of the bean, and display its `date` property. Although this can be done with scriptlets and expressions as before, we can make use of the standard JSP JavaBean actions as follows:

```
<html>

  <head>
    <title>Professional JSP Tag Libraries</title>
  </head>

  <body>
```

Here we have the same HTML template as before, but this time without the import directives, scriptlet, and expression. The `<jsp:useBean/>` action creates an instance of the `com.wrox.jsptaglibs.date.DateBean` class and binds it into the page, storing it in the page context under the name of `dateBean`:

```
<jsp:useBean id="dateBean"
             class="com.wrox.jsptaglibs.date.DateBean"
             scope="page"/>
```

Once this is done, we can simply use the `<jsp:getProperty/>` action to retrieve the `date` property of our new instance and display it on the page:

```
    <h1>The date is <jsp:getProperty name="dateBean" property="date"/></h1>

  </body>

</html>
```

The result of this is that we have now created a reusable class (`DateBean`) and also have a much more concise and readable JSP page. However, what's missing here is that the date isn't displayed in a format appropriate to the user's locale because we've not implemented the formatting inside the bean, so we get something like this:

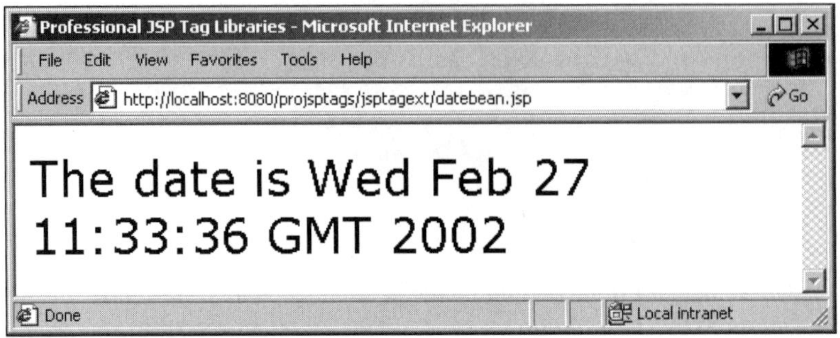

How can the date be properly formatted using this example?

One solution would be to add another method to our bean that formats the date before returning it to be displayed on the page. This way, we encapsulate the logic required to create the appropriate `java.text.DateFormat` object into a class, therefore making it reusable. This sounds like a great idea but how does the bean know about the locale of the client? A simple solution is to have the JSP page pass in the locale as an argument to the method that will format the date. With this change, the bean now looks as follows:

```
package com.wrox.jsptaglibs.date;

import java.io.Serializable;
import java.text.DateFormat;
import java.util.Date;
import java.util.Locale;

public class FormattedDateBean implements Serializable {

  private Date date;

  public FormattedDateBean() {
    // set the date property to the current date
    this.date = new Date();
  }

  public Date getDate() {
    return this.date;
  }

  public void setDate(Date newDate) {
    this.date = newDate;
  }

  public String formatDate(Locale locale) {
    // using the specified locale, create an appropriate date format
    DateFormat df = DateFormat.getDateInstance(DateFormat.MEDIUM, locale);

    return df.format(date);
  }
}
```

So far so good, and all we need to do now is to execute the appropriate method on our new bean:

```
<html>
  <head>
    <title>Professional JSP Tag Libraries</title>
    <link rel="stylesheet" href="../page.css">
  </head>

  <body>

    <jsp:useBean id="dateBean"
                 class="com.wrox.jsptaglibs.date.FormattedDateBean"
                 scope="page"/>
```

As before, we can use the `<jsp:useBean/>` action to create an instance of the JavaBean. However, the standard family of JSP JavaBean actions don't allow us to call arbitrary methods on our beans – especially those that take arguments. For this reason, we've had to resort to a small expression again to call the appropriate method, passing the locale of the client as an argument:

```
    <h1>The date is <%= dateBean.formatDate(request.getLocale()) %></h1>

  </body>

</html>
```

The result we get is something like this:

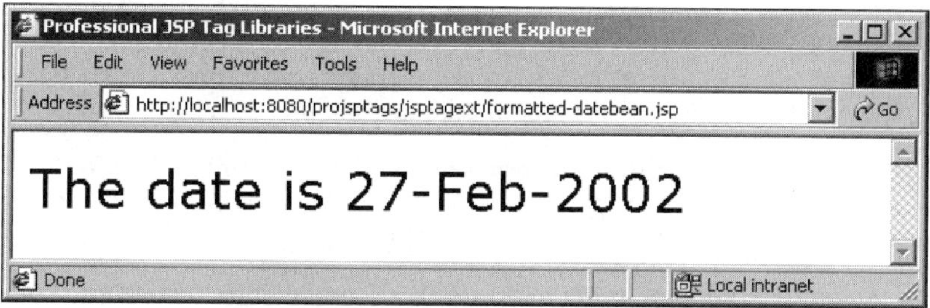

Although we have achieved the desired end result of displaying the current date to the user in a format that they are familiar with, we've had to introduce some Java code to achieve this. Although our JavaBean is reusable elsewhere in our web application, there is now additional complexity associated with using it – that is, creating an expression to tell the bean the locale to which it should format the date.

Ideally, we would like to skip this step and have the JavaBean work this out for itself, but unfortunately for us JavaBeans are not aware of the context in which they are running. In reality, they are just reusable software components that encapsulate some data and related functionality independently of the environment in which they are created – be it a web container or a standalone GUI application. Fortunately, JSP 1.1 introduced a mechanism whereby we can extend the actions available – JSP tag extensions.

JSP Tag Extensions

JSP tag extensions, or **custom tags** as they are informally known, are a portable mechanism for encapsulating reusable functionality, and primarily used by page authors – people who are more concerned with the presentation of the application rather than how it works behind the scenes.

In the same way that the `<jsp:useBean/>` tag wraps up the functionality needed to instantiate a named JavaBean, custom tags are a way of wrapping up common and customized functionality so that it can be reused easily on the page. This functionality includes recurring and repetitive tasks such as generating dynamic content, performing business logic, and accessing data.

Once built, tags are bundled up and deployed as **tag libraries** (also commonly known as **taglibs)** and it's at this stage that they can be used in different JSP containers and reused within:

- A single page
- The pages of a web application
- Separate web applications

On an implementation level, custom tags are simply Java classes that implement a specific interface – in this case, the `javax.servlet.jsp.tagext.Tag` interface. We'll be looking at this in the following chapters, but first of all, why should we use custom tags?

The Need for Custom Tags

One of the goals and best practices associated with developing JSP pages is that they should contain as little Java code (for example, presentation and/or business logic) as possible. This makes for a clean JSP page that is easy to read, easy to understand, and most importantly, easy to maintain. Before custom tags, a combination of JavaBeans and scriptlets was generally used to provide this type of logic although, as we've seen, this can make the pages harder to read and maintain.

Another issue is that while moving the date formatting functionality into a JavaBean was certainly a step in the right direction, we still needed to utilize some Java code in the page to give the bean some information about the environment in which it is running.

JSP pages have access to all sorts of useful information about the environment and context in which they are running. This information is made available through implicit page variables and include:

- The request – `request`
- The response – `response`
- The HTTP session – `session`
- The JSP page context – `pageContext`
- The servlet context – `application`

One of the reasons that custom tags are such an appealing technology is that they have access to the same environment and contextual information as the JSP page in which they are running. To use the example of displaying the date to the user, a custom tag could look up the locale of the client from the HTTP request and use this knowledge to format the date appropriately.

Using a Custom Tag

Moving back to the date example, if we were to use `<simple:date/>` (our custom tag) instead of the `<jsp:useBean/>` action and related expression, our JSP might look like the following example:

```
<html>

  <head>
    <title>Professional JSP Tag Libraries</title>
  </head>
```

We now tell the JSP container where to locate the tag library using the following directive, we'll learn more about this in the next chapter:

```
  <%@ taglib uri="/simpleTaglib" prefix="simple" %>

  <body>

    <h1>The date is <simple:date/></h1>

  </body>

</html>
```

We've eliminated all traces of Java code from the page and therefore have a JSP page which is much more readable than before. In terms of maintainability and reusability, all of the functionality required to format and output the current date in a format appropriate to the locale of the client is now encapsulated within the `<simple:date/>` custom tag. Building custom tags involves writing some Java code and an XML file describing the semantics of how the tag is used on the page. We'll discuss the detailed implementation of these in the next chapter.

JavaBeans vs. Custom Tags

Now that we understand what a custom tag is, it does raise the question of when to use JavaBeans and when to use custom tags. The simple answer is that it is possible to perform many tasks using either. The more complex answer is whichever is the best for the job. In Chapter 8 we take a detailed look into this question, but equipped with our current knowledge we can deduce the following rules of thumb:

- Use JavaBeans when knowledge of the environment is not required – for example, when representing business objects or storing state
- Use custom tags when knowledge of the environment is required – for example, when generating content

Summary

This chapter has introduced the two paradigms for generating dynamic content – embedding content into logic and embedding logic into content. We've shown how Java servlets and JSP pages map onto each of these paradigms respectively, and we've seen some examples of how a simple HTML page containing dynamic content can be implemented. In doing this, we also looked at some of the issues that should be taken into account, namely:

- Maintainability
- Readability
- Reusability

As a result, we've seen and highlighted how introducing Java code as scriptlets can reduce the readability of a JSP page and although it wasn't too much of a problem in our simple example, most real-world implementations are typically more complex. To resolve this, we followed up by exploring how the functionality contained within a JSP page can be moved into a reusable software component – a JavaBean.

This does go some way to solving the issues mentioned above, but unfortunately JavaBeans don't know about the environment in which they are running and short scriptlets would again have to be introduced to equip them with this knowledge.

Finally, we introduced custom tags and demonstrated how the same example HTML page could be generated without the need for any additional Java code. To wrap up, we briefly compared JavaBeans to custom tags and were able to deduce a couple of high-level rules of thumb. With these in mind, let's move on to the next chapter which will take us through a step-by-step guide to building, deploying, and using our first custom tag.

LONDON

2

Simple Tags

As we saw in the previous chapter, custom tags are a portable mechanism for encapsulating reusable functionality. In reality, this functionality is wrapped up in a regular Java class that implements a specific interface – the `Tag` interface from the `javax.servlet.jsp.tagext` package, available in JSP 1.1 and above.

In this chapter, we'll take a look at:

- The tag syntax
- The `Tag` interface
- The tag lifecycle
- The interaction of a JSP page with a tag
- The interaction of a tag with its environment
- The use of attributes to customize tag functionality

With this knowledge in place, we can then move on to build our first custom tag. This example will form the basis for later chapters.

Tag Syntax

As the example in the previous chapter demonstrated, the standard JSP tags are written in the form `<jsp:xxx/>` where `xxx` is the name of the tag. An example of this would be the `<jsp:useBean/>` tag. As with XML, tags on a JSP page are made up of two components:

- A prefix
- A name

Prefix

Namespaces in XML documents are a way to prevent name collisions between elements from different **Document Type Definitions** (DTDs) and this has been adopted as part of the way that custom tags are used on a page. In JSP terminology, they are called **prefixes** and are mandatory. In addition to preventing name collisions, the prefix essentially helps us to identify the tag library that the tag came from. Although prefixes are user definable, the JSP specification states that the following are reserved:

- `jsp`
- `jspx`
- `java`
- `javax`
- `servlet`
- `sun`
- `sunw`

This is analogous to the way that Java classes we write ourselves aren't allowed to reside in packages beginning with `java` or `javax`.

> **Although these prefixes are reserved by the JSP specification, the behavior of current JSP containers differs from vendor to vendor. Some allow the use of the prefixes mentioned above, while others do not. In any case, to prevent conflicts with future versions of the JSP specifications (and for the sake of compliance with the specifications), you should not use them.**

Name

The name of a custom tag can be any string of letters, digits, underscores, hyphens, or periods, but must be unique within the context of the tag library in which the tag is described. For example, there couldn't be two tags called `date` in a tag library.

Using Tags on a JSP Page

Custom tags follow the same syntax as the standard JSP actions (and XML) – they have a **start tag**, some optional body content, and a matching **end tag**.

For example, we will give a prefix of `simple` to the first tags that we will build in this chapter. If we were to create a custom tag called `date` that displayed the current date, it could be used on a JSP page with the following syntax:

```
<simple:date>Here is some body content.</simple:date>
```

If the custom tag in this example didn't have any body content, it could be written using the full or shortened syntax:

```
<simple:date></simple:date>
```

or:

```
<simple:date/>
```

In the latter (shortened) form, the start and end tags have been combined, just as with the `<jsp:useBean/>` action.

> **As with Java programming in general, the prefix and name are case-sensitive.**

The Tag Interface

At a minimum, every custom tag must implement the `Tag` interface as this defines the basic contract between a JSP page and the tag itself. At a high level, this involves two parts:

- Making the tag aware of the context/environment in which it is running
- Providing callback methods corresponding to the lifecycle of the tag on the page

To explain this in further detail, let's take a look at the main features of the `Tag` interface itself. The code below shows the complete `Tag` interface and this forms the basis for the discussion over the next few sections:

```
package javax.servlet.jsp.tagext;

import javax.servlet.jsp.JspException;

public interface Tag {

  public final static int SKIP_BODY = 0;
  public final static int EVAL_BODY_INCLUDE = 1;
  public final static int SKIP_PAGE = 5;
  public final static int EVAL_PAGE = 6;

  void setPageContext(PageContext pc);

  void setParent(Tag t);

  Tag getParent();

  int doStartTag() throws JspException;

  int doEndTag() throws JspException;

  void release();
}
```

The Tag Lifecycle

The `Tag` interface defines the contract between a JSP page and a tag used on that JSP page, which means that the methods on this interface provide the API through which the JSP page communicates with the tag. However, interfaces in Java cannot specify the order in which these methods are called.

Fortunately, this order is defined in the JSP specification, ensuring that tags will function correctly in each and every JSP compliant implementation. Let's take a look at the lifecycle of a simple tag initiated when the JSP container encounters the custom tag:

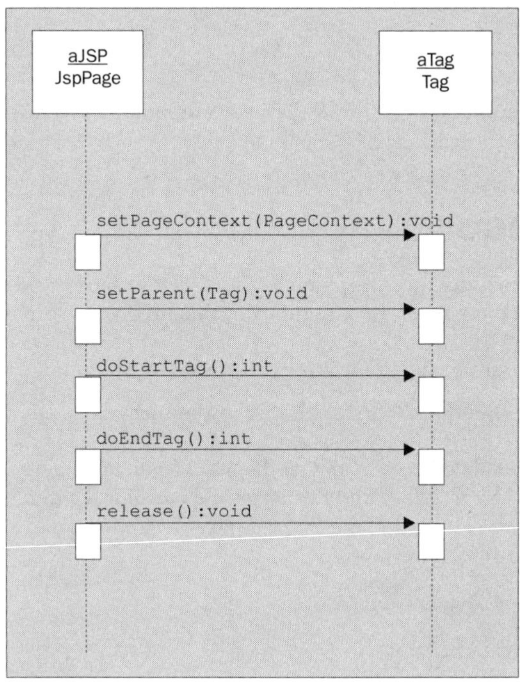

Setting the Page Context

At the first step in a tag's lifecycle, the JSP container makes the tag aware of the environment in which it runs. The `Tag` interface defines the `setPageContext()` method that takes a `javax.servlet.jsp.PageContext` instance as an argument – a convenient wrapper and single point of access for objects that can be used from a JSP page. The instance passed to the tag is the same one that can be referenced in the JSP page using the implicit variable `pageContext`, and originates from the JSP page on which the tag is used. The signature of the `setPageContext()` method is as follows:

```
void setPageContext(PageContext pc);
```

A reference to the JSP page context is useful not only for accessing page variables, but also for accessing the request, the response, and the session object. We'll be looking at its importance shortly.

Setting the Parent

The next step to make the tag aware of its environment is to tell it about its parent. Custom tags can be nested within one another just like XML tags:

```
<prefix:outerTag>
  <prefix:innerTag>Here is some body content.</prefix:innerTag>
</prefix:outerTag>
```

If this is the case, the JSP page simply passes a reference to the closest enclosing tag handler, that is the Java class implementing the `Tag` interface:

```
void setParent(Tag t);
```

A reference to the parent tag is useful in a number of scenarios, for example where nested (child) tags can access information from their parents. If a tag isn't nested, the JSP page will call this method with a `null` argument. Nevertheless, this method will get called.

The Start Tag

Once the context information has been passed to the tag, the JSP page is now ready to start using the functionality contained within the tag. When the JSP page encounters the start tag, the `doStartTag()` method is called on the tag handler, irrespective of whether the custom tag has been written using the full (`<simple:date></simple:date>`) or shortened (`<simple:date/>`) form:

```
int doStartTag() throws JspException;
```

Note that this method could throw a `JspException`. This can be used to notify the JSP container that an exception has occurred during processing. We'll take a closer look at this when we look at how to build our first custom tag.

Finally, the `doStartTag()` method must return an integer. We'll explore this in detail later on, but in the meantime, all we need to know is that the return value determines what happens after the start tag has been processed.

For the purpose of this chapter, the example tag that we develop will have no body content and will therefore require no evaluation of its body. A number of useful constants are defined in the `Tag` interface, one of which is `SKIP_BODY`. Returning this value from the `doStartTag()` method indicates to the JSP container that the body of the tag (if it has any) should be ignored and processing should move on to the end tag.

The `SKIP_BODY` constant represents only one of the possible return values for the `doStartTag()` method and, as we'll see in Chapter 3, a powerful feature of custom tags is that they can programmatically control whether their body content is evaluated or not.

The End Tag

The `doEndTag()` method is called when the end tag is encountered, again irrespective of whether the custom tag has been written using the full or shortened format:

```
int doEndTag() throws JspException;
```

Again, the doEndTag() method can throw a JspException and also requires that an integer value be returned. Instead of SKIP_BODY, we'll return EVAL_PAGE for the purpose of the examples in this chapter. This indicates to the JSP container that processing of the tag has now finished and it should continue processing the remainder of the page.

Releasing State

Once the JSP container has finished with the tag, the final stage of the tag lifecycle is to ensure that any state associated with the tag (such as a database connection) is appropriately released. This is achieved by calling the release() method:

```
void release();
```

Tags should provide an implementation of the release() method to reset any associated state and/or release any resources that they may be holding. A good example is a tag that opens a connection to a database or a remote resource when the tag is created. Here, the code to close the connection can be placed within the release() method. This is just one such example and, as we'll see in later chapters, implementing the release() method in our tags is useful, and a good practice for several reasons.

> *The release() method is not as straightforward as it first seems because of some fairly complex issues around instance pooling of tag handlers. We'll look at this in detail in Chapter 9.*

The TagSupport Class

Before we move on to look at how to build custom tags, we should first take a look at the TagSupport class, also contained within the javax.servlet.jsp.tagext package. We've already established that tag handlers are regular Java classes that implement a specific interface. Writing a tag handler therefore requires implementations for all of the methods in the Tag interface that we've just seen. Although this is not a complex task, the TagSupport class provides a convenient implementation of this interface for us.

Essentially, the TagSupport class just provides default implementations of the methods specified in the Tag interface. The methods to get and set the parent tag and set the page context are shown below:

```
public class TagSupport implements Tag {

  protected PageContext pageContext;
  private   Tag         parent;

  ...

  public void setParent(Tag t) {
    parent = t;
  }

  public Tag getParent() {
    return parent;
  }

  public void setPageContext(PageContext pageContext) {
    this.pageContext = pageContext;
  }
```

> **Notice that there is no `getPageContext()` method and instead the `pageContext` property has been made protected. This makes tag development slightly easier as the `pageContext` variable can be accessed directly in the same way as it can on a JSP page.**

The `doStartTag()` and `doEndTag()` lifecycle methods have each been given a default implementation that does nothing except return the code that is most commonly used:

```
    public int doStartTag() throws JspException {
      return SKIP_BODY;
    }

    public int doEndTag() throws JspException {
      return EVAL_PAGE;
    }

    ...
  }
```

This means that the return code of the `doStartTag()` method indicates that its body should be skipped, while the return code of the `doEndTag()` method indicates that the remainder of the page should be processed. Providing default implementations of these two lifecycle methods reduces the amount of code required to build simple tags (as we'll see shortly).

The PageContext Class

Next, we'll take a quick look at the JSP `PageContext` class. This class resides in the `javax.servlet.jsp` package and is a convenient wrapper and single point of access for the various objects that can be used by a JSP page.

Accessing Implicit JSP Variables

One of the most important features of the `PageContext` class is that it offers a convenient way to access those variables that are made available implicitly on a JSP page. This includes the output stream `out`, and `request`, which is a reference to the underlying `ServletRequest` instance. A full list of the implicit JSP variables is shown below, along with the names of the methods that can be used to access them from a `PageContext` instance:

- `out`
  The current `JspWriter` used to output the contents of the JSP page back to the client. This can be accessed from a JSP page using the implicit `out` object. Through the `PageContext`, it can be accessed using the following method:

```
public JspWriter getOut();
```

- `request`
  The current `ServletRequest` can be accessed on a JSP page using the `request` object, and is available through the `PageContext` using the following method:

```
public ServletRequest getRequest();
```

- response
  In a similar way, the response object can be accessed through the PageContext using the following method:

```
public ServletResponse getResponse();
```

- session
  The current HttpSession instance can be used on a JSP page by referencing the session variable. Once again, this can be accessed through the PageContext:

```
public HttpSession getSession();
```

- exception
  In the event of an unhandled exception, using the page directive makes it possible to define a JSP page to which exceptions can be forwarded. On this **error page**, an implicit variable called exception, which represents the unhandled java.lang.Throwable instance, is available. To access this from the PageContext, the following method can be used:

```
public Exception getException();
```

Accessing Scoped Variables

The PageContext is useful as it also provides a standard way to look up variables that have been previously placed in one of the available scopes – request, page, session, or application. This is made possible through the definition of four constants representing the various scopes, and a family of methods to get and set attributes using a specified scope:

```
public static final int PAGE_SCOPE = 1;
public static final int REQUEST_SCOPE = 2;
public static final int SESSION_SCOPE = 3;
public static final int APPLICATION_SCOPE = 4;
```

```
public Object getAttribute(String name, int scope);
public void setAttribute(String name, Object o, int scope);
public void removeAttribute(String name, int scope);
```

We'll see examples of the use of variables in later chapters.

Including and Forwarding

Finally, the PageContext is useful to us as we can easily forward to, or include the output from, other pages. This functionality is provided for us by the <jsp:forward/> and <jsp:include/> tags respectively and, once again, is supplied by methods on the PageContext class:

```
public void forward(String relativeUrlPath)
   throws ServletException, IOException;

public void include(String relativeUrlPath)
   throws ServletException, IOException;
```

We'll also show their use in tag development in subsequent chapters.

Building our First Tag

Towards the end of Chapter 1 we saw how a custom tag could be used to replace Java code (a scriptlet) in a JSP page. In this case, the code that displayed a date to the user was moved out of the JSP page and into a custom tag. We'll now look at how to build such a tag.

There are five steps to implement a custom tag:

- Write the tag handler
- Write the tag library descriptor file
- Deploy the tag library
- Register the tag library with the web application
- Import the tag library and use it

Writing the Tag Handler

This example tag displays the current date and time in a locale appropriate to the end user. The first step in building a custom tag is to build the tag handler – the Java class that embodies the implementation of the tag. As we've just seen, a good starting point for our tag is the `TagSupport` class:

```
package com.wrox.jsptaglibs.date;

import java.text.DateFormat;
import java.util.Date;
import java.util.Locale;

import javax.servlet.jsp.JspException;
import javax.servlet.jsp.JspTagException;
import javax.servlet.jsp.tagext.TagSupport;

public class DateTag extends TagSupport {
```

We just want to wrap up this functionality into a custom tag so that the JSP page automatically calls it when the tag is encountered on the page. As our custom tag will have no body (that is, it can be used with the shortened syntax of `<simple:date/>`) there are two options open to us:

- We can place this functionality in the `doStartTag()` method that gets called when the start tag is encountered
- We can place this functionality in the `doEndTag()` method that gets called when the end tag is encountered

As our simple tag has no body, it really doesn't matter which option we choose, as the current date will be output in the same place in the resulting HTML page.

We can override the `doStartTag()` method in the tag handler and it's here that we place the functionality associated with the tag. We already know that our tag won't have any body content to be processed, so we (like the `TagSupport` class) can simply return `SKIP_BODY` to indicate this to the JSP container.

As the functionality associated with the custom tag is implemented in the doStartTag() method, there is no need for us to override the doEndTag() method. This is often the case with tag development and is one of the reasons that the TagSupport class provides the default implementations that it does. In this case, we just want the remainder of the page to be processed, as indicated by the default return value (EVAL_PAGE) from the doEndTag() method in the TagSupport class.

The next step is to write the Java code to get the locale of the client and use this information to format the current date appropriately. In the simple JSP page example, we get the locale of the client from the implicit request object. Unfortunately, this variable isn't available to us directly when building tags. Fortunately though, getting a reference to the request object is a simple method call away.

One of the reasons that tags are a better alternative to JavaBeans is that they are aware of the environment in which they are running, and part of the contract between a JSP page and a tag is that the JSP page must provide the tag with this information. It does this by means of the page context and by using this we can easily obtain a reference to the request (and therefore the locale of the client) as follows:

```
  public int doStartTag() throws JspException {

    // get the locale of the client and create an appropriate date format
    Locale loc = pageContext.getRequest().getLocale();
    DateFormat df = DateFormat.getDateInstance(DateFormat.MEDIUM, loc);
```

Also available is the JspWriter, which can be used to write content directly to the output stream. This is called out on a JSP page and is available through a PageContext instance using the getOut() method. With this in mind, we can move on and complete the implementation of the doStartTag() method (and the tag handler) as follows:

```
    try {
      // and write out the formatted date to the page
      pageContext.getOut().write(df.format(new Date()));
    } catch (java.io.IOException ioe) {
      throw new JspTagException(ioe.getMessage());
    }

    // and skip evaluating the body of the tag (as there shouldn't be one)
    return SKIP_BODY;
  }
}
```

The JspWriter instance returned from the getOut() method outputs the formatted date directly to the output stream. As with all input/output calls, there is always a chance that it could fail and it's for this reason that a try-catch block is required around the code that outputs the formatted date. Rather than doing nothing, we can use the error message raised from the IOException and use this to create a JSP specific JspTagException so that we can signal to the JSP page that something has gone wrong.

> **JspTagException is a subclass of JspException and throwing it is a useful way of differentiating those exceptions that are caused by custom tags rather than JSP pages.**

Compiling the tag handler is as simple as compiling any other Java class, but does require that the JSP and tag extension classes are in the CLASSPATH. For an installation of Tomcat 4.0, these can be found in the following location:

```
%TOMCAT_HOME%\common\lib\servlet.jar
```

Writing the Tag Library Descriptor

Once the tag handler class has been written, we need to provide some information to the web container about the tag. We do this through a **tag library descriptor**, also known as a **TLD** file.

What is a Tag Library?

A tag library is a collection of one or more tags, usually related in some way. For example, we might group together all custom tags that help us build HTML forms into a tag library. For the purposes of this example, our tag library will only define a single tag – the date tag.

What is a Tag Library Descriptor?

A TLD is an XML file containing information about a tag library, adhering to a specific XML DTD provided as part of the JSP specification.

> *If you are familiar with custom tags in the JSP 1.1 environment you will notice that the names of some elements have changed in version 1.2 of the JSP specification. Details of these differences can be found in Chapter 11.*

Let's take a look at the TLD file in detail.

Header Information

This is the usual XML header information that states the version of XML used and the DTD that this document should follow:

```
<?xml version="1.0" encoding="ISO-8859-1" ?>
<!DOCTYPE taglib
  PUBLIC "-//Sun Microsystems, Inc.//DTD JSP Tag Library 1.2//EN"
  "http://java.sun.com/dtd/web-jsptaglibrary_1_2.dtd">
```

Tag Library Definition

Next there is the definition of the tag library itself, enclosed within the <taglib> elements:

```
<taglib>

  <tlib-version>1.0</tlib-version>
  <jsp-version>1.2</jsp-version>
  <short-name>simple</short-name>
  <description>Examples for the Simple Tags chapter</description>

</taglib>
```

tlib-version

This represents the version of the tag library and is useful for development purposes and configuration management:

```
<tlib-version>1.0</tlib-version>
```

jsp-version

This states the minimum version of the JSP specification that is required to run the tags:

```
<jsp-version>1.2</jsp-version>
```

short-name

This is a short, abbreviated name for the tag library, mainly for use with tag authoring tools so that they can provide a default prefix. Although it's not really important at this point of time, it is a mandatory element and therefore must be included in the definition of the taglib:

```
<short-name>simple</short-name>
```

description

This is an optional element, and although it's not required, it's good practice to include this as it provides readers with a short description of what a tag library does:

```
<description>Examples for the Simple Tags chapter</description>
```

With the exception of `<description>`, these elements provide the minimum information that is required by the JSP specification for the definition of a tag library. There are also several other optional elements that aren't relevant to the current discussion. For this reason, we'll leave a full explanation until Chapter 11 where we'll be looking at deployment and the descriptor files in detail.

Tag Definition

Up until now, the TLD file only defines the tag library. We must now describe the tags included in the tag library, each of which is contained within the `<tag>` elements as follows:

```
<tag>
  <name>date</name>
  <tag-class>com.wrox.jsptaglibs.date.DateTag</tag-class>
  <body-content>empty</body-content>
  <description>Inserts the current date into the page</description>
</tag>
```

Nested further are yet more elements describing the various properties of the tag.

name

This is the name of the custom tag, and this is how we will refer to it from a JSP page. As our tag will output the current date to the page, we'll call it `date`:

```
<name>date</name>
```

tag-class

The `<tag-class/>` element defines the Java class that represents the implementation of the custom tag and is the fully qualified Java class name of the tag handler. In our example, this is called `DateTag` and resides in the `com.wrox.jsptaglibs.date` package:

```
<tag-class>com.wrox.jsptaglibs.date.DateTag</tag-class>
```

body-content

This is an optional element that gives the JSP container a hint as to what the body of the tags might contain when used in a JSP page. This is useful for a couple of reasons: the JSP container can make optimizations on the way that the tag is used and it can ensure that the tags are used as they were intended.

There are various values for this element, but for now our tag won't have any body between its start and end tags and hence the `empty` value is used:

```
<body-content>empty</body-content>
```

> *We'll be talking more about this in the next chapter where we introduce the other types of body content.*

description

Finally, this is another optional description that indicates the purpose of the tag:

```
<description>Inserts the current date into the page</description>
```

The Complete Tag Library Descriptor File

With the tag library and its tag defined, here is the complete TLD file:

```
<?xml version="1.0" encoding="ISO-8859-1" ?>
<!DOCTYPE taglib
          PUBLIC "-//Sun Microsystems, Inc.//DTD JSP Tag Library 1.2//EN"
                 "http://java.sun.com/dtd/web-jsptaglibrary_1_2.dtd">

<taglib>

  <tlib-version>1.0</tlib-version>
  <jsp-version>1.2</jsp-version>
  <short-name>simple</short-name>
  <description>Examples for the Simple Tags chapter</description>
```

```
  <tag>
    <name>date</name>
    <tag-class>com.wrox.jsptaglibs.date.DateTag</tag-class>
    <body-content>empty</body-content>
    <description>Inserts the current date into the page</description>
  </tag>

</taglib>
```

As tags belong to a tag library, they are nested within the `<taglibs/>` elements alongside the elements that describe the tag library itself.

> **As with all valid XML, the ordering of the elements is important and tag library descriptor files are no different. The order in which the elements have been explained is the order in which they should appear in the TLD. The DTD can be found at http://java.sun.com/dtd/web-jsptaglibrary_1_2.dtd.**

Deploying the Tag Library

Now that we've written the pieces that make up the tag library, the next step is to deploy it. Until now, we've not mentioned anything about where all of these various files reside. So, where do they go? We will answer this shortly.

J2EE Web Applications

For any given web-based application there are usually a number of different components that need to be in place for it to run properly, and they are as follows:

- Java servlets
- JavaServer Pages
- Custom tags
- JavaBeans and supporting Java classes
- Static content (for example HTML, images, Cascading Style Sheets, and so on)
- Third party libraries (for example JDBC drivers, XML parsers, and so on)

In the past, configuration and deployment of these components has been inconsistent not only between projects, but also between servers. For this reason, and to standardize the process, version 2.2 of the Java servlet specification introduced the concept of a single deployable unit known as a **web application**. The idea behind this is that everything needed to run a web application should be included into a single distributable file. This **Web ARchive** (or **WAR**) file is based around the standard JAR file format and defines a standard layout for the components.

> **Web archives can also be used in their exploded (unzipped or unjarred) format. This is particularly useful for development purposes where changes can be made and tested directly rather than having to create the WAR file and redeploy it.**

In addition to this, the way in which web components are configured was also standardized. **Deployment descriptors** are used for configuration as they are for other J2EE components such as Enterprise JavaBeans. Let's recap on the structure of WAR files and find out where those components that are relevant to tag development fit in.

Web Archive File Format

The following diagram shows the layout of a typical web application consisting of all the components usually required to run the application:

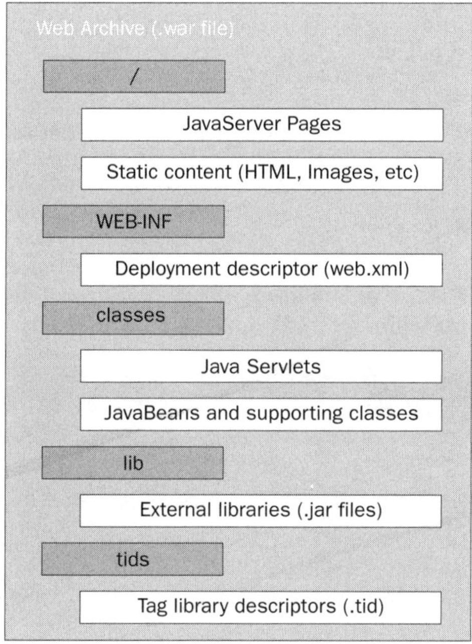

Any static content required by the application is placed at the root of the web application known as the **document root**. This might include HTML files, images, Cascading Style Sheets, PDF files, multimedia files, and so on. To provide structure, the static content can be nested into subdirectories as with regular static web sites. Sitting side-by-side with the static content are the JSP pages themselves, which again can be placed into subdirectories if required.

Next, there is the `WEB-INF` directory and it's under here that the web application deployment descriptor (`web.xml`) can be found. We'll take a closer look at this when we register the tag library with the web application shortly.

> **Although it is possible to place static content and JSP pages underneath the `WEB-INF` directory, these files will not be served up directly to clients.**

Nested beneath the WEB-INF directory are the Java classes required by the web application, including any Java servlets, JavaBeans, and Java classes incorporating the tag functionality. These can be placed in either the classes or the lib directory, in exploded or archived form respectively. The classes directory contains the class files in the directory structure representing the packages and the lib directory contains regular JAR files containing the classes. Placing class files in the classes directory is generally easier during development, while the lib directory is generally used to hold third party libraries such as JDBC drivers or XML parsers.

> **Remember that the JSP page and tag extension classes (those packaged `javax.servlet` and below) are part of the server and therefore do not need to be placed under the web application.**

Finally, we have the TLD files. These can be placed anywhere underneath the WEB-INF directory although it is standard practice to place them under a directory called tlds.

Deploying the Tag Library

The first thing to do is to create a web application structure under the %TOMCAT_HOME%\webapps directory for the application that we are building. For the purpose of this example, we'll call it projsptags. The directory structure for a JSP application is as follows:

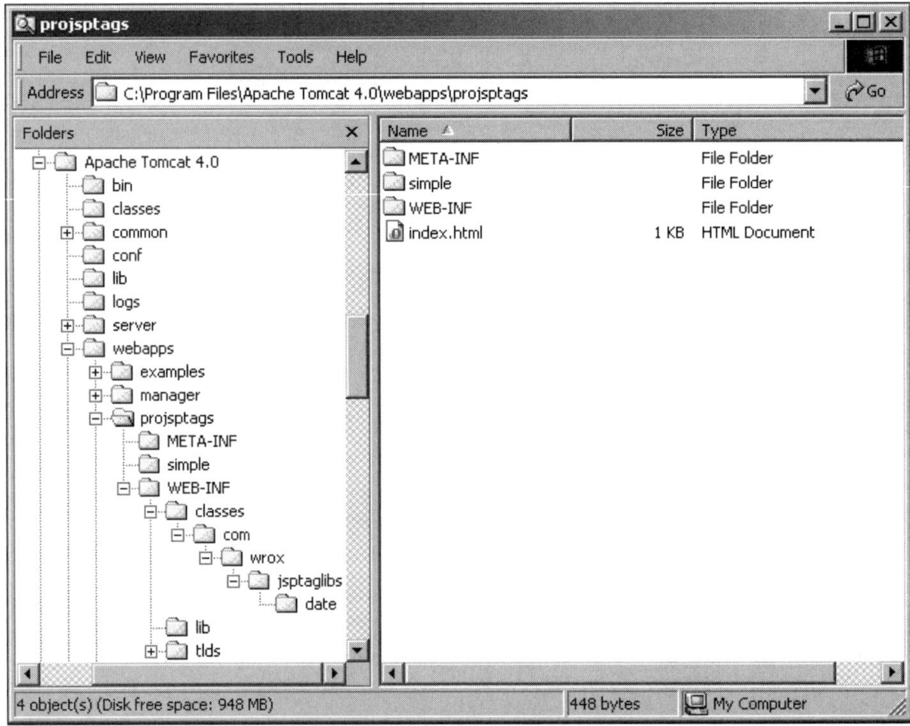

Underneath this directory, first of all there is a directory called `simple` containing the JSP page for the example in this chapter. Following this is a subdirectory called `WEB-INF` and it's here that the `web.xml` file resides, along with the Java classes and the TLD file.

The tag handler that we've just written was called `DateTag` and it was placed in a package called `com.wrox.jsptaglibs.date`. With this in mind, and once it has been compiled, the resulting class file (`DateTag.class`) would be placed under the `WEB-INF\classes\com\wrox\jsptaglibs\date` directory, where the `com\wrox\jsptaglibs\date` directory structure matches the package structure. If we assume that we named the tag library descriptor file `simple.tld`, then this would be placed underneath the `WEB-INF\tlds` directory.

Registering the Tag Library

So far we've written the tag handler, described it with a TLD file, and deployed it into a web application. The next step is to register the tag library with the web application, effectively announcing the existence of the library. To do this, we need to add a small section into the web application deployment descriptor (the `web.xml` file), an example of which is shown below:

```
<?xml version="1.0" encoding="ISO-8859-1"?>

<!DOCTYPE web-app
    PUBLIC "-//Sun Microsystems, Inc.//DTD Web Application 2.3//EN"
    "http://java.sun.com/dtd/web-app_2_3.dtd">

<web-app>

  <taglib>
    <taglib-uri>/simpleTaglib</taglib-uri>
    <taglib-location>/WEB-INF/tlds/simple.tld</taglib-location>
  </taglib>

</web-app>
```

From a JSP tag extensions perspective, the important section of this file is enclosed between the `<taglibs/>` elements defining a tag library. This is saying that there is a tag library defined in the `\WEB-INF\tlds\simple.tld` file, and we'll refer to it as `simpleTaglib` when we come to use it in the JSP page. All we are doing here is defining a mapping between a URI and the location of a TLD file. There can be any number of these uri to location mappings; however, each must be defined within a separate `<taglibs/>` block.

Once you have created this file, you should place it in the `projsptags\WEB-INF` directory.

Importing and Using the Tag Library

With these steps completed, we can now use the tag. The following JSP page is similar to that shown towards the end of Chapter 1 and shows an example of how we can import a tag library and use it in a page. This JSP page is called `date-tag.jsp` and, for the purpose of this example, it is placed in the `projsptags\simple` directory:

```
<html>
  <head>
    <title>Professional JSP Tag Libraries</title>
  </head>
```

In the same way that we must import any Java classes outside of the core `java.lang` package before using them, we must also import the tags in a tag library. Classes are imported on a JSP page using the `page` directive, and similarly, tag libraries are imported using the `taglib` directive.

This says that the JSP page makes use of a tag library, referred to by the specified URI. This URI is the same one that we defined in the `web.xml` file (between the `<taglib-uri/>` elements) and in our example this is `simpleTaglib`:

```
<%@ taglib uri="/simpleTaglib" prefix="simple" %>
```

The `prefix` attribute associates a prefix with the tags in the tag library. For the purpose of our example, we've chosen `simple` as the prefix.

Now that we've imported the tag library, we can use the tag. When we defined the tag in the TLD, we defined its name as `date` and it is referred to as this on the JSP page and not by the name of the tag handler class:

```
    <body>
      <h1>The date is <simple:date/></h1>
    </body>
  </html>
```

The tag is referenced by a prefix that we defined with the `<taglib/>` directive followed by the name of the tag as defined in the TLD file. With this all in place, start up Tomcat and point your browser to the JSP page that has just been written:

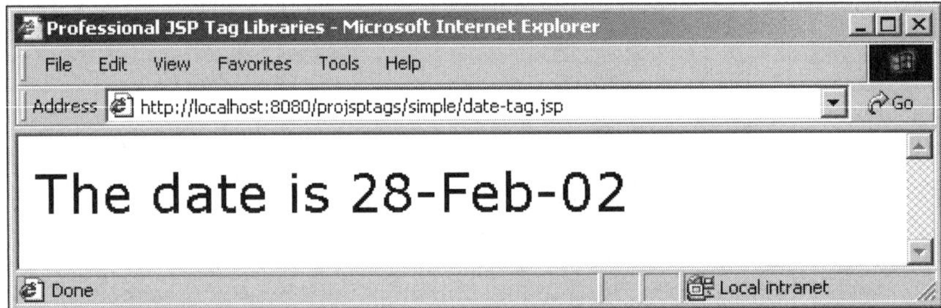

Effort vs. Benefit

That's all there is to creating a custom tag. Although it consists of slightly more work than writing the code directly into a JSP page, the benefits easily outweigh the initial effort required.

In writing this tag, we've moved (and encapsulated) the formatting logic into a reusable software component and maintained the same end result as demonstrated by the examples in Chapter 1. Should we need to modify the way that dates are displayed in our application, all we need to do is modify the tag handler implementation.

However, what if we need to display the date in various formats across the pages of our web application? We could create a new custom tag for each displayable format, but of course this will involve additional work and is also hard to maintain. Instead, we could use **attributes**.

Next, we will look at how attributes can be used to customize the functionality provided by tags. We'll put this into practice by extending the tag that we have just built.

Tag Attributes

Attributes are a way to customize the functionality offered by a tag. For example, if we have a method that formats a date, we might want to implement it so that it takes a specific format rather than coding a new method for each format. This is the same with tags.

Attributes of custom tags are represented in the same way as attributes that are used in regular HTML/XML tags. If we take the `date` tag from the example, we could pass it a value that specifies the exact format of the date we want to display:

```
<attributes:date format="dd-MMM-yyyy"/>
```

A tag can have zero or more attributes, each consisting of a name and a value enclosed within quotes.

Syntax of an Attribute

Attributes, like the tags themselves, also have syntactic rules stating how they can be defined and used on the page. These are split into two parts:

- name
- value

Name

The name must be unique within the context of the tag (in a similar way to tag prefixes). Also, the names of attributes must not start with any of the following strings:

- `jsp`
- `_jsp`
- `java`
- `sun`

> **Although some current JSP container implementations may allow the use of reserved names, they should not be used in order to maintain standards compliance.**

Value

The values of attributes must be quoted in the same way that attributes within XML tags are quoted. To reduce the likelihood that the quotes inside the values themselves must be escaped, attribute values can be quoted between either single or double quotes:

```
<attributes:date format='dd-MMM-yyyy'/>
<attributes:date format="dd-MMM-yyyy"/>
```

Although either type of quotes can be used, it is more common to see values double quoted. No matter which type is used, the start and end quote types must match.

The Tag Lifecycle

We'll look at the implementation specifics behind attributes shortly. However, first let's revisit the tag lifecycle that we introduced earlier, as adding attributes to a tag slightly changes the tag lifecycle. At a high level, a tag attribute maps onto a **property** (in the JavaBeans sense of the term) on the tag handler.

It is essential that the JSP passes on the values of any tag attribute to the tag handler before the processing begins. If this doesn't happen, the tag has no way of accessing the values of its attributes. For this reason, attributes are passed to the tag handler after the calls to the `setPageContext()` and `setParent()` methods, but before the processing of the tag is performed. For example, consider the following tag:

```
<prefix:tag attribute1="xyz" attributeN="123"/>
```

Attributes are processed from left to right, which means that the left-most (or first) attribute specified in the custom tag (`attribute1`) would be set on the tag handler first. A diagrammatic representation is given opposite:

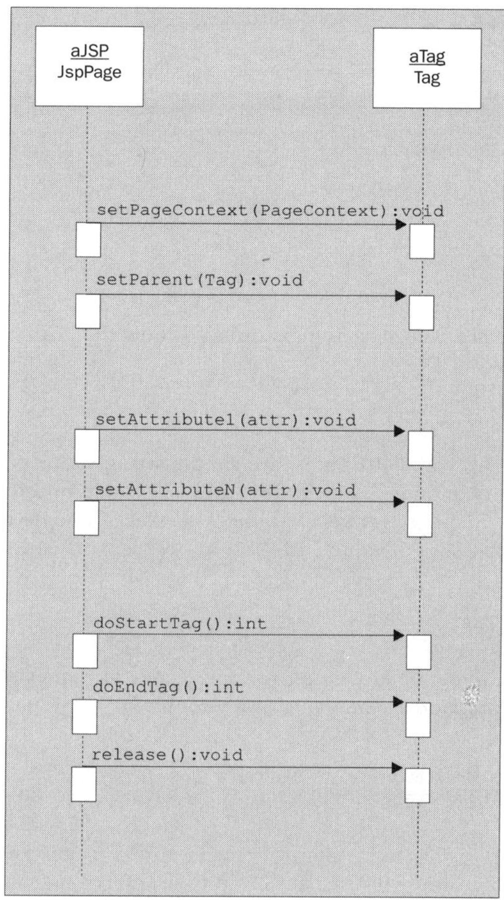

This sequence diagram shows two methods; `setAttribute1()` and `setAttributeN()`, and it's by calling these (in the specified order) that the JSP page passes the value of the two attributes to the tag handler. There must be an appropriately named mutator method that corresponds to the attribute on the tag, following the regular conventions laid out in the JavaBeans specification.

> **Attribute names, like tag prefixes and names, are also case-sensitive.**

This covers the naming conventions behind the methods, but does raise the following questions:

- What is the argument type for these mutators?
- Is `String` the only data type supported?

Prior to answering these questions, we need to take a look at the various types of attributes that are supported.

Types of Attributes

There are various types of attributes that tags support:

- Translation-time values (static)
- Request-time values (dynamic)
- Optional
- Required

Let's take a quick look at these before seeing examples of how they can be used.

Translation-Time

Translation-time attributes (or static attributes) are simple string values hard-coded into the tag surrounded by single or double quotes. Since they are hard-coded into the page, their value is known at **translation time** when the JSP page is translated into a servlet. The date format example given above is an example of a static attribute – the value "dd-MMM-yyyy" is hard-coded onto the page.

Request-Time

Request-time attributes (or dynamic attributes) are the results of **request-time** expressions; for example, the result of a complex expression or the value of a variable on a JSP page as shown below:

```
<% Date today = new Date(); %>
<attributes:date date="<%= today %>"/>
```

> **The terms request-time and run-time are often used interchangeably when referring to JSP pages and custom tags.**

In this case, and as with the standard actions, regular JSP expressions (such as `<%= today %>`) are used as the value of an attribute and again enclosed between quotes.

Required vs. Optional

Attributes can be declared as **required** or **optional**. An example of a required attribute would be the `name` attribute on the `<jsp:useBean/>` action because the name for a bean instance must be specified. On the other hand, attributes that are not marked as required do not have to be provided, for example the `scope` attribute on the `<jsp:useBean/>` action. In this, and the majority of cases, a default value is associated with any one of the optional attributes.

Not supplying a value for a required attribute will result in an error in the compilation of the JSP page. The way in which the error is raised will vary from vendor to vendor, but Tomcat produces the following error message:

According to the TLD attribute <attribute name> is mandatory for tag <tag name>.

Required attributes are a good way of ensuring the correct use of a tag by a web page author and that tags get all of the information that they need to run properly. It is therefore important that tags behave appropriately when optional attributes are not supplied. In the case of the `<jsp:useBean/>` action, a default scope of `page` is assumed if the scope attribute is not explicitly defined. This is a good example of how an attribute can be used to extend the functionality provided by a tag while still allowing the tag to work if it is not provided. Also, it is a good way of ensuring backward compatibility between releases of tag libraries.

Type Conversions

Now that we've learnt about translation-time and request-time values, we can answer the question over argument types. Let's look at the mutator methods for the attributes in a tag handler.

String Values

The easiest case to deal with is where the attributes are simple string values. Here, the mutator methods can be defined to take a `java.lang.String` as an argument. Let's take an example:

```
<prefix:tag attribute1="xyz"/>
```

If `attribute1` is merely a string value, it means that we can define a mutator on the tag handler with the following signature:

```
public void setAttribute1(String attr);
```

When the method is called, the value of the `attr` parameter is the same as it is specified in the JSP page – "`xyz`".

Numerical Values

Now, let's consider the following example:

```
<prefix:tag attribute1="123"/>
```

This time we could do the same and have the value `123` passed to the tag handler as a string. While this may be appropriate, we may instead want to convert this to a numerical value. This isn't hard to achieve, but converting the string to a number ourselves means that we miss out on the JSP container's ability to implicitly perform the conversions for us. If we want the value of `attribute1` to be represented as an integer in the tag handler, all we need to do is define the mutator as taking an `int` argument:

```
public void setAttribute1(int attr);
```

In fact, the conversion also applies if we need to use the wrapper class (from the `java.lang` package) and define the method with the following signature:

```
public void setAttribute1(Integer attr);
```

In either case, the value that gets passed to the method is equivalent to calling `Integer.valueOf(String)` that parses the `String` attribute and returns the appropriate integer value. This is then passed to the tag handler as a primitive or a wrapper respectively.

> **A `NumberFormatException` will be thrown if the value of the attribute does not represent a valid number, is an empty string, or falls outside of the range of an integer in the Java language.**

This conversion also applies to the other numerical types, a full list of which is as follows:

- `byte`
- `short`
- `int`
- `long`
- `float`
- `double`

In all of these cases, the values are converted from a string in a manner equivalent to the appropriate `valueOf(String)`method on the wrapper class. Such conversions are trivial although having the container perform them for us makes the task of writing tag handlers easier.

Boolean Values

Boolean attributes are a user-friendly way to pass information to tags; a good example is indicating to tags whether to turn on or off specific features:

```
<prefix:tag attribute1="true"/>
```

Once again, automatic conversion is provided if the mutator for the attribute uses one of the following signatures:

```
public void setAttribute1(boolean attr);
public void setAttribute1(Boolean attr);
```

Conversion is performed according to the rules of the `valueOf(String)` method, as defined in the `java.lang.Boolean` wrapper class. This states that the `boolean` returned represents the value `true` if the string argument is not `null` and is equal (ignoring case) to the string `"true"`.

Character Values

Attributes can also take the form of single characters as shown below:

```
<prefix:tag attribute1="a"/>
```

Automatic conversion is performed if the mutator method is defined with one of the following two signatures:

```
public void setAttribute1(char attr);
public void setAttribute1(Character attr);
```

Unlike the other types, there is no `Character.valueOf(String)` method that details the process of converting a `String` to a `char`. Instead, when more than a single character is provided as the value of a character attribute, the first character is taken using the `String.charAt(0)` method and the remainder of the string is discarded.

Request-Time Values

The attribute types that we've seen up until now are all applicable to either static (translation-time) or dynamic (request-time) values. However, one of the key differences is that **automatic type conversion** doesn't apply when expressions are used to provide attributes with values. In other words, type conversion only applies to attributes when a static value is used between the quotes. Let's take a look at this by assuming that we have a tag handler with the following mutator method:

```
public void setAttribute1(boolean attr);
```

With the type conversion, this means that we can specify the value of `attribute1` using the following static values:

```
<prefix:tag attribute1="true"/>
<prefix:tag attribute1="false"/>
```

Alternatively, we can specify the value for `attribute1` as request-time expressions, as demonstrated in the examples below:

```
<% boolean b = true; %>
<prefix:tag attribute1="<%= b %>"/>

<% int x = 1; int y = 2; %>
<prefix:tag attribute1="<%= x==y %>"/>
```

Although we achieve the same results, the difference here is that the return type of the expression is the same type as is declared in the mutator method. When request-time values are used, the automatic type conversion is no longer performed and the results of the expression must be the same type as is expected by the tag handler. With this in mind, we can see that the following is not valid:

```
<% String s = "true"; %>
<prefix:tag attribute1="<%= s %>"/>
```

Although the string "true" would be automatically converted, it isn't when an expression is used. Instead, the JSP page will try to find a method called setAttribute1() that takes a String as an argument. This is not the case and hence a compilation error would occur.

Although this doesn't seem important, it opens up a whole new way in which tags can be used. As no conversion is performed, we can use any type of Java object in our tags, including those that we define ourselves, by passing the relevant object reference through to the tag with a request-time expression. We'll see examples of this later on.

Object Values

The final conversion rule to introduce is one that is a new addition to the JSP 1.2 specification. We've just said that when request-time values are used to specify the values of attributes on the page, the parameter type of the corresponding mutator method on the tag handler must match up. For example, if a java.util.Date instance is specified as the value on the page, the tag handler must define the appropriate mutator method that takes a java.util.Date instance.

However, since java.util.Date is a subclass of java.lang.Object, and through the normal rules of parameter conversion in Java, the mutator method can also be written to take Object as a parameter instead.

Ignoring the automatic type conversions that apply to numbers and Boolean values, when a static string is specified on the page as the value of an attribute, the JSP page calls the mutator method that takes a java.lang.String as an argument.

However, with the introduction of JSP 1.2, having the mutator take Object as a parameter additionally means that the same method can be used to take static strings. This provides an additional level of flexibility in passing values to tag handlers, and this means that either an object reference, or a static string can be passed through. An example is the name of a scoped variable that is accessible through the page context. We'll see the importance of this in Chapter 4.

For now, though, and with the theory behind attributes covered, let's now move on to look at how they are implemented and put this knowledge into practice.

Adding a String Attribute

Let's extend the date tag that we built in this chapter by adding an attribute to control how the date is formatted on the page. To do this, we'll allow it to take a static attribute called format as follows:

```
<attributes:date format="dd-MMM-yyyy"/>
```

In this example, the format that is supplied to the tag is the same as is used in the java.text.SimpleDateFormat class.

Modifying the Tag Handler

Let's take a look at how we can modify our tag to make use of an attribute.

The first step is to modify our tag handler implementation so that it too has an attribute (or property) called `format`, along with the appropriate mutator method that meets the naming conventions set up by the JavaBeans specification. As the format is just a simple string, we'll use a `String` property in the tag handler to represent this:

```
private String format;

public void setFormat(String format) {
  this.format = format;
}
```

> **In reality, a mutator and its corresponding property aren't actually required. JSP containers generally make use of introspection with Java's reflection mechanism so all that they are really interested in is the presence of a mutator method that matches with the name of the attribute.**

Once this is in place we can move on to modify the functionality provided by the tag. To do this, we can change the `doStartTag()` method:

```
public int doStartTag() throws JspException {

    DateFormat df;

    if (this.format != null) {
      // use the specified date format
      df = new SimpleDateFormat(this.format);
    } else {
      // get the locale of the client and create an appropriate date format
      Locale loc = pageContext.getRequest().getLocale();
      df = DateFormat.getDateInstance(DateFormat.MEDIUM, loc);
    }

    try {
      // and write out the formatted date to the page
      pageContext.getOut().write(df.format(new Date()));
    } catch (java.io.IOException ioe) {
      throw new JspTagException(ioe.getMessage());
    }

    // and skip evaluating the body of the tag (as there shouldn't be one)
    return SKIP_BODY;
  }
```

We'll define the new `format` attribute as optional and check the `format` property before using it. If a format has been supplied, we'll use it, otherwise we'll default to a format appropriate to the locale of the client.

Modifying the Tag Library Descriptor

Once the tag handler has been modified and assuming that it is packaged in `com.wrox.jsptaglibs.date`, the next step is to enhance our tag definition to indicate that it can now take an (optional) attribute. We do this by adding a small section to the TLD that defines the new attribute. For the purposes of this example, this version of the TLD will be called `attributes.tld` and will, once again, reside under the `WEB-INF\tlds` directory:

```
<?xml version="1.0" encoding="ISO-8859-1" ?>
<!DOCTYPE taglib
  PUBLIC "-//Sun Microsystems, Inc.//DTD JSP Tag Library 1.2//EN"
  "http://java.sun.com/dtd/web-jsptaglibrary_1_2.dtd">

<taglib>

  <tlib-version>1.0</tlib-version>
  <jsp-version>1.2</jsp-version>
  <short-name>attributes</short-name>
  <description>
    Attribute examples for the Simple Tags chapter.
  </description>

  <tag>
    <name>date</name>
    <tag-class>com.wrox.jsptaglibs.date.DateTag2</tag-class>
    <body-content>empty</body-content>
    <description>
      Inserts the current date into the page.
    </description>

    <attribute>
      <name>format</name>
      <required>false</required>
      <rtexprvalue>false</rtexprvalue>
    </attribute>
  </tag>

</taglib>
```

name

This is the name of the attribute, in our case `format`.

required

This is a Boolean flag indicating whether the attribute is required (`true` or `yes`) or not (`false` or `no`). As we would like an optional attribute, we'll set this to `false`.

This element is optional and if not supplied defaults to `false`.

rtexprvalue

This is a Boolean flag indicating whether the value of the attribute is the result of a request-time expression (`true` or `yes`) or simply a translation-time value (`false` or `no`). As we're specifying the date format using a static string, we set this to `false`.

This element is optional and if not supplied defaults to `false`.

Deploying the Tag Library

Deploying the tag library is the same as before and requires a small section in the `WEB-INF\web.xml` file to register the library with the web application:

```
<taglib>
  <taglib-uri>/attributesTaglib</taglib-uri>
  <taglib-location>/WEB-INF/tlds/attributes.tld</taglib-location>
</taglib>
```

Using the Tag

As far as development is concerned, that's all that we need to do to add an attribute to our custom tag. We use the tag in the same way as before, with the exception that we can now specify the exact format in which we want the date displayed:

```
<html>

  <head>
    <title>Professional JSP Tag Libraries</title>
  </head>

  <%@ taglib uri="/attributesTaglib" prefix="attributes" %>

  <body>

    <h1>The date is <attributes:date format="dd-MMM-yyyy"/></h1>

  </body>

</html>
```

When requested through a browser, the result is as follows. Notice how the date has been presented in the format `dd-MMM-yyyy` as we specified in the JSP page:

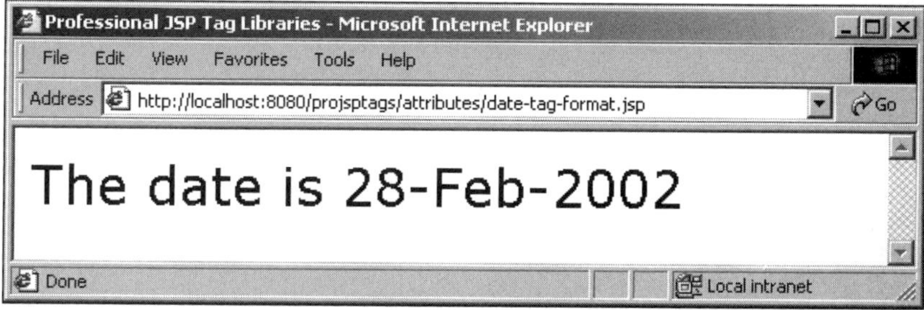

Flexibility and Reusability

We now have a tag that can be used with or without the `format` attribute. This is useful in a number of ways. First, the tag is now more reusable than before as it is more likely to be of use to other pages with different requirements on how the date should be displayed.

Additionally, choosing an optional attribute and ensuring a default behavior has helped to make the tag backwards-compatible. In other words, the tag won't break any existing JSP pages that use it just because we have added an attribute.

Adding an Object Attribute

Let's now take a quick look at how a request-time expression can be used as the value for an attribute. We'll extend the `date` tag further to display an arbitrary date.

Modifying the Tag Handler

The first thing to do is to add a `date` attribute to the tag handler implementation:

```
private Date date;

public void setDate(java.util.Date date) {
  this.date = date;
}
```

As we'd like to display any date, we'll make it so that the tag takes a reference to an existing `java.util.Date` instance as the argument to the mutator method. Remember, attributes can be any Java object. Next, there are further changes to the `doStartTag()` method:

```
public int doStartTag() throws JspException {

  DateFormat df;
  Date d;

  if (this.format != null) {
    // use the specified date format
    df = new SimpleDateFormat(format);
  } else {
    // get the locale of the client and create an appropriate date format
    Locale loc = pageContext.getRequest().getLocale();
    df = DateFormat.getDateInstance(DateFormat.MEDIUM, loc);
  }

  // use a default date (now) if one has not been set
  if (this.date != null) {
    d = this.date;
  } else {
    d = new Date();
```

```
    }

    try {
      // and write out the formatted date to the page
      pageContext.getOut().write(df.format(d));
    } catch (java.io.IOException ioe) {
      throw new JspTagException(ioe.getMessage());
    }

    // and skip evaluating the body of the tag (as there shouldn't be one)
    return SKIP_BODY;
  }
```

As with the format attribute, the date attribute will be optional and therefore we should ensure that the tag works with and without it. If it's not supplied, the default behavior is to simply use the current date.

Modifying the Tag Library Descriptor

Every attribute that we want a tag to support must be defined in the TLD file; otherwise it's inaccessible from the JSP page. In the same way that we did last time, we just need to add another <attribute> section into our taglib descriptor file:

```
<?xml version="1.0" encoding="ISO-8859-1" ?>
<!DOCTYPE taglib
  PUBLIC "-//Sun Microsystems, Inc.//DTD JSP Tag Library 1.2//EN"
  "http://java.sun.com/dtd/web-jsptaglibrary_1_2.dtd">

<taglib>

  <tlib-version>1.0</tlib-version>
  <jsp-version>1.2</jsp-version>
  <short-name>attributes</short-name>
  <description>
    Attribute examples for the Simple Tags chapter.
  </description>

  <tag>
    <name>date</name>
    <tag-class>com.wrox.jsptaglibs.date.DateTag3</tag-class>
    <body-content>empty</body-content>
    <description>
      Inserts the current date into the page.
    </description>

    <attribute>
      <name>format</name>
      <required>false</required>
      <rtexprvalue>false</rtexprvalue>
    </attribute>

    <attribute>
```

```
        <name>date</name>
        <required>false</required>
        <rtexprvalue>true</rtexprvalue>
      </attribute>
    </tag>

  </taglib>
```

Notice here that we've set the `<rtexprvalue/>` flag to `true`, indicating that this attribute can accept values that are the result of a JSP expression.

Using the Tag

Finally, we need to alter our JSP page to use the new functionality:

```
<html>

  <head>
    <title>Professional JSP Tag Libraries</title>
  </head>

  <%@ page import="java.util.Date" %>
  <%@ taglib uri="/attributesTaglib" prefix="attributes" %>

  <body>

    <%
      // 1 day = 1000 * 60 * 60 * 24 = 86400000 milliseconds
      Date tomorrow = new Date();
      tomorrow = new Date(tomorrow.getTime()+86400000);
    %>
    <h1>The date is <attributes:date format="dd-MMM-yyyy"
                                     date="<%= tomorrow %>"/></h1>

  </body>

</html>
```

All we've done here is to get the current date and add the appropriate number of milliseconds to roll it along to tomorrow. This is all performed in a scriptlet, and the resulting `tomorrow` variable is used as the request-time value of the `date` attribute on the new version of the `date` tag:

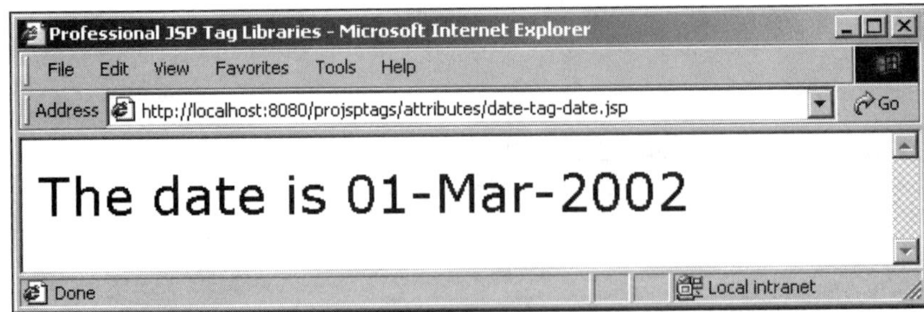

Translation-Time vs. Request-Time Attributes

We've just seen two examples of how to add attributes to tags, and how to subsequently use them for modifying the behavior associated with the tag. One question is, when to use a translation-time attribute and when to use a request-time attribute?

Another question asked frequently is whether there are any additional performance implications in using one type of attribute over the other. This is a hard question to answer as it does vary from vendor to vendor. There is a small degree of processing associated with automatically converting the values of translation-time attributes, but on the other hand some implementations may use Java's reflection mechanism for finding the appropriate mutator method to call when request-time values are used.

Either way, the performance implication of using one over the other is likely to be negligible when compared to the time taken to perform the processing associated with the tag. The best option is to use whichever best suits the type of attribute required. For example, use translation-time values when they can be determined when building the JSP page. On the other hand, use request-time values for passing information between tags, and for passing information between tags and the JSP page itself. We'll see many more examples of this in later chapters.

Summary

This chapter has introduced the basics of tag development. We started out by looking at how tags are represented – both on the page and behind the scenes by way of the `Tag` interface that a tag handler must implement. This includes methods to give the tag knowledge about its environment and the lifecycle methods that provide the functionality associated with a tag.

We looked at the tag lifecycle itself, how JSP pages use tags on the page, and also at how tags can access contextual information. Tags have access to a number of JSP implicit variables such as `out` and `request` through the page context. This is one of the key differentiators over using JavaBeans to encapsulate reusable functionality for use on pages.

We then moved on to building our first tag. Following on from here, we've also seen how attributes can be used to customize the functionality provided by a tag. Here, we looked at the various types of attributes including static (translation-time), dynamic (request-time), optional, and required. We saw some examples of how attribute values can automatically be converted for the tag handler, before moving on to extending the `date` tag to include a couple of attributes.

LONDON

3

Tag Body Content

Up to this point we've looked at some simple tags with and without attributes. All of the examples that we've seen so far had a common feature – the tags had no body. In other words, there was no content between the start and end tags which was highlighted by our use of the shortened form of the tag on the page.

The next step is to introduce the various types of body content that a tag can have and illustrate the purposes for each. We will revisit the tag lifecycle and introduce some of the other return values that are valid for the `doStartTag()` and `doEndTag()` methods. This will demonstrate the ability of custom tags to control those parts of the page that are actually included and rendered in the response sent to the user.

Body Content Types

We've seen that the definition of the tag in the TLD file provides the JSP container with details of the body content of tags. This is done through the optional `<body-content>` element, an example of which is as follows:

```
...
<tag>
  <name>date</name>
  <tag-class>com.wrox.jsptaglibs.date.DateTag</tag-class>
  <body-content>empty</body-content>
  <description>
    Inserts the current date into the page.
  </description>
</tag>
...
```

Here, the body content is defined as empty, which indicates to the JSP container that the tag will contain no body. This is just one of the three possible values that the element can take. The full range of values is:

- empty
- JSP
- tagdependent

> **The <body-content> element is optional in the TLD file; the default value is JSP if it is omitted.**

Let's take a look at each of these values in turn and highlight their meaning when we use the tags on a JSP page.

empty

This states that the body of the tag must be empty (that is, have no content). As we've seen already, empty tags can be written using a long or short format:

```
<prefix:tag></prefix:tag>
<prefix:tag/>
```

From this perspective, body content can be defined as anything that is returned to the client. Therefore, JSP comments are permitted in empty tags as they are stripped during processing. A useful way to document the purpose of the tag on the page is by describing the purpose of the attribute values:

```
<prefix:tag><%-- here is a JSP comment --%></prefix:tag>
```

Something that isn't allowed between empty tags is whitespace. As with the XML specification, whitespace is preserved. This means that whitespace cannot appear between the start and end tags of a tag defined as having empty body content.

The following are examples of body content not permitted between the start and end tags. This includes markup, content, scriptlets, expressions, and HTML comments as they could all return content to the client. The following are all examples of illegal content:

```
<prefix:tag>Here is some content</prefix:tag>
<prefix:tag> </prefix:tag>
<prefix:tag><% ... %></prefix:tag>
<prefix:tag><%= ... %></prefix:tag>
<prefix:tag><!-- here is an HTML comment --></prefix:tag>
```

Including body content in a tag defined as having empty body content will result in a translation-time error.

JSP

A body content of JSP means that the body of the tag may contain regular JSP page elements, including markup, content, scriptlets, expressions, and so on. Additionally, the body content may be empty and can be used with the long or short syntax:

```
<prefix:tag>Here is some content</prefix:tag>
<prefix:tag><% ... %></prefix:tag>
<prefix:tag><%= ... %></prefix:tag>
```

As JSP pages can contain tags it is also valid to have tags as part of the body content, therefore making it possible to nest tags as follows:

```
<prefix:outerTag>
  <prefix:innerTag>Some content inside a nested tag.</prefix:innerTag>
</prefix:outerTag>
```

When JSP is used as the body content type, the content is processed as usual. In other words, scriptlets are executed, expressions are evaluated, and escape character sequences are escaped.

tagdependent

A body content type of tagdependent means that the JSP container will not process the content in any way and instead it is left to the tag to process/evaluate any content. This means that tagdependent body content is left as it is – scriptlets aren't executed, expressions aren't evaluated, and character escape sequences aren't escaped. For example, here is a custom tag that has a SQL statement as its body content:

```
<sql:query>
  SELECT * FROM customer
</sql:query>
```

With potentially large SQL statements, it is clearer to place the SQL statement as body content instead of an attribute. Setting the body content to JSP means that the SQL statement outputs back to the client. Choosing tagdependent on the other hand means that the JSP container ignores the content but does make it available to the tag. As we'll see later, tags can access their body content, which makes it possible for the <sql:query> tag in this example to obtain the SQL statement and execute it on a database.

Once this has been done, the tag could return the results back to the page for display. A tag like this is not really recommended because it breaks the rule about mixing business and presentation logic, but it does illustrate the potential for tagdependent body content.

> *We'll be looking at body tags in Chapter 6 along with some examples of* JSP *and* tagdependent *body content.*

The Tag Interface and Lifecycle Revisited

The previous chapter introduced the Tag interface, but the tags that we looked at were fairly simple with doStartTag() and doEndTag() methods that return SKIP_BODY and EVAL_PAGE respectively. For simplicity, we didn't look at the other valid return codes for these methods. The values of the return codes are constants (static final variables) that are defined within the Tag interface itself:

```
public final static int SKIP_BODY = 0;
public final static int EVAL_BODY_INCLUDE = 1;
public final static int SKIP_PAGE = 5;
public final static int EVAL_PAGE = 6;
```

Notice that there are four constants defined in the Tag interface, two of which we've seen in use already. The constants in the Tag interface can be divided into two groups – those that are valid return values for doStartTag() and those that are valid return values for doEndTag(). In the context of the tag lifecycle, each of these values has a different meaning and can affect the lifecycle of the tag:

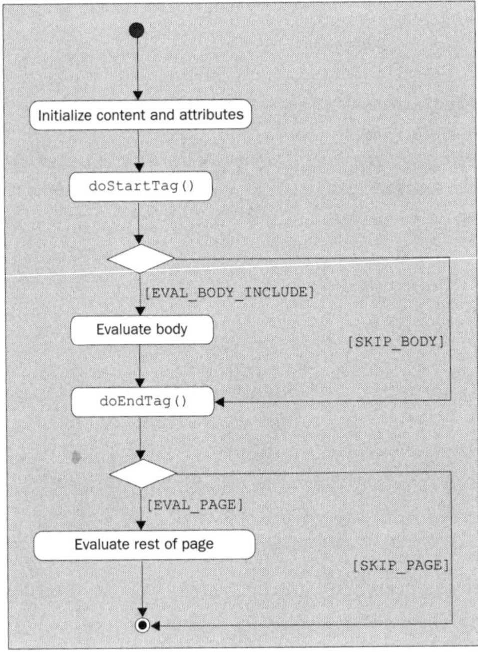

In the first step in the lifecycle of a tag handler the context (parent tag and PageContext) is initialized along with any of the tag's attributes. Following this step is the doStartTag() method. With this as a starting point, let's look in detail at the lifecycle methods, the possible return values, and the way they affect the processing of a page.

Return Values for doStartTag()

Let's first look at those values that are valid return codes for the doStartTag() method – SKIP_BODY and EVAL_BODY_INCLUDE.

SKIP_BODY

The SKIP_BODY return code indicates to the JSP page that we're not interested in processing (or evaluating) the body content of the tag. This could be for several reasons. For example, the tag may not have a body, in which case we're certainly not interested in evaluating it. Alternatively, it may be that we programmatically decide that we don't want the user to see the contents of the tag.

A good example here is a tag that either shows or hides the body of the tag depending on the security roles assigned to the current user, which determines whether the user is authorized to see that content. Another example would be a tag that mimicked a conditional (if) statement. Here, we could skip evaluation of the body if the condition was false.

To tell the JSP page that we don't want the body content of the custom tag evaluated, we simply return SKIP_BODY from the doStartTag() method:

```
public int doStartTag() throws JspException {
  // perform some processing and tell the JSP to skip (ignore)
  // the body of this tag
  return SKIP_BODY;
}
```

EVAL_BODY_INCLUDE

EVAL_BODY_INCLUDE, on the other hand, tells the JSP page that the body content contained between the start and end tags should be included and processed. Again, we simply return EVAL_BODY_INCLUDE from the doStartTag() method:

```
public int doStartTag() throws JspException {
  // perform some processing and tell the JSP to evaluate (include)
  // the body of this tag
  return EVAL_BODY_INCLUDE;
}
```

Return Values for doEndTag()

There are two values that can be returned from the doEndTag() method – EVAL_PAGE and SKIP_PAGE.

EVAL_PAGE

The EVAL_PAGE return code tells the JSP page that the remainder of the page should be processed, or evaluated. This is the most common value returned from the doEndTag() method; an example of its usage is as follows:

```
public int doEndTag() throws JspException {
  // perform some processing and tell the JSP to evaluate (include)
  // the remainder of the page
  return EVAL_PAGE;
}
```

SKIP_PAGE

The `SKIP_PAGE` return code instructs the JSP page to skip the remainder of the page. This is equivalent to placing a "`return`" statement in a scriptlet on a JSP page, which means that everything after that point is ignored. An example of its usage is as follows:

```
public int doEndTag() throws JspException {
  // perform some processing and tell the JSP to skip (ignore)
  // the remainder of the page
  return SKIP_PAGE;
}
```

Now that we've seen the various values that can be returned from the `doStartTag()` and `doEndTag()` methods, let's see a real-world example of this in action by building a tag that only shows its body if the current user is authorized to see it.

Programmatically Including the Body Content

Many web sites allow users to register online for services such as web-based e-mail, e-commerce, discussion forums, and so on. In some cases, registration is essential to access the services provided by the web site, although with many sites, registering simply provides us with additional benefits such as regular updates about the site or the ability to set up preferences and receive personalized content. In this scenario, there are generally two types of users – those that are registered and those that are not. These are called **roles**.

One of the features of the servlet specification is the ability to manage security declaratively from the deployment descriptors. For example, we can define entire sections of a web site as restricted, forcing the users to authenticate themselves with the application before they are allowed into the site. In addition to this, we can also define that only users that belong to a specific role are allowed access to parts of the site.

Imagine that we are building a web site for Wrox to allow visitors to search for information about the currently available books. As part of the web site, users could optionally register so that they can be notified of updates to categories that they are interested in and also so that they can tailor the content of the web site to their interests by specifying their preferences. To enable this, we decide that we need to support two types of users, or roles – one for registered users and one for guests that have not yet registered. To encourage people to register with the site, only registered users can set up their preferences.

Defining the Users

In a real web site, the list of registered users would be dynamic, and probably stored in something like a database. This collection of user information is called a **realm**. For the purposes of this example, however, we'll simply simulate this by defining them in the `tomcat-users.xml` file – the realm file that ships with Tomcat. This file can be found in the `%TOMCAT_HOME%\conf` directory and contains a list of the users that can be authenticated, and the roles that those users are a part of:

```
<tomcat-users>
  <user name="tomcat" password="tomcat" roles="tomcat" />
  <user name="role1"  password="tomcat" roles="role1"  />
  <user name="both"   password="tomcat" roles="tomcat,role1" />
  <user name="simon"  password="password" roles="registered" />
  <user name="guest"  password="" roles="guest" />
</tomcat-users>
```

Here, we have just added two users to the default file – `simon` that is a member of the `registered` role, and `guest` that is part of the `guest` role.

Securing the Site

The next step is to restrict the web site to ensure that only users that log in are allowed to access it. To do this, we simply have to insert the following XML fragment into the web application deployment descriptor.

The first section between the `<security-constraint>` elements defines a collection of secured web resources. In this case, these resources are anything residing underneath `\bodycontent\wrox` of this web application and are only accessible to users that are members of the `registered` and `guest` roles:

```
  <security-constraint>
    <web-resource-collection>
      <web-resource-name>RegisteredUsers</web-resource-name>
      <url-pattern>/bodycontent/wrox/*</url-pattern>
    </web-resource-collection>
    <auth-constraint>
      <role-name>registered</role-name>
      <role-name>guest</role-name>
    </auth-constraint>
  </security-constraint>
```

Following this, the `<login-config>` section defines the mechanism that will be used to allow users to authenticate themselves to this web application:

```
  <login-config>
    <auth-method>BASIC</auth-method>
    <realm-name>Registered Users</realm-name>
  </login-config>
</web-app>
```

Here we are just using BASIC authentication, which is a standard method under HTTP that prompts the user to enter a username and password via a pop-up login window:

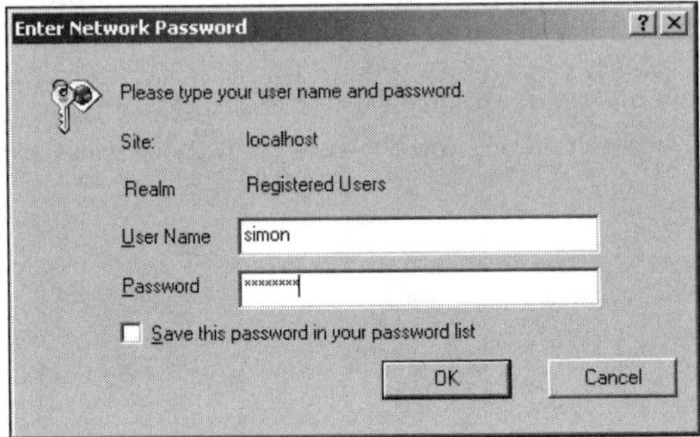

The web container, in this case Tomcat, performs the process of authenticating the user from the username and password that they enter into this window. If successful, access to the requested resource is allowed. If an incorrect username and password is supplied, it will result in an "access denied" error message appearing within the browser.

> *Further information about managing security within web applications can be found in another title in the Wrox series, Professional Java Servlets 2.3 (ISBN 1-861005-61X).*

Building the Menu

Now that the security has been put in place we can move on to build the web site, starting with a static set of menu items on the left-hand side of the page:

```
<html>
  <head>
    <title>Professional JSP Tag Libraries</title>
  </head>

  <body>
    <h1>Wrox books online</h1>

    <b><a href="category.jsp?name=All" target="contentFrame">Books</a></b>
    <br/>

      
    <font size="-2"><a href="category.jsp?name=.NET">.NET</a></font>
    <br/>

      
    <font size="-2"><a href="category.jsp?name=Java">Java</a></font>
    <br/>

      
    <font size="-2"><a href="category.jsp?name=XML">XML</a></font>
    <br/>
```

```
    <br/>
    <b><a href="help.jsp">Help</a></b>
    <br/>
  </body>
</html>
```

This menu allows users to look at specific categories and the result of requesting this page is as follows:

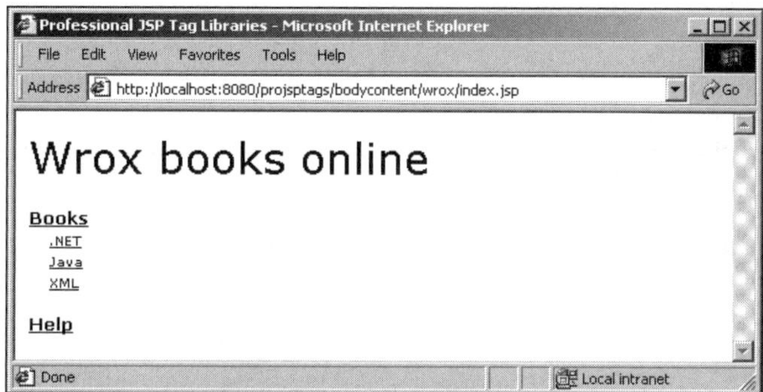

To allow users to manage their preferences when visiting the site, it would be a good idea to give them another menu item called Preferences. However, since this is only available to registered users, we should only render the appropriate hyperlink if the user is a member of the `registered` role.

It is a trivial task to determine whether the user is a member of a specific role by using the `isUserInRole()` method of the `HttpServletRequest` class. However, instead of using Java code on the page we'll build a custom tag to perform this task for us.

Writing the Tag

As we've seen, building tags with attributes is a straightforward task so instead of hard- coding the logic of checking user information, we'll make the tag generic so that it can determine whether the current user is a member of any arbitrary role.

In the same way as we saw in the previous chapter, this tag handler will extend the `TagSupport` class:

```
package com.wrox.jsptaglibs.security;

import javax.servlet.http.HttpServletRequest;
import javax.servlet.jsp.JspException;
import javax.servlet.jsp.tagext.TagSupport;

public class UserInRoleTag extends TagSupport {
```

The attribute that the tag will take is called `role`, which represents the name of a potential user role. As such, we would like to determine whether the user is a member of this role or not. This involves a property and its associated mutator method:

```
    private String role;

    public void setRole(String role) {
      this.role = role;
    }
```

Finally, there is the processing associated with this tag, all wrapped up within the `doStartTag()` method. The logic here says that if the current user is a member of the role specified as an attribute, then they are permitted to see the body content of the tag and the method returns `EVAL_BODY_INCLUDE`. If not, the body content is hidden from them by returning `SKIP_BODY`:

```
    public int doStartTag() throws JspException {

      HttpServletRequest request;
      request = (HttpServletRequest)pageContext.getRequest();

      // check that the user is a member of the specified role
      if (request.isUserInRole(role)) {
        return EVAL_BODY_INCLUDE;
      } else {
        return SKIP_BODY;
      }
    }
  }
```

This tag shows or hides the body content of the tag depending on the role associated with the user. In effect, it performs a simple conditional statement of the form "if the user is in the specified role then show them the body content".

Writing the Tag Library Descriptor

With the tag written, we must of course remember to write the TLD file. In this tag library, we have a single tag called `userInRole` that has a required attribute called `role`. Since we make use of the body content, we define the body content to be `JSP` instead of `empty`:

```
  <?xml version="1.0" encoding="ISO-8859-1" ?>
  <!DOCTYPE taglib
    PUBLIC "-//Sun Microsystems, Inc.//DTD JSP Tag Library 1.2//EN"
    "http://java.sun.com/dtd/web-jsptaglibrary_1_2.dtd">

  <taglib>

    <tlib-version>1.0</tlib-version>
    <jsp-version>1.2</jsp-version>
    <short-name>security</short-name>
    <description>
      Security examples for the Body Content chapter.
    </description>

    <tag>
      <name>userInRole</name>
  <tag-class>com.wrox.jsptaglibs.security.UserInRoleTag</tag-class>
      <body-content>JSP</body-content>
      <description>
        Determines whether the current user is in a particular role.
```

```
    </description>

    <attribute>
      <name>role</name>
      <required>true</required>
      <rtexprvalue>false</rtexprvalue>
    </attribute>
  </tag>

</taglib>
```

Revising the Menu

Once the tag has been successfully deployed, the next step is to use it on the page:

```
<html>
  <head>
    <title>Professional JSP Tag Libraries</title>
  </head>

  <%@ taglib uri="/securityTaglib" prefix="security" %>

  <body>
    <h1>Wrox books online</h1>

    <b><a href="category.jsp?name=All" target="contentFrame">Books</a></b>
    <br/>

      
    <font size="-2"><a href="category.jsp?name=.NET">.NET</a></font>
    <br/>

      
    <font size="-2"><a href="category.jsp?name=Java">Java</a></font>
    <br/>

      
    <font size="-2"><a href="category.jsp?name=XML">XML</a></font>
    <br/>

    <security:userInRole role="registered">
      <br/>
      <b><a href="preferences.jsp">Preferences</a></b>
      <br/>
    </security:userInRole>

    <br/>
    <b><a href="help.jsp">Help</a></b>
    <br/>

  </body>
</html>
```

As we saw in the previous chapter, using the tag is simply a matter of importing the tag library with the `taglib` directive and referring to the tag on the page by the name defined in the TLD file. We're making use of the tag here to only display the Preferences menu item if the current user is a member of the `registered` role. Is this isn't the case then the output is the same as before. If the user is registered, the resulting page is now as follows:

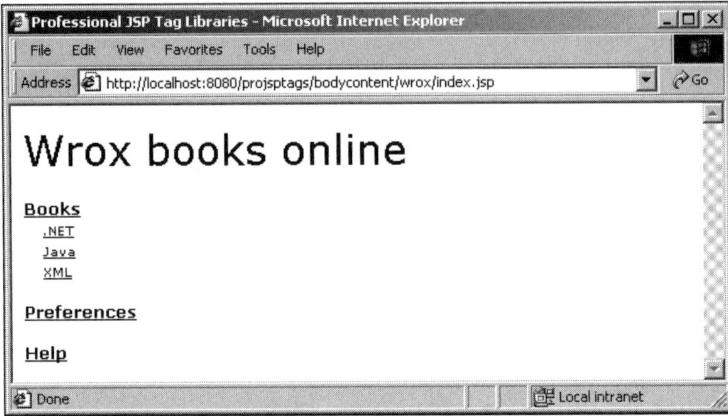

Although we can declaratively define the authentication mechanism through the deployment descriptor, the authorization that we need here must be programmatically determined. Fortunately, this is a simple method call away that, when used, means that we have a single menu that can be used for registered and guest users.

This example has demonstrated two things. First, it has shown that tags have the ability to programmatically determine whether their body content should be skipped or evaluated by returning `SKIP_BODY` or `EVAL_BODY_INCLUDE` from the `doStartTag()` method respectively. In addition to this, we've also illustrated one of the important uses for custom tags on the page, as replacements for short pieces of recurring conditional logic. Moving such logic into custom tags promotes the reusability and maintainability of a JSP-based application while at the same time providing the power and flexibility that conditional programming constructs bring to the page.

Return Codes in Context

Up until now we've only looked at how the return values of the `doStartTag()` and `doEndTag()` methods affect the page when the tags are used in isolation. Let's now consider what happens when the tags are used within some other contexts:

- Included pages
- Forwarded pages
- Nested tags

Let's look at each of these in turn.

Included Pages

Including another JSP page is achieved through the `include` directive or the `<jsp:include/>` action.

Include Directive

The `<include/>` directive statically includes the specified file into the page and is the equivalent of a server-side include. When a file (for example a JSP page fragment) is included into a JSP page, the content of the file gets embedded in source form as it is. Following this, the resulting page is then processed in the normal way.

Consider an included page that contains a custom tag. In general, the body content of a custom tag is self-contained and doesn't affect the remainder of the page from evaluation. For this reason, the behavior associated with the return codes from the `doStartTag()` method is the same as illustrated previously. Returning `SKIP_BODY` instructs the JSP page to ignore the body content of the tag, while returning `EVAL_BODY_INCLUDE` instructs the JSP page to evaluate (include) the body content.

However, the `doEndTag()` method is a different story. Returning `EVAL_PAGE` results in the usual evaluation of the page, but the behavior associated with returning `SKIP_PAGE` is now different. To see how statically including a page changes this, let's look at an example.

First, let's define a parent JSP page that will include another page using the `include` directive:

```
<html>
  <head>
    <title>Professional JSP Tag Libraries</title>
  </head>

  <body>

    (1) Before the include<br/>

    <%@ include file="included-skippage.jsp" %>

    (5) After the include<br/>

  </body>
</html>
```

Here, we have a simple page that uses the `include` directive to include another file, the contents of which are as follows:

```
<%@ taglib uri="/bodycontentTaglib" prefix="bodycontent" %>

(2) Before the tag<br/>

<bodycontent:skipPage>
  (3) In the tag<br/>
</bodycontent:skipPage>

(4) After the tag<br/>
```

This file contains a fragment of JSP page that is to be included and uses a custom tag called `skipPage` that does nothing except return `SKIP_PAGE` from the `doEndTag()` method. Here, we have some numbered points before, inside, and after the tag so that we can see what is going on.

Requesting the parent page will statically include the fragment of JSP page at run-time:

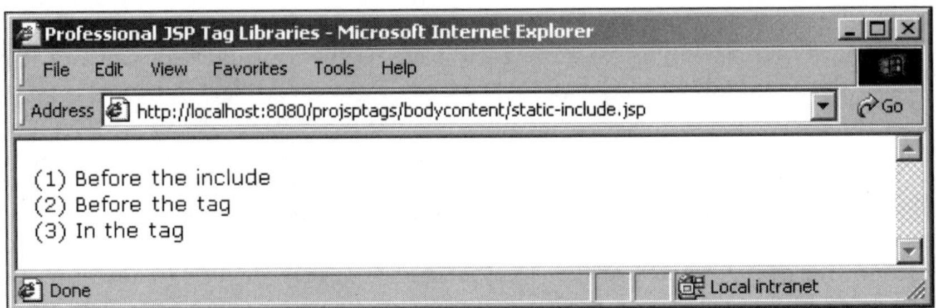

As we can see, returning `SKIP_PAGE` from a tag within a statically included JSP page skips the parent page too. This is because the static include in-lines the included JSP page and then evaluates it. In other words, the contents of the included page become part of the parent JSP page, which is then evaluated as a single page. From here the behavior is the same as before and hence the rest of the parent page is skipped.

Include Action

The `<jsp:include/>` action, on the other hand, processes the request and includes the response into the requesting page. The return codes for `doStartTag()` cause the same behavior as before. However, as the request is treated separately from that of the parent page, the effect of returning `SKIP_PAGE` and `EVAL_PAGE` is different from the static include.

Here, the return codes from the `doEndTag()` apply to the context of the page in which they are used. In other words, as the page is requested separately, only the remainder of the included page is either evaluated or skipped. To illustrate this, let's again look at an example of an included page that contains a tag that instructs the remainder of the page to be skipped. The parent (requesting) page is as follows:

```
<html>
  <head>
    <title>Professional JSP Tag Libraries</title>
  </head>

  <body>

    (1) Before the include<br/>

    <jsp:include page="included-skippage.jsp"/>

    (5) After the include<br/>

  </body>
</html>
```

Here we are using the `<jsp:include/>` action to perform a dynamic (request-time) include of the same page as before. The result of requesting this page is as follows:

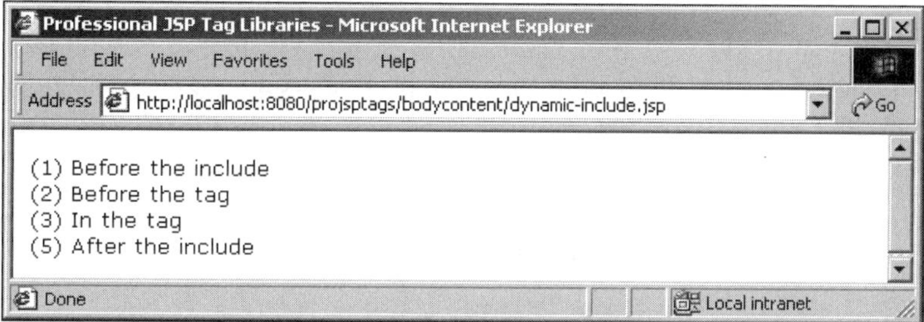

The difference is that only the remainder of the included page has been skipped, leaving the content unaffected after the `<jsp:include/>` action. The JSP page does skip the remainder of the page but the included page has been evaluated separately and only the results have been included.

Forwarded Pages

JSP pages can forward requests on to other JSP pages. As forwards are also evaluated separately from the pages that requested the forward, the return codes of the `doEndTag()` method apply once again only to that context.

Nested Tags

The final context to consider is that of nested tags. The various return values from the `doStartTag()` and `doEndTag()` methods provide the expected results. Returning `EVAL_BODY_INCLUDE` or `EVAL_PAGE` tells the JSP page to evaluate the body and page respectively, while `SKIP_BODY` and `SKIP_PAGE` tells the JSP page to skip the body and page respectively.

Returning `SKIP_BODY` from the `doStartTag()` method in a tag instructs the JSP page to ignore the tag's body content. As the body content is self-contained, the JSP page will only ignore the body content in question. As expected only the body of the nested tag is skipped, leaving the body content of the parent tag unaffected.

On the other hand, returning `SKIP_PAGE` from the `doEndTag()` method of a nested tag tells JSP page to skip the page and the entire page is skipped with no regard for the fact the tag is nested.

Putting it all Together

Let's wrap up the chapter by combining the concepts that we've seen so far into a real-world example, writing some tags that access information stored within cookies.

Following on from the previous example of the Wrox web site, when users revisit the site, we decide that it would be nice to show them a "welcome back" message. One way that this can be achieved is through the use of cookies which, as you know, are small snippets of information (a name-value pair) set by the web server and stored on the user's web browser.

From a development perspective, cookies are easy to use and are accessible through the HttpServletRequest interface. Unfortunately, using them on a JSP page does involve a fair quantity of Java code on the page – something that we are trying to avoid.

Every time the user logs in, the web application will set a cookie called visitorName, and subsequently all that we need to do to show them the personalized message is to find this cookie and display its associated value. If the cookie can't be found, the message isn't shown.

Rather than write the Java code as scriptlets on the page, let's instead build two custom tags – one that searches for the cookie and evaluates its body content if found, and one that simply displays the value associated with a cookie. We could use these tags as follows:

```
<cookie:exists name="visitorName">
    <h2>Welcome back <cookie:value name="visitorName"/></h2>
</cookie:exists>
```

Putting this simple type of conditional logic into the page is often useful from a presentation perspective as it allows parts of the user interface to be hidden or shown depending on whether certain conditions are met. In this case, we are only showing the welcome back message if the cookie can be found.

Determining Whether a Cookie Exists

The first tag to write is the tag that determines whether a specific cookie exists. As before, the first step is to write a tag handler that extends TagSupport:

```
package com.wrox.jsptaglibs.cookie;

import javax.servlet.http.HttpServletRequest;
import javax.servlet.jsp.JspException;
import javax.servlet.jsp.tagext.TagSupport;

public class CookieExistsTag extends TagSupport {
```

As the tag will have one attribute called name, we define the property and its corresponding mutator method:

```
  private String name;

  public void setName(String name) {
    this.name = name;
  }
```

Following this, we have the doStartTag() method where all of the hard work is performed. The tag uses a helper class that gets all of the cookies and checks whether the name matches the name that was supplied through the attribute. If a match is found, the tag instructs the JSP page to evaluate its body content; otherwise the tag instructs the page to skip its body:

```
  public int doStartTag() throws JspException {

    HttpServletRequest request;
    request = (HttpServletRequest)pageContext.getRequest();
```

```
      Cookie cookies[] = request.getCookies();

      CookieHelper helper = new CookieHelper();
      Cookie cookie = helper.getCookie(cookies, name);

      if (cookie != null) {
        // the cookie was found so evaluate the body content
        return EVAL_BODY_INCLUDE;
      } else {
        // the cookie wasn't found so skip the body content
        return SKIP_BODY;
      }
    }
  }
```

Using a helper class in this situation is a good idea since it wraps up the logic required to find a named cookie, making it reusable within other tags that deal with cookies. Custom tags increase the reusability and maintainability of code on a JSP page, but we should also take steps to ensure that our tag handlers do not neglect this too. The implementation for this helper class is as follows:

```
package com.wrox.jsptaglibs.cookie;

import javax.servlet.http.Cookie;

public class CookieHelper {

  public CookieHelper() {}

  public Cookie getCookie(Cookie cookies[], String name) {

    for (int i = 0; i < cookies.length; i++) {
      if (cookies[i].getName().equals(name)) {
        return cookies[i];
      }
    }

    // we've got this far so the specified cookie wasn't found
    return null;
  }
}
```

Displaying the Value of a Cookie

Following this we have the tag that displays the value associated with a specified cookie. Once again this extends the `TagSupport` class and has a single attribute called `name`:

```
package com.wrox.jsptaglibs.cookie;

import java.io.IOException;

import javax.servlet.http.HttpServletRequest;
```

```
import javax.servlet.jsp.JspException;
import javax.servlet.jsp.tagext.TagSupport;

public class CookieValueTag extends TagSupport {

  private String name;

  public void setName(String name) {
    this.name = name;
  }
```

Next is the `doStartTag()` method that again uses the helper class to search through all of the cookies until it finds the one with the same name as that supplied. Once found, the tag simply outputs the value associated with the cookie back to the page using the current `JspWriter` instance. After this has been done, the tag tells the JSP page to skip its body content:

```
  public int doStartTag() throws JspException {

    HttpServletRequest request;
    request = (HttpServletRequest)pageContext.getRequest();
    Cookie cookies[] = request.getCookies();

    CookieHelper helper = new CookieHelper();
    Cookie cookie = helper.getCookie(cookies, name);

    if (cookie != null) {
      try {
        pageContext.getOut().write(cookie.getValue());
      } catch (IOException ioe) {
        throw new JspTagException(ioe.getMessage());
      }
    }

    // and skip the body content for this empty tag
    return SKIP_BODY;
  }
}
```

The Tag Library Descriptor

Now that we've written the tags, we must describe them with a TLD file as before. First, there's the `exists` tag that has a body content of `JSP` and a single, required attribute called `name`:

```
<?xml version="1.0" encoding="ISO-8859-1" ?>
<!DOCTYPE taglib
  PUBLIC "-//Sun Microsystems, Inc.//DTD JSP Tag Library 1.2//EN"
  "http://java.sun.com/dtd/web-jsptaglibrary_1_2.dtd">

<taglib>

  <tlib-version>1.0</tlib-version>
```

```
<jsp-version>1.2</jsp-version>
<short-name>cookie</short-name>
<description>
  Cookie examples for the Body Content chapter.
</description>

<tag>
  <name>exists</name>
  <tag-class>com.wrox.jsptaglibs.cookie.CookieExistsTag</tag-class>
  <body-content>JSP</body-content>
  <description>
    Determines whether a cookie with the specified name exists.
  </description>

  <attribute>
    <name>name</name>
    <required>true</required>
    <rtexprvalue>false</rtexprvalue>
  </attribute>
</tag>
```

This is followed (in the same TLD) by the `value` tag which again has a single attribute called `name`, but this time with a body content of `empty`:

```
  <tag>
    <name>value</name>
    <tag-class>com.wrox.jsptaglibs.cookie.CookieValueTag</tag-class>
    <body-content>empty</body-content>
    <description>
      Displays the value of the cookie with the specified name.
    </description>

    <attribute>
      <name>name</name>
      <required>true</required>
      <rtexprvalue>false</rtexprvalue>
    </attribute>
  </tag>

</taglib>
```

We are demonstrating here a tag library that contains more than one tag. In the same way that Java packages group together related Java classes, it is useful to group together related custom tags into a single tag library. We'll look at this in more detail in Chapter 9.

Using the Tags

After compiling, deploying, and registering the tag library, we can use the tags in a page as follows:

```
<html>
  <head>
    <title>Professional JSP Tag Libraries</title>
  </head>

  <%@ taglib uri="/cookieTaglib" prefix="cookie" %>

  <body>
    <table width="100%">
      <tr>
        <td>
          <h1>Wrox books online</h1>
        </td>
        <td align="right">
          <cookie:exists name="visitorName">
            Welcome back <cookie:value name="visitorName"/>
          </cookie:exists>
        </td>
      </tr>
    </table>
  </body>
</html>
```

If a cookie called `visitorName` had been created on a previous visit to the site, the following page shows the result of using the tags:

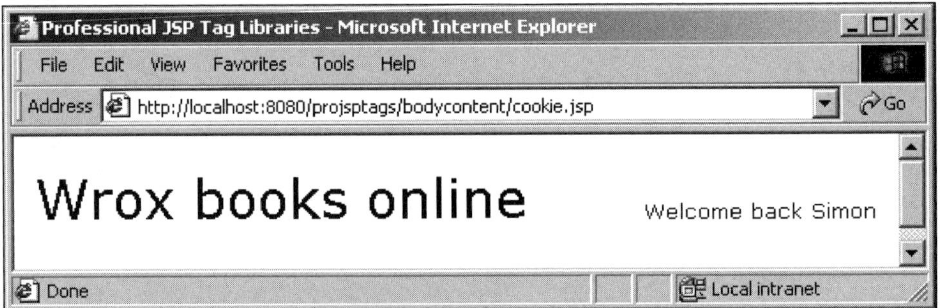

Writing these tags has achieved several things. First, it has further illustrated the power of custom tags and the ability that they have to remove potentially complex code from the page and into reusable components. In addition to this, the examples here have brought together and used several of the features of tags. We've seen yet more examples of how attributes can be used and another real-world example of how a tag might programmatically determine which value to return from the `doStartTag()` method, and therefore whether to evaluate its body content.

Adding the Navigation

As a final example, let's now combine this tag with the security tag that we developed a short while ago. In addition to showing the user a welcome back message, as part of the user preferences we decide that we will allow the user to hide the menu items on the left hand side of the page so that more space can be allocated to the content that they are trying to view. A way to do this is to simply set another cookie to indicate whether they have turned off the navigation or not. For the purposes of this example, this cookie is called `showNavigation` and has a value of `true` or `false`. As a default, the value of this cookie could be set to `false` when the user first visits the site.

Rather than clutter up the page with the HTML behind the menu items, instead we have decided to place this content into a separate JSP page and include it whenever necessary:

```
<html>
  <head>
    <title>Professional JSP Tag Libraries</title>
  </head>

  <%@ taglib uri="/cookieTaglib" prefix="cookie" %>

  <body>
    <table width="100%">
      <tr>
        <td>
          <h1>Wrox books online</h1>
        </td>
        <td align="right">
          <cookie:exists name="visitorName">
            Welcome back <cookie:value name="visitorName"/>
          </cookie:exists>
        </td>
      </tr>
    </table>

    <cookie:existsWithValue name="showNavigation" value="true">
      <%@ include file="navigation.jsp" %>
    </cookie:existsWithValue>
  </body>
</html>
```

We've already developed a couple of tags that deal with cookies, so rather than using Java code on the page to determine whether a named cookie exists with a specified value, we'll again write a tag. This is achieved with the `existsWithValue` tag, the body content of which is evaluated if a named cookie can be found with the specified value. In this example, all that the body content does is to statically include another JSP page that contains the navigation.

Here, the opening and closing `<html>`, `<head>`, and `<body>` tags are missing because it represents a fragment of a page rather than an entire page:

```
<%@ taglib uri="/securityTaglib" prefix="security" %>

<b><a href="category.jsp?name=All" target="contentFrame">Books</a></b>
<br/>

  
<font size="-2"><a href="category.jsp?name=.NET">.NET</a></font>
<br/>

  
<font size="-2"><a href="category.jsp?name=Java">Java</a></font>
<br/>

  
<font size="-2"><a href="category.jsp?name=XML">XML</a></font>
<br/>

<security:userInRole role="registered">
  <br/>
  <b><a href="preferences.jsp">Preferences</a></b>
  <br/>
</security:userInRole>

<br/>
<b><a href="help.jsp">Help</a></b>
<br/>
```

Determining Whether a Specific Cookie Exists

The next thing to do is to write the tag handler for the `existsWithValue` tag. This is a straightforward task since we can once again make use of the `CookieHelper` class:

```
package com.wrox.jsptaglibs.cookie;

import javax.servlet.http.HttpServletRequest;
import javax.servlet.jsp.JspException;
import javax.servlet.jsp.tagext.TagSupport;

public class CookieExistsWithValueTag extends TagSupport {

  private String name;
  private String value;

  public int doStartTag() throws JspException {

    HttpServletRequest request;
    request = (HttpServletRequest)pageContext.getRequest();
    Cookie cookies[] = request.getCookies();

    CookieHelper helper = new CookieHelper();
    Cookie cookie = helper.getCookie(cookies, name);
```

```
    if (cookie != null && cookie.getValue().equals(value)) {
      // the cookie value matched so evaluate the body content
      return EVAL_BODY_INCLUDE;
    } else {
      // the cookie value didn't match so skip the body content
      return SKIP_BODY;
    }
  }

  public void setName(String name) {
    this.name = name;
  }

  public void setValue(String value) {
    this.value = value;
  }
}
```

Modifying the TLD

With the new tag written we can add it in to the TLD file:

```
<?xml version="1.0" encoding="ISO-8859-1" ?>
<!DOCTYPE taglib
  PUBLIC "-//Sun Microsystems, Inc.//DTD JSP Tag Library 1.2//EN"
  "http://java.sun.com/dtd/web-jsptaglibrary_1_2.dtd">

<taglib>

  <tlib-version>1.0</tlib-version>
  <jsp-version>1.2</jsp-version>
  <short-name>cookie</short-name>
  <description>
    Cookie examples for the Body Content chapter.
  </description>

  ...

  <tag>
    <name>existsWithValue</name>
    <tag-class>
      com.wrox.jsptaglibs.cookie.CookieExistsWithValueTag
    </tag-class>
    <body-content>JSP</body-content>
    <description>
      Determines whether a cookie with the specified name and value exists.
    </description>

    <attribute>
      <name>name</name>
      <required>true</required>
      <rtexprvalue>false</rtexprvalue>
```

```
    </attribute>

    <attribute>
      <name>value</name>
      <required>true</required>
      <rtexprvalue>false</rtexprvalue>
    </attribute>
  </tag>

</taglib>
```

Using the Tag

Using the new `existsWithValue` tag on the page as illustrated below demonstrates several things:

```
<cookie:existsWithValue name="showNavigation" value="true">
  <%@ include file="navigation.jsp" %>
</cookie:existsWithValue>
```

First of all, it shows what happens when a JSP fragment that contains other custom tags is statically included in a page. As we'd expect, the fragment is included in the page in its source form. This means, of course, that the content of `navigation.jsp` gets inserted between the `existsWithValue` tags. In turn, as the fragment contains other custom tags, we eventually end up with the scenario where we have further, nested tags to be evaluated on the page.

When a guest user accesses the site, they are still shown the menu but not the Preferences menu item. This works because, although the nested tag (`userInRole`) chooses to skip its body content, the outer (`existsWithValue`) tag doesn't get affected since it has already been evaluated.

Note that we have not implemented the preferences functionality as it would not add anything to the subject at hand.

Splitting up the pages in an application is a common and useful way to increase the maintainability of the site, and the reusability of individual JSP fragments. What this example demonstrates is that it is still possible to do this in conjunction with custom tags – something that is often forgotten about when introducing new technologies such as custom tags.

Summary

In this chapter we introduced tag bodies, and looked at the three different types of tag body content that can be defined in the tag library descriptor (TLD) file.

We then revisited the tag lifecycle and introduced the various return codes that can be returned from the `doStartTag()` and `doEndTag()` methods. Following this, we looked at how the context of the tag affects the behavior associated with each of the return codes. This included a look at statically including content, dynamically including content, forwarding, and finally how nesting tags affects the outcome.

Controlling the page is yet another reason to use custom tags over JavaBeans to encapsulate reusable functionality; for example tags like those that only present their body content to the user if a certain condition is met. While we've only seen simple examples of controlling the page here, the next chapter shows how custom tags can use scripting variables to allow tags and pages to cooperate and share information.

LONDON

Scripting Variables in the Page

Now that we've introduced the various types of tag body content, the next step is to look at JSP scripting variables, specifically around the following areas:

- Using scripting variables in a JSP page
- Using scripting variables to share information between a JSP page and a custom tag
- Using scripting variables to share information between custom tags on a JSP page

In this chapter, we'll see what scripting variables are, how they can be used in conjunction with the implicit `pageContext` variable, and also the standard actions associated with them. We'll then move on and explore how scoped variables can be introduced by custom tags for subsequent use on the page. We'll look at the two mechanisms for declaring scripting variables, namely:

- Declaratively in the TLD file
- Programmatically, by implementing a `TagExtraInfo` class

To wrap up, we'll look at some of the finer points associated with introducing variables into a JSP page, and also some useful conventions for the development of such tags.

Scripting Variables

We've seen that it is possible to declare local variables on the page by using scriptlets. For example, we might use the following scriptlet to declare a variable called `size`:

```
<%
  int size = 0;
%>
```

As we saw in the JSP lifecycle, since the entire JSP page is translated into a single method in a Java servlet, the variables are local to the page on which they are declared. As such, they can be used by other scriptlets and expressions in the page as illustrated below:

```
<%= size %>
```

In essence, they are just regular variables that can be used anywhere on the page.

Java Objects

In addition to scripting variables, JSP pages, like servlets, can create and access Java objects. Once created, these objects can be bound to one of the predefined scopes and subsequently used throughout the pages included by the selected scope. The scopes are as follows:

Page

An object with page scope is only accessible within the JSP page in which it is bound, irrespective of whether the page has been dynamically included within another page, or the request has been forwarded. In these situations, the objects will not be accessible outside the page that created them. This has limited use on a JSP page, but it is more useful when combined with custom tags.

Request

Objects with request scope, on the other hand, are available for the lifetime of the request. In reality, this means until the request has been serviced and a response returned. As these objects are valid for the lifetime of the entire request, they are also available within other included pages and/or Java servlets.

Session

Session-based objects are associated with the HTTP session in which the page is engaged. This is a useful way of storing information throughout a user's session, for example an object representing the user's current details (name, e-mail address, and so on) or a series of objects representing the contents of the user's shopping cart in an online store.

Session-based objects can only be bound and accessed from "session-aware" JSP pages. This is the default, but it can be configured through the JSP `page` directive as shown below:

```
<%@ page session="true" %>
```

Trying to access the session in a page that isn't session-aware will result in an error when the JSP page is translated into its corresponding servlet.

Application

Application scope is used to share information among all of the JSP pages and servlets in a web-based application. Storing objects with this scope is equivalent to storing them in the `ServletContext` – a container for sharing resources accessible by all servlets and JSP pages within a web application. An example here might be a JDBC connection pool that is shared by all pages in an application.

Using Java Objects with JSP

Java objects are very useful for a number of reasons, particularly for storing information about the user's current session. JSP applications must be designed appropriately according to the normal Java application design rules: Java objects should encapsulate the concepts and actors involved. For example, imagine that we have a web application with a `User` class containing information about the current user. This might include a property called `username` to represent the username with which they logged in:

```
package com.wrox.jsptaglibs.scriptingvariables;

public class User {

  private String username;

  public User() {}

  public String getUsername() {
    return this.username;
  }

  public void setUsername(String username) {
    this.username = username;
  }
}
```

Let's look at a couple of different mechanisms for using Java objects like `User` from within a JSP page.

The PageContext Implicit Variable

One way in which objects can be stored and accessed in a particular scope is through the `PageContext`. We introduced the `PageContext` in Chapter 2 and said that it is a convenient single point of access for a number of objects, including those that we write ourselves.

The following constants that are used to represent each of the scopes that we've just looked at are defined in the `PageContext` class:

```
public static final int PAGE_SCOPE = 1;
public static final int REQUEST_SCOPE = 2;
public static final int SESSION_SCOPE = 3;
public static final int APPLICATION_SCOPE = 4;
```

In addition to these constants, there are several methods that we can use to look up, bind, and remove scoped objects, respectively. Each of these methods takes the name of the object and an integer representing the scope in which the object can be found or should be placed:

```
public Object getAttribute(String name, int scope);
public void setAttribute(String name, Object o, int scope);
public void removeAttribute(String name, int scope);
```

In our web application, once the user has successfully logged in, we might want to create an instance of our `User` class and place it to the HTTP session with the following scriptlet on a JSP page:

```
<%@ page import="com.wrox.jsptaglibs.scriptingvariables.User" %>
<%
  User user = new User();

  // set some properties on the user object
  user.setUsername("Simon");

  // and place it into the session
  pageContext.setAttribute("myUser", user, PageContext.SESSION_SCOPE);
%>
```

Here, we have bound an instance of the `User` class into the session under the attribute name of `myUser`. If we wanted to display the user information on another page in the web application we could use the following:

```
<html>
  <head>
    <title>Professional JSP Tag Libraries</title>
  </head>

  <%@ page import="com.wrox.jsptaglibs.scriptingvariables.User" %>

  <body>
    <%
      User user = (User)pageContext.getAttribute("myUser",
                                          PageContext.SESSION_SCOPE);
    %>

    <h1>Wrox books online</h1>
    <h2>Welcome back <%= user.getUsername() %></h2>
  </body>
</html>
```

All we've done here is to use the `PageContext` as a way of accessing the session-scoped `myUser` object. We've declared a variable on the page called `user` and subsequently used this to call a method on it:

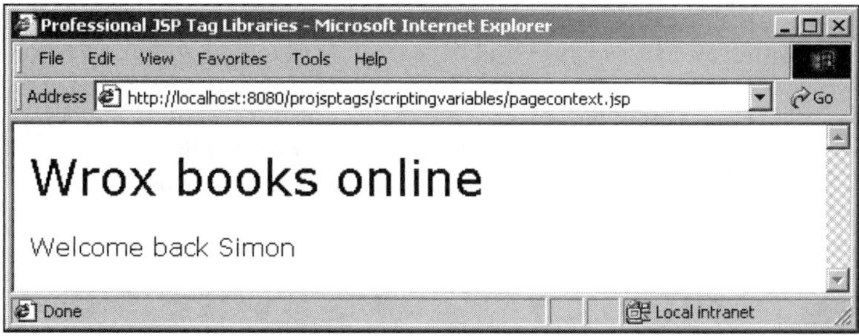

While this works, it does introduce a fair quantity of Java code into the page, which is something we are trying to avoid.

The <jsp:useBean/> Standard Action

The standard `<jsp:useBean/>` action provides a mechanism for accessing and using scoped server-side objects without introducing any Java code into the page. The following snippet demonstrates how the two pieces of functionality can be implemented using the standard actions that are available to us as JSP developers. First is the fragment that creates a `User` instance, sets a property, and binds the instance to the session under the name of `myUser`:

```
<jsp:useBean id="myUser" class="com.wrox.jsptaglibs.scriptingvariables.User"
                         scope="session">
  <jsp:setProperty name="myUser" property="username" value="Simon"/>
</jsp:useBean>
```

In addition to setting a single property as demonstrated here, the `<jsp:setProperty/>` action has the capability to set multiple properties on a JavaBean instance by specifying the property name as `*`. Here, the action looks for all non-null request parameters with names matching the properties on the specified JavaBean and automatically sets them. This is a useful way of setting properties on an object as the result of, for example, submitting an HTML form.

Next is the page that looks up the `User` object from the session and displays the username:

```
<html>
  <head>
    <title>Professional JSP Tag Libraries</title>
  </head>

  <body>
    <jsp:useBean id="myUser"
                 class="com.wrox.jsptaglibs.scriptingvariables.User"
                 scope="session"/>

    <h1>Wrox books online</h1>

    <h2>Welcome back <%= myUser.getUsername() %></h2>
  </body>
</html>
```

Here, the `<jsp:useBean/>` action has made the `myUser` bean available as a scripting variable on the page so that we can use it within an expression on the page.

Of course, we could have used the standard `<jsp:getProperty/>` action here, although what we're showing is that the `<jsp:useBean/>` action looks up the server-side object and creates a scripting variable on the page with the same name that can be used in scriptlets or expressions.

Introducing Scripting Variables from a Tag

We've seen the various ways in which Java objects can be used within JSP pages. We've also seen how the standard actions can introduce scripting variables into the page. Let's now move on to look at how custom tags can introduce scripting variables into the page.

Scope

At a high level, scripting variables can be seen as Java objects that are available through the implicit `PageContext` variable, specifically those that have been inserted into the `PageContext` at some stage during their lifetime using the `setAttribute()` method. This is, however, only half of the story.

The `<jsp:useBean/>` examples we looked at introduced scripting variables that can be used in the rest of the page, but custom tags have slightly more control over this. Variables can be introduced into the page and declared with the following scopes:

- `NESTED`
- `AT_BEGIN`
- `AT_END`

These scopes should not be confused with the scopes applicable to Java objects. Instead, these scopes are applicable to scripting variables and are relative to the custom tag that introduced the variable. The following diagram illustrates this point and provides a summary of the extent of the different scopes:

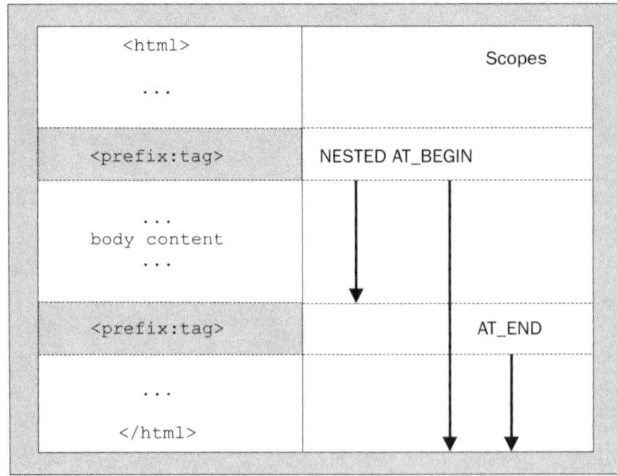

The left section of the diagram represents a JSP page with a custom tag showing its start tag, body content, and end tag. If we imagine that this tag introduces a scripting variable into the page, the right section illustrates the extent of that variable when given each of the possible scopes. The next few sections explain this concept in more detail.

NESTED

Scripting variables introduced with `NESTED` scope are only available for use between the start and end tags of the custom tag that introduced the variable. In other words, the scripting variable is available within the context of the tag's body content.

In the case of the cookie tags in the previous chapter, we could have introduced a `NESTED` variable inside the `cookieExists` tag to represent the value of the cookie. Therefore only content inside the body of the tag could make use of it. This is useful in this situation since the body content of the tag is only evaluated if the cookie (and its value) exists and having a scripting variable available outside the body content wouldn't make sense.

AT_BEGIN

The `AT_BEGIN` scope, on the other hand, indicates that the scripting variable is available for use anywhere in the page after the start tag. It is available within the context of the body content and also after the tag that introduced the variable has ended.

Scripting variables are declared on the page on which they are introduced and hence they are only available until the end of the page is reached, independent of whether the page has been dynamically included in another page.

AT_END

The `AT_END` scope makes scripting variables available after the end tag has been processed. Likewise, scripting variables declared with `AT_END` are only available until the end of the page on which they are introduced.

The `AT_END` scope is useful when the tag that introduces the variable will be used on the page in its shortened form, with the start and end tags combined and having no content. For example, you might have a tag that introduces a variable based on the lookup of a remote object such as an Enterprise JavaBean, in which case you might want it available until the end of the page.

However, if you are unsure of the way the tag will be used on the page then using `AT_BEGIN` is a better option. Say you'd like some initialization of that new variable to be performed within the body of the tag. Using `AT_BEGIN` will make this possible while still allowing the variable to be accessible until the end of the page.

Introducing and Declaring Scripting Variables

Scripting variables are introduced into the page by inserting them into the `PageContext` with the `setAttribute()` method. However, the difference between simply putting a Java object into the `PageContext` and introducing a scripting variable is that the JSP container is responsible for taking this object and making it available on the page as a scripting variable. In other words, the container is responsible for synchronizing the state of the scripting variable with the state of the corresponding Java object in the `PageContext`.

As tag developers, we must provide the JSP container with the information about the scripting variables that we would like to introduce into the page. This is achieved declaratively through the TLD file, or programmatically with a `TagExtraInfo` class. Let's look at an example of each of these in turn.

Declaring Named Variables in the TLD

First, we'll look at declaring a named variable in the TLD file. Consider a web page that allows the user to download a particular file, for example the ZIP file that contains the examples for this book. To aid the user, we also decide to show the size of the file. The first thing to do is to build the tag handler implementation.

The Tag Handler

As we've mentioned, having access to the `PageContext` greatly simplifies the development of a tag that introduces a scripting variable back into the page. In essence, all that we need to do is use the `setAttribute()` method on the `PageContext` to make the object available. With this in mind, here's the implementation of our tag handler:

```
package com.wrox.jsptaglibs.file;

import java.io.File;

import javax.servlet.jsp.JspException;
import javax.servlet.jsp.tagext.TagSupport;

public class FileSizeTag extends TagSupport {

  private String file;
```

Given a URI that points to a file on the web server, this tag uses the `ServletContext` to find out where the file actually resides. With this information, the tag can then use the standard `java.io.File` object to determine the size of the file. One of the caveats about introducing scripting variables back into the page is that they cannot be any of the primitive types – only objects. As the size returned by the `length()` method on the `java.io.File` class is a primitive long, we've wrapped it up in the `java.lang.Long` wrapper class.

The majority of the processing involved in this tag focuses around finding the file and figuring out how large it is:

```
public int doStartTag() throws JspException {
  // get the real path of the file from the container
  String realPath = pageContext.getServletContext().getRealPath(file);

  // we can now find out how large the file is
  File f = new File(realPath);
  Long fileSize = new Long(f.length());
```

Once this has been done, we can introduce the object back into the page using the following code. This binds the specified object (`fileSize` in this case) to the page scope and makes it available under the name of `fileSize`. This is the name that our scripting variable will take when it is made available for use on the page:

```
      // and introduce it into the page
      pageContext.setAttribute("fileSize", fileSize);
      return EVAL_BODY_INCLUDE;
    }

    public void setFile(String s) {
      this.file = s;
    }
  }
```

> **Calling `setAttribute("fileSize", fileSize)` on the `PageContext` without specifying a scope is equivalent to `setAttribute("fileSize", fileSize, PageContext.PAGE_SCOPE)`.**

With the tag processing complete, all that is left to do is to return the appropriate value. Rather than telling the JSP page to skip the body of this tag, we'll instruct the tag to evaluate it. We'll see the reason behind this shortly.

The Tag Library Descriptor

As with most tag development, building the tag handler is only half of the story. Although we've introduced an object into the `PageContext`, we need to tell the JSP page to create a scripting variable so that we can use it in the page.

In the same way that tag attributes are declared in the TLD file, scripting variables that we would like to introduce can also be declared in the TLD as follows:

```
<?xml version="1.0" encoding="ISO-8859-1" ?>
<!DOCTYPE taglib
  PUBLIC "-//Sun Microsystems, Inc.//DTD JSP Tag Library 1.2//EN"
  "http://java.sun.com/dtd/web-jsptaglibrary_1_2.dtd">

<taglib>

  <tlib-version>1.0</tlib-version>
  <jsp-version>1.2</jsp-version>
  <short-name>file</short-name>
  <description>
    File size examples for the Scripting Variables in the Page chapter.
  </description>

  <tag>
    <name>size</name>
    <tag-class>com.wrox.jsptaglibs.file.FileSizeTag</tag-class>
    <body-content>JSP</body-content>
    <description>
      Given a URI, returns a variable representing the size of the file.
    </description>

    <variable>
```

```
      <name-given>fileSize</name-given>
      <variable-class>java.lang.Long</variable-class>
      <declare>true</declare>
      <scope>NESTED</scope>
      <description>The size of a file in bytes.</description>
    </variable>

    <attribute>
      <name>file</name>
      <required>true</required>
      <rtexprvalue>false</rtexprvalue>
    </attribute>
  </tag>

</taglib>
```

Nested between the `<variable/>` elements are the details of the variable that we are introducing into the page.

name-given

This is the name of the scripting variable that we are introducing into the page. As the tag handler implementation binds the object into the `PageContext` under the name `fileSize`, this is the name that we've given to our variable:

```
<name-given>fileSize</name-given>
```

This element is in fact optional and, as we'll see shortly, either it or `<name-from-attribute>` should be supplied.

variable-class

This is the type of the variable that we are introducing into the page. In our case, we use `java.lang.Long` to contain the size of the file:

```
<variable-class>java.lang.Long</variable-class>
```

This is optional and defaults to `java.lang.String` if not specified.

declare

This indicates to the JSP page whether a new scripting variable should be declared on the page (`true` or `yes`) or not (`false` or `no`):

```
<declare>true</declare>
```

In our example, setting this to `true` declares a new variable of type `java.lang.Long` called `fileSize` on the page ready for use. Setting this value to `false` means that a scripting variable called `fileSize` must already be defined in the page, for example in a scriptlet at the top of the page. We'll look at the effects of declaring or not declaring variables towards the end of this chapter.

This element is optional and defaults to `true`.

scope

Earlier in the chapter, we looked at the scopes of scripting variables relative to the tag that introduced them to the page. The `<scope/>` element is where we can specify this, with the value being one of `NESTED`, `AT_BEGIN`, or `AT_END`:

```
<scope>NESTED</scope>
```

Using the `NESTED` scope is the reason that our tag handler implementation returned `EVAL_BODY_INCLUDE` from its `doStartTag()` method. What we're saying here is that the tag will introduce a variable called `fileSize` and it will only be available within the body content of the tag. Skipping the body would mean that we would never be able to use our variable.

Once again this element is optional, with the default value being `NESTED`.

description

This simply provides a short description of the scripting variable for readers of the TLD file:

```
<description>The size of a file in bytes.</description>
```

As with the other `<description/>` elements in the TLD file, this is optional.

Accessing Variables on the Page

Now that we've built the tag and the corresponding tag library descriptor, the next step is to use it. We import the tag library and use the tag in the usual way:

```
<html>
  <head>
    <title>Professional JSP Tag Libraries</title>
  </head>

  <%@ taglib uri="/fileTaglib" prefix="file" %>

  <body>
    <h1>Professional JSP Tag Libraries</h1>
```

In this example, we specify an attribute pointing to the file that we would like to know the size of:

```
<file:size file="/scriptingvariables/examples.zip">
```

Next, we have the body content of the tag. This contains regular JSP content (as specified in the TLD file) including some HTML:

```
The examples for this book can be downloaded as a ZIP file from
```

After generating the hyperlink we have a short expression as shown below:

```
<a href="examples.zip">here</a> (<%= fileSize %> bytes).
```

Although our JSP page does not explicitly declare a variable called `fileSize`, this has been introduced into the page by our custom tag, after which it can be treated as a regular scripting variable. In this example, we simply use an expression to output the value of the variable. Finally, we close off our custom tag:

```
      </file:size>
    </body>
  </html>
```

As we've declared our scripting variable with `NESTED` scope, trying to access it outside of the body content of the custom tag would result in a compilation error of the JSP page, indicating that the variable does not exist.

With our JSP page complete, requesting it generates the following page:

Introducing scripting variables into the page is a useful way to separate content from presentation. We could have built a tag that generated the entire sentence along with the hyperlink and the size of the file. However, this reduces maintainability, as a change to the content requires the tag handler to be modified and redeployed. Also, reusability is reduced as we've effectively hard-coded the content into the tag. As we've mentioned previously, these are both issues that tags can help us solve.

Although we do have a reusable tag, we've still placed a requirement on the users of that tag to work with a scripting variable called `fileSize`. Although this might not be a problem, there may be some circumstances in which it is inappropriate to pre-configure the variable name. A good example of this is the `<jsp:useBean/>` action that allows us to choose the name of the bean with the `id` attribute.

To show how this is also possible from a custom tag, let's revisit our example.

Declaring Variables in the TLD

In a similar way to the `<jsp:useBean/>` action, let's add an `id` property to our tag to specify the name of the scripting variable that it will introduce into the page. We'll start off by modifying the tag handler.

The Tag Handler

The first thing we should do is add a simple `String` property called `id` and a mutator method `setId()` to represent the new string attribute for that property.

As we'll see in later chapters, having an `id` attribute is a fairly common requirement, and for convenience, it has already been implemented for us in the `TagSupport` class as follows:

```
...
  protected String id;

  public void setId(String id) {
    this.id = id;
  }

  public String getId() {
    return id;
  }
...
```

As an `id` property has been implemented on the superclass, the actual processing involved in this tag is pretty much the same as last time:

```
package com.wrox.jsptaglibs.file;

import java.io.File;

import javax.servlet.jsp.JspException;
import javax.servlet.jsp.tagext.TagSupport;

public class FileSizeTag2 extends TagSupport {

  private String file;

  public int doStartTag() throws JspException {
    // ask the container (via the servlet context) for the
    // real path of the file
    String realPath = pageContext.getServletContext().getRealPath(file);

    // we can now find out how large the file is
    File f = new File(realPath);
    Long fileSize = new Long(f.length());
```

The one change is that instead of specifying the name of the scripting variable explicitly, we use the value of the `id` attribute which is accessible using the `getId()` method. This binds the specified object (`fileSize` in this case) to the page scope and this time makes it available under the name specified by the `id` attribute:

```
    // and introduce it into the page
    pageContext.setAttribute(getId(), fileSize);

    return EVAL_BODY_INCLUDE;
  }

  public void setFile(String s) {
    this.file = s;
  }
}
```

> **As the `id` property is marked as protected on the `TagSupport` class, we could have accessed it directly rather than through the `getId()` method. Instead we chose to use the accessor method since it is more maintainable and flexible should we wish to use a different superclass in the future.**

The Tag Library Descriptor

The TLD for the new version of our tag is much the same as last time:

```
<?xml version="1.0" encoding="ISO-8859-1" ?>
<!DOCTYPE taglib
  PUBLIC "-//Sun Microsystems, Inc.//DTD JSP Tag Library 1.2//EN"
  "http://java.sun.com/dtd/web-jsptaglibrary_1_2.dtd">

<taglib>

  <tlib-version>1.0</tlib-version>
  <jsp-version>1.2</jsp-version>
  <short-name>file</short-name>
  <description>
    File size examples for the Scripting Variables in the Page chapter.
  </description>

  <tag>
    <name>size2</name>
    <tag-class>com.wrox.jsptaglibs.file.FileSizeTag2</tag-class>
    <body-content>JSP</body-content>
    <description>
      Given a URI, returns a variable representing the size of the file.
    </description>

    <variable>
      <name-from-attribute>id</name-from-attribute>
      <variable-class>java.lang.Long</variable-class>
      <declare>true</declare>
      <scope>NESTED</scope>
    </variable>

    <attribute>
      <name>id</name>
      <required>true</required>
      <rtexprvalue>false</rtexprvalue>
    </attribute>

    <attribute>
      <name>file</name>
      <required>true</required>
      <rtexprvalue>false</rtexprvalue>
    </attribute>
  </tag>

</taglib>
```

However, there are two changes. The first is that we've added an attribute to the tag called `id` to represent the name of the scripting variable. This is marked as required because we're now asking for the name of the variable rather than assuming it is `fileSize`. This is useful because it provides us with a higher degree of flexibility over the variables that are being introduced into the page and explicitly naming the variable from the page often makes clearer where the variable came from. In addition to this, it can also be useful for the page author to be able to specify the names of the variables so that naming collisions with other variables on the page can be avoided.

Once again, nested between the `<variable/>` elements are the details of the variable that we are introducing into the page. Here is the second difference as we've used the `<name-from-attribute/>` element instead of `<name-given/>`.

name-from-attribute

This represents the name of the scripting variable that we are introducing into the page:

```
<name-from-attribute>id</name-from-attribute>
```

We specified the name that we wanted to give the scripting variable explicitly before, whereas here we say that the name of the variable is the value of the `id` attribute.

> **When declaring variables in the TLD, either the `<name-given/>` or `<name-from-attribute/>` must be specified. Using both is not permitted by the TLD DTD and will result in an error when the JSP container parses the TLD file, usually when the container starts up.**

Accessing Variables on the Page

Now that the tag handler and TLD have been modified, let's look at how to use our modified tag on the page:

```
<html>
  <head>
    <title>Professional JSP Tag Libraries</title>
  </head>

  <%@ taglib uri="/fileTaglib" prefix="file" %>

  <body>
    <h1>Professional JSP Tag Libraries</h1>
```

Once again, we import the tag library and use the tag in a similar way to last time. The difference this time is that we've provided an `id` attribute to the `size2` tag indicating that the scripting variable should be called `sizeOfFile`:

```
    <file:size2 id="sizeOfFile" file="/scriptingvariables/examples.zip">
```

Next, we have the body content of the tag again. This is the same as last time except that we now refer to the scripting variable by its new name:

```
    The examples for this book can be downloaded as a ZIP file from
    <a href="examples.zip">here</a> (<%= sizeOfFile %> bytes).
```

Finally, we close our custom tag:

```
    </file:size2>
    </body>
</html>
```

What we've seen here is that there is some degree of flexibility in how scripting variables can be introduced back into the page. In the examples we've looked at so far, this flexibility has only been around the name of the scripting variable. While this is undoubtedly useful, there are times where the type of the scripting variable is not known. A good example is again the `<jsp:useBean/>` action where the bean can be of any arbitrary class.

Having the flexibility to use un-predetermined types of scripting variables requires the use of a `TagExtraInfo` class.

Declaring Variables with a TagExtraInfo Class

Like the `<variable>` element in the tag library descriptor, as we'll see shortly, the `TagExtraInfo` class can be used to indicate that the associated tag introduces scripting variables into the page. So, why would we want to use a `TagExtraInfo` class when we can define variables in the TLD file? The answer is two-fold:

- Backward compatibility with JSP 1.1 as the `<variable>` element was only introduced in version 1.2 of the specification.
- When more control is required over the scripting variable definitions, such as when the type (class) of the scripting variable is unknown until translation time. In other words, the name of the class can't be hard-coded into the TLD.

Let's take a look at the `TagExtraInfo` class in more detail.

TagExtraInfo

The `TagExtraInfo` class is part of the `javax.servlet.jsp.tagext` package and contains a number of methods to provide additional information and functionality for the tag. The following section of code shows the `TagExtraInfo` class. As we're only interested in how we can specify information about the scripting variables, much of the additional API has been omitted for the moment. We will come back to it in later chapters though:

```
package javax.servlet.jsp.tagext;

public abstract class TagExtraInfo {

  public VariableInfo[] getVariableInfo(TagData data) {
    return new VariableInfo[0];
  }
  ...
}
```

There's only one method that we're interested in here, `getVariableInfo()`, called at translation time to find out the definitions of any scripting variables that the associated tag will be introducing back into the page. If we look at the JSP lifecycle, the first step is to translate the JSP page into the equivalent Java servlet for subsequent compilation. If scripting variables are to be introduced into the page, then the appropriate declarations must be inserted into the resulting servlet code. It's for this reason that the method is called at translation time.

All that our implementations of `TagExtraInfo` will do is return an array of `VariableInfo` instances, each representing a scripting variable that will be introduced into the page. Let's look at the `VariableInfo` class.

VariableInfo

The `VariableInfo` class is also part of the `javax.servlet.jsp.tagext` package. Essentially, it is a data structure for passing around information about the scripting variables that are going to be introduced into the page. The information wrapped up here matches with that defined within the `<variable>` element in the TLD file, namely:

- The name of the scripting variable
- The type of the scripting variable (the class name)
- Whether to declare a new variable (`true` or `false`)
- The scope of the scripting variable (`NESTED`, `AT_BEGIN`, or `AT_END`)

Creating `VariableInfo` objects to represent the information about a scripting variable is achieved through a single constructor specifying each of the properties in turn. Here's the `VariableInfo` class with the implementation details removed for the sake of brevity:

```
package javax.servlet.jsp.tagext;

public class VariableInfo {

  public static final int NESTED = 0;

  public static final int AT_BEGIN = 1;

  public static final int AT_END = 2;

  public VariableInfo(String varName, String className,
                      boolean declare, int scope) { ... }

}
```

As we can see, the constructor allows us to specify each of the four properties associated with scripting variables. For ease of use, three constants are defined representing each of the three scopes that scripting variables can be created with.

Before we move on to look at how a `TagExtraInfo` class can create and return `VariableInfo` instances, let's take a look at the `TagData` class.

TagData

The TagData class also resides in the javax.servlet.jsp.tagext package and represents the translation-time state of a tag's attributes and their associated values. An instance of this is passed to the getVariableInfo() method of the TagExtraInfo class, and it's by using this that we can determine the values of attributes using the following method:

```
public String getAttributeString(String attName);
```

So, why is this useful? Imagine a tag that has a type attribute in a similar way that the standard <jsp:useBean/> tag has an attribute called class, specified on the page by the page author. This type attribute could actually represent the type of a scripting variable that was going to be introduced into the page. If this was the case, we would have no way of knowing which class the page author would specify and therefore couldn't hard-code the type of the scripting variable inside the TLD file.

The TagData class is therefore useful to find out the value of the type attribute and this information can be used in the creation of a VariableInfo object representing the scripting variable.

> **An important point to make here is that it is the translation-time state that is represented here and not the request-time state. Attributes can have translation-time values where they are effectively hard-coded into the page by the page author, or request-time values that are the result of an expression that is evaluated when the page is requested. This is important as the `getAttributeString()` method will only return the value of attributes with static values because request-time values have yet to be evaluated at this point in time.**

Let's take a look at how this all works together in practice.

The Tag Handler

To show an example of how the TagExtraInfo class can be used to provide information about scripting variables, let's build a simple copy of the standard <jsp:useBean/> tag. Our version will have three required attributes as follows:

- id
  The name of the bean
- type
  The name of the fully qualified class of the bean
- scope
  The scope in which the bean can be found – page, request, session, or application

Our tag will look up an existing named and scoped server-side object and make it available to the rest of the page as a scripting variable with the same name. A tag handler for our tag is therefore as follows:

```
package com.wrox.jsptaglibs.scriptingvariables;

import javax.servlet.jsp.PageContext;
import javax.servlet.jsp.JspException;
```

```
import javax.servlet.jsp.tagext.TagSupport;

public class UseBeanTag extends TagSupport {

  private String type;
  private String scope;

  public int doStartTag() throws JspException {
    Object o = null;

    // find the bean in the specified scope
    if (scope.equals("page")) {
      o = pageContext.getAttribute(getId(), PageContext.PAGE_SCOPE);
    } else if (scope.equals("request")) {
      o = pageContext.getAttribute(getId(), PageContext.REQUEST_SCOPE);
    } else if (scope.equals("session")) {
      o = pageContext.getAttribute(getId(), PageContext.SESSION_SCOPE);
    } else if (scope.equals("application")) {
      o = pageContext.getAttribute(getId(), PageContext.APPLICATION_SCOPE);
    }

    // and introduce it into the page
    pageContext.setAttribute(getId(), o);

    return EVAL_BODY_INCLUDE;
  }

  public void setType(String s) {
    this.type = s;
  }

  public void setScope(String s) {
    this.scope = s;
  }
}
```

Once the specified named, scoped object has been found, we simply place it into the page under the same name. As we've seen before, we're using the `getId()` method to get the value of the `id` attribute. Something to notice is that we're not actually using the `type` attribute yet. Instead, the `TagExtraInfo` class uses it.

The TagExtraInfo Class

Now that we've built the tag handler, the next step is to build a `TagExtraInfo` class. To do this, we simply subclass `TagExtraInfo` and override the `getVariableInfo()` method. The TEI class is called behind the scenes at translation time by the JSP container to determine whether any scripting variables are to be introduced by the tags on the page. It then uses this information to generate the Java servlet corresponding to the JSP page, including any code to declare the scripting variables and also to synchronize the state of those variables from the Java objects residing in the `PageContext`.

With this in mind, the implementation of the TEI class for this example is as follows:

```
package com.wrox.jsptaglibs.scriptingvariables;

import javax.servlet.jsp.tagext.TagData;
import javax.servlet.jsp.tagext.TagExtraInfo;
import javax.servlet.jsp.tagext.VariableInfo;

public class UseBeanTagExtraInfo extends TagExtraInfo {
```

To find out the name and type of the variables that have been specified as attributes in the tag, we simply use the `TagData` instance that is passed as an argument to the `getVariableInfo()` method:

```
  public VariableInfo[] getVariableInfo(TagData data) {
    return new VariableInfo[] {
      new VariableInfo(
        data.getId(),
        data.getAttributeString("type"),
        true,
        VariableInfo.AT_BEGIN
      )};
  }
}
```

As our tag will only be introducing a single variable into the page, the `getVariableInfo()` method only returns a single instance of `VariableInfo` in an array. To create the `VariableInfo` instance, we pass the following information to the constructor:

- The name of the scripting variable
- The type (class) of the scripting variable
- Whether we would like to declare a new instance of the scripting variable
- The scope of the scripting variable

> **As we've seen, having an `id` attribute is a fairly common requirement. For this reason, `getId()` is provided as shorthand for `getAttributeString("id")`.**

With the `getVariableInfo()` method complete, this wraps up our `TagExtraInfo` class.

The Tag Library Descriptor

The final step is the tag library descriptor:

```
<?xml version="1.0" encoding="ISO-8859-1" ?>
<!DOCTYPE taglib
  PUBLIC "-//Sun Microsystems, Inc.//DTD JSP Tag Library 1.2//EN"
```

```
  "http://java.sun.com/dtd/web-jsptaglibrary_1_2.dtd">

<taglib>

  <tlib-version>1.0</tlib-version>
  <jsp-version>1.2</jsp-version>
  <short-name>scriptingvariables</short-name>
  <description>
    UseBean examples for the Scripting Variables in the Page chapter.
  </description>

  <tag>
    <name>useBean</name>
    <tag-class>com.wrox.jsptaglibs.scriptingvariables.UseBeanTag</tag-class>
```

The only real difference between the TLD for this and the other tags that we looked at earlier in the chapter is the addition of the `<tei-class>` element. Like the `<tag-class>` element, the value of this is a fully qualified name of a Java class. In this case, the name of the `TagExtraInfo` class that we have implemented for our `useBean` tag:

```
    <tei-class>
      com.wrox.jsptaglibs.scriptingvariables.UseBeanTagExtraInfo
    </tei-class>
    <body-content>JSP</body-content>
    <description>
      Finds the named, scoped object and makes it available on the page.
    </description>

    <attribute>
      <name>id</name>
      <required>true</required>
      <rtexprvalue>false</rtexprvalue>
    </attribute>

    <attribute>
      <name>type</name>
      <required>true</required>
      <rtexprvalue>false</rtexprvalue>
    </attribute>

    <attribute>
      <name>scope</name>
      <required>true</required>
      <rtexprvalue>false</rtexprvalue>
    </attribute>
  </tag>

</taglib>
```

Displaying the Variable with an Expression

When it comes to using our new tag, nothing is really new here:

```
<html>
  <head>
    <title>Professional JSP Tag Libraries</title>
  </head>

  <%@ taglib uri="/scriptingvariablesTaglib" prefix="scriptingvariables" %>

  <body>
```

As we defined the scope of the tag to be `AT_BEGIN`, we can use the shortened form of the tag on the page:

```
    <scriptingvariables:useBean
      id="myUser"
      type="com.wrox.jsptaglibs.scriptingvariables.User"
      scope="session"/>
```

This means that once the tag has been processed, the variable is available for the remainder of the page. Once again, the scripting variable can be used from any scriptlet or expression as demonstrated by the following fragment from the JSP page:

```
    <h1>Wrox books online</h1>
    <h2>Welcome back <%= myUser.getUsername() %></h2>

  </body>
</html>
```

> **When the shortened form is used, the `AT_BEGIN` and `AT_END` scopes are effectively equivalent.**

Alternatively, of course, the variable can be accessed and used with the `<jsp:getProperty/>` tag as illustrated below. This is useful when you only want to access simple properties or don't want to use any Java code on the page:

```
<h2>Welcome back <jsp:getProperty name="myUser"
                                 property="username"/></h2>
```

Either way, the following page is generated:

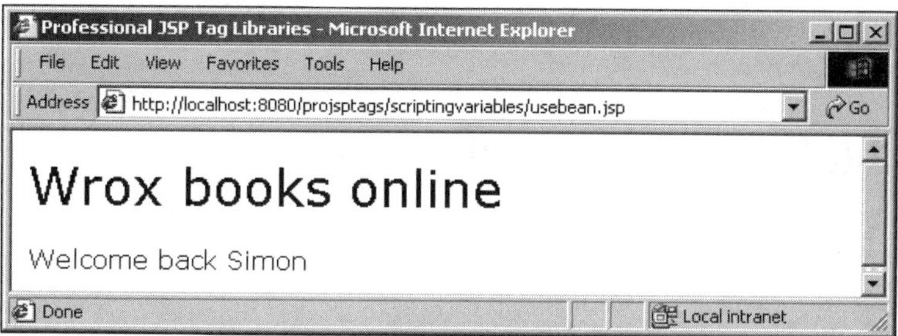

Dynamically determining the properties of scripting variables is a powerful feature of the JSP specification. This opens up a whole new world of opportunity for custom tag development, as we'll see throughout the rest of the book.

Now that we've seen the various ways in which scripting variables can be introduced into the page, let's look at a final, real-world example of how this can be used to replace functionality that is typically written as Java code on the page.

Introducing Remote Information as a Variable

We've already seen examples of how scripting variables can be introduced to represent information with the `<file:size/>` tag, and we've seen how we can build a copy of the `<jsp:useBean/>` action. Let's imagine that the information that we need to display on the page isn't available locally, but instead, it is available over the Internet, perhaps as a web service.

Accessing the Remote Information

For the purpose of this example, a JSP page that generates a dynamic XML document representing the current price of a stock (which for simplicity is just a random number), implements the source of the remote information:

```
<?xml version="1.0" encoding="ISO-8859-1" ?>

<%@ taglib uri="/attributesTaglib" prefix="attributes" %>

<%
  float price = (float)(Math.random() * 1000);
  float change = (float)(Math.random() * 100);
%>

<stock>
  <symbol><%= request.getParameter("symbol") %></symbol>
  <price><%= price %></price>
  <change><%= change %></change>
  <date><attributes:date format="dd-MMM-yyyy HH:mm:ss"/></date>
</stock>
```

The XML document here consists of the stock symbol (code), the price, the change in price, and the current date. Notice here that we're reusing the `date` tag that we built in Chapter 2 to provide us with a nicely formatted date, demonstrating that custom tags don't just have to be used to generate content for HTML documents.

Representing the Information

Rather than access and manipulate the data in the raw XML form, we decide that we would like to wrap it up as a JavaBean as follows:

```
package com.wrox.jsptaglibs.stock;

import java.io.Serializable;
import java.util.Date;

public class Stock implements Serializable {

  private String symbol;
  private float price;
  private float change;
  private Date date;

  public Stock() {}

  public Stock(String symbol, float price, float change, Date date) {
    this.symbol = symbol;
    this.price = price;
    this.change = change;
    this.date = date;
  }

  public String getSymbol() {
    return this.symbol;
  }

  public float getPrice() {
    return this.price;
  }

  public float getChange() {
    return this.change;
  }

  public Date getDate() {
    return this.date;
  }
}
```

Essentially, this JavaBean provides us with a Java representation of the information contained within the XML document and is much easier to use on the page than a reference to an XML document. After all, we can take advantage of the standard `<jsp:getProperty/>` tag to access the information stored within it.

Building the Tag

The next step is to access the XML document and create an instance of our JavaBean to represent it. We could of course write this code straight into the page but instead we'll write a tag to provide a much more maintainable solution that we can reuse in other pages further down the line.

To start off, our tag will have one required attribute called `symbol` that is used to represent the stock that the tag should look up:

```
package com.wrox.jsptaglibs.stock;

import java.io.InputStream;
import java.net.URL;

import javax.servlet.jsp.JspException;
import javax.servlet.jsp.JspTagException;
import javax.servlet.jsp.tagext.TagSupport;

public class StockTag extends TagSupport {

  private String symbol;

  public void setSymbol(String symbol) {
    this.symbol = symbol;
  }
```

Following this is the `doStartTag()` method, which uses the symbol to look up the appropriate stock information. For the purposes of this example we're hard-coding the URL of the remote information source (the dynamically generated XML document). In a real system, this might be specified by a properties file or perhaps passed as an attribute to the tag itself.

All that we are doing here is opening a URL to the specified resource and getting a `java.io.InputStream` with which the data can be read:

```
  public int doStartTag() throws JspException {

    Stock stock;

    try {
      // get the data from the "web service"
      URL url = new
        URL("http://localhost:8080/projsptags/scriptingvariables/
                    get-stock.jsp?symbol=" + symbol);
      InputStream in = url.openStream();
```

Once we have the `InputStream`, we can then pass this on to our `StockFactory`, which is responsible for parsing the XML document and creating a `Stock` JavaBean. Splitting this functionality out of the tag means that it can be reused elsewhere and additionally means that the implementation can be varied without modifying the tag:

```
      // parse it into a stock object and place it in the page
      stock = StockFactory.getInstance().getStock(in);
```

Once we have a `Stock` instance, the next step is to introduce the bean into the page in the same way as we've seen before:

```
      pageContext.setAttribute("stock", stock);
    } catch (Exception e) {
      e.printStackTrace();
      throw new JspTagException(e.getMessage());
    }

    // and skip the body content for this empty tag
    return SKIP_BODY;
  }
}
```

For completeness, the implementation of the singleton `StockFactory` class is as follows. Essentially, it takes an XML document and parses it for the information required to create a `Stock` instance:

```
package com.wrox.jsptaglibs.stock;

import java.io.InputStream;
import java.text.SimpleDateFormat;
import java.util.Date;

import javax.xml.parsers.DocumentBuilder;
import javax.xml.parsers.DocumentBuilderFactory;

import org.w3c.dom.Node;
import org.w3c.dom.Document;

public class StockFactory {

  private static final StockFactory instance = new StockFactory();

  private StockFactory() {}

  public static StockFactory getInstance() {
    return instance;
  }

  public Stock getStock(InputStream in) throws StockException {

    Stock stock;

    try {
      // create a factory and builder - an abstraction for an XML parser
      DocumentBuilderFactory factory = DocumentBuilderFactory.newInstance();
      DocumentBuilder builder = factory.newDocumentBuilder();

      // get a reference to the document
      Document doc = builder.parse(in);
      Node root = doc.getDocumentElement();
      Node node;
```

```
      String symbol;
      float price;
      float change;
      Date date;

      // and now traverse the document for the required information
      // (not forgetting to skip over whitespace in the document)
      node = root.getFirstChild();
      node = node.getNextSibling();
      symbol = node.getFirstChild().getNodeValue();

      node = node.getNextSibling();
      node = node.getNextSibling();
      price = Float.parseFloat(node.getFirstChild().getNodeValue());

      node = node.getNextSibling();
      node = node.getNextSibling();
      change = Float.parseFloat(node.getFirstChild().getNodeValue());

      SimpleDateFormat sdf = new SimpleDateFormat("dd-MMM-yyyy HH:mm:ss");
      node = node.getNextSibling();
      node = node.getNextSibling();
      date = sdf.parse(node.getFirstChild().getNodeValue());

      return new Stock(symbol, price, change, date);
    } catch (Exception e) {
      throw new StockException("Could not parse stock from XML document.");
    }
  }
}
```

Although the example shown here directly manipulates the XML using the Document Object Model (DOM), there are many other options available including the Simple API for XML (SAX), JDOM, XPath, XSLT, and so on. More information about using XML with Java can be found in Professional Java XML from Wrox Press (ISBN 1-861004-01-X), while information about using XML in conjunction with JSP can be found in Professional JSP 2nd Edition from Wrox Press (1-861004-95-8).

Should anything go wrong while creating the `Stock` instance, the following exception is thrown:

```
package com.wrox.jsptaglibs.stock;

public class StockException extends Exception {

  public StockException(String message) {
    super(message);
  }
}
```

The TLD File

The next thing to do is to write the tag library descriptor. The `stock` tag has a single, required, request-time attribute called `symbol` and also declares that it introduces a scripting variable into the page:

```
<?xml version="1.0" encoding="ISO-8859-1" ?>
<!DOCTYPE taglib
  PUBLIC "-//Sun Microsystems, Inc.//DTD JSP Tag Library 1.2//EN"
  "http://java.sun.com/dtd/web-jsptaglibrary_1_2.dtd">

<taglib>

  <tlib-version>1.0</tlib-version>
  <jsp-version>1.2</jsp-version>
  <short-name>stock</short-name>
  <description>
    Stock example for the Scripting Variables in the Page chapter.
  </description>

  <tag>
    <name>stock</name>
    <tag-class>com.wrox.jsptaglibs.stock.StockTag</tag-class>
    <body-content>empty</body-content>
    <description>
      Looks up a stock and introduces a JavaBean into the page.
    </description>

    <variable>
      <name-given>stock</name-given>
      <variable-class>com.wrox.jsptaglibs.stock.Stock</variable-class>
      <declare>true</declare>
      <scope>AT_END</scope>
      <description>A Stock object representing stock details.</description>
    </variable>

    <attribute>
      <name>symbol</name>
      <required>true</required>
      <rtexprvalue>true</rtexprvalue>
    </attribute>
  </tag>
</taglib>
```

Using the Tag

With this in place, we can now use the tag.

```
<html>
  <head>
    <title>Professional JSP Tag Libraries</title>
  </head>

  <%@ taglib uri="/stockTaglib" prefix="stock" %>

  <body>
    <stock:stock symbol='<%= request.getParameter("symbol") %>'/>

    <h1>Stock Price for
      <jsp:getProperty name="stock" property="symbol"/>
    </h1>

    Price : <jsp:getProperty name="stock" property="price"/>
    <br/>
    Change : <jsp:getProperty name="stock" property="change"/>
    <br/>
    Date : <jsp:getProperty name="stock" property="date"/>
  </body>
</html>
```

When requested with a parameter called `symbol`, the result of the page is as follows:

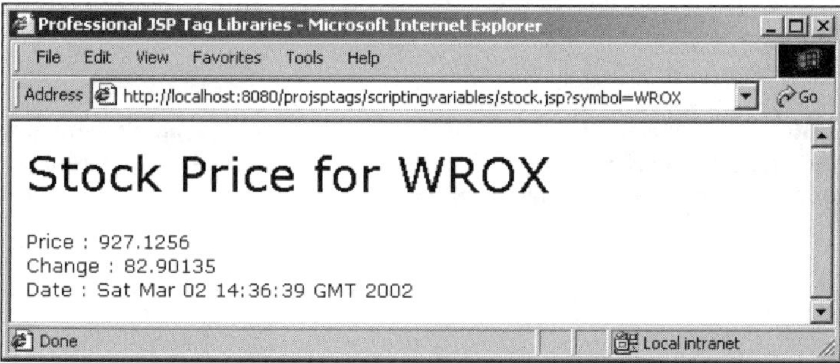

This example demonstrates another powerful, real-world use for introducing scripting variables into the page. Here, we've wrapped up access to a remote data source and introduced the information that we need as a scripting variable on the page.

Another important part of this example is that the variable introduced is a JavaBean that consists of a number of properties. This is generally preferable to introducing each property individually, as it reduces the number of variables that get declared on the page and decreases the likelihood of a naming collision with other variables. Also, we've provided a mechanism for page authors to obtain and use the information provided by our remote data source. Not only is it hidden away from the page, it is easy to use, maintainable, and reusable.

As a final topic, and now that we understand how scripting variables can be introduced in the page, let's see how we can define whether new scripting variables are created or not, and what implications this has.

Declaring New Scripting Variables

When defining scripting variables, either through the TLD or with a `TagExtraInfo` class, we can indicate whether we would like a new variable to be declared or not. So what happens if we request that new variable to be declared? Let's answer this and look at how the scope of scripting variables can affect the outcome.

AT_BEGIN and AT_END

As scripting variables scoped `AT_BEGIN` and `AT_END` are available for the remainder of the page, the JSP page declares a new variable outside the body content of the tag. In other words, just before the start tag and just after the end tag, respectively. If we remember that a JSP page is translated into a Java servlet, there is nothing special about declaring variables. If we look back to our `<file:size/>` tag and imagine that it introduces the `fileSize` variable with a scope of `AT_END`, a variable will be declared in the generated servlet code after every ending `</file:size>` tag:

```
java.lang.Long size;
```

The problem with declaring a new variable along with every use of the tag is that the resulting servlet code will contain a number of identical declarations. With the JSP effectively being a single method in a servlet, the Java compiler will see these declarations and a compilation error will occur. After all, it is invalid to declare the same variable more than once.

A simple workaround is to manually declare a variable at the top of the page in a scriptlet with the same name and then specify that a new variable should not be declared in the TLD or `TagExtraInfo` class. Of course, a JSP page will not compile if a tag relies on an existing scripting variable in the page that has not been declared.

> **Doing this reduces the reusability of the tag since it places additional dependencies on the page, and therefore on the page author wishing to use the tag. For this reason it is not recommended that tags rely on variables being declared on the page using scriptlets.**

NESTED

Variables declared with `NESTED` scope are generally shielded from such compilation errors. During the translation phase of a JSP page, start tags are translated into calls on the tag handler's `doStartTag()` method, while end tags are translated into calls to the `doEndTag()` method. There are various ways in which this can be written, but generally the servlet code is written in such a way that the processing between the start and end tags is hidden from the rest of the page.

This is analogous to declaring a variable within a {...} block, for example as part of a `for` loop, where the variable is only visible within the block such as the variable `myString` in the code snippet illustrated below:

```
for (int i = 0; i < myArray.length; i++) {
  String myString = myArray[i];
}
```

With variables hidden between the start and end tags, the same tag can be reused on the page without problems.

The only complication is of course specifying in the TLD or `TagExtraInfo` class that a new variable shouldn't be declared. In the same way as before, the tag is now relying on an existing variable to use.

Rules of Thumb

Choose to declare a new variable when introducing nested variables, or when the tag will only be used once per page. Alternatively, ensuring that page authors can specify the name of the scripting variable is another way in which to overcome the problems of multiple variable declarations with the same name.

Conventions

Finally, and before we wrap up, let's look at a couple of conventions that are commonplace when introducing scripting variables into the page.

Sharing Objects and Cooperating Tags

As we've seen with the standard actions, often it is appropriate for tags to cooperate. For example, the `<jsp:useBean/>` tag locates and makes objects available while the `<jsp:getProperty/>` accesses properties on those objects. When tags do need to cooperate on the page, a useful convention is to use a common naming standard to clarify the relationship. An example of this is as follows:

```
<jsp:useBean id="myUser"
             class="com.wrox.jsptaglibs.scriptingvariables.User"
             scope="session"/>
<jsp:getProperty name="myUser" property="username"/>
```

Here, the tag that is introducing the object uses the `id` attribute to define the name of the object in the page. Any tags that wish to subsequently use this object specify the name of the object using the `name` attribute. Removing the need to hard-code the name of the object in both tags in this example makes them much more reusable independently later on down the line.

Defining Objects

Should the need arise for building a tag that makes available several objects for use on a page, the JSP specification suggests that this is encapsulated in a custom tag called `defineObjects`. This tag would then be used at the top of the JSP page, making it clear that objects are being introduced into the page. An example of this is as follows:

```
<html>
  <head>
    <title>Professional JSP Tag Libraries</title>
  </head>

  <%@ taglib uri="/defineObjectsTaglib" prefix="define" %>
  <define:defineObjects/>
```

```
    <body>

      ...

    </body>
  </html>
```

Examples of objects introduced into a page might be a database connection, user information retrieved from the session, a user's shopping cart, remote object (EJB) references, and so on. Wrapping up the functionality associated with locating these objects is a simple way to reduce the complexity associated with the page, along with providing a consistent and maintainable way in which the variables can be introduced into the pages of web applications.

Summary

This chapter has moved on to show another important use for custom tags: introducing scripting variables into the page. Although tags are able to generate content, doing so can decrease the maintainability and reusability of tags as they are tied to the specific page or application in which they are used. Introducing scripting variables provides opportunities for reuse whereby the tags perform some processing and the JSP page presents the results of that processing. We've seen this in our `<file:size/>` tag example.

To see how this is achieved, we first looked at the new JSP 1.2 mechanism for defining scripting variables that uses the `<variable/>` element in the TLD file. This allows us to define the various properties of our scripting variables, including the name, the type, whether we would like a new variable declared on the page, and finally the scope (`NESTED`, `AT_BEGIN`, or `AT_END`).

Defining scripting variables in the TLD file provides a certain degree of flexibility in the naming of scripting variables on the page. This can either be specified directly with the `<name-given>` element, or through another attribute on the tag with the `<name-from-attribute>` element.

We then moved on to look at how the `TagExtraInfo` class can also be used to define the scripting variables that a tag will introduce into the page. This does require the implementation of a simple class, but provides much more flexibility as the values of other attributes can be used in the definition of the scripting variables. The example we looked at here was similar to the `<jsp:useBean/>` tag where the scripting variable class is not known until translation time.

To wrap up the chapter, we looked at how a tag can be used to access information from a remote data source and make it available on the page as a scripting variable for ease of use.

We then moved on to look at the differences between declaring new scripting variables versus not declaring them, and also highlighted some of the pitfalls of each. Finally, we looked at some useful conventions for cooperating tags and those that introduce several objects into the page.

The next chapter builds on the principles of controlling the page (from the previous chapter) and introducing scripting variables by combining them to show how tags can be used to perform iteration on a JSP page.

LONDON

5

Iteration Tags

This chapter builds on the material from the previous chapters, and introduces the `IterationTag` interface which is now a part of the JSP 1.2 specification. Iteration tags – tags that implement the `IterationTag` interface – are an extension of regular tags and have further capabilities to control their body content. The tags that we've seen up until now programmatically determine whether their body content is to be included or skipped. Iteration tags programmatically include their body content over and over again. In other words, they evaluate their bodies iteratively.

In addition to this, we'll also look at how scripting variables can be introduced into the page throughout these re-evaluations. This technique is useful because it can be used to provide iteration over a collection of Java objects on a JSP page. To demonstrate this, we'll implement a tag that iterates over a collection. To wrap up the chapter, we'll also see an example of how tags can be built to perform iteration implicitly behind the scenes, rather than explicitly.

Iterating on a JSP Page

There are several ways that iterations can be performed on a JSP page, including using Java scriptlets to wrap up `for` and `while` loops. For example, the entire block to be iterated over could be wrapped up in a scriptlet.

Alternatively, of course, the start and end braces that demarcate the iteration could be wrapped up in separate scriptlets as follows:

```
<%
  for (int i = 0; i < myArray.length; i++) {
%>
  ... content to be displayed on each iteration ...
<%
  }
%>
```

An Iteration Example

Imagine an online bookshop that presents the user with a list of all the books that it sells. In such an application, we might have a class to represent a book as follows:

```
package com.wrox.jsptaglibs.common;

import java.io.Serializable;

public class Book implements Serializable {

  private String isbn;
  private String title;

  public Book() {}

  public Book(String isbn, String title) {
    this.isbn = isbn;
    this.title = title;
  }

  public String getIsbn() {
    return this.isbn;
  }

  public void setIsbn(String isbn) {
    this.isbn = isbn;
  }

  public String getTitle() {
    return this.title;
  }

  public void setTitle(String title) {
    this.title = title;
  }
}
```

For simplicity, this representation of a book consists of the ISBN (for this example, the unique identifier) and the title, both of which are strings. To keep things simple, we will not use a database to retrieve the list of books. Instead, we just have a simple class that maintains a collection of hard-coded `Book` instances. We will use this class when iterating in the JSP page:

```
package com.wrox.jsptaglibs.common;

import java.util.HashMap;
import java.util.Collection;

public class BookManager {

  private static BookManager instance = new BookManager();

  private HashMap books = new HashMap();

  private BookManager() {
    Book book;

    book = new Book("1861002092", "Beginning JSP Web Development");
    books.put(book.getIsbn(), book);

    book = new Book("1861004958", "Professional JSP 2nd Edition");
    books.put(book.getIsbn(), book);

    book = new Book("1861005512", "Professional JSP Site Design");
    books.put(book.getIsbn(), book);
  }

  public static BookManager getInstance() {
    return instance;
  }

  public Book getBook(String isbn) {
    return (Book)books.get(isbn);
  }

  public Book[] getBooksAsArray() {
    return (Book[])books.values().toArray(new Book[0]);
  }

  public Collection getBooksAsCollection() {
    return books.values();
  }
}
```

The important methods in this class are `getBooksAsArray()` which returns an array of `Book` instances, `getBooksAsCollection()` which returns a `java.util.Collection` of `Book` instances, and `getBook()` which finds and returns a specific instance of a book.

Iterating with Scriptlets

Now that we've defined these classes, the next step is to write a JSP page that will show a list of the books. Here, we can use two scriptlets – one to start the iteration, and one to end it:

```
<html>
  <head>
    <title>Professional JSP Tag Libraries</title>
  </head>

  <%@ page import="com.wrox.jsptaglibs.common.Book" %>
  <%@ page import="com.wrox.jsptaglibs.common.BookManager" %>

  <body>
    <h1>Wrox books online</h1>
```

The first scriptlet retrieves the array of `Book` instances and starts the `for` loop to provide the iteration:

```
    <%
      Book[] books = BookManager.getInstance().getBooksAsArray();
      Book book;

      for (int i = 0; i < books.length; i++) {
        book = books[i];
    %>
```

We then display the content on each iteration:

```
      <p>
        <b><%= book.getTitle() %></b>
        <br/>
        ISBN : <%= book.getIsbn() %>
      </p>
```

The second scriptlet closes the loop:

```
    <%
      }
    %>

  </body>
</html>
```

Here, we're displaying the title and ISBN of each book. The JSP page produces the following output:

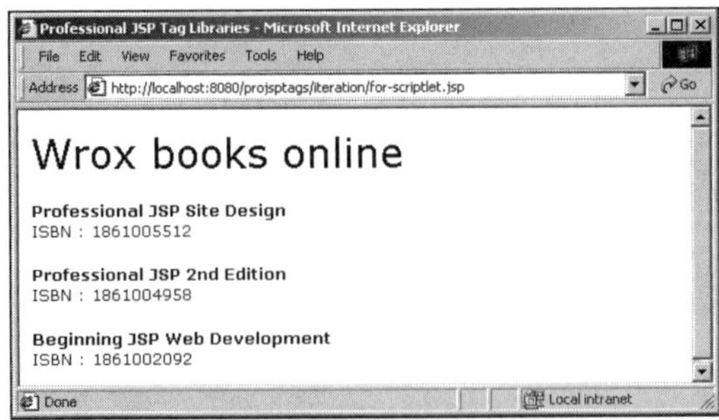

While this page generates the desired result, this technique does introduce a fair quantity of Java code into it. We are ultimately trying to avoid this because page authors not familiar with Java may be nervous when dealing with a page that contains Java code.

Let's look at how custom tags can help us to achieve the same result.

The IterationTag Interface

The `IterationTag` interface (from the `javax.servlet.jsp.tagext` package) was introduced in version 1.2 of the JSP specification. It provides a simplified mechanism for performing iterations on the page and should be implemented by tag handlers that wish to repeatedly evaluate their body content. Iteration was previously possible, but was achieved using the `BodyTag` interface – the subject of the next chapter.

> *Iteration is still possible with the `BodyTag` interface although it entails more of a performance hit because of the additional flexibility that it provides over the `IterationTag` interface. Therefore, the `IterationTag` interface is the preferred way to achieve iteration in JSP 1.2.*

`IterationTag` is an extension of the standard `Tag` interface and adds another tag lifecycle method – `doAfterBody()` called after the body of the tag has been evaluated. The interface also features a new constant (`EVAL_BODY_AGAIN`), specifically as a return value for this new method. The `IterationTag` interface is as follows:

```
package javax.servlet.jsp.tagext;

import javax.servlet.jsp.JspException;

public interface IterationTag extends Tag {

  public final static int EVAL_BODY_AGAIN = 2;

  int doAfterBody() throws JspException;
}
```

The IterationTag Lifecycle

There is a subtle difference in the lifecycle of tags that implement the `IterationTag` interface as compared to the other interfaces. The following activity diagram summarizes this lifecycle:

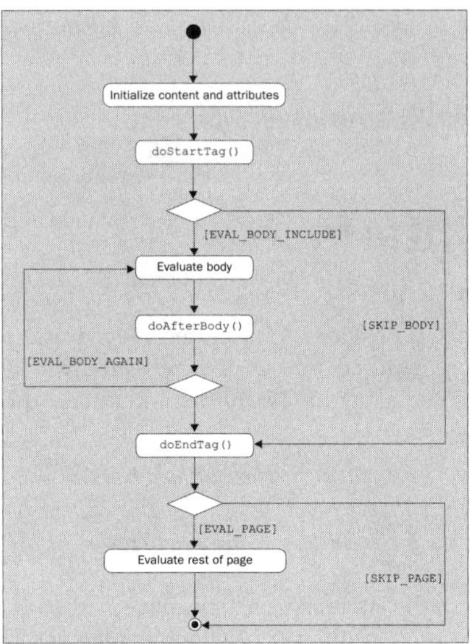

The first step in the lifecycle is the same as we have seen in Chapter 3 – the tag is initialized. The contextual information (such as references to its parent tag and the `PageContext`) is set on the tag handler, in addition to any attributes that the tag might use. Following this is the `doStartTag()` method. Let's take a look at the behavior associated with this, and the other lifecycle methods, in turn.

The doStartTag() Method

The behavior associated with the `doStartTag()` method is the same as we've seen before, and it is called when the start tag is encountered. Returning `SKIP_BODY` tells the JSP page that the body of the tag should be skipped (or ignored), and returning `EVAL_BODY_INCLUDE` tells the JSP page that the body should be evaluated.

The doAfterBody() Method

The `doAfterBody()` method is essentially what makes `IterationTag` different from the standard `Tag` interface. This method is called after the body of the tag has been evaluated. It's here that we can determine whether the body of the tag should be re-evaluated.

> **If `SKIP_BODY` is returned from the `doStartTag()` method, the body is not evaluated and therefore `doAfterBody()` is never called. Hence, we return `EVAL_BODY_INCLUDE` in the `doStartTag()` method if we want the tag to iterate.**

Like the other lifecycle methods, `doAfterBody()` can return one of two values. The first one of these is `SKIP_BODY` and, as with `doStartTag()`, this tells the JSP page that the body should be skipped and should not be re-evaluated.

The second return value is `EVAL_BODY_AGAIN` as introduced in the `IterationTag` interface. Returning this value from the `doAfterBody()` method instructs the JSP page that the body should be evaluated again. Re-evaluating the body leads to another call of `doAfterBody()` that can again return `EVAL_BODY_AGAIN` to re-evaluate the body content further. This loop continues until the `doAfterBody()` method returns `SKIP_BODY` to signal that no more iteration is required.

> **As with regular looping constructs such as `while` loops, it is possible to create an infinite loop by not even returning `SKIP_BODY` from the `doAfterBody()` method, potentially causing a `StackOverflowError` or crashing the JSP container.**

The doEndTag() Method

The `doEndTag()` method is called when the end tag is encountered. Returning `EVAL_PAGE` tells the JSP page to evaluate the rest of the page, while returning `SKIP_PAGE` tells it to skip the rest of the page.

The TagSupport Class Revisited

In Chapter 2 we were introduced to the `TagSupport` class, where we saw that it provides a default implementation of the `Tag` interface as a convenient starting point for developing custom tags. What we didn't see, however, was the actual definition of the `TagSupport` class and how it fits in with the rest of the `javax.servlet.jsp.tagext` package. The following class diagram summarizes these relationships:

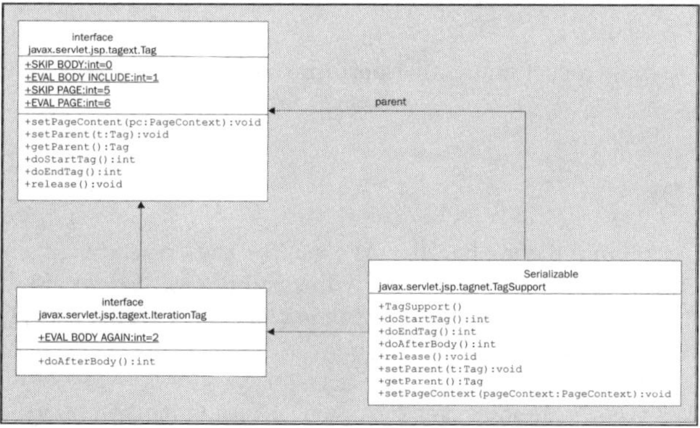

As we can see, the `TagSupport` class implements the interface `IterationTag`, which in turn extends the `Tag` interface by adding an additional method – `doAfterBody()`.

> *In addition to this, the `TagSupport` class maintains a reference to a `Tag` instance called `parent`. This is the parent tag handler reference and is set by the JSP container through the `setParent()` method.*

The following code snippet from the `TagSupport` class shows the default implementations of the lifecycle methods. `TagSupport` actually implements the `IterationTag` interface – which means that it provides a convenient starting point for building custom tags that provide iteration too:

```
package javax.servlet.jsp.tagext;
...
public class TagSupport implements IterationTag {

  public int doStartTag() throws JspException {
    return SKIP_BODY;
  }

  public int doEndTag() throws JspException {
    return EVAL_PAGE;
  }
```

In addition to the default implementations of the `doStartTag()` and `doEndTag()` methods there is also a default implementation of `doAfterBody()`. This returns `SKIP_BODY`, telling the JSP page that another evaluation of the body content is not required:

```
  public int doAfterBody() throws JspException {
    return SKIP_BODY;
  }
  ...
}
```

Now that we've looked at the `IterationTag` interface, let's see what we can do with it.

A for Loop

As an example of how to build a custom tag that performs iteration, let's develop a generic iteration tag that implements a `for` loop.

The Tag Handler

The first step, as usual, is to build the tag handler. We can use the `TagSupport` class as a starting point. We would like to replace the scriptlets on the JSP page with custom tags. We can do this by replacing the opening scriptlet that starts the iteration with the start tag, and the close the scriptlet with the end tag as follows:

```
<%
  Book[] books = BookManager.getInstance().getBooksAsArray();
  Book book;
%>
<iteration:for ...>

  <% book = books[i]; %>

  <p>
    <b><%= book.getTitle() %></b>
    <br/>
    ISBN : <%= book.getIsbn() %>
  </p>

</iteration:for>
```

For this to work, the tag will need to evaluate its body content a number of times. When we write a `for` loop, we specify the range of values over which we would like to iterate. In the same way, our tag needs to know about:

- The starting value (where to iterate from)
- The ending value (where to iterate to)

As we've already seen, details such as these can be passed to the tag as attributes. For the tag, the starting and ending values will be called `from` and `to`, both of which are integers. The other important point about the tag is that since the counter variable (`i` in the previous example) is no longer available, the tag will have to introduce it back into the page. With this in mind, our tag handler is as follows:

```
package com.wrox.jsptaglibs.iteration;

import javax.servlet.jsp.JspException;
import javax.servlet.jsp.tagext.TagSupport;

public class ForTag extends TagSupport {

  private int from = 0;
  private int to;

  private int index;

  public void setFrom(int i) {
    this.from = i;
  }

  public void setTo(int i) {
    this.to = i;
  }
```

As we're implementing a `for` loop, the tag needs to keep track of its location in the loop. We can do this by way of a counter variable, called `index` for the purpose of this tag. This is the same as the counter variable called `i` that we used in the `for` loop in the previous example.

Next there is the `doStartTag()` method, which is only called once per tag and this makes it a good place to set up any internal state required by the tag. In this example, the method sets up the counter variable to the starting value represented by the `from` attribute:

```
public int doStartTag() throws JspException {
  // setup the counter variable
  index = from;
```

With this set, we can move on to determine whether we need to evaluate the body content of the tag. This is done by comparing the value of the counter variable (that we've just initialized) to that of the `to` attribute. If we've not reached the end of the loop, we can introduce the value of the counter variable into the page. As we saw in the previous chapter, this is achieved by using the `setAttribute()` method on the `PageContext`:

```
    if (index < to) {
      // put the first index into the page
      pageContext.setAttribute("index", new Integer(index));
```

> **Remember that only objects can be introduced into the page so primitive types must be introduced through their corresponding wrapper class. In this case we are using the `java.lang.Integer` wrapper class.**

Finally, we tell the JSP page that the body content of the tag should be evaluated and return `EVAL_BODY_INCLUDE`:

```
      // and include the body
      return EVAL_BODY_INCLUDE;
```

Alternatively, if we've already reached the value of the `to` attribute, we simply skip the body content by returning `SKIP_BODY`:

```
    } else {
      // there are no elements so skip the body
      return SKIP_BODY;
    }
  }
```

The `doAfterBody()` method is called following the evaluation of the body content. The first step here is to increment the counter variable as we have again gone round the loop. Once again, we check whether we have reached the end of the range of values and introduce the incremented counter variable into the page if this is not the case:

```
    public int doAfterBody() throws JspException {
      // increment the counter
      index++;

      if (index < to) {
        // put the next index into the page
        pageContext.setAttribute("index", new Integer(index));
```

Returning `EVAL_BODY_AGAIN` ensures that the body content is re-evaluated:

```
        // and instruct the JSP engine to re-evaluate the body of this tag
        return EVAL_BODY_AGAIN;
```

The `doAfterBody()` method is repeatedly called after body evaluation until it returns `SKIP_BODY` to signal that the end of the array has been reached and that no more iteration is required:

```
      } else {
        // there are no more elements so skip the body
        return SKIP_BODY;
      }
    }
  }
```

In this case, as with the majority of tag handlers that extend the `TagSupport` class, we can simply use the default implementation of the `doEndTag()` method that tells the JSP page to evaluate the rest of the page.

The Tag Library Descriptor

Following this is the tag library descriptor:

```
<?xml version="1.0" encoding="ISO-8859-1" ?>
<!DOCTYPE taglib
  PUBLIC "-//Sun Microsystems, Inc.//DTD JSP Tag Library 1.2//EN"
  "http://java.sun.com/dtd/web-jsptaglibrary_1_2.dtd">

<taglib>

  <tlib-version>1.0</tlib-version>
  <jsp-version>1.2</jsp-version>
  <short-name>iteration</short-name>
  <description>
    Examples for the Iteration Tags chapter.
  </description>

  <tag>
    <name>for</name>
    <tag-class>com.wrox.jsptaglibs.iteration.ForTag</tag-class>
    <body-content>JSP</body-content>
    <description>
      Iterates over a specified array of objects.
    </description>

    <variable>
      <name-given>index</name-given>
      <variable-class>java.lang.Integer</variable-class>
      <declare>true</declare>
      <scope>NESTED</scope>
    </variable>

    <attribute>
      <name>from</name>
      <required>false</required>
      <rtexprvalue>true</rtexprvalue>
    </attribute>

    <attribute>
      <name>to</name>
      <required>true</required>
      <rtexprvalue>true</rtexprvalue>
    </attribute>
  </tag>

</taglib>
```

Here, we say that our tag takes two attributes (from and to), both of which can be the result of a request-time expression. Also, we've specified that the from attribute is optional (hence a default value of zero in the tag handler) while the to attribute is required.

Finally, as this tag introduces a variable called index back into the page, we have a <variable/> element in our TLD file that declares this. Of course we could have used a TagExtraInfo class to declare this variable, but as we already know that it will be a java.lang.Integer called index, there is no additional benefit in doing so.

Using the Tag

Once deployed, the final step is to use our tag. This is straightforward and all that we've done is replaced the opening and closing scriptlets with the start and end tags respectively:

```
<html>
  <head>
    <title>Professional JSP Tag Libraries</title>
  </head>

  <%@ page import="com.wrox.jsptaglibs.common.Book" %>
  <%@ page import="com.wrox.jsptaglibs.common.BookManager" %>

  <%@ taglib uri="/iterationTaglib" prefix="iteration" %>

  <body>
    <h1>Wrox books online</h1>

    <%
      Book[] books = BookManager.getInstance().getBooksAsArray();
      Book book;
    %>
```

Here, we pass the start and end values to the for loop:

```
    <iteration:for from="0" to="<%= books.length %>">

      <% book = books[index.intValue()]; %>

      <p>
        <b><%= book.getTitle() %></b>
        <br/>
        ISBN : <%= book.getIsbn() %>
      </p>

    </iteration:for>
  </body>
</html>
```

Although an optional attribute, the value of from is set to zero to highlight its usage in this example. The value of the to attribute on the other hand is determined from the value of a request-time expression that gets the length of the array containing Book instances.

Since the counter variable is now introduced into the page through a `java.lang.Integer` instance called `index`, there is a minor change to the body content of the tag.

The results are the same as the previous example that used scriptlets, but they show that it is possible to remove iteration logic from the JSP page and into a custom tag. Although the `for` tag does have its uses, and does go some way to eliminate scriptlets on the page, we still have separate steps (and scriptlets) for iterating and finding the next variable (in this case a `Book` instance) in the array. An alternative solution is to wrap up both together in a single tag.

A while Loop

Let's now look at how the `IterationTag` interface can be used to build a tag representing a `while` loop. We'll use the same `Book` and `BookManager` classes to generate the same page as before, although this time we'll use a `while` loop to iterate over a collection of objects.

Iterating with Scriptlets Revisited

Before we look at how to implement a `while` loop with a custom tag, let's see how it might be done using a scriptlet or two. Once again, we have the opening and closing sections of the loop wrapped up in separate scriptlets on the page.

This time, the starting scriptlet contains the logic to find the collection and set up the `Iterator`:

```
<%
  Collection books = BookManager.getInstance().getBooksAsCollection();
  Iterator iterator = books.iterator();
  Book book;

  while (iterator.hasNext()) {
    book = (Book)iterator.next();
%>
```

The closing scriptlet is, of course, the same as last time in that it simply closes off the loop.

As the body content is the same as the previous example, the end result is the same. Let's see how this functionality can be replicated with a custom tag.

The Tag Handler

Instead of just introducing a variable into the page that represents the current count, ideally we would like to have a tag that provides the iteration facility along with functionality to introduce each subsequent element in the collection into the page. This will simplify the page by moving the Java code out of the JSP page and into tags. For this to work, the tag will need to iterate over the collection and introduce a scripting variable back into the page. For this reason, there are a few things that our tag needs to know about:

- The name by which we can reference each element in the collection
- The type (class) of the elements in the collection
- The `java.util.Collection` to iterate over

As we saw in the previous chapter, details such as these can be passed to the tag as attributes. For our iteration tag, these details will be as follows:

- `id`
  The name of the scripting variable to be introduced
- `type`
  The name of the fully qualified class of the elements in the collection
- `collection`
  The `java.util.Collection` to be iterated over

With this in mind, the source for the tag handler is as follows:

```
package com.wrox.jsptaglibs.iteration;

import java.util.Collection;
import java.util.Iterator;

import javax.servlet.jsp.JspException;
import javax.servlet.jsp.tagext.TagSupport;

public class IteratorTag extends TagSupport {

  private String type;
  private Collection collection;

  private Iterator iterator;

  public void setType(String s) {
    this.type = s;
  }

  public void setCollection(Collection coll) {
    this.collection = coll;
  }
```

As usual, we have the appropriate properties and mutators that represent the attributes of our tag. As we saw in the previous chapter, the `TagSupport` class provides a default implementation (`getId()` and `setId()`) of the `id` attribute; we can use this feature here too. In addition, we also have an instance variable to store a `java.util.Iterator` instance. This will be used to manage and track our progress through the collection.

Next, we have the `doStartTag()` method. As this is called only once, it's here that we can create an `Iterator` and associate it with our instance variable. We then need to figure out whether the collection contains any elements, and whether we subsequently need to evaluate the body content of the tag at all. This is performed using the `hasNext()` method on the `Iterator` instance. If there are elements in the collection, we need to get the first element and make it available (introduce it) to the page under the name specified by the `id` attribute. Following this, the `doStartTag()` method simply needs to return `EVAL_BODY_INCLUDE` to instruct the JSP page to evaluate the body content:

```
  public int doStartTag() throws JspException {
    // setup the iterator to be used
    iterator = collection.iterator();
```

```
    if (iterator.hasNext()) {
      // if there are elements, put the first one into the
      // page under the name provided by the "id" attribute
       pageContext.setAttribute(getId(), iterator.next());
      // and include the body
      return EVAL_BODY_INCLUDE;
```

On the other hand, if the collection is empty and there are no elements to iterate over, the `doStartTag()` method can simply return `SKIP_BODY`. In doing so, the body content of the tag is not evaluated and therefore the `doAfterBody()` method isn't called:

```
    } else {
      // there are no elements, so skip the body
      return SKIP_BODY;
    }
  }
```

Once the body content of the tag has been evaluated, the `doAfterBody()` method is called on the tag handler to determine whether another evaluation is required. Performing another evaluation is only required if there are yet more elements in the collection. This can again be checked using the `hasNext()` method on the `Iterator` instance:

```
  public int doAfterBody() throws JspException {
    if (iterator.hasNext()) {
      // if there are more elements, put the next one into the
      // page under the name provided by the "id" attribute
      pageContext.setAttribute(getId(), iterator.next());
```

Once again, if there are more elements, we can introduce the next one into the page in the same way as before, following which the `doAfterBody()` method returns `EVAL_BODY_AGAIN` to signal that another evaluation of the body content is required. Following this evaluation, the `doAfterBody()` method is called on the tag handler repeatedly until it returns `SKIP_BODY`, which tells the JSP page that no more evaluations are necessary:

```
      // and instruct the JSP engine to re-evaluate the body of this tag
      return EVAL_BODY_AGAIN;
    } else {
      // there are no more elements so skip the body
      return SKIP_BODY;
    }
  }
}
```

The TagExtraInfo Class

As we are introducing each element of the collection into the JSP page, we need to communicate this to the JSP container. We saw in the previous chapter that there are two ways in which variables can be declared – in the TLD or with a `TagExtraInfo` class. In this example, we don't know the type of the scripting variables until translation time in the same way that the `<jsp:useBean/>` action doesn't know the type of the JavaBeans that it will be introducing. For this reason, we must build a `TagExtraInfo` class:

```
package com.wrox.jsptaglibs.iteration;

import javax.servlet.jsp.tagext.TagData;
import javax.servlet.jsp.tagext.TagExtraInfo;
import javax.servlet.jsp.tagext.VariableInfo;

public class IteratorTagExtraInfo extends TagExtraInfo {

  public VariableInfo[] getVariableInfo(TagData data) {
    return new VariableInfo[] {
      new VariableInfo(data.getId(), data.getAttributeString("type"),
        true, VariableInfo.NESTED)
    };
  }
}
```

Here we're saying that we will be introducing a scripting variable, the name of which will be specified by the `id` attribute and the type will be specified by the `type` attribute. As the scripting variable that we introduce will represent each element in the collection in turn, we've chosen that a new variable will be declared and selected `NESTED` for the scope. After all, the elements of the collection only make sense in the context of the body content of the iteration tag.

The Tag Library Descriptor

The tag library descriptor for this example is shown below:

```
<?xml version="1.0" encoding="ISO-8859-1" ?>
<!DOCTYPE taglib
  PUBLIC "-//Sun Microsystems, Inc.//DTD JSP Tag Library 1.2//EN"
  "http://java.sun.com/dtd/web-jsptaglibrary_1_2.dtd">

<taglib>

  <tlib-version>1.0</tlib-version>
  <jsp-version>1.2</jsp-version>
  <short-name>iteration</short-name>
  <description>
    Examples for the Iteration Tags chapter.
  </description>

  <tag>
    <name>iterate</name>
    <tag-class>com.wrox.jsptaglibs.iteration.IteratorTag</tag-class>
    <tei-class>
      com.wrox.jsptaglibs.iteration.IteratorTagExtraInfo
    </tei-class>
    <body-content>JSP</body-content>
    <description>
      Iterates over a specified java.util.Collection instance.
    </description>

    <attribute>
      <name>id</name>
      <required>true</required>
      <rtexprvalue>false</rtexprvalue>
    </attribute>
```

```
    <attribute>
      <name>type</name>
      <required>true</required>
      <rtexprvalue>false</rtexprvalue>
    </attribute>

    <attribute>
      <name>collection</name>
      <required>true</required>
      <rtexprvalue>true</rtexprvalue>
    </attribute>
  </tag>

</taglib>
```

There's nothing new in here, although we are using a request-time expression for the `collection` attribute so that an object reference (to a `java.util.Collection`) can be passed through to the tag from the page.

Using the Tag

As in the previous example, we've replaced the opening and closing scriptlets with the start and end tags respectively:

```
<html>
  <head>
    <title>Professional JSP Tag Libraries</title>
  </head>

  <%@ page import="java.util.Collection" %>
  <%@ page import="com.wrox.jsptaglibs.common.BookManager" %>
  <%@ taglib uri="/iterationTaglib" prefix="iteration" %>

  <body>
    <h1>Wrox books online</h1>

    <%
      Collection books = BookManager.getInstance().getBooksAsCollection();
    %>

    <iteration:iterate id="book" type="com.wrox.jsptaglibs.common.Book"
                       collection="<%= books %>">

      <p>
        <b><%= book.getTitle() %></b>
        <br/>
        ISBN : <%= book.getIsbn() %>
      </p>

    </iteration:iterate>
  </body>
</html>
```

Once we have the `Collection` of `Book` instances that we would like to iterate over, we simply pass this reference into the `iterate` tag. This is made possible because we defined the value of the `collection` attribute to be the result of a request-time expression. When the page is requested, the results are identical to those shown earlier.

Once again, we have seen here that it is possible to replace trivial logic and scriptlets on a page with a generic custom tag, something that is certainly beneficial for page authors that aren't familiar with the Java language. In addition to this, we've combined the steps involved in performing the iteration and finding the next element in the collection into a single, easy to use tag. For the final example, let's take this a step further.

Iterating Implicitly

The examples of the `IterationTag` interface that we've seen so far have all allowed iteration on the page explicitly. This means that the page author had to explicitly specify some of the details such as the range of the loop or the variables that should be introduced to perform iteration. Having a generic tag that provides the capability to iterate over any collection is useful and, no doubt, you'll find yourself using it repeatedly. However, just because we can build such tags doesn't mean that we always have to present such a raw interface to the page author. Instead, we can present them with a façade that uses the `IterationTag` interface behind the scenes.

Often when building web sites, it is useful to be able to display a list of hyperlinks based upon files in a directory. For example, you might want to show a list of documents in a specific directory, or perhaps a series of thumbnails showing photos, or images of products that an online store sells:

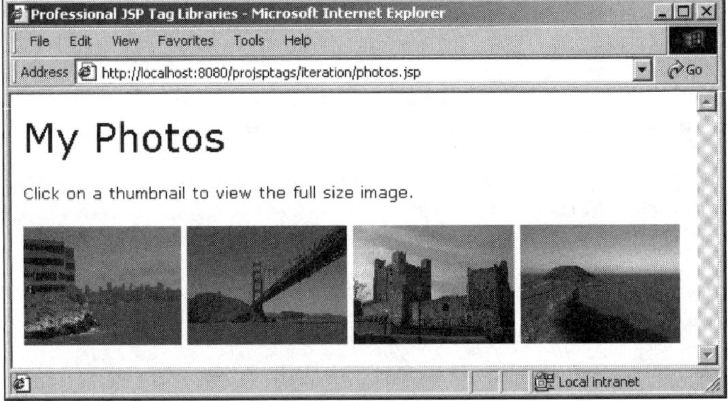

As we've seen, such a page could easily be generated with the tags that we've developed in this chapter, in conjunction with some Java scriptlets that determine which files reside in the directory. In this example, however, let's present the page author with a simplified tag as follows:

```
... start of page ...

<directory:list path="/" filter=".jpg" recursive="true">
  ... thumbnail to be displayed ...
</directory:list>

... end of page ...
```

Here, instead of iterating explicitly over a collection of Java objects, the `list` tag will determine the files that match the specified criteria and provide the iteration implicitly for us. The body content can then be written so that it displays a thumbnail and hyperlink of each file that the tag finds. Let's see how this could be built.

The first thing to do is to define a JavaBean with which to represent the files that are found. Rather than present a reference to the physical file back to the page, we'll present a simplified representation consisting of the filename, the URI from which the file can be reached, and also the date that the file was last modified:

```
package com.wrox.jsptaglibs.directory;

import java.io.Serializable;
import java.util.Date;

public class FileEntry implements Serializable {

  private String name;
  private String uri;
  private Date date;

  public FileEntry(String name, String uri, Date date) {
    this.name = name;
    this.uri = uri;
    this.date = date;
  }

  public String getName() {
    return this.name;
  }

  public String getUri() {
    return this.uri;
  }

  public Date getDate() {
    return this.date;
  }
}
```

Now that we can represent the files, let's move on to the tag.

The list Tag

The purpose of this tag is to find all files within a specific directory and provide iteration over them. In addition to this, the tag will filter out those files that don't match the specified criteria. The tag therefore takes three attributes:

- The path, specified by a URI, in which the files can be found
- The filter that should be applied to the filenames
- A flag to indicate whether the search should be recursive, checking subdirectories

With these attributes in mind, we can start building the tag. First of all are the properties and their corresponding mutator methods:

```
package com.wrox.jsptaglibs.directory;

import java.io.File;
import java.util.ArrayList;
import java.util.Date;
import java.util.Iterator;
import java.util.List;

import javax.servlet.ServletContext;
import javax.servlet.http.HttpServletRequest;
import javax.servlet.jsp.JspException;
import javax.servlet.jsp.JspTagException;
import javax.servlet.jsp.tagext.TagSupport;

public class DirectoryListingTag extends TagSupport {

  private String path;
  private String filter;
  private boolean recursive = false;

  public void setPath(String path) {
    this.path = path;
  }

  public void setFilter(String filter) {
    this.filter = filter;
  }

  public void setRecursive(boolean recursive) {
    this.recursive = recursive;
  }
```

Next are a couple of instance variables that are used to maintain state during the invocation of this tag. The first of these is a `java.util.Iterator` instance as we've seen before, and the second is a string that is used to store the current context path – the path under which the pages in this web application can be accessed through. For example, this might be something like `/projsptags`:

```
private Iterator iterator;
private String contextPath;
```

Next is the `doStartTag()` method where the majority of the work is performed. First of all we get the physical path that corresponds to where the files accessible by the specified URI can be found on the local disk:

```
  public int doStartTag() throws JspException {

    ServletContext ctx = pageContext.getServletContext();
    String realPath = ctx.getRealPath(path);
```

Then we get the context path and store it away for use later on:

```
      HttpServletRequest request;
      request = (HttpServletRequest)pageContext.getRequest();
      contextPath = request.getContextPath();
```

Now that we have this information we can move on to gather a list of the files that match the specified criteria. To do this, we create an empty list and call the `findFiles()` helper method. We will see the implementation of the `findFiles()` method in a moment:

```
      List fileEntries = new ArrayList();
      findFiles(path, realPath, fileEntries);
      iterator = fileEntries.iterator();
```

Following this, the tag becomes a regular iteration tag as we've seen before. It uses the list of files that was found in the helper method and if some were found, it introduces the first one into the page and returns `EVAL_BODY_INCLUDE`. If no files were found, the body content is skipped by returning `SKIP_BODY`:

```
      if (iterator.hasNext()) {
        pageContext.setAttribute("file", iterator.next());
        return EVAL_BODY_INCLUDE;
      } else {
          return SKIP_BODY;
      }
    }
```

Likewise, the `doAfterBody()` method is also very similar to those that we've seen before, returning `EVAL_BODY_AGAIN` or `SKIP_BODY` appropriately:

```
  public int doAfterBody() throws JspException {
    if (iterator.hasNext()) {
      pageContext.setAttribute("file", iterator.next());
      return EVAL_BODY_AGAIN;
    } else {
      return SKIP_BODY;
    }
  }
```

The only piece of the puzzle that we've not looked at is the `findFiles()` helper method. This method is provided with three parameters – a path (represented by a URI), the corresponding real path representing a physical directory, and a `java.util.List`. The purpose of this method is to find the files in that directory that match the criteria in the `filter` attribute. This is achieved by using the standard `java.io.File` class to create a "representation" of the directory. Once it has this, the `listFiles()` method can be called on it to obtain a list of all of the files that reside in the directory:

```
  private void findFiles(String path, String realPath, List fileEntries) {

    // remove the trailing slash as this is not necessary
    if (path.endsWith("/")) {
      path = path.substring(0, path.length()-1);
    }

    File file = new File(realPath);
    File files[] = file.listFiles();
```

Following this we can simply loop over each of the files that was found and, for the purposes of this example, simply check whether the file extension matches that specified by the tag's `filter` attribute. If this is the case, we simply wrap up some information about the file as an instance of our `FileEntry` class and add it to the list of files that we've found:

```
FileEntry entry;
String uri;

for (int i = 0; i < files.length; i++) {
  file = files[i];

  if (file.getName().endsWith(filter)) {
    // create a FileEntry object representing it
    uri = contextPath + path + "/" + file.getName();
    entry = new FileEntry(file.getName(), uri,
                          new Date(file.lastModified()));

    fileEntries.add(entry);
  }
```

The other piece of functionality that the tag provides is the ability to recursively check subdirectories to find matching files there too. If the current file is actually a directory and this functionality is required, we simply call the `findFiles()` method again, this time passing through information about the subdirectory:

```
      if (recursive && file.isDirectory()) {
        findFiles(path + "/" + file.getName(),
                  realPath + "/" + file.getName(), fileEntries);
      }
    }
  }
}
```

The Tag Library Descriptor

Next is the TLD file that describes the tag. Here, all we are saying is that the `list` tag has three attributes – `path` and `filter` which are mandatory, and `recursive` which is optional. In addition to this, the tag also declares that it introduces a scripting variable called `file`, of type `com.wrox.jsptaglibs.directory.FileEntry`:

```
<?xml version="1.0" encoding="ISO-8859-1" ?>
<!DOCTYPE taglib
  PUBLIC "-//Sun Microsystems, Inc.//DTD JSP Tag Library 1.2//EN"
  "http://java.sun.com/dtd/web-jsptaglibrary_1_2.dtd">

<taglib>

  <tlib-version>1.0</tlib-version>
  <jsp-version>1.2</jsp-version>
  <short-name>directory</short-name>
  <description>
    Listing example for the Iteration Tags chapter.
```

```
  </description>

  <tag>
    <name>list</name>
    <tag-class>com.wrox.jsptaglibs.directory.DirectoryListingTag</tag-class>
    <body-content>JSP</body-content>
    <description>
      Looks up a directory and iterates for each file found.
    </description>

    <variable>
      <name-given>file</name-given>
      <variable-class>
        com.wrox.jsptaglibs.directory.FileEntry
      </variable-class>
      <declare>true</declare>
      <scope>NESTED</scope>
      <description>An individual file entry.</description>
    </variable>

    <attribute>
      <name>path</name>
      <required>true</required>
      <rtexprvalue>false</rtexprvalue>
    </attribute>

    <attribute>
      <name>filter</name>
      <required>true</required>
      <rtexprvalue>false</rtexprvalue>
    </attribute>

    <attribute>
      <name>recursive</name>
      <required>false</required>
      <rtexprvalue>false</rtexprvalue>
    </attribute>
  </tag>

</taglib>
```

Using the Tag

Using the tag is very straightforward. It demonstrates how we can easily build a page that displays a list of hyperlinked thumbnail images like we saw in the previous screenshot:

```
<html>
  <head>
    <title>Professional JSP Tag Libraries</title>
  </head>

  <%@ taglib uri="/directoryTaglib" prefix="directory" %>
```

```
  <body>
    <h1>My Photos</h1>

    <p>
      Click on a thumbnail to view the full size image.
    </p>

    <directory:list path="/" filter=".jsp" recursive="true">

      <a href="<jsp:getProperty name="file" property="uri"/>">
        <img src="<jsp:getProperty name="file" property="uri"/>"
             border="0" width="218" height="96"></a>

    </directory:list>
  </body>
</html>
```

Although this example produces the same result that can be achieved by using a generic iteration tag, there is an important difference here in the way that the tags are used and perceived. As developers, iterating is something that we are familiar with, and use on a day-to-day basis. However, it is worth bearing in mind that those building the pages might not always be as familiar with these programming techniques as we are. By building this tag, we have addressed a specific need and presented it in a non-programming specific way. This has helped achieve the goal of producing similar results using custom tags and subsequently made the page more understandable to those people who maintain it.

Summary

This chapter has combined several of the concepts that we've seen up until this point in the book. We introduced the `IterationTag` interface by showing how custom tags can be built that conditionally evaluate and re-evaluate their body content. The examples that we looked at showed how iteration logic written using Java scriptlets could be replaced with such tags. We also showed how a generic iteration tag could be written that introduces a scripting variable into the page for each element in a collection.

Additionally, we've seen how instance variables can be used in a tag handler to maintain its state between calls of the various lifecycle methods. The examples that we saw here made use of either a `java.util.Iterator` or a counter variable for tracking and managing their progress through the loops.

Although trivial, iterations are commonplace in many pages and are also good candidates for custom tags for the following reasons:

- Increased maintainability, quality, and reusability, as the page authors use the tags instead of raw Java code
- Provides a more natural interface for page authors unfamiliar with the Java language, especially when iteration combines introduction of each subsequent element into the page

The `IterationTag` interface was introduced in version 1.2 of the JSP specification. The ability to programmatically evaluate and re-evaluate the body content of a tag was previously available by implementing the `BodyTag` interface. The `IterationTag` interface is preferred over the `BodyTag` owing to its increase in performance. The next chapter builds on the material covered in this chapter by introducing the `BodyTag` interface and showing how it adds even more flexibility in the evaluation of its body content.

LONDON

6

Body Tags

The previous chapter introduced the `IterationTag` interface, which was introduced as part of version 1.2 of the JSP specification. We saw that this is a very useful and convenient mechanism to programmatically evaluate and re-evaluate a tag's body. Before version 1.2, however, the `BodyTag` interface was used to perform such tasks.

In this chapter we will look at the `BodyTag` interface, showing how it extends the functionality available over tags that implement the `IterationTag` interface. We will also see why we would want to implement such a tag with the `BodyTag` interface when the `IterationTag` is sufficient. We'll also revisit the tag lifecycle and introduce yet another value that can be returned from the `doStartTag()` method, along with two more methods that are part of `BodyTag`'s lifecycle. To demonstrate this, we'll go through the steps required to build the following types of tags:

- A tag that represents a `while` loop
- Tags that filter/transform their body content

To wrap up the chapter, we'll again look at the types of tag body content, in particular `JSP` and `tagdependent`, in more detail.

The BodyTag Interface

The `BodyTag` interface (from the `javax.servlet.jsp.tagext` package) is the last of the three interfaces that a custom tag handler can implement, and also the one that is the largest and most complex. `BodyTag` extends the `IterationTag` interface, adding another constant, and two more methods – one to set a reference to a `BodyContent` object and the other that can be used to initialize it.

The complete interface is as follows:

```
package javax.servlet.jsp.tagext;

import javax.servlet.jsp.JspException;

public interface BodyTag extends IterationTag {

  public final static int EVAL_BODY_BUFFERED = 2;

  void setBodyContent(BodyContent b);

  void doInitBody() throws JspException;
}
```

Before we look at how this affects the tag lifecycle, let's recap on what the `JspWriter` is.

JspWriter

When writing JSP pages, one of the implicit page variables available to us is the `out` variable. Back in Chapter 2 we said that the `JspWriter` was effectively the output stream through which content made its way back to the client. A `JspWriter` is in fact just a subclass of `java.io.Writer`, and as such, has a number of methods for printing the values of primitive types and objects.

The current `JspWriter` can be accessed on a JSP page by using the implicit variable called `out`, and also through the `PageContext` object by using the `getOut()` method. This is particularly useful when building custom tags because the tags themselves can also output information back to the page through the current `JspWriter` instance. An example of this can be seen in the tags that we built back in Chapter 2, a snippet of which is as follows:

```
try {
  // and write out the formatted date to the page
  pageContext.getOut().write(df.format(new Date()));
} catch (java.io.IOException ioe) {
  throw new JspTagException(ioe.getMessage());
}
```

Here, we simply get a reference to the current `JspWriter` and output the formatted date. As this is an I/O operation, something could of course go wrong and hence `IOException` must be caught. If successful, the formatted date is written back to the page. Let's now take a look at `BodyContent`.

BodyContent

The `BodyContent` class is a specialized `JspWriter`, and as such also has methods to print and output primitive and object values. However, what is different about the `BodyContent` class is that any values written through it are not written automatically back to the page.

A `BodyContent` instance is like a temporary scratchpad that can be used to assemble content. Values are written to a `BodyContent` object in the same way as to a `JspWriter`. The definition of the `BodyContent` class is as follows:

```
package javax.servlet.jsp.tagext;

import java.io.Reader;
import java.io.Writer;
import java.io.IOException;

import javax.servlet.jsp.JspWriter;

public abstract class BodyContent extends JspWriter {

  public void flush() throws IOException {
    throw new IOException("Illegal to flush within a custom tag");
  }

  public void clearBody() {
    ...
  }

  public abstract Reader getReader();

  public abstract String getString();

  public abstract void writeOut(Writer out) throws IOException;

  public JspWriter getEnclosingWriter() {
    ...
  }
}
```

Although a subclass of `JspWriter`, there are several key differences between a `BodyContent` and a `JspWriter`. The first of these is that although `BodyContent` inherits all of the methods that allow primitive and object values to be printed to it, these values are not written directly back to the page. Not writing the output directly back to the page allows us to retrieve and manipulate the content that has been written to the `BodyContent` object. The content can be accessed through the `getString()` and `getReader()` methods, while it can be cleared using the `clearBody()` method.

We've already said that a `BodyContent` instance is like a temporary scratchpad, and this is reinforced by the fact that a `BodyContent` has an enclosing `JspWriter` instance associated with it. As we'll see shortly, this enclosing `JspWriter` instance is assigned when the tag is used on the page and represents the output stream to which the content of the `BodyContent` instance will be written to when we finish assembling and manipulating it. So how do these `BodyContent` objects get created and why are they useful? Let's answer this by first looking at the tag lifecycle.

The BodyTag Lifecycle

As discussed earlier, the `BodyTag` interface introduces more methods and this once again means that the lifecycle of tag handlers that implement this interface are subtly different from before. The following activity diagram summarizes this:

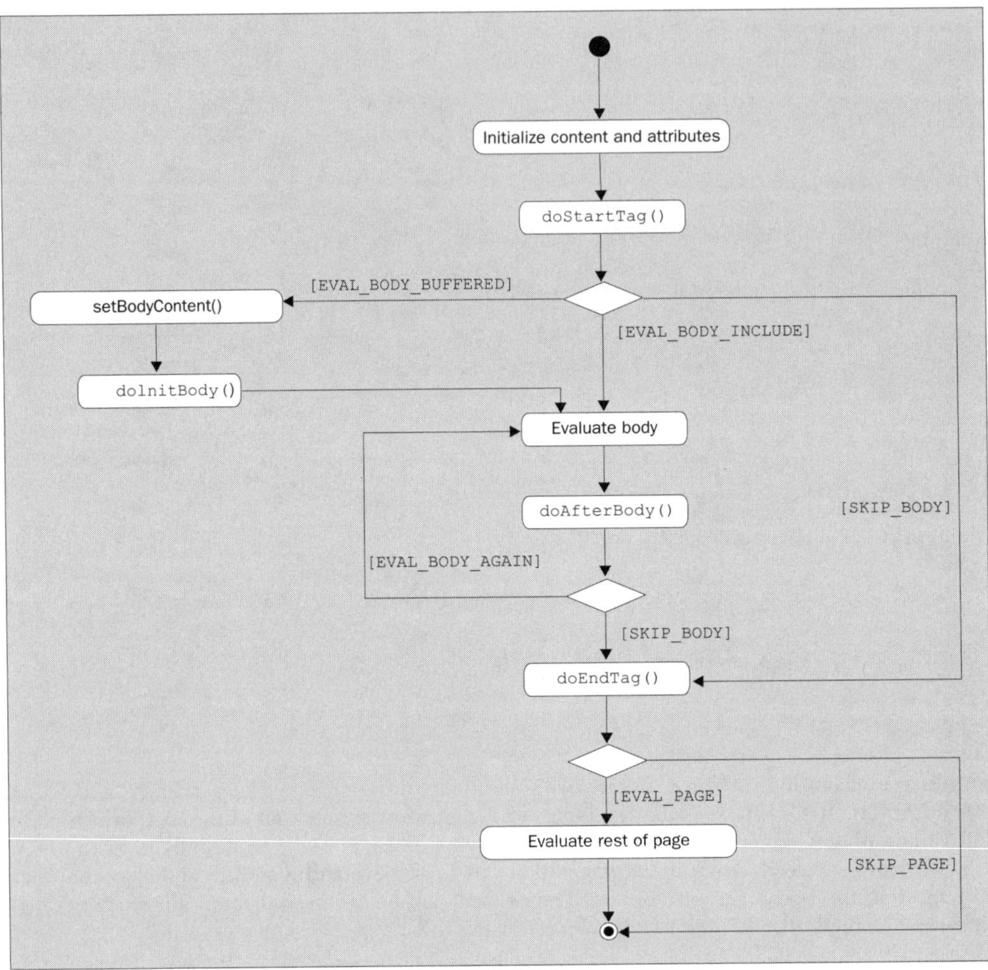

As usual, the first step is to initialize the tag by way of its context and any attributes. Let's take a look through each of the existing and new lifecycle methods in turn.

The doStartTag() Method

The behavior associated with tags implementing the `IterationTag` interface remains unchanged from that we've seen before. The `BodyTag` interface, however, is slightly different. It too can return `SKIP_BODY` or `EVAL_BODY_INCLUDE` (as we have seen in Chapter 3), and these tell the JSP page to skip or evaluate the body content respectively.

> **With `doStartTag()` returning `SKIP_BODY` or `EVAL_BODY_INCLUDE`, evaluation is the same as that associated with the `IterationTag` interface. After all, the `BodyTag` interface extends `IterationTag`.**

However, the BodyTag interface introduces another constant that can be returned from the doStartTag() method – EVAL_BODY_BUFFERED:

```
public final static int EVAL_BODY_BUFFERED = 2;
```

Returning this value instructs the JSP page to evaluate the body content, but additional steps are included before this happens. We'll see what these steps are, below.

The setBodyContent() Method

The first of these additional steps is that the JSP page creates a new BodyContent object and passes this to the tag handler using the setBodyContent() method. This BodyContent object represents the body content of the custom tag and is therefore only valid until the end tag is reached. Behind the scenes, this new BodyContent object becomes the implicit out variable, which means that any content generated between the start and end tags is written to the BodyContent object and not the usual JspWriter. Instead, the JspWriter becomes the enclosing writer for the BodyContent instance:

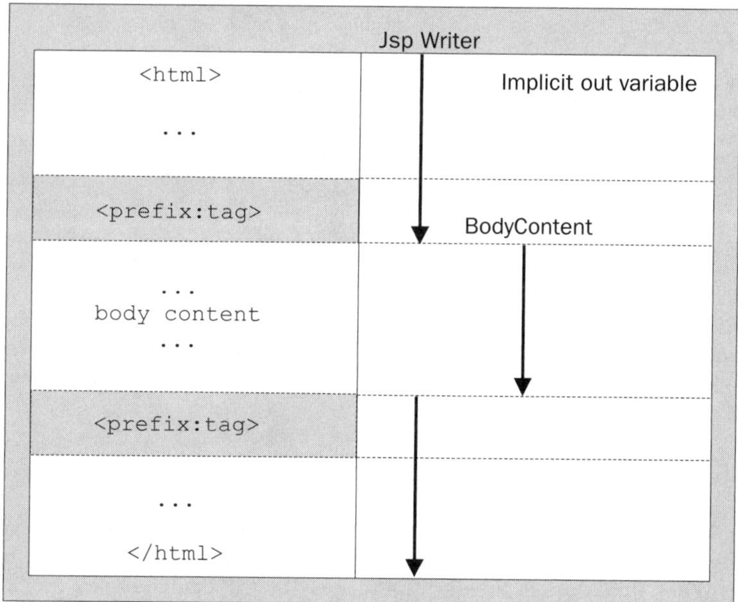

Following the end tag, the original enclosing JspWriter instance (and therefore the implicit out variable) is restored.

As BodyContent is a subclass of JspWriter, it is therefore possible for a BodyContent object to be the enclosing writer for another BodyContent object. In other words, it is possible to nest tags that implement the BodyTag interface, each tag handler having its own BodyContent instance to represent its body content. This is useful in circumstances where each nested tag needs to assemble its own content, which is then re-assembled or manipulated in the outer tags. A diagrammatic representation of how each tag gets its own BodyContent instance is as follows:

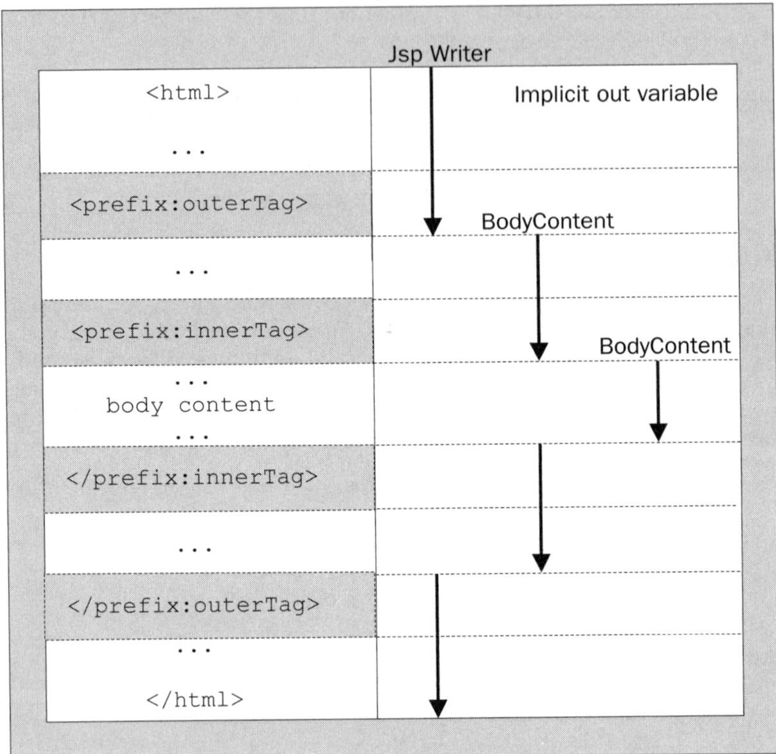

The `PageContext` maintains a stack of `JspWriter` and `BodyContent` instances so that it can keep track of which one is currently active. In a regular JSP page containing no tags implementing the `BodyTag` interface, the implicit `out` variable represents the `JspWriter` instance that can be used to output content directly to the page as illustrated below:

```
<% out.println(myString); %>
```

Each time a start tag implementing the `BodyTag` interface is encountered on the page, a new `BodyContent` object is pushed onto the top of the stack, and the previous instance becomes the **enclosing writer**. When this happens, behind the scenes, the JSP container sets the implicit `out` variable to point to the new `BodyContent` object on the top of the stack.

From a page author's perspective, nothing seems different or unusual, and they can still output content with the implicit `out` variable. However, what is actually happening here is that any content being written out at this point in time is being written into the `BodyContent` instance – the temporary scratchpad.

Subsequently, when the corresponding end tag is encountered, the `BodyContent` object is popped off the stack. This has the effect of restoring the enclosing writer (the previous instance), and once again, the JSP container resets the implicit `out` variable to what it was before the `BodyContent` object was pushed onto the stack.

Once it has been popped off the stack, the content stored within it disappears and can never be retrieved again. For this reason, and as we'll demonstrate shortly, the content residing within a BodyContent instance must be manually written back to the page through the enclosing writer.

The doInitBody() Method

This is the other new method that features as part of the BodyTag interface and is called after the setBodyContent() method. Since this method is called after the BodyContent instance has been set on the tag handler, this is a more appropriate place to perform initialization of the body content. For example, to start writing to the BodyContent before the body of the tag is written into it. Alternatively, this method can be used to set up scripting variables, or even to set up internal state used by this invocation of the tag which is dependent on there being body content to be manipulated.

> **The doInitBody() method is only called after setBodyContent(), which subsequently is only called if doStartTag() returns EVAL_BODY_BUFFERED. For this reason it is only called once per tag and not once for each evaluation of the body content.**

The doAfterBody() Method

The behavior associated with the doAfterBody() method is the same as we've seen in the previous chapter with the IterationTag interface. It is called after the body of the tag has been evaluated, and a tag handler should implement this to return either EVAL_BODY_AGAIN or SKIP_BODY to instruct the JSP page to re-evaluate the body or skip it.

The doEndTag() Method

The doEndTag() method, as usual, is called when the end tag is encountered and tag handlers can return EVAL_PAGE or SKIP_PAGE to tell the JSP page to evaluate or skip the rest of the page, respectively.

An additional use of the doEndTag() method when implementing the BodyTag interface is that this is the ideal point at which the content of the BodyContent instance can be written out to the enclosing JspWriter. We'll see an example of this shortly.

The BodyTagSupport Class

In the previous chapter we saw that the TagSupport class implements the IterationTag interface by supplying a default implementation of the lifecycle methods. In a similar way, the BodyTagSupport class (from the javax.servlet.jsp.tagext package) provides a default implementation of the methods found in the BodyTag interface. As BodyTag extends IterationTag, the TagSupport class can serve as a starting point for the BodyTagSupport class:

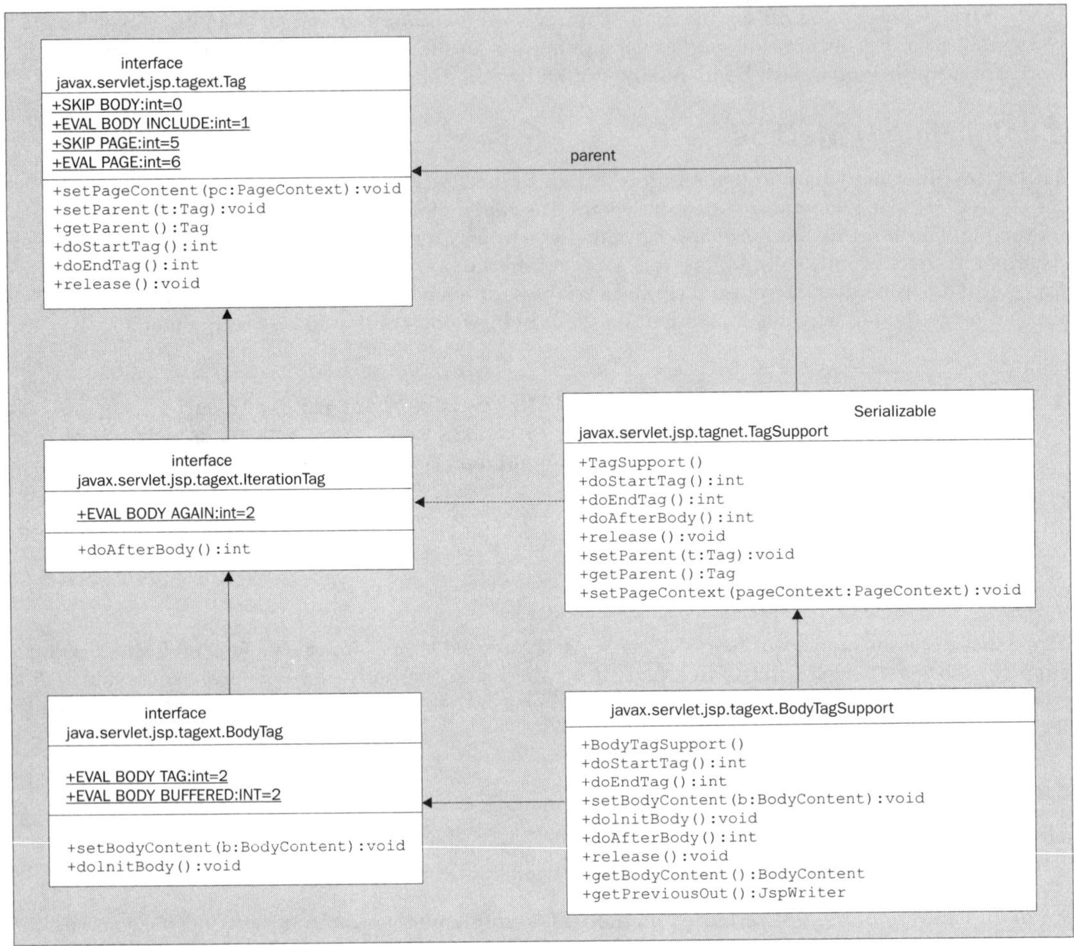

`EVAL_BODY_TAG` is a valid return value for both the `doStartTag()` and `doAfterBody()` methods, being equivalent to returning `EVAL_BODY_BUFFERED` and `EVAL_BODY_AGAIN` respectively. This has been deprecated as of version 1.2 of the JSP specification in favor of `EVAL_BODY_BUFFERED` and `EVAL_BODY_AGAIN` which are seen as more meaningful.

In terms of the implementation details, the `BodyTagSupport` class is as follows:

```
package javax.servlet.jsp.tagext;

import java.io.Writer;
import java.util.Hashtable;

import javax.servlet.jsp.JspException;
```

```
import javax.servlet.jsp.JspWriter;
import javax.servlet.jsp.tagext.BodyTag;
import javax.servlet.jsp.tagext.BodyContent;
import javax.servlet.jsp.tagext.TagSupport;

public class BodyTagSupport extends TagSupport implements BodyTag {

  protected BodyContent bodyContent;

  public int doStartTag() throws JspException {
    return EVAL_BODY_BUFFERED;
  }

  public int doEndTag() throws JspException {
    return super.doEndTag();
  }

  public void setBodyContent(BodyContent b) {
    this.bodyContent = b;
  }

  public void doInitBody() throws JspException {
  }

  public int doAfterBody() throws JspException {
    return SKIP_BODY;
  }

  public void release() {
    bodyContent = null;

    super.release();
  }

  public BodyContent getBodyContent() {
    return bodyContent;
  }

  public JspWriter getPreviousOut() {
    return bodyContent.getEnclosingWriter();
  }
}
```

The implementation is fairly straightforward. The important features are the instance variable that keeps a reference to a `BodyContent` object and its corresponding accessor and mutator methods.

In addition to this, there is a convenient method that can be used to obtain the enclosing `JspWriter` called `getPreviousOut()`. This is important because it is the mechanism whereby we can write the contents of the current `BodyContent` instance back to the `JspWriter` instance that was previously on the top of the stack before the invocation of this tag. Failing to write the contents back to the previous writer will result in content loss.

> **The `getPreviousOut()` method is a convenient method supplied by the `BodyTagSupport` class. It is equivalent to calling `getEnclosingWriter()` on the `BodyContent` instance.**

With our look at the BodyTag interface complete, let's look at some examples of how it can be used.

Iteration – A while Loop

The first example is an alternative way to implement the iteration tag that can be used to output the list of books in an online bookshop as we saw in the previous chapter. The difference here is that a BodyContent object will be used to capture the content of the tag.

While this example doesn't really take advantage of maintaining a tag's body content object, it does demonstrate the principles involved and shows how iteration can be implemented with JSP 1.1.

The Tag Handler

As usual, the first step is to write the tag handler. The full implementation is as follows:

```
package com.wrox.jsptaglibs.body;

import java.io.IOException;
import java.util.Collection;
import java.util.Iterator;

import javax.servlet.jsp.JspException;
import javax.servlet.jsp.JspTagException;
import javax.servlet.jsp.tagext.BodyTagSupport;

public class IteratorTag extends BodyTagSupport {

  private String type;
  private Collection collection;

  private Iterator iterator;

  public void setType(String s) {
    this.type = s;
  }

  public void setCollection(Collection coll) {
    this.collection = coll;
  }
```

One of the interesting and different features of this new implementation is that the doStartTag() method returns EVAL_BODY_BUFFERED instead of EVAL_BODY_INCLUDE. This value instructs the JSP page to create a new BodyContent object to capture the evaluated body content of the tag. Of course, BodyTagSupport provides a default implementation of setBodyContent(), so we don't have to maintain this reference ourselves. In addition to this, it also provides a default (empty) implementation of the doInitBody() method so we don't have to implement this either if we choose:

```
public int doStartTag() throws JspException {
  iterator = collection.iterator();
  if (iterator.hasNext()) {
    pageContext.setAttribute(getId(), iterator.next());
    return EVAL_BODY_BUFFERED;
  } else {
    return SKIP_BODY;
  }
}

public int doAfterBody() throws JspException {
  if (iterator.hasNext()) {
    pageContext.setAttribute(getId(), iterator.next());
    return EVAL_BODY_AGAIN;
  } else {
    return SKIP_BODY;
  }
}
```

The other change to this implementation of the tag handler is the addition of a doEndTag() method. Previously, we relied on the default implementation provided by the TagSupport class that simply instructed the JSP page to evaluate the rest of its content. This time, however, there is an additional step required before the JSP page can evaluate itself.

Since doStartTag() returns EVAL_BODY_BUFFERED, a new BodyContent object is created to capture the evaluation of the body content of the tag. When the end tag is encountered, the contents of this temporary area need to be written back to the enclosing writer if they are to be seen on the page. For this reason, our implementation of the doEndTag() method does exactly this:

```
  public int doEndTag() throws JspException {
    if (bodyContent != null) {
      try {
        bodyContent.writeOut(getPreviousOut());
      } catch (IOException ioe) {
        throw new JspTagException(ioe.getMessage());
      }
    }
    return EVAL_PAGE;
  }
}
```

Something to notice in the implementation of the doEndTag() method is that we are performing a check for the bodyContent reference not being null. As we saw when we revisited the tag lifecycle, it is possible for a tag handler implementing the BodyTag interface to return one of three values from the doStartTag() method, with only EVAL_BODY_BUFFERED causing a new BodyContent object to be created.

Since the `doEndTag()` method will be called regardless of whether a `BodyContent` object is created, it's always good practice to check that it exists before trying to use it. Failing to do so will of course cause a `NullPointerException` to be thrown. While this isn't a problem in this example, it is particularly important when dealing with a tag handler containing a `doStartTag()` method that programmatically determines its return value.

The TagExtraInfo Class

Here we're introducing a scripting variable representing the current element in the collection back into the page, and therefore need a `TagExtraInfo` class. This is actually the same as the one used in the example of the previous chapter, but is included here for completeness:

```
package com.wrox.jsptaglibs.body;

import javax.servlet.jsp.tagext.TagData;
import javax.servlet.jsp.tagext.TagExtraInfo;
import javax.servlet.jsp.tagext.VariableInfo;

public class IteratorTagExtraInfo extends TagExtraInfo {

  public VariableInfo[] getVariableInfo(TagData data) {
    return new VariableInfo[] {
      new VariableInfo(data.getId(), data.getAttributeString("type"),
        true, VariableInfo.NESTED)
    };
  }
}
```

The Tag Library Descriptor

Finally the TLD, which is similar to the one we saw in the previous chapter:

```
<?xml version="1.0" encoding="ISO-8859-1" ?>
<!DOCTYPE taglib
  PUBLIC "-//Sun Microsystems, Inc.//DTD JSP Tag Library 1.2//EN"
  "http://java.sun.com/dtd/web-jsptaglibrary_1_2.dtd">

<taglib>

  <tlib-version>1.0</tlib-version>
  <jsp-version>1.2</jsp-version>
  <short-name>body</short-name>
  <description>
    Examples for the Body Tags chapter.
  </description>

  <tag>
    <name>iterate</name>
    <tag-class>com.wrox.jsptaglibs.body.IteratorTag</tag-class>
    <tei-class>com.wrox.jsptaglibs.body.IteratorTagExtraInfo</tei-class>
    <body-content>JSP</body-content>
    <description>
```

```
      Iterates over a specified java.util.Collection instance.
    </description>

    <attribute>
      <name>id</name>
      <required>true</required>
      <rtexprvalue>false</rtexprvalue>
    </attribute>

    <attribute>
      <name>type</name>
      <required>true</required>
      <rtexprvalue>false</rtexprvalue>
    </attribute>

    <attribute>
      <name>collection</name>
      <required>true</required>
      <rtexprvalue>true</rtexprvalue>
    </attribute>
  </tag>

</taglib>
```

Using the Tag

Considering that the majority of the development (including defining the `Book` and `BookManager` classes) involved in building this tag was the same as we saw in the previous chapter, it will probably come as no surprise that its usage is also the same. After all, the work involved in creating `BodyContent` objects is performed behind the scenes and therefore doesn't affect the way in which the tag is used:

```
<html>
  <head>
    <title>Professional JSP Tag Libraries</title>
  </head>

  <%@ page import="java.util.Collection" %>
  <%@ page import="com.wrox.jsptaglibs.common.BookManager" %>

  <%@ taglib uri="/bodyTaglib" prefix="body" %>

  <body>
    <h1>Wrox books online</h1>

    <%
      Collection books = BookManager.getInstance().getBooksAsCollection();
    %>

    <body:iterate id="book" type="com.wrox.jsptaglibs.common.Book"
                  collection="<%= books %>">

      <p>
```

```
        <b><%= book.getTitle() %></b>
        <br/>
        ISBN : <%= book.getIsbn() %>
      </p>

    </body:iterate>
  </body>
</html>
```

This result of executing this JSP page is the same as we have seen in the previous chapter.

The Tag Handler Revisited

Before we look at the next example, let's consider what happens if the code that writes the contents of the `BodyContent` object back to the enclosing writer is removed. Looking back to our tag handler, this code was implemented in the `doEndTag()` method:

```
public int doEndTag() throws JspException {
  if (bodyContent != null) {
    try {
      bodyContent.writeOut(getPreviousOut());
    } catch (IOException ioe) {
      throw new JspTagException(ioe.getMessage());
    }
  }
  return EVAL_PAGE;
}
```

Removing this code means that although the body content of the tag is evaluated into the `BodyContent` object that the JSP page instantiates, it goes no further. Once the processing of the tag has finished and the enclosing `JspWriter` is restored, the `BodyContent` object is lost forever. The result of requesting such a page is like the following:

```
  <body>
    <h1>Wrox books online</h1>


  </body>
</html>
```

> **Omitting the code that writes the contents of the `BodyContent` object back to the enclosing writer is a common error that is easy to make when developing body tags.**

Why would we want to implement such a tag with the `BodyTag` interface when the `IterationTag` interface is sufficient? The answer is two-fold. First, tags that wanted to perform iteration before version 1.2 of the JSP specification didn't have the `IterationTag` interface and therefore had to use the `BodyTag` interface; and second, performing iteration this way gives us much more control over the generated output.

For example, perhaps it is useful to generate some header information before the body content. In this situation, the `doInitBody()` method might be a good place in the lifecycle to do this. In addition to this, once the body content has been evaluated and the iterations performed, it is possible to further manipulate the body content. An example here might be filtering or transforming the content in some way.

In the majority of cases, however, the `IterationTag` is sufficient for performing iteration on a JSP page. After all, the implementation is straightforward and doesn't incur the additional overhead of creating and manipulating `BodyContent` objects. For those cases where it is a requirement to programmatically modify the content in some way, the `BodyContent` object offers us the ability to do this. Let's take a look at such an example.

Manipulating the Body Content

Our second example of how the `BodyTag` interface will show how evaluated body content can be manipulated. One of the features of the example web application that accompanies this book (downloadable from http://www.wrox.com/) is to look at the source code for the examples through the web browser. An example of this is like the following:

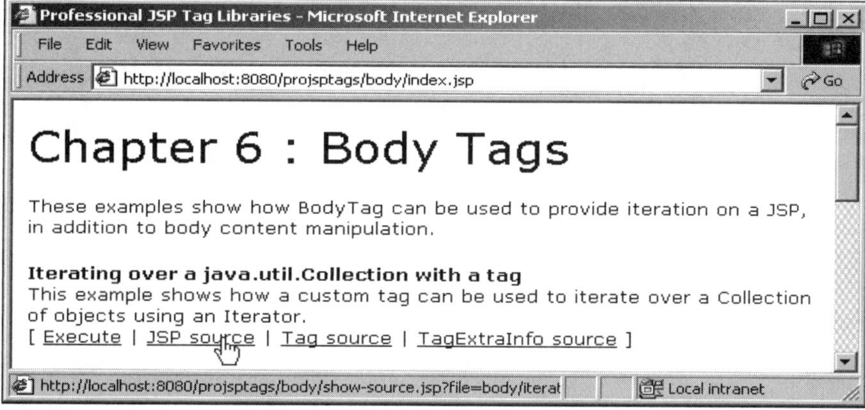

As we can see, with the mouse hovering over the JSP source link, the status bar shows us that clicking on this link will take us to a page called `show-source.jsp` with a parameter called `file` representing the name of the file that should be displayed. When requested, this page will find this particular file and display it (as it is, with no compilation) on the page. Let's look at how this could be implemented.

An include Tag

The first step is to write a simple tag that finds a file, reads its contents, and writes it back out to the page:

```
package com.wrox.jsptaglibs.body;

import java.io.BufferedReader;
import java.io.InputStream;
```

```
import java.io.InputStreamReader;
import java.io.IOException;

import javax.servlet.jsp.JspException;
import javax.servlet.jsp.JspTagException;
import javax.servlet.jsp.tagext.TagSupport;

public class IncludeTag extends TagSupport {

  private String file;

  public int doStartTag() throws JspException {
    try {
      InputStream in;
      BufferedReader br;

      in = pageContext.getServletContext().getResourceAsStream(file);
      br = new BufferedReader(new InputStreamReader(in));

      String line = br.readLine();

      while (line != null) {
        pageContext.getOut().println(line);

        line = br.readLine();
      }

      br.close();

    } catch (IOException ioe) {
      throw new JspTagException(ioe.getMessage());
    }

    return SKIP_BODY;
  }

  public void setFile(String s) {
    this.file = s;
  }
}
```

Our tag has a single attribute called `file` that represents a URI to the file that we would like to include. Once we have this, we can use the `ServletContext` to get a `java.io.InputStream` to the file so we can read it in line-by-line and write it back to the page.

Effectively, this tag performs a static include of the file rather than a dynamic include as would be performed if we were to use the `<jsp:include/>` action. This is important because it's the source code that we would like to display and not the results of running it. Consequently, performing a static include means that meaningful HTML tags end up in the page and are therefore rendered by the browser.

One way to solve this problem would be to change the content type of the response to try and mislead the browser into thinking that it was plain text. This is not an ideal solution, however, as it restricts the degree to which we can present the information, because plain text cannot present a rich set of fonts and styles.

A filter Tag

An alternative solution is to filter out all of the HTML (and JSP) tags and replace them with ones that can be rendered in a browser. For example, we can replace the left and right angle brackets (< and >) with their HTML escaped equivalents `<` and `>` respectively. This has the desired effect of changing the source code so that the JSP container won't try to run it, and making it presentable in a browser.

The next issue is how to filter the content generated by the `include` tag that we just wrote. The simple answer is to nest the tags as follows, indicating that we will filter any content that is generated as part of the `include` tag:

```
<body:filter>
  <body:include file="<%= file %>"/>
</body:filter>
```

With regular tags (those that implement the `Tag` or `IterationTag` interfaces), any content that is generated goes straight back to the current `JspWriter` instance, accessible through the `pageContext.getOut()` method. If this happens to be the writer instance associated with the page, we write the content straight back to the page and can't modify it. If the `filter` tag is implemented as a `BodyTag` whose body content is evaluated into a `BodyContent` object, we can step in and filter the content before writing it back to the page. The full implementation for this tag is as follows:

```
package com.wrox.jsptaglibs.body;

import java.io.IOException;

import javax.servlet.jsp.JspException;
import javax.servlet.jsp.JspTagException;
import javax.servlet.jsp.JspWriter;
import javax.servlet.jsp.tagext.BodyTagSupport;

public class FilterTag extends BodyTagSupport {
```

This is a straightforward tag and contains only two methods. From a tag lifecycle perspective, all we need to do is return `EVAL_BODY_BUFFERED` from the `doStartTag()` method to indicate that we would like the body content evaluated into a `BodyContent` object, and, as no iteration is required, return `SKIP_BODY` from the `doAfterBody()` method. As the `BodyTagSupport` class provides a default implementation of the `doStartTag()` and `doAfterBody()` methods that matches these requirements, the only lifecycle method that we need to implement is `doEndTag()`:

```
public int doEndTag() throws JspException {
  if (bodyContent != null) {
    try {
```

The first step is to get a copy of the body content. It is a simple method call away:

```
      String content = bodyContent.getString();
```

Now that we have the content, we need to filter it to replace characters in the content with their HTML escaped counterparts that can be displayed in the browser. For simplicity, this code has been moved into a helper method called `filter()`:

```
content = filter(content);
```

The next step is to clear the current body content of the tag:

```
bodyContent.clearBody();
```

Next, we need to write the filtered copy of the content back into the `BodyContent` object:

```
bodyContent.print(content);
```

Finally, we need to ensure that the contents of the `BodyContent` object get written back to the enclosing `JspWriter` so that they are displayed on the page and return `EVAL_PAGE`, telling the JSP page to evaluate the rest of it as usual:

```
        bodyContent.writeOut(getPreviousOut());
      } catch (IOException ioe) {
        throw new JspTagException(ioe.getMessage());
      }
    }
    return EVAL_PAGE;
  }
```

It's here that the work associated with this tag is performed and the reason for implementing it in the `doEndTag()` method is that we need to wait until the body content has been evaluated (that is the file has been included) before we can start manipulating it. Finally we have the `filter()` method:

```
  private String filter(String s) {
    StringBuffer buf = new StringBuffer(s.length());

    int length = s.length();
    for (int i = 0; i < length; i++) {
      switch (s.charAt(i)) {
        case '<' :
          buf.append("&lt;");
          break;
        case '>' :
          buf.append("&gt;");
          break;
        case '&' :
          buf.append("&amp;");
          break;
        default :
          buf.append(s.charAt(i));
      }
    }
    return buf.toString();
  }
}
```

The Tag Library Descriptor

The next step of course is to write the tag library descriptor. In this example, our TLD contains descriptions of both the tags that we've implemented here:

```
<?xml version="1.0" encoding="ISO-8859-1" ?>
<!DOCTYPE taglib
  PUBLIC "-//Sun Microsystems, Inc.//DTD JSP Tag Library 1.2//EN"
  "http://java.sun.com/dtd/web-jsptaglibrary_1_2.dtd">

<taglib>

  <tlib-version>1.0</tlib-version>
  <jsp-version>1.2</jsp-version>
  <short-name>body</short-name>
  <description>
    Examples for the Body Tags chapter.
  </description>

  <tag>
    <name>include</name>
    <tag-class>com.wrox.jsptaglibs.body.IncludeTag</tag-class>
    <body-content>empty</body-content>
    <description>
      Includes the specified file into the page statically.
    </description>

    <attribute>
      <name>file</name>
      <required>true</required>
      <rtexprvalue>true</rtexprvalue>
    </attribute>
  </tag>

  <tag>
    <name>filter</name>
    <tag-class>com.wrox.jsptaglibs.body.FilterTag</tag-class>
    <body-content>JSP</body-content>
    <description>
      Filters its body content into a form displayable on HTML pages.
    </description>
  </tag>

</taglib>
```

Using the Tag

We've already seen how the pair of tags are going be used, but for completeness, here's the full JSP page:

```
<html>
  <head>
    <title>Professional JSP Tag Libraries</title>
    <link rel="stylesheet" href="../page.css">
  </head>

  <%@ taglib uri="/bodyTaglib" prefix="body" %>
```

First, we get the `file` parameter from the request and place it in a variable called `file`:

```
  <%
    String file = request.getParameter("file");
  %>

  <body>
    <h1>Source for <%= file %></h1>
```

Following this are our tags, surrounded by HTML `<pre>` tags to ensure that whitespace in the source code is maintained:

```
    <pre>
      <body:filter>
        <body:include file="<%= file %>"/>
      </body:filter>
    </pre>
  </body>
</html>
```

Clicking on the hyperlink in the previous screenshot produces the following page showing the source code for the iteration example that we saw earlier in the chapter:

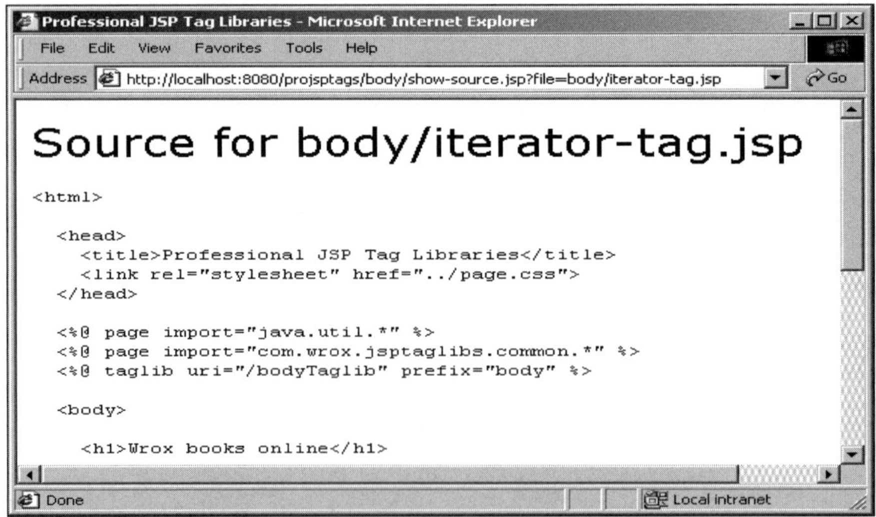

The source of the JSP page is shown in the browser and has not been executed. This is because we filtered out all of the important characters and replaced them with their viewable counterparts. Viewing the source of the resulting page will highlight how extensive the filtering has been:

```
<html>
  <head>
    <title>Professional JSP Tag Libraries</title>
  </head>

 <body>
    <h1>Source for bodytag/iterator-tag.jsp</h1>

    <pre>


&lt;html&gt;
  &lt;head&gt;
    &lt;title&gt;Professional JSP Tag Libraries&lt;/title&gt;
    &lt;link rel="stylesheet" href="../page.css"&gt;
  &lt;/head&gt;
  &lt;%@ page import="java.util.*" %&gt;
  &lt;%@ page import="com.wrox.jsptaglibs.common.*" %&gt;

  &lt;%@ taglib uri="/bodyTaglib" prefix="body" %&gt;

  &lt;body&gt;

    &lt;h1&gt;Wrox books online&lt;/h1&gt;

    &lt;%
      Collection books = BookManager.getInstance().getBooksAsCollection();
    %&gt;

    &lt;body:iterate id="book" type="com.wrox.jsptaglibs.common.Book"
                  collection="&lt;%= books %&gt;"&gt;

      &lt;p&gt;
        &lt;b&gt;&lt;%= book.getTitle() %&gt;&lt;/b&gt;
        &lt;br&gt;
        ISBN : &lt;%= book.getIsbn() %&gt;
      &lt;/p&gt;

    &lt;/body:iterate&gt;

  &lt;/body&gt;
&lt;/html&gt;

    </pre>
  </body>
</html>
```

The important point here is that only the content between the HTML <pre> tags has been filtered. This corresponds with the body content of the filter tags and illustrates the use of a BodyContent as a separate, temporary scratchpad that can be used to manipulate and assemble complex content.

Before we wrap up this chapter, there's one body content type that can be defined in the TLD that we've not really looked at in any detail up until now – `tagdependent`.

tagdependent Body Content

We touched upon `tagdependent` body content back in Chapter 3 when we introduced the different types of body content that can be defined in the TLD.

A body content of `empty` implies that the start and end tags have no content between them, while `JSP` means that the tag's body content may contain regular JSP elements such as JSP tags, scriptlets, expressions, and so on. Most of the examples that we've seen up until now have used a body content type of `JSP`, including those tags that have performed multiple evaluations of their body content to provide iteration on a JSP page.

With `tagdependent` however, none of this applies and it is left up to the tag to process and evaluate its body content. To demonstrate this, let's look again at the previous example, a snippet of which is as follows:

```
<body:filter>
  <body:include file="<%= file %>"/>
</body:filter>
```

In this example, the `filter` tag was declared with a body content type of `JSP`. This means that the body content (highlighted) is evaluated as usual. If we were to change this to `tagdependent`, the JSP page would no longer evaluate the body content and the result would be like the following:

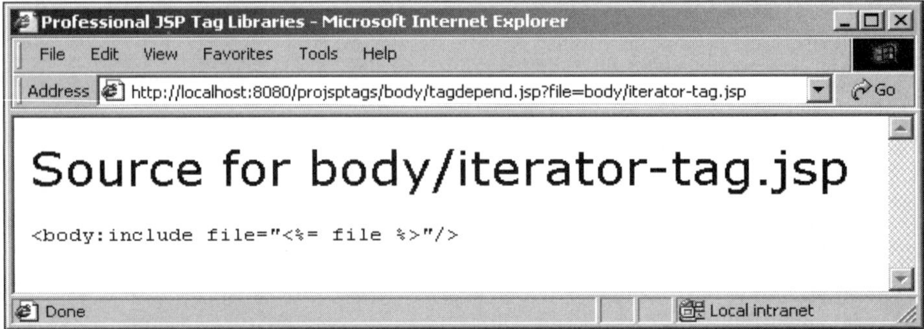

Here, the body content of the tag is not evaluated and the emphasis is now on the tag to process it. So what can we use this for? There are, in fact, many good uses including interpreting code written in other languages, for example mixing ColdFusion or Microsoft ASP with JSP. Essentially, `tagdependent` body content is useful where we don't want the JSP page to evaluate it, or simply where the JSP page doesn't know how to evaluate it. Let's wrap up the chapter by taking a look at such an example.

Manipulating Tag Dependent Body Content

Our final example of the `BodyTag` interface demonstrates a scenario where we don't want the body content of the tag evaluated.

Imagine that we are writing a series of Java training courses for publication on a web site like the Java Developer Connection (http://developer.java.sun.com/developer/). Being an in-depth technical course, we decide that we'd like to include several code examples. For a while now, integrated development environments (IDEs) have been able to highlight specific parts of a source code document and to help readers get a better feeling for the Java language, we decide that we'd also like to provide a similar facility whereby the keywords that make up the Java language are highlighted in some way.

A Keyword Highlighting Tag

Implementing this is straightforward and all that we need to do is to write the Java source code that we are showing the reader on the page, and wrap it up inside a custom tag. This custom tag will subsequently read this body content and highlight the Java keywords that it finds.

Since we don't want the body content executed in anyway, we'll once again build a tag handler that extends the `BodyTagSupport` class. In the TLD, we can then define the body content to be `tagdependent`. After all, we want to display the Java code rather than have it executed when the JSP is requested:

```
package com.wrox.jsptaglibs.learning;

import java.io.BufferedReader;
import java.io.InputStream;
import java.io.InputStreamReader;
import java.io.IOException;
import java.io.StreamTokenizer;
import java.util.HashSet;
import java.util.Set;

import javax.servlet.ServletContext;
import javax.servlet.jsp.JspException;
import javax.servlet.jsp.JspTagException;
import javax.servlet.jsp.JspWriter;
import javax.servlet.jsp.tagext.BodyTagSupport;

public class KeywordHighlightingTag extends BodyTagSupport {
```

While the Java code to be displayed will make up the body of the tag, it will be useful to allow a couple of optional attributes to be supplied specifying how the Java keywords should be highlighted on the page. For this reason, we have two properties called `startTag` and `endTag`. These are simply the HTML tags that should be placed either side of the Java keyword to highlight it on the page. By default we've just decided to use the HTML bold tags:

```
  private String startTag = "<b>";
  private String endTag = "</b>";

  public void setStartTag(String s) {
    this.startTag = s;
  }
  public void setEndTag(String s) {
    this.endTag = s;
  }
```

As with the previous example, all of the hard work is performed when the end tag is encountered, because this is when the body content is available to us. First of all we check that body content is present and if it is, we get the contents as a string:

```
  public int doEndTag() throws JspException {
    if (bodyContent != null) {
      try {
        String content = bodyContent.getString();
```

Now that we have the body content, we then ask the `highlight()` method to highlight the Java keywords for us:

```
        content = highlight(content);
```

With the content manipulated, we then clear the original body content and replace it with our newly-highlighted version:

```
        bodyContent.clearBody();
        bodyContent.print(content);
```

Finally, we must not forget to write it back to the enclosing writer, otherwise it will never be displayed on the page:

```
        bodyContent.writeOut(getPreviousOut());
      } catch (IOException ioe) {
        throw new JspTagException(ioe.getMessage());
      }
    }
    return EVAL_PAGE;
  }
```

Next is the `highlight()` method:

```
  private String highlight(String s) throws IOException {
    StringBuffer buf = new StringBuffer(s.length());
```

The first step here is to load the Java keywords from a flat text file with another helper method. For the purposes of this example, `String` objects representing the keywords are just loaded into a `java.util.Set` instance:

```
    Set keywords = loadKeywords();
```

The highlighting mechanism here is implemented with the help of an instance of a `java.io.StreamTokenizer`. It's a fairly complex class to use, but the first step involves defining how the stream should be parsed:

```
    StreamTokenizer st = new StreamTokenizer(bodyContent.getReader());
    st.resetSyntax();
    st.eolIsSignificant(true);
    st.slashSlashComments(false);
```

```
    st.slashStarComments(false);
    st.wordChars(48, 122); // these are the characters '0' to 'z'
```

Once this has been configured, we simply loop over all of the tokens provided by the tokenizer and determine whether we've found a keyword that needs to be highlighted. The `StreamTokenizer` provides information about the type of token that is currently available through its `ttype` property.

The only tokens that we are really interested in looking at are those of type `TT_WORD` – basically anything that isn't a single character or a number. Once we come across a word, we simply test whether it is a Java keyword and if so, we wrap it up inside the start and end tags that we use to highlight. Following this, and in all other cases, the token is then added into a `StringBuffer` representing the highlighted version of the body content:

```
    while (st.nextToken() != StreamTokenizer.TT_EOF) {

      if (st.ttype == StreamTokenizer.TT_WORD) {
        if (keywords.contains(st.sval)) {
          buf.append(startTag + st.sval + endTag);
        } else {
          buf.append(st.sval);
        }
      } else if (st.ttype == StreamTokenizer.TT_NUMBER) {
          buf.append(st.nval);
      } else if (st.ttype == StreamTokenizer.TT_EOL) {
          buf.append("<br/>");
      } else {
          buf.append((char)st.ttype);
      }
    }
    return buf.toString();
  }
```

The final method in the tag is the one that loads the list of Java keywords from a flat text file. This is achieved using the `getResourceAsStream()` method on the `ServletContext`. We can then create a `java.io.Reader` instance, read in the file line-by-line and add each keyword to a `java.util.Set` object:

```
  private Set loadKeywords() throws IOException {
    Set keywords = new HashSet();

    ServletContext sc = pageContext.getServletContext();
    InputStream in = sc.getResourceAsStream("/WEB-INF/keywords.txt");
    BufferedReader br = new BufferedReader(new InputStreamReader(in));
    String line;

    line = br.readLine();
    while (line != null) {
      keywords.add(line);
      line = br.readLine();
    }
    br.close();
    return keywords;
  }
}
```

The Tag Library Descriptor

The next step is to write the TLD which describes the tag as having `tagdependent` body content and two optional attributes:

```
<?xml version="1.0" encoding="ISO-8859-1" ?>
<!DOCTYPE taglib
  PUBLIC "-//Sun Microsystems, Inc.//DTD JSP Tag Library 1.2//EN"
  "http://java.sun.com/dtd/web-jsptaglibrary_1_2.dtd">

<taglib>

  <tlib-version>1.0</tlib-version>
  <jsp-version>1.2</jsp-version>
  <short-name>learning</short-name>
  <description>
    Learning examples for the Body Tags chapter.
  </description>

  <tag>
    <name>highlight</name>
    <tag-class>
      com.wrox.jsptaglibs.learning.KeywordHighlightingTag
    </tag-class>
    <body-content>tagdependent</body-content>
    <description>
      Highlights Java keywords used in the body content of this tag.
    </description>

    <attribute>
      <name>startTag</name>
      <required>false</required>
      <rtexprvalue>false</rtexprvalue>
    </attribute>

    <attribute>
      <name>endTag</name>
      <required>false</required>
      <rtexprvalue>false</rtexprvalue>
    </attribute>
  </tag>

</taglib>
```

Using the Tag

With the tag deployed, using it is straightforward and all we've done is wrap up some example Java code inside the new `highlight` tag. For clarity, the two optional attributes have been included to illustrate their usage:

```
<html>
  <head>
    <title>Professional JSP Tag Libraries</title>
  </head>

  <%@ taglib uri="/learningTaglib" prefix="learning" %>

  <body>
    <h1>Writing a JavaBean</h1>

    <p>
      Here is an example JavaBean, used to represent a book:
    </p>

    <pre>
      <learning:highlight startTag="<b>" endTag="</b>">
        package com.wrox.jsptaglibs.common;

        import java.io.Serializable;
        import java.util.*;

        /**
         * Represents a book.
         *
         * @author    Simon Brown
         */
        public class Book implements Serializable {

        ... content of class omitted for brevity ...

        }
      </learning:highlight>
    </pre>
  </body>
</html>
```

Since the body content has been defined as `tagdependent`, the Java code in the JSP isn't executed when the JSP is requested. In fact, nothing at all happens to `tagdependent` body content – custom tags aren't processed and scriptlets/expressions aren't executed. It is entirely up to the tag to process it and the result of requesting the page is as follows:

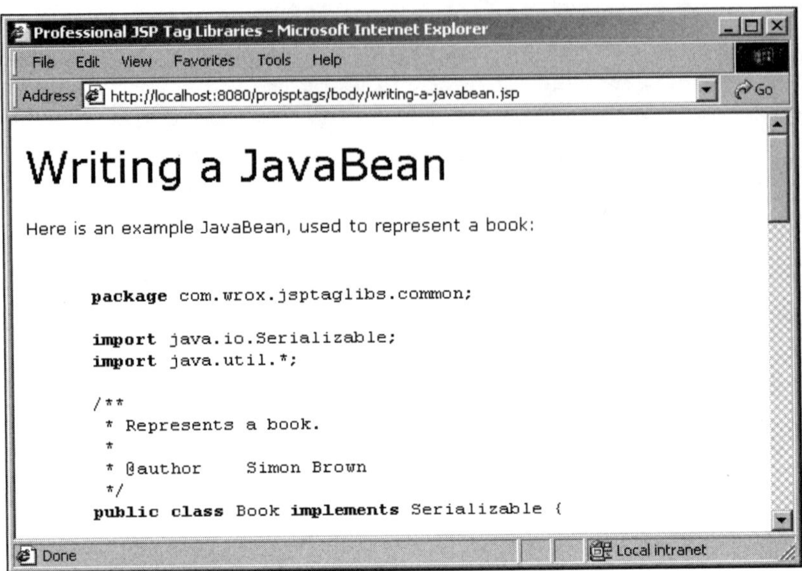

As we can see, this produces the desired result in that all of the Java keywords within the body content of the tag have been highlighted in bold.

JSP vs. tagdependent Body Content

On a final note, while `tagdependent` body content does have its uses, you'll probably find yourself using a body content of `JSP` more often. As demonstrated by the `filter` tag, `JSP` body content is generally more useful because it does provide the ability to use JSP elements and other custom tags between the start and end tags. This can therefore be used to dynamically generate the body content.

With `tagdependent`, however, the body content must be explicitly written between the start and end tag since even simple JSP elements, such as the `include` directive, will not be processed. In either situation, implementing the `BodyTag` interface will provide you with a very powerful way to post-process the body content – something that isn't possible with the `Tag` or `IterationTag` interfaces.

Summary

This chapter introduced `BodyTag`, the last of the three interfaces that a tag handler can implement. The `Tag` interface is the most straightforward, with `IterationTag` and `BodyTag` interfaces extending the capabilities to include re-evaluation of the body content and manipulation of that body content respectively.

We then looked the `JspWriter` and `BodyContent` classes. We also revisited the tag lifecycle and illustrated how body tags slightly modify this to allow `BodyContent` objects to be created when the `doStartTag()` method of the tag handler returns the `BodyTag` specific `EVAL_BODY_BUFFERED` value.

The BodyContent class is simply a specialized JspWriter and serves as a temporary scratchpad in which content can be evaluated, retrieved, and manipulated before being written back to the page. We looked at a couple of examples of how the BodyContent object can be used by implementing a tag that performed iteration, and a tag that filtered its content. With this knowledge in place, we took a slightly more detailed look at tagdependent body content and discussed why it was useful and how the responsibility is on the tag handler to evaluate it.

We've now covered all of the basic types of custom tags, from those that have attributes to those that can programmatically evaluate and manipulate their body content. The next chapter takes this yet another step further by looking at how custom tags can cooperate on the page.

LONDON

7

Cooperating Tags

We have touched upon this topic in some of the earlier examples already but, in the majority of cases, we have only looked at how tags are built and used on the page on their own. This chapter puts into practice many of the ideas that we've looked at so far and shows several ways in which tags can cooperate with each other on the page. Allowing tags to cooperate on the page opens up new ways in which they can be used to help build JSP pages by allowing more sophisticated functionality to be built than is possible with a single tag alone. A good example of this is that cooperating tags can help to remove complex conditional logic and Java from the page and into reusable components.

There are several ways in which tags can cooperate, including:

- With a scripting variable
- With a scoped attribute – both implicitly and explicitly
- By accessing parent tags

We'll walk through each of these techniques of cooperation and show examples of how each of them works. To wrap up, we'll look at how the coupling between cooperating tags can be minimized and finally, some rules of thumb for determining the appropriate technique of cooperation.

What is Cooperation?

Before we dive into some examples, let's first define what we mean by cooperation. Cooperation between tags can be simply defined as the tags working together to achieve a common goal. Although servlets, JSP pages, and custom tags can all cooperate by sharing information through common resources such as the `Session` object, the cooperation that we are most interested in here is the cooperation of tags within the page.

The most common reason why tags might want to cooperate on a page is to exchange information. Although the cooperation between the tags in such a situation is basic, as we will see shortly it does illustrate a common usage pattern. On an advanced level, a nested tag could explicitly ask its parent tag for some information, or even to perform some processing.

Cooperation is typically achieved by nesting tags on the page, and in essence there are two paradigms of cooperation. In the first, the parent (or outer) tag passes information to its child (nested) tags; and in the second, the child tags request information from their parent. The examples that we will look at in this chapter encompass both of these.

Cooperation with a Scripting Variable

A feature of many web sites is a set of links, or menu items, in the left hand frame or section of the page representing the areas of the web site that users can visit. In many cases these are simply static links but in others they are dynamic, perhaps sourced from a database or a configuration file. In an online bookstore, these links might represent the categories that the users can browse:

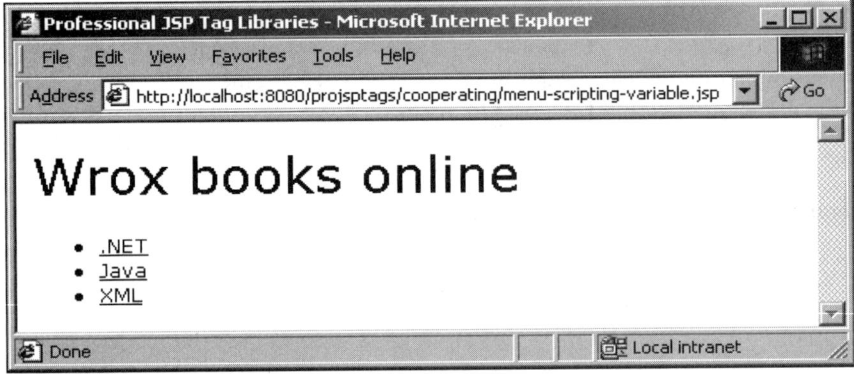

Such a list could easily be generated with the `iterate` tag that we developed in Chapter 5. However, let's present the page author with a much-simplified pair of tags as follows:

```
... start of page ...

<ul>
  <menu:showMenu menu="... the menu to be displayed ...">
    <li><menu:showMenuItem item="... the menu item to be displayed ..."/>
  </menu:showMenu>
</ul>

... end of page ...
```

We would like to generate a menu that simply consists of one or more menu items. Here, the `showMenu` tag takes the menu to be displayed and iterates over the body content for each item in the menu, during which we can render the menu item with the `showMenuItem` tag. Let's see how this could be built.

Representing the Menu

The first thing to do is to define some Java classes to represent a menu structure. First of all there is the `MenuEntry` class. Since menus can be hierarchical and arbitrarily deep, `MenuEntry` is the abstract class for menus and menu items. It contains a `name` property that will be displayed, and a URL that will form the hyperlink on the page:

```
package com.wrox.jsptaglibs.menu;

import java.io.Serializable;

public abstract class MenuEntry implements Serializable {

  private String name;
  private String url;

  public MenuEntry(String name, String url) {
    this.name = name;
    this.url = url;
  }

  public String getName() {
    return this.name;
  }

  public void setName(String name) {
    this.name = name;
  }

  public String getUrl() {
    return this.url;
  }

  public void setUrl(String url) {
    this.url = url;
  }
}
```

Next is `MenuItem` with a property called `target` for storing the name of the HTML frame or window in which the link should be opened. For example, it may be the case that some menu items (for example, links to external sites) open new windows:

```
package com.wrox.jsptaglibs.menu;

public class MenuItem extends MenuEntry {

  private String target;

  public MenuItem(String name, String url) {
    super(name, url);
  }

  public String getTarget() {
```

```
    return this.target;
  }

  public void setTarget(String target) {
    this.target = target;
  }
}
```

Finally, Menu maintains a collection of MenuEntry instances that in turn can be menu items, or further nested menus:

```
package com.wrox.jsptaglibs.menu;

import java.util.ArrayList;
import java.util.Collection;
import java.util.Iterator;

public class Menu extends MenuEntry {

  private Collection menuEntries;

  public Menu(String name, String url) {
    super(name, url);

    this.menuEntries = new ArrayList();
  }

  public void add(MenuEntry menuEntry) {
    menuEntries.add(menuEntry);
  }

  public Iterator menuEntries() {
    return menuEntries.iterator();
  }
}
```

Although this model allows a nested hierarchy, we won't be taking advantage of it until Chapter 11.

The final class to build is called MenuManager. In a real system, the menu structure might be generated dynamically, perhaps from information stored within a database. For the purposes of this example, however, we will just use a singleton class that builds up a menu.

```
package com.wrox.jsptaglibs.menu;

import java.util.HashMap;

public class MenuManager {

  private static MenuManager instance = new MenuManager();

  private HashMap menus = new HashMap();
```

```
  private MenuManager() {
    Menu root = new Menu("/", "home.jsp");
    root.add(new MenuItem(".NET", "category.jsp?name=dotnet"));
    root.add(new MenuItem("Java", "category.jsp?name=java"));
    root.add(new MenuItem("XML", "category.jsp?name=xml"));

    menus.put("main", root);
  }

  public static MenuManager getInstance() {
    return instance;
  }

  public Menu getMenu(String name) {
    return (Menu)menus.get(name);
  }
}
```

Since there might be several different menus for any web application, this class has a method `getMenu()` with which clients can look up the one that they are interested in. For this example, we will just use a menu called `main`. Now that the menu structure can be represented in memory, we can build the tags.

The showMenu Tag

The purpose of this tag is to take a `Menu` instance as an attribute, iterate over the menu items, and introduce each one into the page as a scripting variable. For this reason, we have the usual property that represents an attribute, and a mutator method that accepts the attribute:

```
package com.wrox.jsptaglibs.menu;

import java.util.Iterator;

import javax.servlet.jsp.JspException;
import javax.servlet.jsp.tagext.TagSupport;

public class ShowMenuTag extends TagSupport {

  private Menu menu;

  private Iterator iterator;

  public void setMenu(Menu menu) {
    this.menu = menu;
  }
```

Next is the `doStartTag()` method, and essentially this is the same as we saw in the previous iteration examples. First, we set up the `Iterator` that the tag will use. We then check whether the body content should be evaluated by seeing if there are elements to iterate over. If this is the case, we introduce the first menu item into the page under the name `item`:

```
    public int doStartTag() throws JspException {
      // setup the iterator to be used
      iterator = menu.menuEntries();

      if (iterator.hasNext()) {
        // if there are menu items, put the first one into the
        // page under the name "item"
        pageContext.setAttribute("item", iterator.next());

        // and include the body
        return EVAL_BODY_INCLUDE;
      } else {
        // there are no menu items so skip the body
        return SKIP_BODY;
      }
    }
```

Following this is the `doAfterBody()` method, which is again similar to those used last time:

```
    public int doAfterBody() throws JspException {
      if (iterator.hasNext()) {
        // if there are more menu items, put the first one into the
        // page under the name "item"
        pageContext.setAttribute("item", iterator.next());

        // and instruct the JSP engine to re-evaluate the body of this tag
        return EVAL_BODY_AGAIN;
      } else {
        // there are no more menu items so skip the body
        return SKIP_BODY;
      }
    }
  }
```

The showMenuItem Tag

Since each menu item should be rendered as a hyperlink, we'll use a custom tag to wrap this functionality up for us. All that it does is take a `MenuItem` instance as an attribute and generates the appropriate HTML:

```
  package com.wrox.jsptaglibs.menu;

  import java.io.IOException;

  import javax.servlet.jsp.JspException;
  import javax.servlet.jsp.JspTagException;
  import javax.servlet.jsp.tagext.TagSupport;

  public class ShowMenuItemTag extends TagSupport {

    private MenuItem item;

    public int doStartTag() throws JspException {
```

```
    try {
      StringBuffer buf = new StringBuffer();

      buf.append("<a href=\"");
      buf.append(item.getUrl());
      buf.append("\">");
      buf.append(item.getName());
      buf.append("</a>");

      pageContext.getOut().write(buf.toString());
    } catch (IOException ioe) {
      throw new JspTagException(ioe.getMessage());
    }

    // and skip the body content for this empty tag
    return SKIP_BODY;
  }

  public void setItem(MenuItem item) {
    this.item = item;
  }
}
```

The Tag Library Descriptor

Next is the TLD file that describes both of the tags:

```
<?xml version="1.0" encoding="ISO-8859-1" ?>
<!DOCTYPE taglib
  PUBLIC "-//Sun Microsystems, Inc.//DTD JSP Tag Library 1.2//EN"
  "http://java.sun.com/dtd/web-jsptaglibrary_1_2.dtd">

<taglib>

  <tlib-version>1.0</tlib-version>
  <jsp-version>1.2</jsp-version>
  <short-name>menu</short-name>
  <description>
    Menu examples for the Cooperating Tags chapter.
  </description>
```

The first of these is called showMenu and has a single, required attribute:

```
  <tag>
    <name>showMenu</name>
    <tag-class>com.wrox.jsptaglibs.menu.ShowMenuTag</tag-class>
    <body-content>JSP</body-content>
    <description>
      Iterates over all of the menu items in a menu.
    </description>

    <variable>
      <name-given>item</name-given>
```

```
      <variable-class>com.wrox.jsptaglibs.menu.MenuItem</variable-class>
      <declare>true</declare>
      <scope>NESTED</scope>
      <description>The next MenuItem instance.</description>
    </variable>

    <attribute>
      <name>menu</name>
      <required>true</required>
      <rtexprvalue>true</rtexprvalue>
    </attribute>
  </tag>
```

Then there's the `showMenuItem` tag again with a single, required attribute:

```
  <tag>
    <name>showMenuItem</name>
    <tag-class>com.wrox.jsptaglibs.menu.ShowMenuItemTag</tag-class>
    <body-content>empty</body-content>
    <description>
      Generates a hyperlink for a menu item.
    </description>

    <attribute>
      <name>item</name>
      <required>true</required>
      <rtexprvalue>true</rtexprvalue>
    </attribute>
  </tag>

</taglib>
```

Using the Tag

Using the tag is very straightforward, and for this example, we'll use the `MenuManager` class to get a reference to the menu that we would like to display:

```
<html>
  <head>
    <title>Professional JSP Tag Libraries</title>
  </head>

  <%@ page import="com.wrox.jsptaglibs.menu.*" %>
  <%@ taglib uri="/menuTaglib" prefix="menu" %>

  <body>
    <h1>Wrox books online</h1>

    <%
      Menu menu = MenuManager.getInstance().getMenu("main");
    %>

    <ul>
```

```
        <menu:showMenu menu="<%= menu %>">
          <li><menu:showMenuItem item="<%= item %>"/>
        </menu:showMenu>
      </ul>
    </body>
  </html>
```

This example demonstrates that it is possible for tags to cooperate on the page. The `showMenu` tag introduces a scripting variable called `item` into the page, while the nested `showMenuItem` tag uses this reference to generate the appropriate hyperlink.

Using a request-time expression to pass information between tags works well, but does bring with it a couple of consequences. First, we've had to allow the `showMenuItem` tag to take request-time expressions and this means that Java code can be used to specify the value for the attribute. Although in this case the Java code is very simple, the expression could feasibly be very complex. In this situation, the page would once again contain Java code, which we are trying to avoid. Additionally, the syntax of request-time expressions is not easily readable – especially when a large expression with plenty of brackets and other non-alphanumeric characters is used.

The other consequence of using a scripting variable to pass information to a tag is that a variable is actually defined within the page. Scripting variables are certainly very useful but if they are simply used for passing values between tags, it does seem a little wasteful to always declare them. Let's look at a better way in which information can be exchanged between tags.

Cooperation with a Scoped Attribute

Another way in which tags can exchange information is through the page context. Instead of creating a scripting variable, a tag can use the page context as a facility to store information and references to other objects. Any tags that subsequently wish to use this information can simply look up the information using the page context.

This mechanism also has other benefits; attributes stored within the page context can be associated with several scopes – `page`, `request`, `session`, and `application`. This means that tags can share information regardless of whether they are on the same page or not.

For two tags to make use of the page context, they must agree on one piece of information – the name of the attribute residing in the page context that they wish to share. There are two ways in which this can be achieved: implicitly and explicitly.

Cooperating Implicitly on the Page

In the previous example, the nested `showMenuItem` tag had an attribute that represented the menu item to be rendered. This was an explicit exchange of information because we explicitly passed the tag the information it required. Alternatively, we can let the `showMenuItem` tag find its own information as illustrated by the following JSP fragment:

```
... start of page ...

    <ul>
```

```
      <menu:showMenu menu="<%= menu %>">
        <li><menu:showMenuItem/>
      </menu:showMenu>
    </ul>

... end of page ...
```

Instead of the showMenu tag creating and introducing a scripting variable, it can bind the MenuItem instance into the page context during each iteration and let the tag find it rather than specifying it in the page.

From a development perspective, nothing much has changed with the showMenu tag. We have again set an attribute called item in the page context. Although this is the same as last time, we won't be including the variable description in the TLD file because we don't want a scripting variable declared on the page.

When declaring a scripting variable, it is possible to declare its scope as NESTED, meaning that it is only available between the start and end tags. However, the smallest scope in which attributes can be placed within the page context is page, which means that they are available for the entire length of the page.

To mimic the NESTED scope of scripting variables and ensure that attributes aren't available outside the scope in which they could be used, it is a good idea to remove the attributes from the page context when they are finished with. A good place to do this is in the doEndTag() method:

```
package com.wrox.jsptaglibs.menu;

import java.util.Iterator;

import javax.servlet.jsp.JspException;
import javax.servlet.jsp.tagext.TagSupport;

public class ShowMenuImplicitTag extends TagSupport {

  private Menu menu;

  private Iterator iterator;

  public int doStartTag() throws JspException {
    // setup the iterator to be used
    iterator = menu.menuEntries();

    if (iterator.hasNext()) {
      // if there are menu items, put the first one into the
      // page context under the name "item"
      pageContext.setAttribute("item", iterator.next());

      // and include the body
      return EVAL_BODY_INCLUDE;
    } else {
      // there are no menu items so skip the body
      return SKIP_BODY;
    }
  }
```

```
  public int doAfterBody() throws JspException {
    if (iterator.hasNext()) {
      // if there are more menu items, put the first one into the
      // page context under the name "item"
      pageContext.setAttribute("item", iterator.next());

      // and instruct the JSP engine to re-evaluate the body of this tag
      return EVAL_BODY_AGAIN;
    } else {
      // there are no more menu items so skip the body
      return SKIP_BODY;
    }
  }

  public int doEndTag() throws JspException {
    pageContext.removeAttribute("item");

    return EVAL_PAGE;
  }

  public void setMenu(Menu menu) {
    this.menu = menu;
  }

}
```

With the showMenu tag written, the next step is to write the showMenuItem tag to use the page context rather than having it passed as a reference to a MenuItem. This version of the tag is much shorter than the previous because it doesn't have any attributes. Instead, the tag uses the page context to find the attribute (called item) that the showMenu tag inserted into it:

```
package com.wrox.jsptaglibs.menu;

import java.io.IOException;

import javax.servlet.jsp.JspException;
import javax.servlet.jsp.JspTagException;
import javax.servlet.jsp.tagext.TagSupport;

public class ShowMenuItemImplicitTag extends TagSupport {

  public int doStartTag() throws JspException {

    // find the attribute placed into the page context by the parent tag
    MenuItem item = (MenuItem)pageContext.findAttribute("item");

    // check that it was found
    if (item == null) {
      throw new JspTagException("The menu item could not be found");
    }

    try {
      StringBuffer buf = new StringBuffer();
```

```
        buf.append("<a href=\"");
        buf.append(item.getUrl());
        buf.append("\">");
        buf.append(item.getName());
        buf.append("</a>");

        pageContext.getOut().write(buf.toString());
      } catch (IOException ioe) {
        throw new JspTagException(ioe.getMessage());
      }

      // and skip the body content for this empty tag
      return SKIP_BODY;
    }
  }
```

An additional piece of logic in this version of the tag is to check that the object it looks up from the `PageContext` is not `null`. Since we're no longer explicitly supplying this reference, it could be the case that the object doesn't exist. Perhaps another tag or scripting element on the page has removed this object from the `PageContext`, or maybe the tag has not been used correctly on the page, for example if the tag wasn't nested inside the `showMenu` tag. Therefore, instead of silently failing, the tag handler throws a `JspTagException` to signal to the page author that something has gone wrong.

> *Further information about error handling and how tags can validate how they are used on the page can be found in Chapter 10.*

For completeness, here's the TLD to illustrate that the tags are now much simpler to define too:

```
<?xml version="1.0" encoding="ISO-8859-1" ?>
<!DOCTYPE taglib
  PUBLIC "-//Sun Microsystems, Inc.//DTD JSP Tag Library 1.2//EN"
  "http://java.sun.com/dtd/web-jsptaglibrary_1_2.dtd">

<taglib>

  <tlib-version>1.0</tlib-version>
  <jsp-version>1.2</jsp-version>
  <short-name>menu</short-name>
  <description>
    Menu examples for the Cooperating Tags chapter.
  </description>

  <tag>
    <name>showMenu</name>
    <tag-class>com.wrox.jsptaglibs.menu.ShowMenuImplicitTag</tag-class>
    <body-content>JSP</body-content>
    <description>
      Iterates over all of the menu items in a menu.
    </description>

    <attribute>
      <name>menu</name>
      <required>true</required>
```

```
      <rtexprvalue>true</rtexprvalue>
    </attribute>
  </tag>

  <tag>
    <name>showMenuItem</name>
    <tag-class>com.wrox.jsptaglibs.menu.ShowMenuItemImplicitTag</tag-class>
    <body-content>empty</body-content>
    <description>
      Generates a hyperlink for a menu item.
    </description>
  </tag>

</taglib>
```

Notice that the showMenu tag no longer introduces any scripting variables, while the showMenuItem tag no longer has any attributes. This, therefore, means that the usage of the tags on the page is now simplified:

```
<ul>
  <menu:showMenu menu="<%= menu %>">
    <li><menu:showMenuItem/>
  </menu:showMenu>
</ul>
```

Of course, this still generates the same result.

The use of attributes stored in the page context is a good way for tags to cooperate and exchange information. Using an implicit attribute does clean up the page, but can introduce some problems of its own. First, it is less apparent that the showMenuItem tag is cooperating with the showMenu tag, although even less obvious is where the MenuItem instances are coming from.

One of the problems that can arise is that there is nothing stopping another tag on the page using an attribute with the same name. Although we have taken steps to ensure that the item attribute isn't visible outside the showMenu tag, it is possible to overwrite an existing attribute called item, which was used elsewhere in the page. The results from such a bug could be very strange and also incredibly hard to track down.

In a best-case scenario, an exception might be thrown from the JSP container to indicate that something has gone wrong such as, for example, a ClassCastException because the named object residing in the PageContext is of the wrong type. In this case, the developer will know that something is wrong and can take steps to correct it, assuming that checks are in place to monitor the occurrence of exceptions. On the other hand, incorrect information from the new object might be displayed on the page.

Allowing tags to cooperate implicitly on the page does make those tags easy to use since the page author doesn't have to ensure that the correct information is passed to the child tag because it simply finds this out for itself. However, to solve the problems associated with tags cooperating through an implicitly named attribute, the page author could explicitly supply the name of the attribute.

Cooperating Explicitly on the Page

Explicitly supplying the name of an attribute is a good way of dealing with the problems just outlined and is used by the standard <jsp:useBean/> family of actions that are part of the JSP specification. An example that we've seen already in the book is as follows:

```
<jsp:useBean id="dateBean"
             class="com.wrox.jsptaglibs.date.DateBean"
             scope="page"/>

<h1>The date is <jsp:getProperty name="dateBean" property="date"/></h1>
```

Here, the <jsp:useBean/> tag creates an object and binds it into the page context under the name specified by the id attribute – in this case dateBean. Following this, the <jsp:getProperty/> tag uses the name attribute as a way for the page author to define the name of the object that it uses. Instead of the tags implicitly agreeing upon a name for the attribute, the page author now performs this task. This is a much more flexible solution as it can help to prevent collisions and clashes between any other objects that are placed in the page context, and is also very easy to implement.

First, we need to modify the showMenu tag so that it can accept an attribute called id, and bind the MenuItem instances into the page context under this name rather than item. Since this tag handler already extends the TagSupport class, we don't actually have to write the code to implement the id attribute because it is already written for us. The only thing that we have to change is to use the id attribute instead of the string "item" where we set and remove the page context attribute:

```
package com.wrox.jsptaglibs.menu;

import java.util.Iterator;

import javax.servlet.jsp.JspException;
import javax.servlet.jsp.tagext.TagSupport;

public class ShowMenuExplicitTag extends TagSupport {

  private Menu menu;

  private Iterator iterator;

  public int doStartTag() throws JspException {
    // setup the iterator to be used
    iterator = menu.menuEntries();

    if (iterator.hasNext()) {
      // if there are menu items, put the first one into the
      // page context under the name provided by the "id" attribute
      pageContext.setAttribute(getId(), iterator.next());

      // and include the body
      return EVAL_BODY_INCLUDE;
    } else {
      // there are no menu items so skip the body
      return SKIP_BODY;
    }
```

```
  }

  public int doAfterBody() throws JspException {
    if (iterator.hasNext()) {
      // if there are more menu items, put the next one into the
      // page context under the name provided by the "id" attribute
      pageContext.setAttribute(getId(), iterator.next());

      // and instruct the JSP engine to re-evaluate the body of this tag
      return EVAL_BODY_AGAIN;
    } else {
      // there are no more menu items so skip the body
      return SKIP_BODY;
    }
  }

  public int doEndTag() throws JspException {
    pageContext.removeAttribute(getId());

    return EVAL_PAGE;
  }

  public void setMenu(Menu menu) {
    this.menu = menu;
  }
}
```

> **The `id` attribute is already implemented and this is a good reason to use the `TagSupport` (or `BodyTagSupport`) class as a start point for tag handlers.**

Next is the `showMenuItem` tag that requires minimal changes:

```
package com.wrox.jsptaglibs.menu;

import java.io.IOException;

import javax.servlet.jsp.JspException;
import javax.servlet.jsp.JspTagException;
import javax.servlet.jsp.tagext.TagSupport;

public class ShowMenuItemExplicitTag extends TagSupport {

  private String name;

  public int doStartTag() throws JspException {

    // find the attribute placed into the page context by the parent tag
    MenuItem item = (MenuItem)pageContext.findAttribute(name);

    // check that it was found
    if (item == null) {
      throw new JspTagException("The menu item could not be found");
```

```
    }

    try {
      StringBuffer buf = new StringBuffer();

      buf.append("<a href=\"");
      buf.append(item.getUrl());
      buf.append("\">");
      buf.append(item.getName());
      buf.append("</a>");

      pageContext.getOut().write(buf.toString());
    } catch (IOException ioe) {
      throw new JspTagException(ioe.getMessage());
    }

    // and skip the body content for this empty tag
    return SKIP_BODY;
  }

  public void setName(String name) {
    this.name = name;
  }
}
```

Here, we have just added the code to implement a `name` attribute, and subsequently use this instead of the "`item`" string once more.

Here's the TLD to illustrate the difference in the tags. This time we have two additional required, non request-time expression attributes `id` and `name`:

```
<?xml version="1.0" encoding="ISO-8859-1" ?>
<!DOCTYPE taglib
  PUBLIC "-//Sun Microsystems, Inc.//DTD JSP Tag Library 1.2//EN"
  "http://java.sun.com/dtd/web-jsptaglibrary_1_2.dtd">

<taglib>

  <tlib-version>1.0</tlib-version>
  <jsp-version>1.2</jsp-version>
  <short-name>menu</short-name>
  <description>
    Menu examples for the Cooperating Tags chapter.
  </description>

  <tag>
    <name>showMenu</name>
    <tag-class>com.wrox.jsptaglibs.menu.ShowMenuExplicitTag</tag-class>
    <body-content>JSP</body-content>
    <description>
      Iterates over all of the menu items in a menu.
    </description>
```

```
      <attribute>
        <name>id</name>
        <required>true</required>
        <rtexprvalue>false</rtexprvalue>
      </attribute>

      <attribute>
        <name>menu</name>
        <required>true</required>
        <rtexprvalue>true</rtexprvalue>
      </attribute>
    </tag>

    <tag>
      <name>showMenuItem</name>
      <tag-class>com.wrox.jsptaglibs.menu.ShowMenuItemExplicitTag</tag-class>
      <body-content>empty</body-content>
      <description>
        Generates a hyperlink for a menu item.
      </description>

      <attribute>
        <name>name</name>
        <required>true</required>
        <rtexprvalue>false</rtexprvalue>
      </attribute>
    </tag>

  </taglib>
```

Of course, changing the tags also means changing the JSP page on which they are used:

```
      <ul>
        <menu:showMenu id="item" menu="<%= menu %>">
          <li><menu:showMenuItem name="item"/>
        </menu:showMenu>
      </ul>
```

Here, we are now explicitly specifying the name of the page context attribute to be used. Again, the same results are generated.

Although using explicitly named attributes is slightly more work than before, the relationship between the tags is now clear again. Additionally, since the page author can specify the attribute names, there is less of a chance that name clashes will occur. If they do, at least the tag handler doesn't have to be modified, recompiled, and redeployed.

The examples in this chapter until now have shown how it is possible for parent tags to pass on information to the child tags. Let's now turn this on its head and see how child tags can access information from the parent tags.

Cooperation with Access to Parent Tags

Making information available for child tags is a useful way of providing them (and also tag bodies) with the information that they need to perform the task in hand. However, there may be times where having the parent tag push this information out is not appropriate. For example, pushing information into the page context does mean that it is accessible by other nested custom tags but, depending on the scope, that information could also be accessible from other servlets or JSP pages. This may or may not be a desirable side effect because these other components could accidentally corrupt the information, once again leading to all kinds of bugs and unpredictable behavior.

Another reason why pushing information out might not be appropriate is when that information is changing frequently over a short period of time. A good example here is when information changes frequently within the body content of a custom tag such as an iteration tag that publishes contextual information (current index, how many elements remaining, and so on) in addition to a variable representing the next element. Rather than continually pushing out this updated data, it would be better and more efficient for nested tags to query their parent and ask for the information only when needed.

As with many of the facets of custom tag development, there are several ways in which child tags can gain access to their parent tags:

- Using the `getParent()` method on the `Tag` interface
- Using the `findAncestorWithClass()` method on the `TagSupport` class

Let's look at each of these in turn.

Getting Access to the Parent

When the tag lifecycle was introduced earlier in the book, we saw that one of the steps that the container performs when it encounters a tag is to call the `setParent()` method on the corresponding tag handler instance. This method, defined on the `Tag` interface, makes tags aware of the parent tag in which they are nested:

```
void setParent(Tag t);
```

> **If a tag is not nested within any other custom tags, the `setParent()` method would get called with a `null` parameter.**

Also specified on the `Tag` interface is the `getParent()` method, a default implementation of which is provided by the `TagSupport` class. This method returns a reference to the parent tag handler instance of type `Tag`, or `null` if the tag isn't nested. The mechanism behind this is very simple, but offers a great deal of opportunity for building some quite complex tags. Let's look at an example.

Conditional Processing with Tags

Consider a page that displays information about books in an online store. To build such a page, we could use the `Book` and `BookManager` classes from the previous chapters and write a JSP page that presents the user with all the information about a book. The unique ID (ISBN) of the book could be specified as a parameter when the JSP page is requested:

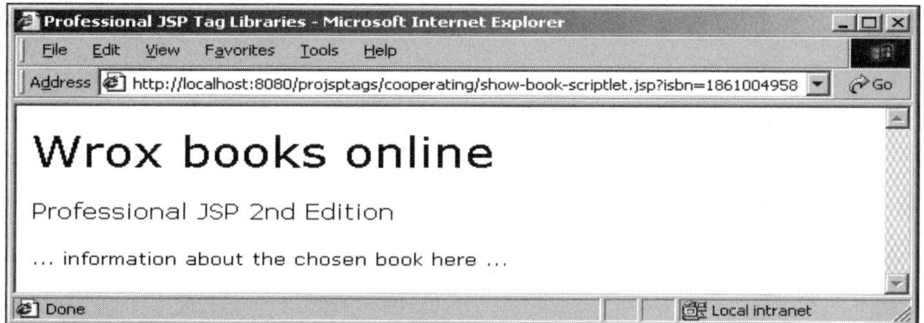

Of course, through an error somewhere, it is possible that the page could be requested with an incorrect or blank ISBN. In this case, rather than show the user a nasty stack trace, we would instead like to show a page indicating that a book could not be found:

Here, we are saying that if a book can be found, show the information to the user; otherwise show a page indicating that a book couldn't be found. Typically, this type of logic would be embedded into the JSP page using Java scriptlets, an example of which is as follows:

```
<html>
  <head>
    <title>Professional JSP Tag Libraries</title>
  </head>

  <%@ page import="com.wrox.jsptaglibs.common.*" %>

  <body>
    <h1>Wrox books online</h1>

    <%
      String isbn = request.getParameter("isbn");
      Book book = BookManager.getInstance().getBook(isbn);
```

```
      if (book == null) {
    %>
        Sorry, no book was found.
    <%
      } else {
    %>
        <h2><%= book.getTitle() %></h2>
        ... information about the chosen book here ...
    <%
      }
    %>
  </body>
</html>
```

This technique is effective but does introduce a fair quantity of Java code into the page. In addition to this, the structure of the page is now more difficult to read because of the increased number of scriptlets to start and end the various conditions of the `if` block. To resolve these problems, we could build a tag-based solution as follows:

```
<html>
  <head>
    <title>Professional JSP Tag Libraries</title>
  </head>

  <%@ page import="com.wrox.jsptaglibs.common.*" %>
  <%@ taglib uri="/logicTaglib" prefix="logic" %>

  <body>
    <h1>Wrox books online</h1>

    <%
      String isbn = request.getParameter("isbn");
      Book book = BookManager.getInstance().getBook(isbn);
    %>

    <logic:if value="<%= book %>">

      <logic:undefined>
        Sorry, no book was found.
      </logic:undefined>

      <logic:default>
        <h2><%= book.getTitle() %></h2>
        ... information about the chosen book here ...
      </logic:default>

    </logic:if>
  </body>
</html>
```

This is a cleaner page in terms of the quantity of Java code, and also the structure is clearer. This is also a great example of cooperating tags implicitly. Let's see how they work by building each tag in turn.

The if Tag

The first tag to build is the parent of the other tags that demarcates the block of conditional processing – the if tag:

```
package com.wrox.jsptaglibs.logic;

import javax.servlet.jsp.JspException;
import javax.servlet.jsp.tagext.TagSupport;

public class SingleConditionIfTag extends TagSupport {
```

Instead of supplying a condition to the if tag, we'll simply give it the value that we would like to test. In the example, this is just a Book reference that was obtained from the lookup at the top of the page. To be generic, we'll allow the value attribute to take any Java object reference and this is reflected in its implementation:

```
  private Object value;

  public void setValue(Object value) {
    this.value = value;
  }
```

The tags nested inside the if tag obviously require access to the value of this attribute, and although we could insert it into the page context as we've seen in the previous examples, we will provide an accessor method so that the nested tags can explicitly ask for it instead:

```
  public Object getValue() {
    return this.value;
  }
```

When writing if blocks in Java, only the code within the first matching condition will be executed. We would like the same functionality replicated by our if tag, and therefore we have another property in our tag handler called matchFound. This Boolean flag is used to indicate whether a matching condition block has been found. To start with, the value of this flag is set to false:

```
  private boolean matchFound = false;
```

Alongside this property are the accessor and mutator methods for it:

```
  public boolean getMatchFound() {
    return this.matchFound;
  }

  public void setMatchFound(boolean b) {
    this.matchFound = b;
  }
```

The final part of the if tag is, of course, the tag-related implementation details. In this case, all we want the tag to do is process its body content. After all, the nested tags are where the real work is performed:

```
    public int doStartTag() throws JspException {
      // and include the body
      return EVAL_BODY_INCLUDE;
    }
  }
```

The condition Tag

The next tag to build is the one that determines whether the value specified to the `if` tag is undefined. For the purpose of this example, undefined means either a `null` reference, or in the case of a `java.lang.String`, a length of zero. Essentially, this tag needs to get the value given to the `if` tag and determine whether it is undefined. If this is the case, the tag should signal to the `if` tag that a matching condition has been found and evaluate its own body content. If the value isn't undefined, the tag should simply skip the evaluation of its body content following which the next condition tag can perform its check.

As the actual processing involved in all condition tags is almost the same, this is a good opportunity to introduce an abstract class from which they can all extend. As usual, this class will extend `TagSupport`:

```
  package com.wrox.jsptaglibs.logic;

  import javax.servlet.jsp.JspException;
  import javax.servlet.jsp.tagext.TagSupport;

  public abstract class ConditionTag extends TagSupport {
```

Each concrete implementation of a condition tag will need to provide an implementation of the following method:

```
    public abstract boolean match(Object value);
```

The `value` parameter is a reference to the value supplied to the attribute on the `if` tag and this method is where the specifics of the condition tag will be implemented. For example, the undefined tag will check whether the value of the parameter is `null`. We'll see shortly how the value supplied to the `if` tag is passed to the `match()` method.

Following this is the implementation of the common processing for all conditional tags. The evaluation of the condition needs to happen in the `doStartTag()` method so that the body content can be appropriately evaluated or skipped:

```
    public final int doStartTag() throws JspException {
```

The first thing to do is to get a reference to the parent `if` tag. We can do this using the `getParent()` method but, of course, we must remember to cast it to the appropriate tag handler:

```
    // get a reference to the parent "if" tag
    SingleConditionIfTag tag = (SingleConditionIfTag)getParent();
```

Casting the resulting `Tag` reference implies that you are certain about how the tags have been nested and used on the page. For example, it might be the case that the enclosing tag isn't the `if` tag that you were expecting, perhaps because the page author has nested the tags incorrectly. We'll see how this issue can be addressed shortly.

The next part is to check whether a matching condition has already been found. If not, we can call the `match()` method to check whether this condition matches. This is where the `if` tag's accessor method for the value attribute is used:

```
    // if a matching condition hasn't been found yet, evaluate
    // this condition
    if (!tag.getMatchFound() && match(tag.getValue())) {
```

If the `match()` method returns `true`, the condition tag needs to signal to the `if` tag that a match has been found. Following this, the body content is evaluated:

```
      // the condition matched so evaluate the body of this tag
      tag.setMatchFound(true);

      return EVAL_BODY_INCLUDE;
```

If a match has already been found, or this condition didn't match, the JSP page is told to skip the body content:

```
      } else {
        // the condition didn't match, so skip the body content
        return SKIP_BODY;
      }
    }
  }
```

The undefined Tag

Now that the abstract class is written, we can provide an implementation for the `undefined` tag. Here, only an implementation of the `match()` method is provided that checks for a `null` value, or an empty string:

```
  package com.wrox.jsptaglibs.logic;

  public class UndefinedTag extends ConditionTag {

    public boolean match(Object value) {
      if (value instanceof String) {
        String s = (String)value;
        return (s == null || s.length() == 0);
      } else {
        return value == null;
      }
    }
  }
```

The default Tag

The implementation of the `default` tag is simpler still. What we're saying here is that this condition matches any value – it's like the `else` condition of an `if` block:

```
package com.wrox.jsptaglibs.logic;

public class DefaultTag extends ConditionTag {

  public boolean match(Object value) {
    return true;
  }
}
```

The Tag Library Descriptor

As usual, there is the TLD file that describes the tag library. First of all there's the header information:

```
<?xml version="1.0" encoding="ISO-8859-1" ?>
<!DOCTYPE taglib
  PUBLIC "-//Sun Microsystems, Inc.//DTD JSP Tag Library 1.2//EN"
  "http://java.sun.com/dtd/web-jsptaglibrary_1_2.dtd">

<taglib>

  <tlib-version>1.0</tlib-version>
  <jsp-version>1.2</jsp-version>
  <short-name>logic</short-name>
  <description>
    Logic examples for Cooperating Tags chapter.
  </description>
```

Following this, there is the `if` tag with its single, request-time expression called `value`:

```
  <tag>
    <name>if</name>
    <tag-class>com.wrox.jsptaglibs.logic.SingleConditionIfTag</tag-class>
    <body-content>JSP</body-content>
    <description>
      Used to represent a block of conditional processing.
    </description>

    <attribute>
      <name>value</name>
      <required>true</required>
      <rtexprvalue>true</rtexprvalue>
    </attribute>
  </tag>
```

Then there's the `undefined` tag with no attributes:

```
  <tag>
    <name>undefined</name>
    <tag-class>com.wrox.jsptaglibs.logic.UndefinedTag</tag-class>
```

```
    <body-content>JSP</body-content>
    <description>
      Nested within an if tag, this checks whether the value supplied
      to the if tag is undefined (null or an empty string).
    </description>
  </tag>
```

Finally, there's the `default` tag which again has no attributes:

```
  <tag>
    <name>default</name>
    <tag-class>com.wrox.jsptaglibs.logic.DefaultTag</tag-class>
    <body-content>JSP</body-content>
    <description>
      Nested within an if tag, this is a catchall. The body content
      is displayed if the previous conditions have not matched.
    </description>
  </tag>

</taglib>
```

Using the Tags

To summarize how the tags work, let's again consider the JSP page on which they are used. Here, the `Book` reference is passed as a request-time expression to the `if` tag which asks the JSP page to evaluate its body content. Nested beneath the `if` tag are the various conditions. In turn, each condition is evaluated and if matched, the body content of that condition is evaluated. The cooperation between the child tags and their parent is twofold. First, the condition tags ask the `if` tag whether a matching condition has already been found. Second, they ask the `if` tag for the value that it was given to test.

This is a good example of a different type of implicit cooperation where the child tag asks for the information, rather than retrieving it from a central location into which it has been pushed by the parent tag. Although not apparent in this simple example, this practice is of benefit here. The `if` tag could, of course, have made the information available through the page context. However, nothing stops `if` tags from being nested inside other `if` or condition tags. If this were the case, the innermost tags would overwrite the information stored in the page context. This action could introduce some interesting bugs, which would not be easy to track down.

This, in fact, raises another question. What if the condition tags were nested indirectly beneath the `if` tag? In other words, what if the `if` tag wasn't their closest enclosing parent?

Finding a Particular Parent

In this example, the condition tags need access to their parent `if` tag handler because it is the mechanism through which they access the value to be tested and find out whether a condition has already been matched. If the `getParent()` method returns the closest nested parent tag handler, it may be the case that it isn't the right one.

One way to solve such a problem is to check whether the reference returned by the getParent() method is of the correct type by using the instanceof operator. If not, its parent could be accessed and again checked. However, since this sort of functionality is frequently required when writing cooperating custom tags, the TagSupport class provides the following static method as a convenience:

```
public static final Tag findAncestorWithClass(Tag from, Class klass)
```

This method does all of the hard work for us and given a reference to a tag handler (such as this for example), will walk up the hierarchy of parent tag handlers until it finds one assignable with type klass, or until the outer most custom tag is found in which case null is returned. For example, we can rewrite the following line from the ConditionTag class:

```
SingleConditionIfTag tag = (SingleConditionIfTag)getParent();
```

as follows:

```
SingleConditionIfTag tag =
    (SingleConditionIfTag)findAncestorWithClass(this,
                                            SingleConditionIfTag.class);
```

Notice that we still have to cast the resulting tag handler reference, but using this method instead of getParent() makes our tag handlers more resilient to how they are used on the page. No matter how many levels of nested tags are between the if tag and the condition tags, this method will always find the closest if tag.

Reducing the Coupling Between Tags

One of the consequences of using direct references to tag handlers is that the child tags are coupled to their parent tag. In the examples that we've just seen, the condition tags are tightly coupled to the if tag, which means that it is more difficult to reuse them at a later date.

As it stands, the if tag only allows a single condition to be matched. If we wanted to introduce another version of this tag to allow multiple conditional blocks to be matched, we would have to modify the condition tags too.

One way to reduce the coupling between tags is to use regular Java interfaces in conjunction with the findAncestorWithClass() method. For example, we could create an interface called IfTag that defined the three methods that the child tags make use of:

```
package com.wrox.jsptaglibs.logic;

public interface IfTag {

  public Object getValue();

  public boolean getMatchFound();
  public void setMatchFound(boolean b);

}
```

The `SingleConditionIfTag` would then implement the interface and following this, we can use the `findAncestorWithClass()` method to look up the closest parent tag handler that implements this interface:

```
IfTag tag = (IfTag)findAncestorWithClass(this, IfTag.class);
```

In doing so, we can easily swap the implementations of the tags and use any version on the page without modifying any code within the tag handlers. Where references to tag handlers are to be used, this is certainly a good idea for improving the future maintainability and reusability of the tags.

Rules of Thumb

Let's wrap up this chapter by looking at some rules of thumb for choosing the appropriate mechanism for cooperating and exchanging information.

Although using scripting variables does imply the use of Java code in the page, there are times when this practice may be more appropriate than using the page context. For example, it may be the case that in addition to a nested tag, you have some other nested functionality that relies on a scripting variable that is introduced to the page.

For the majority of cases, however, using the page context is a better option because it generally leads to less Java code within the page, and the use of cryptic request-time expressions is also reduced.

Needless to say, the use of explicitly named page context attributes is better than using implicitly named attributes. Here, the page author has control over the names that are used for the attributes leading to a reduction in the risk of name collisions, and also making the relation of tags on a page more apparent. Of course, implicitly named attributes are much easier for page authors to use, so if this is required, a good compromise is to allow the page author to optionally specify the names of the attributes. This way, the tag is easy to use and can be easily changed if a name collision does occur.

There are, however, times when using the page context is not appropriate. For example, when information frequently changes, or when information should not be made accessible to anything other than the tags that need it. A page scope of `tag` would be ideal for preventing anything other than nested tags accessing such information, but unfortunately it isn't available in the current version of the JSP specification. In this situation, getting a reference to the actual tag handler is a better solution. This also has a side effect in that the functionality on the parent tag handler can also be called if necessary.

Another scenario that may point to using direct references to the tag handlers is when there is a defined structure to how the tags are used on the page. We've seen this in the examples already where a condition tag such as `undefined` must be used within the bounds of an `if` tag.

Part of the JSP specification allows validators to be built that can check how tags are used on the page. We'll be looking at these in Chapter 10.

Summary

This chapter has looked at yet another type of custom tag – those that cooperate on the page. Cooperation between custom tags can take several forms, although the most common use is for the exchange of information. Other uses, however, include child tags directly using and calling functionality on their parent tags. There are several ways in which this can be achieved, and during the chapter we have seen examples of some of these ways.

We have also demonstrated the use of inheritance when building tags. Although this is nothing revolutionary, it is something that is often overlooked when building custom tags because tag handlers themselves are generally fairly small and simple classes.

Using variables or attributes for inter-tag communication is a good way of building loosely coupled tags. However, accessing parent tag handlers introduces a coupling between tags that can limit the reusability of tags further down the line. As a solution, we followed up this discussion by looking at how Java interfaces can be used to reduce this coupling. Finally, each mechanism is suited to a specific problem and to wrap up the chapter, we looked at some rules of thumb for determining the appropriate one.

The first part of the book introduced custom tags and showed how to build them. With this knowledge, we can now move on to the second part of the book which takes a look at the advanced topics related to JSP tag development. This starts with the next chapter that explores the question of whether to use custom tags or JavaBeans for a given problem, as well as looking at tag usage patterns.

LONDON

8

Tag Patterns

The first section of this book looked at how to build custom tags by taking a step-by-step approach through simple tags, tags with attributes, iteration tags, body tags, and cooperating tags. This chapter starts the second section by looking at some of the more advanced topics around JSP tag development. Before we move on to look at some of the common uses, or usage patterns, for custom tags, we'll look at the frequently asked question of whether to use JavaBeans or custom tags to encapsulate server-side functionality for use with JSP pages.

We'll start off by looking at how the key characteristics of JavaBeans and custom tags affect the tasks to which they are best suited. We'll then explore this question by taking a look behind the scenes and consider some scenarios from which this question might arise and determine some rules of thumb.

We then build upon this knowledge by looking at some examples of the common uses for tag extensions when developing JSP pages. These include:

- Performing actions on the page
- Performing logic on the page
- Replacing the standard HTML tags, particularly for building HTML forms
- Accessing enterprise resources (for example, EJB and JMS)

Again, some more rules of thumb will be discussed and we'll wrap up the chapter with some recommendations.

Common Uses for Tags

There are many ways in which tags can be used on the page, but ultimately they all help to achieve a common goal – to wrap up actions that are performed on a JSP page and move Java code away from the page. With closer inspection, we can see that although all tags focus on this common goal, there are many ways in which they are used on the page. These can be seen as tag, or usage, patterns.

To help illustrate how patterns are useful when dealing with custom tags, let's first take a quick detour into the world of patterns.

Design Patterns

Patterns are ideas that have been proven to be useful over and over again. Design patterns more specifically are now seen as an important part of the software development process as they capture reusable solutions to common problems, and provide a common language with which to describe them. One of the first books published on the topic, *Design Patterns, Elements of Reusable Object-Oriented Software* from *Addison-Wesley (ISBN 0-201633-61-2)* describes 23 common design solutions with which many developers are now familiar and use on a daily basis. Since their inception, many other patterns in software development have been documented, including some directly related to J2EE development.

J2EE Patterns

The J2EE patterns catalog documents a number of patterns that provide solutions to frequently encountered problems in the design and implementation of J2EE applications. These are broken down into patterns spanning:

- **The Presentation Tier**
  Components responsible for presenting information to the user, built with technologies such as Java servlets and JSP
- **The Business Tier**
  Components encapsulating the business functionality of an application such as Enterprise JavaBeans
- **The Integration Tier**
  Components that access enterprise information systems such as relational databases through JDBC and legacy systems through the Java Connector Architecture

These patterns provide reusable solutions to common problems associated with performance and also help structure J2EE applications.

More information on the patterns contained within the J2EE patterns catalog can be found at http://developer.java.sun.com/developer/technicalArticles/J2EE/patterns/.

View Helpers

One of the J2EE presentation tier patterns is particularly relevant here – View Helpers. In web applications, JavaServer Pages and Java servlets often represent the view of information and are responsible for presenting this information back to the user. The View Helper pattern is a way of taking logic embedded in the view (for example scriptlets inside a JSP page) and wrapping it up as reusable functionality for use on other view components.

Problem

If we assume that JSP pages are used to build the views in a web application, an easy way of rendering information for the user is to make use of Java scriptlets on the page. As we've mentioned previously, using scriptlets is something that we are ultimately trying to avoid. After all, there are several different types of people that write JSP pages – web designers who are responsible for the look and feel, and Java developers who write the core functionality behind the web application. Too much Java code in the page creates several problems:

- Increased maintenance through copy and paste reuse across the web application.
- Reduced readability because business logic, content, and presentation are mixed together. This is especially true for web designers that might not understand complex Java code.
- Greater likelihood that pages could be broken by accidentally removing fragments of Java code.

Solution

To solve these problems, embedded functionality can be moved into helper components and subsequently reused across the web application. Creating reusable components increases maintainability as it moves complex functionality away from the page, and as a result, the pages once again become more readable.

There are several areas in which this pattern is applicable, including:

- Data retrieval (for example, getting data to display)
- Logic related to presentation of data but not to formatting (for example, determining whether a particular piece of data should be displayed)
- General presentation-layer related logic (for example, iterating over a collection of data items)

Many of the examples shown in this chapter are in fact implementations of the View Helper pattern, where functionality has been taken away from scriptlets in the JSP page and encapsulated into helper components. However, on an implementation level, these helpers could be built as either JavaBeans or custom tags and raises the question of which of these two technologies should be used to encapsulate such functionality for use with JSP pages. We did briefly touch upon this in Chapter 1, but before we move on to look at the examples in this chapter, let's answer this question in more detail.

Custom Tags vs. JavaBeans

To answer this question, we'll start off by discussing how JavaBeans and tags can be used on a page, following which we'll further explore this by taking a look behind the scenes. With this behind us, we'll then consider some scenarios from which this question might arise and determine some rules of thumb. These scenarios include:

- Generating dynamic content (for example, HTML or text)
- Representing information

Characteristics of a JavaBean

A JavaBean is a reusable software component that we can use to encapsulate state, behavior, and business logic. This is actually true of classes and components in OO systems in general though. Technically, a JavaBean is more than this, as it must adhere to the standards and conventions defined within the JavaBeans specification.

> **The JavaBeans specification can be downloaded from the Sun web site at http://java.sun.com/products/javabeans/.**

The main features that we are interested in here are as follows:

- The presence of a default, zero arguments constructor
- The naming convention for property accessors (getters) and mutators (setters)
- Implementation of the `java.io.Serializable` interface

The JavaBeans architecture is a model for building reusable components for use in any sort of Java application. In the same way that Java is platform-independent and can run anywhere, JavaBeans are Java technology-independent and can run anywhere there is Java. As a final point, they encapsulate data and functionality independently of the environment in which they are created – be it a web container or a standalone GUI application.

Using Scriptlets and Expressions

As we saw in Chapter 1, there are various ways in which JavaBeans can be used on a JSP page. The first of these methods is to use a scriptlet in the JSP page to instantiate the JavaBean and subsequently use an expression to call its methods.

Using the Standard Actions

The other way in which JavaBeans can be used on a JSP page is by using the `<jsp:useBean/>` family of actions. These standard actions are a very powerful mechanism for using JavaBeans on a JSP page and work because JavaBeans adhere to the set of standards and conventions outlined earlier.

The zero arguments constructor means that the `<jsp:useBean/>` tag can instantiate the class through Java's reflection mechanism. Also, the naming convention for the accessors and mutators provides the `<jsp:getProperty/>` and `<jsp:setProperty/>` actions with a way in which to find the appropriate method to call – getting and setting a particular property on the bean.

Using these standard actions is preferable to directly calling the accessor and mutator methods for a couple of reasons. First of all, using them reduces the need to use Java code on the page. This provides a simplified interface to the beans and is useful for page authors that might not have the same level of knowledge in Java as we do, and it also reduces the temptation to use Java code elsewhere in the page. A side-effect of using the standard actions is that the JavaBeans don't have to be available as scripting variables in the page, providing slightly more flexibility than if expressions were used.

> *In terms of performance, using the standard actions does generally result in more Java code being generated than if an expression was used directly on the page. However, the JSP specification states that containers can optimize this and if they can guarantee that the result produced is the same.*

The one thing that isn't possible using this standard family of actions is the ability to call arbitrary methods. The `<jsp:getProperty/>` and `<jsp:setProperty/>` tags allow us to call the accessor and mutator methods associated with a JavaBean's property because of standards that are defined for the naming of such methods. For example, the accessor method for a property called `date` must be called `getDate()`, while the mutator method must be called `setDate()`. Using these rules, the standard tags can locate the appropriate method on the specified JavaBean and call it.

Combining Standard Actions with Java

Although there is nothing preventing other arbitrary methods being defined on a JavaBean, calling them requires knowledge that they are there. As there are no special rules governing the naming convention of these additional methods, without specifying the entire method name it would be difficult for a standard set of tags to call them. For this reason, methods that are not property accessors and mutators must be called on a JSP page using Java code in scriptlets and/or expressions.

Ultimately this is something that we are trying to avoid as it negatively impacts reusability and maintainability; we would also have to modify each scriptlet and expression in every JSP page where that method was used should we wish to change it in some way.

In addition to this, using such code on the page places more responsibility onto the clients of this bean because they must now pass the appropriate arguments through to the method. Since JavaBeans can be used on a JSP page, this also means that more responsibility is placed on the page author.

With this in mind, let's now look at custom tags.

Characteristics of a Custom Tag

A custom tag is a portable mechanism for encapsulating reusable functionality for use on JSP pages. This functionality is wrapped within a tag handler, a Java class that implements `javax.servlet.jsp.tagext.Tag` or one of its sub-interfaces such as `IterationTag` or `BodyTag`.

As we've seen, there are five steps to implementing a custom tag. They are as follows:

- Write the tag handler
- Write the tag library descriptor file
- Deploy the tag library
- Register the tag library with the web application
- Import the tag library and use it

There are more steps involved in writing, deploying, and using a custom tag than a JavaBean. Although this is the case, we have gained improvements on the reusability and maintainability.

In comparison to a JavaBean implementation, a tag is much more aware of the environment in which it is running and it can trivially find out information through the page context. This is ideal from a reusability perspective because the tag is now much easier to use. Also, from a maintainability perspective, using the tag doesn't require any additional Java code. This means that the tag is self-contained and any changes to the functionality provided by the tag require only a change to the tag itself.

Customizing a Tag's Behavior

Customizing the behavior offered by a JavaBean can be achieved by modifying the methods, or perhaps by providing different versions of those methods that take different parameters. Although we can provide different variations of a custom tag by providing different versions of it, it is often useful to customize a tag's behavior. For this reason, custom tags can make use of attributes.

As we've previously seen, attributes are simply name-value pairs specified during assembly of the JSP page on which the tag is being used. These name-value pairs are similar to those seen in regular XHTML or XML tags, with an example being the `action` attribute on an XHTML `form` tag. When the page is requested, the values associated with any tag attributes are passed through to the tag handler via mutator methods conforming to the JavaBeans naming conventions.

Tags are more easily configured on the page than JavaBeans through the use of attributes on the page. Where we would have to call a method with Java code passing the relevant parameters to customize the behavior provided, custom tags support customization through simple attributes on the page. No additional Java code is required on the page and once again the functionality associated with the tag is self-contained. In addition to this, attributes can be marked as optional and this allows many ways in which the individual features of a tag can be customized by the page author.

There are certainly more steps involved in custom tag development, but in reality these additional steps are fairly small, and depending on the complexity, building a library shouldn't take very long at all.

Behind the Scenes

Let's now take a look at how JavaBeans and custom tags are used from a different perspective – behind the scenes. In other words, let's look at what actually happens when JavaBeans and custom tags are used on a JSP page. We've already looked at the lifecycle of a JSP page in Chapter 1, but to recap, the request for a particular JSP page involves translating it into a Java servlet and then compiling the resulting servlet. This is then loaded into the web container where it is used to service the request and generate the response.

Although the output of the translation process is a regular Java servlet, the translation process itself is fairly complex and many different things happen behind the scenes. Basically, the entire JSP page is transformed into a single method within the resulting servlet. Any static content (for example, HTML) is wrapped up in `out.print()` statements, while Java source code contained within scriptlets, expressions, and declarations gets inserted into the servlet as is.

The examples that we saw in Chapter 1 showed that it is possible to make use of JavaBeans or custom tags on a JSP page. In these situations, how is this represented in the resulting Java servlet?

Fortunately this is possible to answer. Many of the web and application servers available (including Tomcat) keep the source code to the translated Java servlets and by looking at this we can establish what happens behind the scenes when JavaBeans and custom tags are used on the page.

With Tomcat 4.0, the source code for the translated JSP pages can be found in the `%TOMCAT_HOME%\work\localhost` directory.

JavaBeans

Let's first take a look at how JavaBeans are used in conjunction with the `<jsp:useBean/>` family of tags, using the following example that we saw back in Chapter 2:

```
<html>

  <head>
    <title>Professional JSP Tag Libraries</title>
  </head>

  <body>

    <jsp:useBean id="dateBean"
                 class="com.wrox.jsptaglibs.date.DateBean"
                 scope="page"/>

    <h1>The date is <jsp:getProperty name="dateBean" property="date"/></h1>

  </body>

</html>
```

The first step here is that the JavaBean (of type `com.wrox.jsptaglibs.date.DateBean`) is instantiated and bound into the `page` scope under the name of `dateBean`.

The way that the `<jsp:useBean/>` tag works is that it first of all tries to find an existing instance of the specified bean in the specified scope and makes it available for use on the page. If this fails and a bean isn't available, the tag will create a new instance. For the purpose of this example, we'll assume that a bean called `dateBean` doesn't already exist and therefore that the `<jsp:useBean/>` tag is simply instantiating it.

Next, the `<jsp:getProperty/>` tag is used to display the `date` property on the `dateBean` instance. Effectively, this involves looking through the available scopes (`page`, `request`, `session`, and `application`) for the JavaBean called `dateBean`. Once this has been found, the appropriate accessor method can be called on the instance to retrieve the property. In this case, the method is called `getDate()` and returns the value of the `date` property.

When the JSP page is translated into a Java servlet, the JSP engine generates all of the code required to perform the functionality provided by the standard tags. A prototypical example of this is as follows:

This is based around the actual code generated by Tomcat 4.0, for our `DateBean` *example:*

```
... start of page ...
com.wrox.jsptaglibs.date.DateBean dateBean = null;

try {
  dateBean = (com.wrox.jsptaglibs.date.DateBean)
             java.beans.Beans.instantiate(getClass().getClassLoader(),
             com.wrox.jsptaglibs.date.DateBean");

  pageContext.setAttribute("dateBean", dateBean, PageContext.PAGE_SCOPE);
} catch (Exception e) {
  throw new ServletException("Cannot create bean.", e);
}

out.write("<h1>The date is ");
out.print(((com.wrox.jsptaglibs.date.DateBean)
           pageContext.findAttribute("dateBean")).getDate());
out.write("</h1>");
... end of page ...
```

As this demonstrates, Java's reflection mechanism can be used to instantiate JavaBeans and this is why it is important to have a zero arguments constructor. The `<jsp:getProperty/>` action has been translated into a simple line of Java code that looks up the bean through the page context and calls the appropriate accessor method.

This is made possible because of the naming conventions behind JavaBean properties. From an implementation perspective, this is all pretty much standard Java code. After all, it's the process that translates the JSP page to a Java servlet where all of the clever work is done.

Custom Tags

So how does this Java code compare to that generated when custom tags are used? Let's again use one of the previous examples from Chapter 2 to illustrate this:

```
<html>

  <head>
    <title>Professional JSP Tag Libraries</title>
  </head>

  <%@ taglib uri="/attributesTaglib" prefix="attributes" %>
```

```
  <body>

    <h1>The date is <attributes:date format="dd-MMM-yyyy"/></h1>

  </body>

</html>
```

As the functionality associated with a custom tag (the tag handler) is implemented as a Java class, the first step is to create a new instance to service the request. The tag is then told about the environment in which it is running (the page context) and following this a reference to its parent tag is also set.

Next, the mutator method associated with any supplied attributes is called on the tag handler to set the values of the attributes. After this, the lifecycle methods are called and, in the case of our example, these consist of just the `doStartTag()` and `doEndTag()` methods. Finally, when the tag is finished with, the `release()` method is called to reset any state associated with the tag.

What we're saying here is that a Java object is created and then its methods are called in the same way as for JavaBeans. A prototypical example of this is as follows:

This code is again based upon that generated by Tomcat 4.0 but simplified for the purposes of this example.

```
... start of page ...

com.wrox.jsptaglibs.date.DateTag t
                            = new com.wrox.jsptaglibs.date.DateTag();
t.setPageContext(pageContext);
t.setParent(null);
t.setFormat("dd-MMM-yyyy");

try {
  if (t.doStartTag() != javax.servlet.jsp.tagext.Tag.SKIP_BODY) {
    ... body content would be here ...
  }

  if (t.doEndTag() == javax.servlet.jsp.tagext.Tag.SKIP_PAGE) {
    return;
  }
} finally {
  t.release();
}

... end of page ...
```

As this shows, again the translation process generates standard Java code. Showing this helps to understand what is going on behind the scenes and also that, apart from the increased number of method calls, tag handlers aren't that dissimilar to JavaBeans.

What are the Differences?

Both custom tags and JavaBeans can be used very easily on a JSP page and the observation that tags and beans aren't that dissimilar raises some interesting points.

Tag handlers can implement the `java.io.Serializable` interface and therefore we could implement tag handlers as JavaBeans. After all, they are instantiated through the zero arguments constructor and have attributes with mutator methods conforming to the conventions laid out by the JavaBeans naming conventions. As we saw in the last chapter, it is also useful for tags to define accessor methods for their attributes so that nested (child) tags can access them. This tends to suggest that the tag handlers can in fact be JavaBeans if they choose.

On the other hand, JavaBeans are not tags because of one simple fact – they don't implement the `javax.servlet.jsp.tagext.Tag` interface. Although a JavaBean could implement this interface, it would be meaningless outside the context of a web container that supported Java servlets and JSP pages.

With all of these factors in mind we are now in a good position to answer the question about which component model to use to wrap up functionality for use on JSP pages – custom tags or JavaBeans?

To answer this question, let's look at some scenarios and deduce some rules of thumb. The scenarios that we'll look at are:

- Generating dynamic content (such as HTML)
- Representing information

Generating Dynamic Content

The examples that we've seen in this chapter involve generating a small amount of dynamic content: returning the current date back to the user. As we've seen, a JavaBean isn't really appropriate in this example because JavaBeans don't know about the environment in which they are running. Custom tags, however, do know about their environment and can access a large quantity of information through the `PageContext` class, including the following implicit JSP page variables:

- `out`
  The current `JspWriter` instance
- `request`
  The current `ServletRequest` that is being serviced
- `response`
  The current `ServletResponse`
- `session`
  The `HttpSession` representing the client's session

This is useful, not only for accessing information, but having access to the current `JspWriter` means that custom tags can write output directly back to the page. JavaBeans, on the other hand, don't have this information and therefore can't write directly back to the page. Of course they could be provided with a reference to the current `JspWriter`, although another frequently used alternative is to generate a string representing the content and return this to the page so that it can be written out.

One of the reasons behind not using Java servlets to generate dynamic content is that the content becomes hard-coded into the sourcecode. This is bad for maintainability because changing the content to be generated requires the servlet to be edited, recompiled, and redeployed. The same is true here of JavaBeans generating dynamic content – hard-coded content is not good. In fact, the same maintainability problems are applicable to custom tags.

However, given the choice between using JavaBeans or tags, tags are more suitable because of their knowledge of the environment. Additionally, the behavior associated with custom tags can be easily customized by page authors through the use of tag attributes. In general, custom tags are also easier for page authors to use, as they will be more familiar than Java code and JavaBeans.

Although custom tags are more appropriate to use for generating dynamic content, we still don't get away from the maintainability problems associated with hard-coding content into sourcecode. Additionally, mixing content and presentation can be bad because changing one often means changing the other. This is another issue entirely and is covered in depth in Chapter 9. For completeness, however, the key guidelines for alleviating these issues are:

- Externalize the style information
- Externalize the presentation
- Internationalization

As Chapter 9 illustrates, there are several ways in which these can be achieved, including the use of Cascading Style Sheets (CSS) and introducing scripting variables back into the page.

Rule of Thumb

Custom tags are a preferable choice to JavaBeans for generating content because of their knowledge of the environment in which they are running, plus the fact that they can be customized through the use of tag attributes. Of course JavaBeans can be provided with such information, although they should really be designed to run and be reused independently of any particular environment.

With this in mind, however, the quantity of content generated from tags should be minimal to reduce the problems associated with maintainability in the future.

Representing Information

From the examples that we've seen so far and our look behind the scenes, it is very tempting to say that custom tags have the competitive edge over JavaBeans. After all, they have a much greater knowledge of their environment, can be customized easily, and can be implemented as JavaBeans if necessary. However, using custom tags is not always the most appropriate method and sometimes JavaBeans will be a more appropriate solution.

As we'll see shortly, a more common use for JavaBeans is as containers for information required in the web container, including the following:

- Business information from a persistent data source
- Information about the user's current session
- Carriers of data between components, internally and externally

For example, if there is some state that we need to maintain during the user's interaction with the system, we could define a JavaBean in which to hold this information. An example here might be a bean to represent the contents of the user's shopping cart in an e-commerce application. In this example, the JavaBean might contain a number of properties such as the username and a collection of items that they have added to their cart.

This JavaBean would then be bound to the user's current session using the `HttpSession` interface. To make it a JavaBean, there would be a default, zero arguments constructor along with accessors and mutators for each of the properties that are defined in the bean.

Making the JavaBean implement `java.io.Serializable` means that the information can be distributed around a cluster of web containers or simply used to transport data between servers, as serialized Java objects should this be required. Utilizing this bean in a web application would probably be achieved through the `<jsp:useBean/>` family of standard actions which would instantiate the bean the first time around and bind it into the `session` scope. On subsequent pages, the `<jsp:useBean/>` action would be used to look up the bean, after which further information could be stored and retrieved.

Pooling of Tag Handler Instances

Although a custom tag can be a JavaBean for representing information, a tag would not be appropriate because this is not what tags are designed for. Instead, they represent actions that can occur on the page. Behind the scenes, the web container manages tag handlers, with some implementations improving performance by **pooling** tag handler instances, thereby reducing the overhead in object creation every time a tag handler is required. We've already seen the prototypical example of Java code that might be generated to support the use of custom tags on the page. Let's see how the pooling of tag handler instances might affect this:

At the time of writing, Tomcat 4.0 doesn't yet support the pooling of tag handler instances. However, while others such as BEA WebLogic and Tomcat 3.3 do support this optional part of the JSP specification, such code is vendor-specific and for simplicity has been abstracted out of the following code snippets.

```
... start of page ...

com.wrox.jsptaglibs.date.DateTag t = ... get tag handler instance from pool ...
t.setPageContext(pageContext);
t.setParent(null);
t.setFormat("dd-MMM-yyyy");

try {
  if (t.doStartTag() != javax.servlet.jsp.tagext.Tag.SKIP_BODY) {
    ... body content would be here ...
  }

  if (t.doEndTag() == javax.servlet.jsp.tagext.Tag.SKIP_PAGE) {
    return;
  }
} finally {
  ... return tag handler instance back to pool ...
}

... end of page ...
```

In this example, instead of instantiating another tag handler, an instance is requested from the pool. As the web container maintains this pool, the actual code is vendor-specific although the principle is the same. When the handler has completed its processing, the instance can be returned to the pool for subsequent use by other pages. This is permitted by the JSP specification and therefore places some restrictions on how tag handlers can be programmed and subsequently used.

The JSP specification guarantees that only a single thread of execution will operate on any given tag handler at any given time. This provides a safety net around tag development in that tags are generally considered thread-safe. Of course, tag handlers can make use of shared resources that may require synchronization, but the tag handler instances themselves will only ever be used by one thread at a time.

Suppose we take an example where tag handlers might be pooled by the web container. When a page containing a tag is requested, an unused tag handler instance is retrieved from the pool and used to service the request. On completion of the request, the tag handler is then returned to the pool. Custom tags only ever span across a single JSP page. In other words, the starting and ending tags always appear on the same page. This means that at most, a tag handler will be active for the lifetime of a request on a page.

Lifetime of a JavaBean

Taking our shopping cart example again, we've already determined that the bean will be used to store information relating to the contents of the user's shopping cart for the duration of the user's session. In other words, this bean will be available for use from the moment it is created and bound to the HTTP session, until the moment that the session becomes invalidated. This could be for a number of reasons, including the user logging out or the session simply timing out because no requests have been made for a predetermined period of time. What this indicates is that JavaBeans can be long-lived components, demonstrated by the fact that they can exist in the session for any length of time.

Lifetime of a Custom Tag

Custom tags, on the other hand, are short-lived container-managed components whose purpose is to perform actions on one page. Although in practice it is possible to store a reference to a tag handler within the HTTP session for use in later pages, doing so is not recommended. In this scenario, and if the web container did implement a pool for tag handler instances, it is first of all not possible to tell whether the web container is using this particular instance to service another request. If this were the case, it is no longer possible for the container to guarantee that only one thread of execution is operating upon the tag handler and a corruption of data or system failure could occur.

In addition to this, the web container may have overwritten any state saved within the stored tag handler instance because the same instance has since been used to service other requests. For these reasons, it is not advisable that the tag handler instances are stored for use outside of the scope in which they are used on the page. In other words, references to tag handlers should not be used after the `doEndTag()` method of that handler has been executed.

Rule of Thumb

Tag handlers are not suitable for representing and storing information in the same way JavaBeans are. It is best to use JavaBeans for representing state and leave custom tags for representing actions that happen on those JavaBeans.

Recommendations

Looking at these scenarios has provided us with some basis on which to make some recommendations for the use of JavaBeans and custom tags on JSP pages.

JavaBeans

JavaBeans are environment-independent, reusable software components, governed by a strict set of rules relating to what constitutes a JavaBean. JavaBeans can be long-lived and it is therefore recommended that they be used to represent information and/or state inside the web container, or as carriers of data.

Custom Tags

Custom tags are components for encapsulating reusable functionality for use on JSP pages. This functionality is wrapped up inside tag handlers – regular Java classes that implement a specific interface. As tag handlers are regular Java classes, there is nothing stopping them from being JavaBeans too. However, tag handlers are thread-safe, container-managed components, and are specifically created to help service a particular request. Even if the web container pools them, they are still used to service individual requests and are therefore seen as short-lived.

It is recommended that custom tags be used to represent actions on JSP pages, such as generating dynamic content, accessing other resources, or performing actions upon the data represented by JavaBeans.

Naming Conventions

A good way to help determine whether a component should be a JavaBean or custom tag, and therefore establish the division of roles, is to use the following guidelines on naming conventions.

JavaBeans as Nouns

As JavaBeans represent information and business objects, they should be named as nouns. Examples here include `ShoppingCart`, `Customer`, and `Order`. Essentially this maps back to the process whereby we might pick the nouns out of a requirements specification to identify the business objects in a software system. These objects mainly represent data, although they may also consist of a small amount of associated functionality.

Custom Tags as Verbs

Custom tags, on the other hand, perform actions that control the page in some way: access information or manipulating the information contained within beans. For this reason, tags should be named as verbs. Examples here include `useBean` (from the standard `<jsp:useBean/>` tag), `iterate`, and `include`.

Although such naming conventions could be adopted, there are situations in which they might not the most appropriate. For example, a tag that generates an HTML submit button could be named `<generateSubmitButton/>`, although it might be more meaningful to call it `<submit/>` as HTML authors will be familiar with this. Nevertheless, this example represents that the tag can be named as an action and is therefore a good fit.

Now that we understand why tags are better suited to performing actions on the page, let's look at some of the common uses, or usage patterns.

Performing Actions on the Page

Our first example illustrates the principles defined by the View Helper pattern by demonstrating how embedded logic in Java scriptlets can be moved out of the page and into reusable components.

Iterating with Scriptlets

As we saw in Chapter 5, there are several ways in which iteration can be achieved on a JSP page. One such example is to use scriptlets to start and end the block of code we want to iterate over. To demonstrate this, imagine that we wish to display a list of books on a JSP page.

To represent a book we just have a regular JavaBean called `Book`. As we saw, it implements the `java.io.Serializable` interface, has a zero arguments constructor, and has accessor and mutator methods for each of its properties (`isbn` and `title`). For the purpose of showing how to perform iteration on a JSP page, we didn't use a database to retrieve a list of books; instead, we just have a simple class called `BookManager` that maintains a collection of hard-coded `Book` instances.

With these two classes, we can write a JSP page that presents a list of all books to the user as follows:

```
<html>

  <head>
    <title>Professional JSP Tag Libraries</title>
  </head>

  <%@ page import="com.wrox.jsptaglibs.common.Book" %>
  <%@ page import="com.wrox.jsptaglibs.common.BookManager" %>

  <body>
    <h1>Wrox books online</h1>

    <%
      Book[] books = BookManager.getInstance().getBooksAsArray();
      Book book;

      for (int i = 0; i < books.length; i++) {
        book = books[i];
    %>

      <p>
        <b><%= book.getTitle() %></b>
        <br/>
        ISBN : <%= book.getIsbn() %>
      </p>

    <%
      }
    %>

  </body>

</html>
```

This JSP page is fairly straightforward and has two scriptlets representing the start and end of the iteration block, implemented in this case as a `for` loop. These two scriptlets contain regular JSP page content that is evaluated on each iteration of the loop. This block contains some JSP expressions to output the values of the current book – specifically to output the title and ISBN:

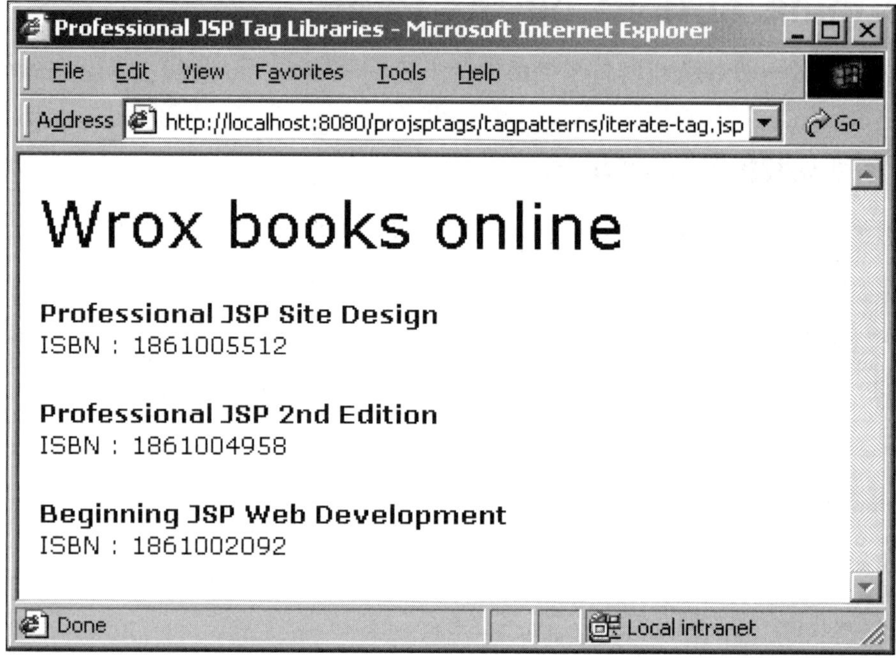

While this produces the desired result, there is obviously a reasonable amount of Java code on the page. As highlighted earlier, this is something that we are trying to avoid for reasons of maintainability, readability, and reusability.

Iterating with Custom Tags

One solution to these problems is to use a custom tag to provide the iteration facility on a JSP page. As we've discussed, a tag is a good fit in this situation because it represents an action that happens on the page. Where we currently have Java scriptlets that define the start and end blocks of the iteration, the start and end custom tags could be used in their place. By replacing these with the `iterate` tag that we built in Chapter 5, we can see how this transforms the page:

```
<html>

  <head>
    <title>Professional JSP Tag Libraries</title>
  </head>

  <%@ page import="java.util.Collection" %>
  <%@ page import="com.wrox.jsptaglibs.common.BookManager" %>
```

```
<%@ taglib uri="/iterationTaglib" prefix="iteration" %>

<body>

  <h1>Wrox books online</h1>

  <%
    Collection books = BookManager.getInstance().getBooksAsCollection();
  %>

  <iteration:iterate id="book" type="com.wrox.jsptaglibs.common.Book"
                     collection="<%= books %>">

    <p>
      <b><jsp:getProperty name="book" property="title"/></b>
      <br/>
      ISBN : <jsp:getProperty name="book" property="isbn"/>
    </p>

  </iteration:iterate>

</body>

</html>
```

As we are now using a custom tag to introduce a scripting variable back into the page on each iteration, we can subsequently use the standard `<jsp:getProperty/>` tag to further clean the page of Java code. This of course generates the same HTML page as before.

While we've seen this example before, it is useful to demonstrate the power that tags have to perform actions on the page. Next, let's look at another example where we are performing a different type of action. Here, instead of controlling the page, we'll use a custom tag to wrap up the logic to perform a specific task.

Using Resource Bundles with Scriptlets

One of the differentiating factors that makes Java stand out from other languages is its support for internationalization (i18n) – the ability to create applications that can be adapted to run in different languages and locales without requiring changes to the sourcecode. This is possible, in part, through a feature called resource bundles that contain locale-specific resources. For example, you may have bundles for all of the labels and messages in your application. One of these could be in English, one in French, and so on. Rather than hard-coding messages into your sourcecode, instead you externalize this information.

With the explosion of the Web, it is now possible, and increasingly more likely, that the applications we develop will be used by people whose first language isn't the same as ours. For this reason, another useful action that can be performed on the page is accessing resource bundles so that messages and labels can be displayed in the appropriate language.

Writing a Properties Backed Resource Bundle

There are several ways in which resource bundles can be written but essentially it is a simple process of building up a list of name-value pairs representing the locale-specific resources that we would like to externalize from the application code. For example, here is a properties file called `myResources.properties` representing the resources that we might use in a web application:

```
username=Username
password=Password
login=Login
```

Of course, in addition to this you would also define a resource bundle for the other languages that you wish to support. For example, the same resource bundle for the French language version would be called `myResources_fr.properties`:

```
username=Votre Compte
password=Mot de passe
login=Ouvrir session
```

Using a Resource Bundle

Once the resource bundles have been defined, the next step is to use them. This is straightforward and involves using the factory method `getBundle()` on the `ResourceBundle` class itself, specifying the name of the resource bundle (the base name) and the locale for which the bundle should be located:

```
<html>

  <head>
    <title>Professional JSP Tag Libraries</title>
  </head>

  <%@ page import="java.util.ResourceBundle" %>

  <body>

    <%
      ResourceBundle bundle;
      bundle = ResourceBundle.getBundle("myResources", request.getLocale());
    %>
```

Once we have a reference to a `ResourceBundle` instance, we can then go on and use it to display the localized resources that are stored within it. This is achieved with the `getString()` method which takes a parameter corresponding to the name of the key we wish to use:

```
    <h1>Wrox books online</h1>

    <form action="process-logon.jsp">

      <%= bundle.getString("username") %>
      : <input type="text" name="username" size="16">
```

```
        <br/>
        <%= bundle.getString("password") %>
        : <input type="password" name="password" size="16">

        <br/><br/>
        <input type="submit"
               value="<%= bundle.getString("login") %>">

      </form>

    </body>

  </html>
```

When requested, and assuming that the user is based in an English-speaking locale, the result is as follows, demonstrating that the keys have been substituted with the appropriate values from the resource bundle:

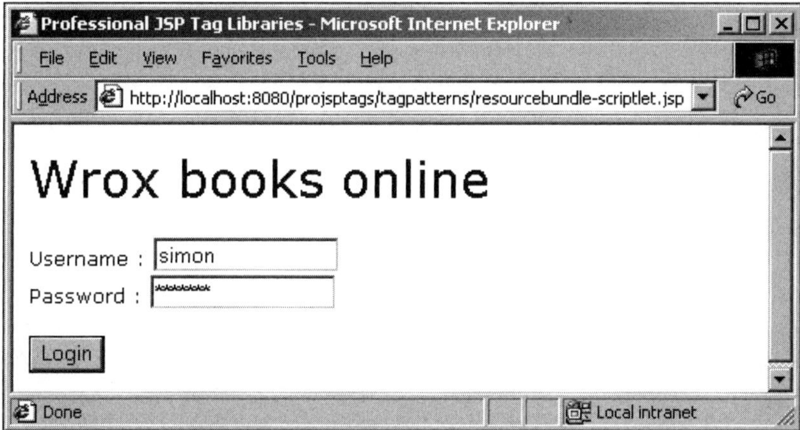

On the other hand, a French-speaking user might see the following:

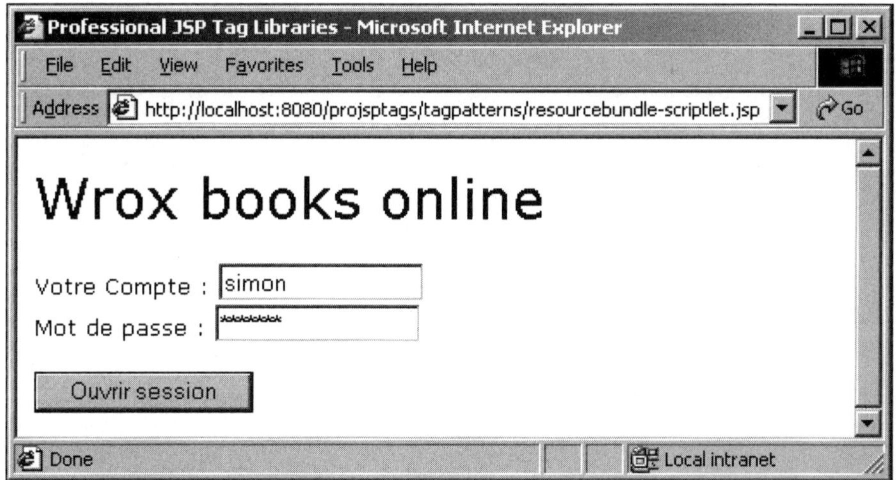

As this demonstrates, using resource bundles is straightforward and particularly worthwhile if you are thinking of attracting a worldwide audience. Once again, we have introduced some Java code into the page and since page authors are the people that are going to primarily be concerned with the localized presentation of information, it makes sense to move this code out of the page and into custom tags.

Using Resource Bundles With Custom Tags

As we're about to see, performing an action on the page doesn't have to be confined to a single custom tag. In the example that we just saw, there are two distinct actions – locating the resource bundle, and using it; both of which can be wrapped up into tags.

The ResourceBundle Tag

The first tag that we'll build is the `resourceBundle` tag that will allow page authors to locate a named resource bundle and subsequently use it on the page. When locating a `ResourceBundle` instance, we must supply the base name and the locale. Since custom tags are aware of the environment in which they are running, we can get away without asking the page author to specify the locale, instead only asking them for the base name of the bundle:

```
package com.wrox.jsptaglibs.i18n;

package com.wrox.jsptaglibs.i18n;

import java.util.Locale;
import java.util.ResourceBundle;

import javax.servlet.jsp.JspException;
import javax.servlet.jsp.tagext.TagSupport;

public class ResourceBundleTag extends TagSupport {

  private String baseName;

  public void setBaseName(String s) {
    this.baseName = s;
  }
```

This just leaves the processing associated with the tag. In this case, all we would like to do is find the resource bundle and make it available through the page context by the name that is specified by the `id` attribute:

```
  public int doStartTag() throws JspException {

    // get the locale and then find the appropriate resource bundle
    Locale loc = pageContext.getRequest().getLocale();
    ResourceBundle bundle = ResourceBundle.getBundle(baseName, loc);

    // and place it into the page context for use later on
    pageContext.setAttribute(getId(), bundle);

    // skip the body content as there shouldn't be one
    return SKIP_BODY;
  }
}
```

The message Tag

Once we've located the resource bundle, the next thing to do is use it. As we saw in Chapter 7, using a named attribute in the page context is a good way of allowing tags to access shared information and therefore cooperate. The `message` tag will simply look up the resource bundle in the page context and, using a specified key, find its corresponding value, and output this back onto the page.

With this in mind, the tag handler is as follows:

```
package com.wrox.jsptaglibs.i18n;

import java.io.IOException;
import java.util.ResourceBundle;

import javax.servlet.jsp.JspException;
import javax.servlet.jsp.JspTagException;
import javax.servlet.jsp.JspWriter;
import javax.servlet.jsp.tagext.TagSupport;

public class MessageTag extends TagSupport {

  private String key;
  private String name;

  public int doStartTag() throws JspException {

    // find the specified resource bundle
    ResourceBundle bundle = (ResourceBundle)pageContext.getAttribute(name);

    try {
      // and write out the message
      JspWriter out = pageContext.getOut();

      out.write(bundle.getString(key));
    } catch (IOException ioe) {
      throw new JspTagException(ioe.getMessage());
    }

    // skip the body content as there shouldn't be one
    return SKIP_BODY;
  }

  public void setName(String s) {
    this.name = s;
  }

  public void setKey(String s) {
    this.key = s;
  }
}
```

The Tag Library Descriptor

Here is the tag library descriptor for the above tag handlers:

```
<?xml version="1.0" encoding="ISO-8859-1" ?>
<!DOCTYPE taglib
  PUBLIC "-//Sun Microsystems, Inc.//DTD JSP Tag Library 1.2//EN"
  "http://java.sun.com/dtd/web-jsptaglibrary_1_2.dtd">

<taglib>

  <tlib-version>1.0</tlib-version>
  <jsp-version>1.2</jsp-version>
  <short-name>i18n</short-name>
  <description>
    I18N examples for the Tag Patterns chapter.
  </description>

  <tag>
    <name>resourceBundle</name>
    <tag-class>com.wrox.jsptaglibs.i18n.ResourceBundleTag</tag-class>
    <body-content>empty</body-content>
    <description>
      Locates the specified resource bundle.
    </description>

    <attribute>
      <name>id</name>
      <required>true</required>
      <rtexprvalue>false</rtexprvalue>
    </attribute>

    <attribute>
      <name>baseName</name>
      <required>true</required>
      <rtexprvalue>false</rtexprvalue>
    </attribute>
  </tag>

  <tag>
    <name>message</name>
    <tag-class>com.wrox.jsptaglibs.i18n.MessageTag</tag-class>
    <body-content>empty</body-content>
    <description>
      Displays a message associated with a key.
    </description>

    <attribute>
      <name>name</name>
      <required>true</required>
      <rtexprvalue>false</rtexprvalue>
    </attribute>

    <attribute>
      <name>key</name>
      <required>true</required>
      <rtexprvalue>false</rtexprvalue>
    </attribute>
  </tag>

</taglib>
```

Using the Tags

Using the tags on the page is then simply a matter of replacing the scriptlet and expressions that we used in the previous version:

```
<html>

  <head>
    <title>Professional JSP Tag Libraries</title>
  </head>

  <%@ taglib uri="/i18nTaglib" prefix="i18n" %>

  <body>

    <i18n:resourceBundle id="bundle" baseName="myResources"/>

    <h1>Wrox books online</h1>

    <form action="process-logon.jsp">

      <i18n:message name="bundle" key="username"/>
        : <input type="text" name="username" size="16">
      <br/>
      <i18n:message name="bundle" key="password"/>
        : <input type="password" name="password" size="16">

      <br/></br/>
      <input type="submit"
             value="<i18n:message name="bundle" key="login"/>">

    </form>

  </body>

</html>
```

This certainly cleans up the page and also makes it much more intuitive to figure out what is going on while generating the same result as before. In addition to this, we've also negated the need to explicitly look up the locale. Tags having access to their environment is another contributing factor to use custom tags.

Rules of Thumb

Replacing the scriptlets that are responsible for providing the iteration facility on a JSP page is a good use for custom tags for several reasons. From a software engineering and technical perspective, we increase the maintainability of our application because we've moved the Java code away from each page in which it is used and replaced it with a reusable component – a custom tag. From a usage perspective, the page author doesn't have to know about the complexities associated with iterating over a collection of Java objects.

As Java developers generally build custom tags, there is always a danger that tags are built to represent the sort of fine-grained actions that programmers would typically perform. For example, when using a `for` loop to iterate over an array, a programmer would write the `for` loop with one statement to provide the counter facility, and use a separate statement to retrieve the element corresponding to the current index from an array. An example of such an implementation is as follows:

```
... start of page ...

<%
  Book[] books = BookManager.getInstance().getBooksAsArray();
  Book book;

  for (int i = 0; i < books.length; i++) {
    book = books[i];
%>

  ... content to be displayed on each iteration ...

<%
  }
%>

... end of page ...
```

In this implementation there are two distinct parts to the iteration – looping with a counter variable and getting the corresponding element from the array. Since writing code in this way is so common, an easy mistake to make is to write a custom tag implementation that maps directly onto the steps involved:

```
... start of page ...

<%
  Book[] books = Books.getBooksAsArray();
%>

<iteration:for from="0" to="<%= books.length %>">

  <iteration:getBean id="book" array="<%= books %>"/>

  ... content to be displayed on each iteration ...

</iteration:for>

... end of page ...
```

Here we have two custom tags. The first performs a loop with a counter variable while the second wraps up the corresponding element from the array specified as an attribute. This approach does work and removes the majority of the Java code from the page and places it into reusable components. However, the problem here is with the usage of the tags.

There are two different types of people that write JSP pages – Java developers and web designers. While Java developers are familiar with the Java language and don't mind using it on the page, web designers may not be so familiar with it. Even though we have moved some Java code out of the page and replaced it with custom tags, the usage of these tags still requires some knowledge of how the mechanism behind arrays works. This will seem easier to Java developers than it will for web designers.

In addition to this, even if Java developers are responsible for putting the page together, web designers may still be involved in transforming the look and feel. In this situation, the page will certainly seem overcomplicated and much more difficult to understand.

For these reasons, it is a good idea to try to strive for fairly coarse-grained actions. The `iterate` tag is a good example of this as it wraps up several steps into an easy-to-use tag. A single tag is a much more natural interface to use for achieving the desired end goal, and it provides an understanding of what is happening on the page to a wider range of people with varying skill levels.

However, single tags aren't always appropriate. If we look back to the resource bundle tags, we could have simply used a single tag called `message`. However, in this situation the page author would have had to specify the name of the resource bundle and the name of the key. Doing this would probably introduce performance problems by always looking up the `ResourceBundle`. In addition to this, we've reduced the maintainability of the page because the name of that bundle has to be specified everywhere that the `message` tag is used. Splitting the actions up over a set of cooperating tags in this case was more practical and more efficient.

Having a more natural interface for page authors to use on the page is an important part of the process behind building custom tag libraries. Although this interface can be kept consistent throughout a web application by reusing the tags in a tag library, the next application might make use of a different set of tags, even though they might provide the same functionality.

> *For this reason, a new Java Specification Request (JSR) has been approved to create the JSP Standard Tag Library (JSTL) – a standard set of tags for performing common tasks (such as iteration) that can be used across JSP containers. A more in-depth look along with some examples of the JSTL is in Chapter 12.*

Performing Logic on the Page

The next example of a good use for custom tags is to perform logic on the page. Deterministic behavior is important in all applications, with the ability to perform conditional checks using `if` statements almost taken for granted. In the same way that these conditional checks are performed in Java classes, they are often required on the JSP pages within a web application to determine which particular information to show to the user.

Let's go back to our application that displays information about books to the user. Here, a list of hyperlinked book titles could be shown that will take the user to more detail about that particular book. To indicate to the requested page which book should be displayed, the ISBN (the unique key) of the book should be encoded into the URL as part of the query string:

http://localhost/projsptags/show-book.jsp?isbn=1861004958

The requested page will then use the `isbn` parameter to look up the appropriate book and display the relevant information to the user. With this information appended to the URL, users could always manually alter the `isbn` parameter, or worse, remove it entirely. Because of this situation, our JSP page should take precautions to ensure that the user is presented with an appropriate message rather than just throwing a nasty Java stack trace.

Conditional Programming with Scriptlets

Conditional behavior on a page could be implemented using several Java scriptlets, essentially as one large `if`. If a book can be found then we show the user the appropriate information about it, otherwise we show them an error message:

```
<html>

  <head>
    <title>Professional JSP Tag Libraries</title>
  </head>

  <%@ page import="com.wrox.jsptaglibs.common.*" %>

  <body>

    <h1>Wrox books online</h1>

    <%
      String isbn = request.getParameter("isbn");
      Book book = BookManager.getInstance().getBook(isbn);

      if (book == null) {
    %>
        Sorry, no book was found.
    <%
      } else {
    %>
        <h2><%= book.getTitle() %></h2>
        ... information about the chosen book here ...
    <%
      }
    %>

  </body>

</html>
```

Requesting the page properly, with an ISBN, means that the page will look up the appropriate `Book` instance and present the information to the user:

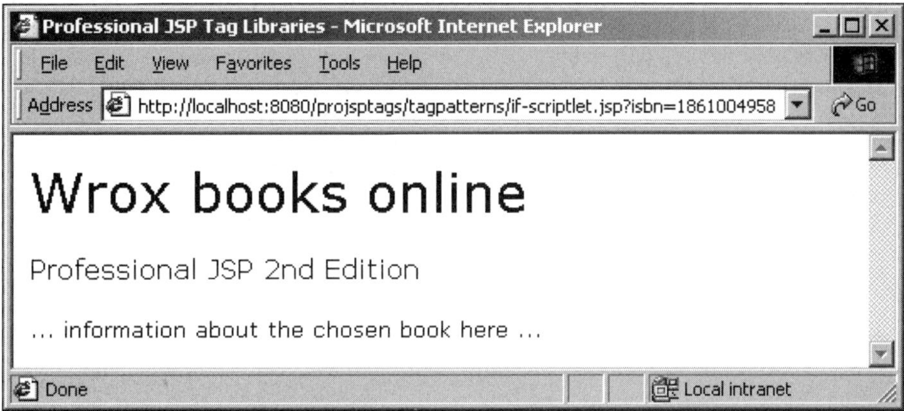

On the other hand, requesting the page with an invalid ISBN, or not specifying it at all, generates the following page showing an error message:

Providing conditional behavior such as this is much more appropriate from the user's perspective. After all, presenting them with a Java stack trace will probably put them off coming back to your site.

In achieving this, as we can see from the example JSP page, there is not only a fair amount of Java code in the page, but the page is now increasingly more difficult to read because of the scriptlets dispersed throughout. Also, we have exposed the complexities associated with conditional checking, including the check for `null`. This is something that web designers certainly won't want to see.

Conditional Programming with Custom Tags

Custom tags are a good solution to the problems described above. Essentially, all we are doing is performing an action on the page to check whether a book has been found. If this is the case we display some content related to the book, otherwise we show the user some other content containing an error message. This type of behavior is well suited to custom tags because tags have programmatic control over whether their body content is evaluated and hence shown to the user.

Instead of wrapping up the conditional statements inside Java scriptlets, they can instead be wrapped inside custom tags. To illustrate this, let's see how the tags that we built in Chapter 7 can be used to improve the page:

```
<html>

  <head>
    <title>Professional JSP Tag Libraries</title>
  </head>

  <%@ page import="com.wrox.jsptaglibs.common.Book" %>
  <%@ page import="com.wrox.jsptaglibs.common.BookManager" %>
  <%@ taglib uri="/logicTaglib" prefix="logic" %>

  <body>

    <h1>Wrox books online</h1>

    <%
      String isbn = request.getParameter("isbn");
      Book book = BookManager.getInstance().getBook(isbn);
    %>
```

First of all we have a tag called `if` indicating that we are going to be evaluating the value specified by the `book` scripting variable. This represents the start of the conditional block. Next, and nested underneath the `if` tag, are the conditions that we wish to evaluate. We have a tag called `undefined` and this checks whether the book variable (supplied to the outer `if` tag) is `null`. If this is the case, the body content of this tag is evaluated, showing the user a message about how a book couldn't be found in the same way as before:

```
    <logic:if value="<%= book %>">

      <logic:undefined>
        Sorry, no book was found.
      </logic:undefined>
```

The other tag that we have here is called `default`. This acts as a catch-all, the body content of which is only evaluated if the previous conditions (in this case `undefined`) did not match. In this example, and as we've seen, the default behavior is to show some more information about the selected book. As this new example illustrates, the page is now cleaner and contains significantly less Java code and Java scriptlets:

```
        <logic:default>
          <h2><%= book.getTitle() %></h2>
          ... information about the chosen book here ...
        </logic:default>

      </logic:if>

    </body>

  </html>
```

Rules of Thumb

As with the iteration example, custom tags are a great way to remove excess Java code from the page and place it into reusable components. This time, however, we're using a tag's ability to programmatically control the evaluation of its body content to determine what gets displayed to the user.

We've already mentioned that there is a danger that tags are implemented to map directly on to the steps involved when implementing the same action using Java code, and this is applicable here too. It is possible to create quite complex conditions using Java, for example using Boolean ANDs and ORs along with the other conditional operators that are available to us as Java developers.

There are two dangers here. The first is that this complex logic is implemented within the page. Irrespective of whether custom tags or scriptlets are used, complex conditional processing will undoubtedly confuse those that have to maintain the page in the future. The other danger is that the tags map onto concepts that will be understood only by programmers. For this reason, the same recommendations about the tags being a more natural interface apply here too. The names given to tags are often a good way to provide this natural interface and this is why the `undefined` tag is not named `null` – after all, `null` might not mean much to non-programmers.

Replacements for Standard HTML Tags

A common requirement when building web applications is to build HTML forms to capture information from the user. If we take our example of presenting the user with a list of book titles again, an alternative way of displaying this list to the user is using a drop-down list box – an HTML select control. These types of controls normally reside within an HTML form, and the value (option) selected by the user is sent back to the server when the form is submitted.

The HTML behind these drop-down lists is fairly straightforward and is written using the standard `select` tag. For the purposes of our example, we'll also make use of the `name` attribute. This is the name of the control on the form and also the name of the parameter sent back to the server representing the user's selection:

```
<select name="isbn">
  ... options ...
</select>
```

Nested within the HTML select tag are the items that are to be displayed in the list. These items can be made up of two parts – a visible **label** and a hidden **value**. Each item to be displayed is wrapped up inside the standard option tags:

```
<option value="1861005512">Professional JSP Site Design</option>
```

In this example, Professional JSP Site Design is the visible label while 1861005512 is the hidden value. When the form is submitted back to the server, the hidden value corresponding to the selected item in the drop-down list is matched up with the name of the control and sent back as a name-value pair.

Generating HTML with Scriptlets

Let's take a look at how such a control could be dynamically generated by a JSP page. To do this, we'll again use our list of Book objects. On our JSP page, we'll have a drop-down list containing the titles of the books, while the ISBNs will be used as the hidden values:

```
<html>

  <head>
    <title>Professional JSP Tag Libraries</title>
  </head>

  <%@ page import="java.util.Collection" %>
  <%@ page import="java.util.Iterator" %>
  <%@ page import="com.wrox.jsptaglibs.common.Book" %>
  <%@ page import="com.wrox.jsptaglibs.common.BookManager" %>

  <body>

    <h1>Wrox books online</h1>

    <form method="post">
```

The select tag is written using standard HTML straight into the page. As the list of options is not known until run-time, these must be built up and added to the select tag one by one. To do this we will use some Java code in a scriptlet that iterates over the collection of Book instances and generates the appropriate option tag:

```
      <select name="isbn">
        <%
          Collection books;
          books = BookManager.getInstance().getBooksAsCollection();
          Iterator iterator = books.iterator();

          Book book;
          while (iterator.hasNext()) {
            book = (Book)iterator.next();
        %>
          <option value="<%= book.getIsbn() %>">
            <%= book.getTitle() %>
          </option>
        <%
          }
        %>
```

When the iteration is complete, all the `option` tags have been completed and so the `select` tag can be closed off:

```
        </select>
        <input type="submit" value="Submit">

      </form>

    </body>

  </html>
```

When requested through a browser, the results of this JSP page are as follows.

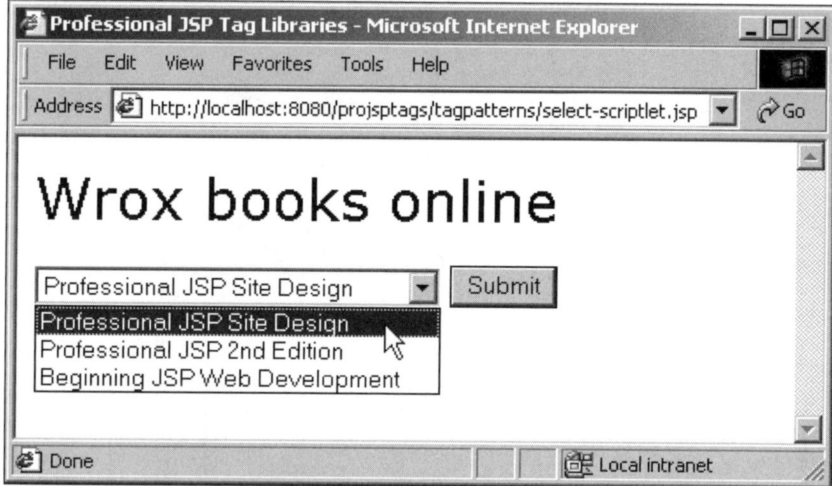

As with all of the other examples, there is far too much Java code in the page and the problems around maintainability and readability will rear their ugly heads again – especially if there is more than one drop-down list on the page.

Generating HTML with Custom Tags

As we're performing an action on the page (in this case generating an HTML control), custom tags are yet again a good fit. One solution is to remove the Java code that performs the iteration with the `iterate` tag that we saw earlier:

```
  <html>

    <head>
      <title>Professional JSP Tag Libraries</title>
    </head>

    <%@ page import="java.util.Collection" %>
    <%@ page import="com.wrox.jsptaglibs.common.BookManager" %>
```

```
<%@ taglib uri="/iterationTaglib" prefix="iteration" %>

<body>

  <h1>Wrox books online</h1>

  <form method="post">

    <select name="isbn">
      <%
        Collection books;
        books = BookManager.getInstance().getBooksAsCollection();
      %>

      <iteration:iterate id="book"
                         type="com.wrox.jsptaglibs.common.Book"
                         collection="<%= books %>">
```

In addition to removing the scriptlets that perform the iteration, because we are now using a custom tag that introduces a scripting variable back into the page on each iteration, we can use the standard `<jsp:getProperty/>` tag to further avoid Java code:

```
        <option value="<jsp:getProperty name="book" property="isbn"/>">
          <jsp:getProperty name="book" property="title"/>
        </option>

      </iteration:iterate>
    </select>

    <input type="submit" value="Submit">

  </form>

</body>

</html>
```

This undoubtedly offers some improvements in terms of maintainability and also makes the page easier to understand and more readable for those people that aren't Java programmers. However, the logic required to create this control is still exposed in the page. In other words, we have a series of fine-grained actions once again representing the steps required to produce the desired result.

Another way in which custom tags can be used is to wrap up all of the functionality required to generate the HTML select control. From a usability perspective this makes a lot of sense. First of all, it removes all of the individual steps out of the page and into an easy to use, reusable component. This is good news for maintainability and will increase the readability of our page – especially if more than one select control is needed. Let's first of all see how such a tag could be used on the page:

```
<html>

  <head>
```

```
    <title>Professional JSP Tag Libraries</title>
  </head>

  <%@ page import="java.util.Collection" %>
  <%@ page import="com.wrox.jsptaglibs.common.BookManager" %>

  <%@ taglib uri="/htmlTaglib" prefix="html" %>

  <body>

    <h1>Wrox books online</h1>

    <form method="post">

      <%
        Collection books;
        books = BookManager.getInstance().getBooksAsCollection();
      %>

      <html:select name="isbn" label="title" value="isbn"
        collection="<%= books %>"/>

      <input type="submit" value="Submit">

    </form>

  </body>

</html>
```

The page is much shorter and hence much more readable. This single tag wraps up all of the steps involved in generating the HTML to render a select control and is customized by four attributes:

- `name`
  The name of the control in the form
- `collection`
  The `java.util.Collection` of JavaBeans that will be used to populate the list of options
- `label`
  The name of the property on those JavaBeans that will be used as the visible label
- `value`
  The name of the property on those JavaBeans that will be used as the hidden value

Let's take a closer look at how this tag works by looking at its tag handler class. First of all we have the usual properties and mutator methods corresponding to the attributes that the tag will take:

```
package com.wrox.jsptaglibs.html;

import java.beans.PropertyDescriptor;
import java.io.IOException;
import java.lang.reflect.PropertyDescriptor;
```

```
import java.util.Collection;
import java.util.Iterator;

import javax.servlet.jsp.JspException;
import javax.servlet.jsp.JspTagException;
import javax.servlet.jsp.JspWriter;
import javax.servlet.jsp.tagext.TagSupport;

public class SelectTag extends TagSupport {

  private Collection collection;
  private String name;
  private String label;
  private String value;

  public void setName(String name) {
    this.name = name;
  }

  public void setLabel(String label) {
    this.label = label;
  }

  public void setValue(String value) {
    this.value = value;
  }

  public void setCollection(Collection coll) {
    this.collection = coll;
  }
```

Following this we have the `doStartTag()` method where all of the processing is performed. Assuming that all of the tag attributes are mandatory, the first step is to create an `Iterator` over the `Collection` of JavaBeans:

```
  public int doStartTag() throws JspException {
    Iterator iterator = collection.iterator();
```

Next we get a reference to the current `JspWriter` so that we can output content back to the page:

```
    try {
      JspWriter out = pageContext.getOut();
```

With this done, we can then output the starting `select` tag:

```
      out.print("<select name=\"");
      out.print(name);
      out.print("\">");
```

The options that will be displayed are nested underneath the `select` tag. To generate this HTML, all the tag needs to do is iterate over the collection of JavaBeans and create the appropriate string representing the option.

When we use the tag on the page, it can take two attributes representing the names of properties on the JavaBeans – one for the visible label and one for the hidden value. Getting the value of a property from a JavaBean is a straightforward process and requires the use of Java's reflection mechanism. Here, we are creating a `java.lang.reflect.PropertyDescriptor` object representing a specific, named property on the bean. We can then use this object to invoke the `getXxx()` method associated with that property:

```
    while (iterator.hasNext()) {
          Object o = iterator.next();

      PropertyDescriptor labelPD =
        new PropertyDescriptor(label, o.getClass());

      PropertyDescriptor valuePD =
        new PropertyDescriptor(value, o.getClass());

      out.print("<option value=\"");

      out.print(
        valuePD.getReadMethod().invoke(o, new Object[] {}).toString());
      out.print("\">");

      out.print(
        labelPD.getReadMethod().invoke(o, new Object[] {}).toString());
      out.print("</option>");
    }
```

In our example, the collection that is being passed into the tag is a collection of `Book` instances. We then set the value of the tag's `label` attribute to be `title`, while the `value` attribute is set to be `isbn`. When run, this reflection code locates and calls the corresponding accessor methods (`getTitle()` and `getIsbn()` respectively) on the `Book` instances, using the results to generate the `option` tag. Of course, we could have hard-coded these properties, but using the reflection mechanism is a good way of making the tag generic, and hence reusable on other pages in our web application.

Following the generation of the `option` tags, the ending `select` tag is sent back to the page:

```
      out.print("</select>");

    } catch (Exception e) {
      throw new JspTagException(e.getMessage());
    }
```

As we're using the shortened form of our tag on the page, combining the start and end tags, we can simply return SKIP_BODY as we are not interested in processing the tag's body:

```
        return SKIP_BODY;
    }
  }
```

The result of using the single tag is the same as we saw with the scriptlet.

To confirm that the tag is generating the correct HTML code, a good way to check is by looking at the source of the page through the browser. In this example, the HTML that is being generated is as follows:

Some additional blank lines in the generated HTML have been removed for clarity.

```
<html>

  <head>
    <title>Professional JSP Tag Libraries</title>
  </head>

  <body>

    <h1>Wrox books online</h1>

    <form method="post">

      <select name="isbn">
         <option value="1861005512">Professional JSP Site design</option>
         <option value="1861004958">Professional JSP 2nd Edition</option>
         <option value="1861002092">Beginning JSP Web Development</option>
      </select>

      <input type="submit" value="Submit">

    </form>

  </body>

</html>
```

The generated HTML may not be as neatly laid out as HTML we might write ourselves, but the output is still the same to the user.

Rules of Thumb

Writing replacements for the standard HTML controls is often debated within the JSP community. One view says that custom tag replacements are harder for web authoring tools to deal with because the content and presentation of the HTML is now wrapped up inside a custom tag. In addition to this, HTML tags are standardized, well known, and therefore easy to understand. On the other hand, building replacements for the standard tags takes a great deal of the work out of building HTML pages which in turn leads to a decrease in the time taken to build a site, and therefore the time to market.

The example shown in this section is very straightforward, although there are many other enhancements that could be made. If we take an HTML text field as another example, a custom tag could be built that generates the text field with a specified name as an attribute. It is often useful to perform client-side validation of the contents of text fields before they are submitted back to the browser.

An example here is checking that a mandatory field on a form has been filled in. This type of validation is often done using JavaScript and therefore has to be manually coded into the HTML page. By using a custom tag to generate the HTML text field, this functionality could automatically be included. Not only do page authors get the HTML text field built, but they also get the client-side validation script too.

There is of course a downside to mimicking the standard HTML tags. While our example generated basic HTML for a select control, it does make it harder for web designers to customize the look and feel because the HTML code is embedded within a tag handler class. There are several ways around this and these are discussed in the next chapter.

In addition to this, the standard HTML tags have many attributes allowing them to be customized extensively. Mimicking the entire set of behaviors entails mimicking the entire set of attributes too. This is not a complex piece of development but is time consuming nonetheless. In this situation, it is worth being pragmatic about implementing just a subset of the behaviors.

> *Another option is to use a third party tag library of which there are now several. One of the most widely adopted of these is shipped with the Struts Framework from the Jakarta Project (http://jakarta.apache.org/struts/). Struts is an open source framework that provides an implementation of a complete Model 2 framework – an MVC style architecture whereby actions and business logic that operate on the data (the model) are decoupled from the views that present that information to the user.*
>
> *This decoupling brings with its own set of challenges and for this reason Struts comes complete with several tag libraries that help in building HTML-based web applications. One of these tag libraries (called `html`) consists of replacements for the majority of the standard tags for building HTML forms and provides integration with the rest of the framework, particularly with respect to accessing information from the model. A more detailed discussion on the Struts features is in Chapter 12.*

Building replacements for the standard HTML tags is certainly a good use of custom tags as they again represent an action that is performed on the page. Wrapping up the steps required to generate HTML controls is a good way to increase the maintainability and readability of the pages within web applications. At the same time, it can make it harder to customize the look and feel at a later date. The next chapter looks at how these problems can be addressed, but the key rule of thumb here is not to place too much presentation and formatting-related code into the tag handlers.

Accessing Enterprise Resources

The last example that we'll look at in this chapter is the use of enterprise resources from within JSP pages. The other examples that we've seen up until now have all been fairly straightforward and represent simple actions on the page. These actions, such as iteration and generating HTML, are all related to the presentation of information and for this reason are quite likely to be understood and used by people other than Java developers who author the page.

For even the most simple web applications, there will probably come a time when information gathered from, or presented to, the user will be stored using a persistent data source of some kind. To use some examples, this data could be accessed directly from a relational database such as Oracle, or even through Enterprise JavaBeans running within an application server such as BEA WebLogic. However the data gets from the data source to the user, there will ultimately need to be some interaction from the presentation tier – JSP pages and servlets.

More information about Enterprise JavaBeans can be found in Professional EJB from Wrox Press (ISBN 1-861005-08-3).

When writing J2EE applications, enterprise resources such as EJBs and database connections are typically made available through the Java Naming and Directory Interface (JNDI) – a standard, hierarchical interface for registering and subsequently retrieving references to objects. For example, when the application server starts up, the resources are made available and bound into the JNDI tree. During the lifetime of the application, other components such as JSP pages and servlets will use JNDI to find these resources so that they can use them.

Using Remote Objects with Scriptlets

To show how a remote object such as an EJB might be used from a JSP page, let's imagine that our `Book` instances can be looked up through a session bean called `RemoteBookManager`, running inside an application server. This session bean has a single method that takes an ISBN and returns the appropriate `Book` instance to the caller. To recap, building an EJB involves writing three classes:

- A remote interface specifying the public API that the EJB provides clients
- A bean implementation providing the functionality behind the interface
- A home interface through which instances of the EJB are created

As with the other examples in the book, the complete source code is available to download from the Wrox Press website (http://www.wrox.com/). Also included in the download are the EJB deployment descriptors and instructions on how to deploy into Sun's J2EE 1.3 Reference Implementation, downloadable from http://java.sun.com/j2ee/download.html/.

The Remote Interface

For the purposes of this example, the `RemoteBookManager` bean will provide clients with the ability to look up a specific `Book` instance. The remote interface for this session bean is as follows:

```
package com.wrox.jsptaglibs.ejb;

import java.rmi.RemoteException;
import javax.ejb.EJBObject;

import com.wrox.jsptaglibs.common.Book;
public interface RemoteBookManager extends EJBObject {

  public Book getBook(String isbn) throws RemoteException;

}
```

The Bean Implementation

Next up is the implementation of the bean, this time called `RemoteBookManagerBean`:

```
package com.wrox.jsptaglibs.ejb;

import java.rmi.RemoteException;
import javax.ejb.SessionBean;
import javax.ejb.SessionContext;

import com.wrox.jsptaglibs.common.Book;
import com.wrox.jsptaglibs.common.BookManager;

public class RemoteBookManagerBean implements SessionBean {

  public void ejbActivate() {
  }

  public void ejbPassivate() {
  }

  public void setSessionContext(SessionContext ctx) {
  }

  public void ejbCreate() {
  }

  public void ejbRemove() {
  }

  public Book getBook(String isbn) {
    return BookManager.getInstance().getBook(isbn);
  }
}
```

The majority of the methods on this class are required because we are implementing the `javax.ejb.SessionBean` interface, although we have provided an implementation of the `getBook()` method too.

The Home Interface

The session bean also has a home interface called `RemoteBookManagerHome`:

```
package com.wrox.jsptaglibs.ejb;

import java.rmi.RemoteException;
import javax.ejb.CreateException;
import javax.ejb.EJBHome;

public interface RemoteBookManagerHome extends EJBHome {

  public RemoteBookManager create() throws RemoteException, CreateException;

}
```

The Deployment Descriptors

The final step to building an EJB is to write the deployment descriptor – an XML file that describes the bean and its behavior while running in the EJB container:

```
<?xml version="1.0" encoding="Cp1252"?>

<!DOCTYPE ejb-jar
  PUBLIC '-//Sun Microsystems, Inc.//DTD Enterprise JavaBeans 2.0//EN'
  'http://java.sun.com/dtd/ejb-jar_2_0.dtd'>

<ejb-jar>

  <display-name>BookManager</display-name>

  <enterprise-beans>
    <session>
      <display-name>RemoteBookManager</display-name>
      <ejb-name>RemoteBookManager</ejb-name>
      <home>com.wrox.jsptaglibs.ejb.RemoteBookManagerHome</home>
      <remote>com.wrox.jsptaglibs.ejb.RemoteBookManager</remote>
      <ejb-class>com.wrox.jsptaglibs.ejb.RemoteBookManagerBean</ejb-class>
      <session-type>Stateless</session-type>
      <transaction-type>Container</transaction-type>
      <security-identity>
        <description></description>
        <use-caller-identity></use-caller-identity>
      </security-identity>
    </session>
  </enterprise-beans>

  <assembly-descriptor>
    <container-transaction>
      <method>
        <ejb-name>RemoteBookManager</ejb-name>
        <method-intf>Remote</method-intf>
        <method-name>getBook</method-name>
        <method-params>
          <method-param>java.lang.String</method-param>
        </method-params>
      </method>
      <trans-attribute>NotSupported</trans-attribute>
    </container-transaction>
  </assembly-descriptor>

</ejb-jar>
```

If this session bean is deployed into an application and bound into JNDI with the name `ejb/bookManager`, the following JSP page shows how the home interface is looked up and subsequently used from a JSP page:

```
<html>

<head>
    <title>Professional JSP Tag Libraries</title>
    <link rel="stylesheet" href="../page.css">
  </head>

  <%@ page import="javax.naming.Context" %>
  <%@ page import="javax.naming.InitialContext" %>
  <%@ page import="javax.rmi.PortableRemoteObject" %>
  <%@ page import="com.wrox.jsptaglibs.common.Book" %>
  <%@ page import="com.wrox.jsptaglibs.ejb.RemoteBookManager" %>
  <%@ page import="com.wrox.jsptaglibs.ejb.RemoteBookManagerHome" %>

  <body>

    <h1>Wrox books online</h1>

    <%
      Context context = new InitialContext();
      RemoteBookManagerHome home;
      String jndiName = "ejb/bookManager";

      home = (RemoteBookManagerHome)PortableRemoteObject.narrow(
        context.lookup(jndiName), RemoteBookManagerHome.class);

      RemoteBookManager manager = home.create();
      Book book = manager.getBook(request.getParameter("isbn"));
    %>

    <h2><%= book.getTitle() %></h2>
    ... information about the chosen book here ...

  </body>

</html>
```

This example is similar to that shown earlier in that when requested, the `isbn` parameter is added to the query string telling the page which book should be displayed.

As this page illustrates, using EJBs from within JSP means that more classes have to be imported. In this example, we are importing the classes required for using JNDI and getting a reference to a remote object. In addition to this, we have a fair quantity of Java code embedded in the page just to facilitate the lookup of the remote object – even though this is just a simple example.

Using Remote Objects with Custom Tags

Once again, we are performing an action here and custom tags are a good fit. Basically, we can use a custom tag to hide all of this complexity and reduce the number of page directives that we have to use to import the required classes. In the example, there are three key pieces of information that we need to take into account when looking up the EJB home interface:

- The name of the variable with which to reference the EJB home
- The JNDI name of the EJB home
- The fully qualified class name of the EJB home

We could of course build a custom tag that locates only a specific type of EJB home by hard-coding this information. However, this isn't a very reusable solution. Instead, we could build a custom tag that is generic enough to be able to look up any type of EJB home. To do this, we simply need to externalize these key pieces of information. A simple way to do this is to customize the tag using the above as attributes.

To see how this works in practice, let's first see how such a tag can be used on the page:

```
<html>

  <head>
    <title>Professional JSP Tag Libraries</title>
  </head>

  <%@ page import="com.wrox.jsptaglibs.common.*" %>
  <%@ page import="com.wrox.jsptaglibs.ejb.*" %>
  <%@ taglib uri="/ejbTaglib" prefix="ejb" %>

  <body>

    <h1>Wrox books online</h1>

    <ejb:useRemoteBean id="home"
                       type="com.wrox.jsptaglibs.ejb.RemoteBookManagerHome"
                       jndiName="ejb/bookManager"/>

    <%
      RemoteBookManager manager = home.create();
      Book book = manager.getBook(request.getParameter("isbn"));
    %>

    <h2><%= book.getTitle() %></h2>
    ... information about the chosen book here ...

  </body>

</html>
```

We now have a single custom tag called `useRemoteBean` that is responsible for looking up the EJB home interface. In doing so, the tag introduces a variable into the page with the name that is specified by the `id` attribute. Once this action has been performed, the home interface can be used as normal and the page produces the same results.

As this new version of the page shows, there is now much less Java code, fewer page directives, and less complexity. The tag handler itself is also fairly straightforward and all that we've really done here is move the code that looked up the EJB home into the `doStartTag()` method.

Building the Tag

First of all we have the usual properties and mutator methods corresponding to the attributes that our tag will take:

```
package com.wrox.jsptaglibs.ejb;

import java.rmi.RemoteException;
import javax.rmi.PortableRemoteObject;
import javax.naming.InitialContext;
import javax.naming.NamingException;
import javax.servlet.jsp.JspException;
import javax.servlet.jsp.JspTagException;
import javax.servlet.jsp.tagext.TagSupport;

public class UseRemoteBeanTag extends TagSupport {

  private String jndiName;
  private String type;

  public void setJndiName(String s) {
    this.jndiName = s;
  }

  public void setType(String s) {
    this.type = s;
  }
```

Following this we have the `doStartTag()` method. As mentioned, this is really just the same code that was used on the JSP page to look up the EJB home through JNDI, with the exception that we are introducing the remote reference back into the page:

```
  public int doStartTag() throws JspException {
    try {
      InitialContext ctx = new InitialContext();

      Object remoteBean = null;
      Class remoteClass = Class.forName(type);

      // look up the bean, checking that it is of the type expected
      remoteBean = PortableRemoteObject.narrow(
        ctx.lookup(jndiName), remoteClass);

      // and introduce the reference into the page
      pageContext.setAttribute(id, remoteBean);
    } catch (ClassNotFoundException cnfe) {
      throw new JspTagException(cnfe.getMessage());
    } catch (NamingException ne) {
      throw new JspTagException(ne.getMessage());
    }

    // and evaluate the body
    return SKIP_BODY;
  }
}
```

Building the TagExtraInfo class

Since this tag is introducing a scripting variable into the page, we must also build the TEI class, which for completeness is as follows:

```
package com.wrox.jsptaglibs.ejb;

import javax.servlet.jsp.tagext.TagData;
import javax.servlet.jsp.tagext.TagExtraInfo;
import javax.servlet.jsp.tagext.VariableInfo;

public class UseRemoteBeanTagExtraInfo extends TagExtraInfo {

  public VariableInfo[] getVariableInfo(TagData data) {
    return new VariableInfo[] {
      new VariableInfo(data.getId(), data.getAttributeString("type"),
        true, VariableInfo.AT_BEGIN)
    }
  }
}
```

The Tag Library Descriptor

Finally, here is the TLD:

```
<?xml version="1.0" encoding="ISO-8859-1" ?>
<!DOCTYPE taglib
  PUBLIC "-//Sun Microsystems, Inc.//DTD JSP Tag Library 1.2//EN"
  "http://java.sun.com/dtd/web-jsptaglibrary_1_2.dtd">

<taglib>

  <tlib-version>1.0</tlib-version>
  <jsp-version>1.2</jsp-version>
  <short-name>ejb</short-name>

  <description>
    EJB examples for the Tag Patterns chapter.
  </description>

  <tag>
    <name>useRemoteBean</name>
    <tag-class>com.wrox.jsptaglibs.ejb.UseRemoteBeanTag</tag-class>
    <tei-class>com.wrox.jsptaglibs.ejb.UseRemoteBeanTagExtraInfo</tei-class>
    <body-content>JSP</body-content>
    <description>
      Looks up, and places into the page, a reference to a remote object.
    </description>

    <attribute>
      <name>id</name>
      <required>true</required>
      <rtexprvalue>false</rtexprvalue>
```

```
      </attribute>

      <attribute>
        <name>type</name>
        <required>true</required>
        <rtexprvalue>false</rtexprvalue>
      </attribute>

      <attribute>
        <name>jndiName</name>
        <required>true</required>
        <rtexprvalue>false</rtexprvalue>
      </attribute>
    </tag>

  </taglib>
```

In addition to wrapping up the functionality to look up a remote object into a reusable component, another benefit of this approach is that the custom tag could be extended to cache references to remote objects if necessary.

As looking up remote objects is an expensive process in terms of the associated network overhead, we could create a cache of the looked-up references and hand them out to subsequent calls instead of going back across the network. This is something that would be harder to maintain if it was embedded as a scriptlet on a JSP page – particularly if that scriptlet was copied and pasted into other pages in the application.

Accessing Enterprise JavaBeans is a good example of how enterprise resources might be used from the page. To wrap up the chapter, let's also look at how another type of resource can be accessed and subsequently used – JMS.

Using JMS

The Java Message Service (JMS) is an abstraction through which messages can be sent over Message Oriented Middleware (MOM), such as IBM MQSeries and SonicMQ. Such enterprise messaging systems have been around for a while now, although the introduction of JMS has certainly seen an increase in their usage.

JMS offers two messaging paradigms – **point-to-point** (p2p) and **publish-subscribe** (pub/sub). With p2p, messages are sent to a queue and received by a single recipient. With pub/sub, messages are published onto a topic, and can be picked up by many recipients.

> *A more in-depth look at JMS can be found in Professional JMS Programming from Wrox Press (ISBN 1-861004-93-1).*

Sending JMS Messages with Scriptlets

Sending a message to a topic with JMS requires several steps. First of all a connection to the JMS server (also known as a **provider**) is made, following which a session is created. Once we have a session on the server, a topic is then looked up through JNDI. Finally, and only once this has been done, we can use some of the other JMS specific classes to start creating and sending messages. Let's take a look at how this might be achieved with a scriptlet on a JSP page.

Since using JMS involves looking up objects through JNDI, the first thing that we have to do is import the relevant classes:

```
<html>
  <head>
    <title>Professional JSP Tag Libraries</title>
  </head>

  <%@ page import="javax.naming.Context"%>
  <%@ page import="javax.naming.InitialContext"%>
  <%@ page import="javax.jms.Message" %>
  <%@ page import="javax.jms.Session" %>
  <%@ page import="javax.jms.Topic" %>
  <%@ page import="javax.jms.TopicConnection" %>
  <%@ page import="javax.jms.TopicConnectionFactory" %>
  <%@ page import="javax.jms.TopicPublisher" %>
  <%@ page import="javax.jms.TopicSession" %>
```

Next is the body of the JSP. If we imagine that this page is invoked after a customer has purchased a book from an online store, we might wish to send a message to the department in the company that package up books and ship them out to the customer.

> **While this is not a book about J2EE design principles, JSP pages are and should only be concerned with the issues around presenting information to the user. For this reason, sending JMS messages directly from the web tier of an application is not always the best solution. Although it can be useful in small applications, a better solution is to adopt the Model 2 architecture. For the purposes of this chapter, the example here serves the purpose of illustrating how enterprise resources other than EJB can be accessed and used through a custom tag library.**

```
  <body>
    <h1>Wrox books online</h1>

    <p>
      Thank you for your order.
    </p>
```

Following this is the Java scriptlet that actually creates and sends the message. First we need to get a reference into the JNDI tree so that various objects can be looked up later on in the process:

```
    <%
      Context context = new InitialContext();
```

Next we need to get a connection to the JMS provider by looking up a `TopicConnectionFactory` through JNDI. This factory provides us with an easy way to open a connection:

```
      TopicConnectionFactory factory;
      factory =
       (TopicConnectionFactory)context.lookup("jms/TopicConnectionFactory");
        TopicConnection connection = factory.createTopicConnection();
```

With a connection started, the next step is to create a session with which we will actually create the messages:

```
      TopicSession topicSession = connection.createTopicSession(false,
                                  Session.AUTO_ACKNOWLEDGE);

      Message message = topicSession.createTextMessage("The order is ...");
```

Once a message has been created, we must then look up a topic through JNDI representing the destination to which we would like to send the message:

```
      Topic topic = (Topic)context.lookup("jms/Topic");
```

Finally, we create a publisher object from the existing session and use this to send the message before closing it and the connection down:

```
      TopicPublisher publisher = topicSession.createPublisher(topic);
      publisher.publish(message);

      topicSession.close();
      connection.close();
    %>
  </body>
</html>
```

Sending messages to queues (the p2p model) is a very similar process, but as you can see, there are several non-trivial steps to sending a JMS message. This is certainly something that the page authors probably wouldn't like to see on the page, and furthermore, including such logic on the page certainly increases the maintainability of the application should JMS messages need to be sent from other pages. Let's once again see how tags can help.

Sending JMS Messages with Tags

As custom tags wrap up reusable functionality, let's build a small tag library that makes it easy for page authors to send JMS messages. In the example that we have seen, the message that we created subsequently got sent out on a topic using the pub/sub model. To see how tags can be used to remove this type of Java code away from the page and into reusable components, let's first of all see how such a set of tags could be used:

```
<html>
  <head>
    <title>Professional JSP Tag Libraries</title>
  </head>

  <%@ taglib uri="/jmsTaglib" prefix="jms" %>

  <body>
    <h1>Wrox books online</h1>

    <p>
      Thank you for your order.
    </p>

    <jms:sendMessage topic="jms/Topic"
                     topicConnectionFactory="jms/TopicConnectionFactory">
      <jms:textMessage>The order is ...</jms:textMessage>
    </jms:sendMessage>
  </body>
</html>
```

In this example we have two tags that are cooperating on the page – `sendMessage` and `textMessage`. Here, the inner `textMessage` tag is responsible for creating the message that we would like to send using JMS, while the outer `sendMessage` tag is responsible for actually opening the connection, starting the session and sending the message.

Part of the JMS specification allows different types of messages to be sent. Examples here include text messages where the message body is simply plain text, map messages where the body of the message is name-value pairs, and byte messages where the contents of the message can be binary content such as images or serialized Java objects. For this reason, and rather than forcing only text messages to be used, we've decided to split out the process of creating the message from the process involved in sending it. Therefore, sending a different type of message simply involves using a different inner tag.

Let's see how the tags themselves can be written.

The SendMessage Tag

First of all is the `sendMessage` tag. It has two attributes that correspond to the name of the `Topic` and the `TopicConnectionFactory` respectively:

```
package com.wrox.jsptaglibs.jms;

import javax.naming.Context;
```

```
import javax.naming.InitialContext;

import javax.jms.Message;
import javax.jms.Session;
import javax.jms.Topic;
import javax.jms.TopicConnection;
import javax.jms.TopicConnectionFactory;
import javax.jms.TopicPublisher;
import javax.jms.TopicSession;

import javax.servlet.jsp.JspException;
import javax.servlet.jsp.JspTagException;
import javax.servlet.jsp.tagext.TagSupport;

public class SendMessageTag extends TagSupport {

  private String topicName;
  private String topicConnectionFactoryName;

  public void setTopic(String topic) {
    this.topicName = topic;
  }

  public void setTopicConnectionFactory(String tcf) {
    this.topicConnectionFactoryName = tcf;
  }
```

Following this are some instance variables that are used to maintain state while the tag is performing its processing. The important ones here are `session` and `message` which also have associated accessor/mutator methods – we'll be seeing why this is shortly:

```
  private Context context;
  private TopicConnection connection;
  private TopicSession session;
  private Message message;

  public Session getSession() {
    return this.session;
  }

  public void setMessage(Message message) {
    this.message = message;
  }
```

Next is the `doStartTag()` method. Since the message is built during the body content of the tag, all that this does is use a helper method to initialize the instance properties of the tag by starting the JMS connection and session:

```
  public int doStartTag() throws JspException {
    try {
      init();
    } catch (Exception e) {
```

```
        throw new JspTagException(e.getMessage());
      }

      return EVAL_BODY_INCLUDE;
    }

    private void init() throws Exception {
      context = new InitialContext();

      TopicConnectionFactory factory;
      factory = (TopicConnectionFactory)context.lookup(
        topicConnectionFactoryName);

      connection = factory.createTopicConnection();

      session = connection.createTopicSession(false,
        Session.AUTO_ACKNOWLEDGE);
    }
```

Finally is the `doEndTag()` method and, using a helper method, it's here that the message actually gets sent:

```
    public int doEndTag() throws JspException {
      try {
        sendMessage();
      } catch (Exception e) {
        throw new JspTagException(e.getMessage());
      }

      return EVAL_PAGE;
    }

    private void sendMessage() throws Exception {
      Topic topic = (Topic)context.lookup(topicName);

      TopicPublisher publisher = session.createPublisher(topic);
      publisher.publish(message);

      session.close();
      connection.close();
    }
  }
```

The TextMessage Tag

The `textMessage` tag is nested between the start and end `sendMessage` tags on the page and it is here that the content of the message to be sent is assembled. As there are various other types of JMS messages that can be created and sent, we have decided to introduce an abstract tag handler from which they can all extend:

```
package com.wrox.jsptaglibs.jms;

import javax.jms.Message;
import javax.jms.Session;

import javax.servlet.jsp.JspTagException;
import javax.servlet.jsp.JspException;
import javax.servlet.jsp.tagext.BodyTagSupport;

public abstract class MessageTag extends BodyTagSupport {
```

```
    public int doStartTag() throws JspException {
      return EVAL_BODY_BUFFERED;
    }

    public int doEndTag() throws JspException {
      try {
        SendMessageTag tag;
        tag = (SendMessageTag)findAncestorWithClass(this,
          SendMessageTag.class);
        tag.setMessage(createMessage(tag.getSession()));
      } catch (Exception e) {
        throw new JspTagException(e.getMessage());
      }

      return EVAL_PAGE;
    }

    protected abstract Message createMessage(Session session)
      throws Exception;
  }
```

This tag handler extends the `BodyTagSupport` class and therefore provides tags with the ability to capture and manipulate their body content if they wish. Once again, all of the real work is carried out in the `doEndTag()` method where, in this case, the tag finds the closest enclosing `sendMessage` tag to which it passes the JMS message that should be sent. An abstract method called `createMessage()` on this class is the source of the message and, as follows, is implemented by the `textMessage` tag:

```
package com.wrox.jsptaglibs.jms;

import javax.jms.Session;
import javax.jms.Message;

public class TextMessageTag extends MessageTag {

  protected Message createMessage(Session session) throws Exception {

    String messageText = "";

    if (bodyContent != null) {
      messageText = bodyContent.getString();
      bodyContent.clear();
    }

    return session.createTextMessage(messageText);
  }
}
```

All that this subclass does is provide an implementation of the `createMessage()` method whereby the body content of the tag is captured and used as the content to create a new JMS `TextMessage`. After this message has been created and passed back to the `sendMessage` tag, the message is sent before the JMS session and connection are closed down.

Once again we have demonstrated how some non-trivial functionality can be extracted from a JSP page and wrapped up inside a tag library. Using tags in this situation has again provided us with a more maintainable solution, but in addition to this it provides a much more usable and reusable solution. Where the useRemoteBean tag helped us to access an enterprise resource, the JMS tags that we've just built allow us to easily perform a recurring task using enterprise resources rather then just accessing them.

The Tag Library Descriptor

Here is the TLD for the above tag handler:

```
<?xml version="1.0" encoding="ISO-8859-1" ?>
<!DOCTYPE taglib
  PUBLIC "-//Sun Microsystems, Inc.//DTD JSP Tag Library 1.2//EN"
  "http://java.sun.com/dtd/web-jsptaglibrary_1_2.dtd">

<taglib>

  <tlib-version>1.0</tlib-version>
  <jsp-version>1.2</jsp-version>
  <short-name>jms</short-name>
  <description>
    JMS examples for the Tag Patterns chapter.
  </description>

  <tag>
    <name>sendMessage</name>
    <tag-class>com.wrox.jsptaglibs.jms.SendMessageTag</tag-class>
    <body-content>JSP</body-content>
    <description>
      Sends a text message to a JMS queue or topic.
    </description>

    <attribute>
      <name>topic</name>
      <required>true</required>
      <rtexprvalue>false</rtexprvalue>
    </attribute>

    <attribute>
      <name>topicConnectionFactory</name>
      <required>true</required>
      <rtexprvalue>false</rtexprvalue>
    </attribute>
  </tag>

  <tag>
    <name>textMessage</name>
    <tag-class>com.wrox.jsptaglibs.jms.TextMessageTag</tag-class>
    <body-content>JSP</body-content>
    <description>
      Creates a JMS text message.
    </description>
  </tag>

</taglib>
```

Rules of Thumb

Looking at these examples has once again shown us that we can gain improvements in the maintainability and readability of our pages. However, something else that we have concluded is that introducing a reusable component is a good way to implement performance improvements. Building a reusable tag means that any enhancements to the tag are immediately available to those pages that make use of the tag.

Something else that we've not yet considered is that the `useRemoteBean` tag doesn't just have to be used to look up EJB home references. We're using JNDI to locate a remote object but haven't actually specified that the remote object must be an EJB. Other objects that are usually stored and made available through JNDI include:

- `javax.sql.DataSource` objects representing connections to persistent data stores such as relational databases
- `javax.jms.Topic` and `javax.jms.Queue` objects representing the destinations to which JMS (Java Message Service) messages can be sent to and received from

From a conceptual point of view, these types of objects are different to the EJB home interface that we saw before. Where the EJB home interface was a way of accessing functionality provided by that EJB, these objects represent resources used within J2EE applications. Looking them up through JNDI is still performed in the same way, but the way in which they are used is different. To use an example, sending a message to a topic with JMS requires several steps. First of all a connection to the JMS server (provider) is made, following which a session is created. Once we have a session on the server, a topic is then looked up through JNDI. Finally, and only once this has been done, we can use some of the other JMS-specific classes to start creating and sending messages.

Although wrapping the lookup for a remote object into a custom tag is useful, only programmers familiar with JMS will know about the other steps required to send a message. In this scenario it is often a good idea to look at the audience for your tags.

If the tags are to potentially be used by anybody involved in the project regardless of whether they are familiar with Java and JMS, then it is probably best to wrap up all of the steps required to send a message into a single `sendMessage` tag. On the other hand, if it is just Java developers that will be writing the page it is still worth wrapping up the functionality into custom tags. If a certain degree of flexibility is required then writing a series of tags to wrap up each small step in the process is still useful. After all, the benefits of moving code out from the page and into reusable components still apply – maintainability is increased and development time is decreased.

Where performing iterations on the page is a fairly simple task that is easy to understand, accessing and using enterprise resources is somewhat more complex. For this reason, it will probably be the case that only Java developers will ever write and maintain these sorts of pages. If this is the case, the tags can be finer grained and more aligned to the steps involved in the process.

Recommendations

Walking through the examples in this chapter has provided several different perspectives on the use of custom tags and additionally, some rules of thumb. Moving code embedded in JSP pages into reusable custom tags is certainly something to be recommended for reasons of maintainability, readability, and the potential for decreasing the time taken to build a web application. There are various ways in which this can be achieved, and therefore some recommendations are useful.

In general, it is recommended that the tags themselves represent fairly coarse-grained actions. We saw this with the iteration example where combining the steps associated with performing the iteration and getting the next element was wrapped up into a single tag. This not only provides a more natural interface, but is also easier to use on the page.

A side effect of making tags coarse-grained is that it shields the page from the inner workings of the individual steps involved. If we wanted to use a different method of iteration, using just a single `iterate` tag would mean that only the tag itself would have to be modified. If separate tags were used to represent the individual steps, this would probably mean more work in changing the tags and the pages on which they were used. Introducing more work is not what tags are about.

Summary

The focus of this chapter has not been so much on how to build tags, but rather how tags can best be used on the page. The purpose of this chapter was to look at some of the common uses for tags, and to start off we looked at how design and J2EE patterns are relevant, in particular by looking at the View Helper pattern.

View Helpers can be implemented using JavaBeans or custom tags, so the next thing that we looked at was a discussion of when to use JavaBeans and when to use custom tags to wrap up such functionality. In doing so, we looked at some of the key characteristics of both technologies and, by taking a look behind the scenes, managed to deduce some rules of thumb.

JavaBeans are long-lived, environment-independent components and are best used for representing information that is required in the web tier – be it session information or information from a persistent data source. Custom tags, on the other hand, are short-lived, container-managed components and are therefore best used to represent actions that occur on the page. This includes, for example, generating dynamic content, manipulating the data represented by JavaBeans, accessing EJBs and using JMS.

Custom tags are best used to reduce the Java code present in JSP pages – code that is usually used to perform actions or process information stored using JavaBeans. Another way to look at it is that custom tags are the glue between the JSP pages, JavaBeans, and other resources.

Throughout all of the examples in this chapter there has been a common theme – removing the scriptlets out of the page and into reusable components. Java code in the page is something that we should really try to avoid if possible for several reasons. First of all there is the maintainability aspect. Having Java code on a JSP page promotes a copy and paste style of reuse. This means that should the logic require a change or bug fix further down the line, all occurrences of the code must be changed.

Another reason why it is a good idea to move Java code out of the page is that everybody involved in the development of a JSP-based web application may not be familiar with Java. A good example here is web designers that are responsible for the look and feel of the site. Having a long, seemingly complex page containing lots of Java source code may not only confuse them, but also will probably make their job of transforming the page into a creative masterpiece more difficult.

While looking at the example uses of custom tags, some interesting rules of thumb were introduced. Tags can be built to represent any type of action that is performed on a JSP page. For this reason, some thought should go into how the tag will be used and who will be using it.

As developers, we are much more aware that actions are often made up of one or more smaller steps. With this in mind, developing tags that represent these smaller actions is easily done and while it may remove the Java code from the page, the complexities associated with performing each step may still be exposed to the page. We saw an example of this when looking at how an HTML select control can be generated. Instead of using tags to perform each of the steps associated with generating the control, we built a single tag that wrapped up the entire action. Making tags represent coarse-grained actions provides a more natural interface making the page much more readable by everybody involved in development.

The next chapter looks at some of the design issues around custom tags, including some recommendations for how the issues around mixing content and presentation can be addressed.

LONDON

9

Designing Tags and Tag Libraries

While looking at how to build custom tags, a common underlying theme throughout many of the chapters in this book has been about the best practices associated with tag development. This chapter opens up this discussion further to include best practices relating to the design and development of tags and tag libraries. The topics that we'll be looking at in this chapter include:

- How OO design applies to tags and tag libraries
- How the expected audience affects the design and naming of tags
- How to separate content and presentation
- How to build tags that support static (translation-time) or dynamic (request-time) values for attributes

To wrap up the chapter, we'll take a look at some general best practices for custom tag development by focusing on the tag lifecycle and performance.

What Makes a Good Tag Library?

One of the first questions that we'll tackle in this chapter is: what makes a good tag library? Custom tags are an extremely flexible feature of the JSP specification and this flexibility means that almost any JSP functionality can be built using them. In designing a good tag library, ultimately there are several factors to take into account, including granularity and the end-user.

One of the key factors in designing a good tag library is to think about how the tags will be used on the page. Like HTML, JSP pages use the concept of tags to make up the page. The syntax may be different, but from this perspective, tags can simply be thought of as page elements. However, they are really more than this. In JSP pages, tags are the building blocks that allow page authors to write complex pages by assembling tags in the correct order. These tags provide an abstraction that the page author can make use of, an example here being the HTML tag that allows text to be rendered in a bold typeface. Custom tags can replicate this type of behavior but of course they can do much more than this. From this perspective, custom tags are reusable software components.

Component-based development (CBD) is still a relatively new methodology for designing software systems where instead of decomposing the system down into objects, you break it down into components. These components are subsequently broken down into their constituent objects, but the components become the building blocks of the system through the interfaces that they provide. When talking about JSP, custom tags can be viewed as the building blocks of the page or, in other words, the components of which it is made. After all, the page authors use the tags, and the tags provide a well-defined interface, although behind the scenes they may well consist or one or more objects.

Whether looking at CBD or OO development, there are several important factors to good design. One of these is reusability which has been a common theme throughout the preceding chapters. The key to a good tag library is identifying opportunities for reuse. This can be on several levels.

Of course, reusability on the code and class level is always a good thing and something that we are always on the lookout for. However well a tag library meets its specific objectives, it will be even better if it can be reused. Here, we can look for reuse of tags between the pages in an individual web application, or even between different web applications, and hence projects, in an organization. So how do we go about making sure that the tags and tag libraries that we build are reusable?

Object-Oriented Design Principles

A good object can be described as one that has **high cohesion** and **low coupling**. In other words, a good object is one that performs a targeted set of functionality (it is cohesive) while having few, if any, dependencies on other objects (it isn't tightly coupled).

The benefits of designing loosely coupled objects include being able to reuse them in conjunction with other objects through **composition**. With composition, objects are simply used together to provide some specialized functionality, and typically this functionality is provided through a simplified interface or façade. Other important benefits include increased maintainability and improved quality. So how does this translate to custom tag design?

OO Design Principles Translated to Custom Tags

OO design principles are just as relevant to building custom tags as they are to regular component and OO-based solutions. What we're saying here is that custom tags should also be highly cohesive and loosely coupled.

Like objects, tags should be small reusable building blocks from which to build web applications. One difference here between designing objects and designing tags is that objects are generally built with developers as the target audience.

However, while custom tags can be built for the same audience, their remit is much wider in that they can be designed solely for use by non-programmer page authors whose job it is to concentrate on the look and feel of the JSP pages rather than how they work behind the scenes. This difference in audience also brings about an interesting point about how tags can and should be designed. We'll be looking at this shortly.

Despite these differences in audience, one thing that does carry over to the world of custom tags is that tags should also be able to be reused in conjunction with other tags through composition. A good example here is a tag that provides iteration on a JSP page. Such a tag is an ideal candidate for reuse through composition because there are so many places and scenarios in which a generic iteration tag can be used in conjunction with other tags, and additionally, other scripting elements in the page.

One final point to mention is that inheritance is just as useful when building tag handlers as it is when building regular Java classes. Tag handlers are generally fairly small, simple classes and the use of this powerful OO feature is often forgotten. Inheritance can provide a quicker way to build collections of related tags such as those with a large number of common attributes. In addition to reducing effort, there are also the benefits of increased maintainability and quality.

OO Design Principles Translated to Tag Libraries

So we've looked at how OO principles apply equally well to tags, but what about tag libraries? How do we design a good tag library?

In essence, the same principles apply here too. Tag libraries should provide a focused suite of functionality (highly cohesive), while at the same time not being dependent on many (ideally any) other tag libraries by having as few external dependencies as possible (loosely coupled).

As an abstraction, consider the following. We've already said that tags are reusable software components, and if we carry this abstraction forward, we can say that tag libraries are really a grouping for such components – they are the packages in which those components reside. Ideally, these packages should only contain related tags.

To put it another way and use an analogy, we can think of tags as Java classes and tag libraries as Java packages. Once again, and like the core Java packages, each package groups together a related set of classes to form a cohesive collection.

When building Java solutions, ideally we aim to maximize reuse at both the class and package levels, which translated to tags means that we should look for reusability at the tag and tag library levels. This actually turns out to be a good analogy, and applying the same principles to tag development as you do when designing regular Java systems is a good basis on which to design tags and tag libraries.

Having loosely coupled tag libraries permits reuse in isolation. For example, you may have a tag library that deals with collections (for example several ways of iterating over them), or perhaps a tag library for dealing with remote objects such as Enterprise JavaBeans. Splitting these disparate sets of functionality into separate tag libraries means that it is possible to use and reuse them independently of other tag libraries. Of course, the danger here is having too many small tag libraries, each with a very small number of tags. For this reason, try to be pragmatic when determining the contents of a tag library.

As a rule of thumb, somewhere between four and eight tags in a tag library seems a good starting point, but of course it does depend on the requirements.

Tags as Proxies to Existing Functionality

One final thing to mention about designing tags is that they are JSP-specific. When you implement tag handlers, you build Java classes that make use of the `Tag` interface, and subsequently have access to the infrastructure that is a part of the JSP specification. For this reason, custom tags are really only useful within a JSP environment. In fact, the fact that tags know about their environment is one of the key reasons for using them over regular JavaBeans.

However, there may be times where the functionality that you wish to use has already been wrapped up as a JavaBean, or simply that the functionality might be better placed into a JavaBean. Examples here include a third party library, or perhaps you are building presentation layer logic that you wish to use over multiple presentation layers such as JSP, Swing, and web services. In this situation, and rather than reinventing the wheel, it might be more appropriate to wrap up the functionality as JavaBeans and simply provide a JSP-specific proxy for that functionality through custom tags. Since custom tags are JSP-specific, wrapping up functionality inside environment-independent components such as JavaBeans means that the functionality can easily be used from other presentation technologies that aren't reliant on JSP-specific features.

Now that we've looked at some of the principles of designing good tags and tag libraries, let's now look at how the audience can affect the end result.

Remember Your Audience

As mentioned, building tags can be quite different from regular component-based development because of the potentially different audience that is involved. Where we might build components for use by other developers, there are often many people in different roles that are involved in building web applications.

First of all there are the developers that figure out how the web site will work and put it together from a "behind the scenes" perspective. As developers, we are used to programming and are also used to the types of fine-grained actions that are generally required to perform all but the simplest of tasks.

In addition to the developers, there might be a team of web designers that help put the site together from a "look and feel" perspective. These people may not be as programming-savvy as the developers but certainly have the edge when it comes to turning dull HTML pages into creative masterpieces.

Potentially, any custom tags that we build will be used by both of these types of people. The involvement of these two different sets of end users raises some interesting questions over the granularity of the tags. It is always better to be on the safe side, which means that it is better to build tags that will be useful and understood by people that are not as proficient in Java programming as we might be even though it may involve some overheads.

Let's consider an HTML select list that is rendered by the browser as a drop-down list. This is effectively a list of HTML `<option>` tags, wrapped inside a `<select>` tag. Generating such lists based upon a collection of objects is fairly trivial but of course there are a couple of ways that it can be done. First of all, we could just build up the list by using an `iterate` tag to iterate over a collection. In doing this, we would build up each option individually as follows:

```
<select name="isbn">
  <%
    Collection books = BookManager.getInstance().getBooksAsCollection();
  %>

  <iteration:iterate id="book"
                     type="com.wrox.jsptaglibs.common.Book"
                     collection="<%= books %>">

    <option value="<jsp:getProperty name="book" property="isbn"/>">
      <jsp:getProperty name="book" property="title"/>
    </option>

  </iteration:iterate>
</select>
```

This does work but represents the sort of fine-grained actions that developers are generally used to, where the list is built up one row at a time. To somebody who is less technical, this might not seem logical and this, therefore, makes the page harder to understand and to maintain. A better solution in this scenario is to build a custom tag that generates the entire select list:

```
<%
  Collection books = BookManager.getInstance().getBooksAsCollection();
%>

<html:select name="isbn" label="title" value="isbn"
             collection="<%= books %>"/>
```

The tag now encapsulates all of the functionality required to generate the drop-down list and consequently is now fairly coarse-grained. However, from a usability perspective it is now much easier to use and requires less effort on the part of the person putting together the page.

Custom tags are there to wrap up this sort of reusable functionality, but they also reduce effort, and save time. If more flexibility is required, breaking down the single `select` tag into a collection of smaller, cooperating tags is a good solution although it does introduce more tags and increases the future maintenance effort. At the end of the day, think about who is going to be using your tag libraries and use this to influence how the tags are designed and built.

Naming Conventions

The final point to look at in this section is that of naming conventions. In the discussion of whether to use custom tags or JavaBeans to wrap up reusable functionality in Chapter 8, one of the conclusions made was that tags are best suited to performing actions on the page. As such, it was recommended that tags be named after these actions, or as verbs. The standard `<jsp:useBean/>` tag is a good example, with another being a tag that performs iteration could be named `iterate` rather than `iterator`.

Naming tags after actions tends to make the page on which they are used easier to read and understand. Of course there may be times where such a naming convention isn't appropriate, again, because of the intended audience of the tag. An example here is the `select` tag that we've just seen. This could have been named `generateSelectList` although `select` is more meaningful to people familiar with building HTML pages. Be pragmatic and try to choose a name that best expresses the intent of the tags, again, taking into account the potential audience.

As demonstrated by the earlier examples, the tag handler classes have generally been named following regular Java naming conventions. For example, the tag handler that performs iteration is called `IteratorTag`. As only those people that maintain the tags will ever see this name, it could be called anything. The name that is assigned to the tag in the TLD is much more important. After all, it's by using this name that page authors will make use of the tag and choosing a good name can really help to clarify the purpose and meaning on the JSP page on which it is being used.

Now that we've looked at some of the theoretical sides to designing custom tags, let's turn our focus to some development practices, starting with a discussion on how content and presentation can be kept separate when building them.

Content and Presentation

As some of the early examples in the book illustrate, it is very easy to mix together content (what we are displaying) with the presentation (how we are displaying it). Mixing content and presentation is all too easy to do because it is easy for custom tags to generate HTML dynamically.

Let's demonstrate this with a tag similar to the `<file:size/>` example as discussed in Chapter 4:

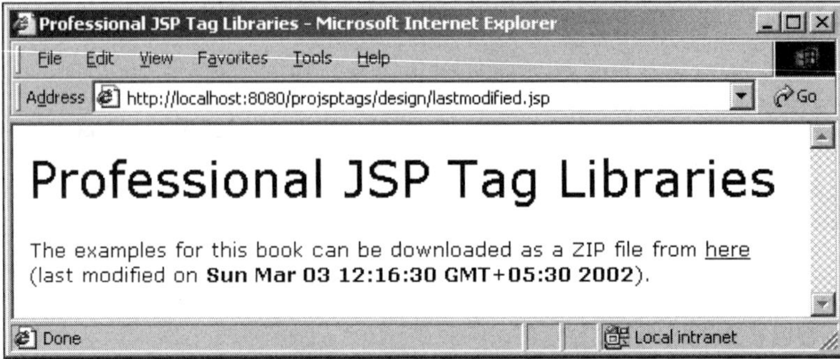

In this example, we simply have a message with a hyperlink to download a file. Following this is the date that the file was last modified as a useful aid to help the user decide whether they wish to actually download the file or not. The relevant part of this JSP page is as follows:

```
<%@ taglib uri="/fileTaglib" prefix="file" %>

The examples for this book can be downloaded as a ZIP file from
<a href="examples.zip">here</a>

(<file:lastModified file="/examples.zip"/>).
```

Here, we have a simple custom tag called `lastModified` that generates a small snippet of HTML indicating the last modified date of the specified file:

```
package com.wrox.jsptaglibs.file;

import java.io.File;
import java.io.IOException;
import java.util.Date;

import javax.servlet.jsp.JspException;
import javax.servlet.jsp.JspTagException;
import javax.servlet.jsp.JspWriter;
import javax.servlet.jsp.tagext.TagSupport;

public class FileLastModifiedTag extends TagSupport {

  private String file;

  public int doStartTag() throws JspException {
    // ask the container (via the servlet context) for the
    // real path of the file
    String realPath = pageContext.getServletContext().getRealPath(file);

    // we can now find out when the file was last modified
    File f = new File(realPath);
    Date lastModified = new Date(f.lastModified());

    // and generate some dynamic content
    try {
      JspWriter out = pageContext.getOut();
      out.write("last modified on <b>" + lastModified + "</b>");
    } catch (IOException ioe) {
      throw new JspTagException(ioe.getMessage());
    }

    return SKIP_BODY;
  }

  public void setFile(String s) {
    this.file = s;
  }
}
```

This example clearly demonstrates the mixing of content (the last modified date of the file) and its presentation. While the content is determined at run-time, the presentation of that content is hard-coded into the tag handler, in this case by wrapping up the last modified date of the file in HTML bold tags and by simply using the default formatting of that date.

There are several problems with this. The first of these is that we've reduced the maintainability of the tag handler because we would have to modify, recompile, and redeploy the tag handler should we wish to change some feature of the tag due to a change in requirements. Leading on from this, the tag handler is now also less reusable.

After all, this tag can't be used to display the last modified date of a file in a more readable format because the presentation has been hard-coded. Additionally, the tag can't be reused to show a different style or message since this too has been hard-coded into the tag. Meeting all of these potential requirements would mean either different tags, or modification followed by recompilation, and redeployment. Either way, some rework is necessary.

Fortunately there are several ways in which such issues can be addressed, so let's take a look at them in turn.

Externalizing the Style

If a tag does need to generate dynamic content (for example HTML) that includes embedded styles, one solution to the problem of hard-coding the style element is to externalize it using Cascading Style Sheets (CSS). Instead of generating HTML that includes references to the bold tag, we could instead output references to a CSS style with the HTML `<span>` tag:

```
<span class="dateStyle">...</span>
```

Now that we're only using references to a particular style, the actual implementation of that style can vary from page to page, and application to application. This does go some way to solving the problem but it is a little inconvenient to have a different style sheet for each page that needs it. In addition to this, the presentation of the content is still hard-coded in terms of the message and the formatting.

The best way in which this tag can be made reusable is if it doesn't include any presentation at all. In some cases, such as tags that generate HTML form controls, this will not be possible in which case using external styles will certainly help to increase the reusability. The next question is, therefore: how can the presentation be externalized?

Externalizing the Presentation

Basically, removing the presentation from custom tags implies that the JSP page will be generating all of the dynamic content. In reality, this is what they were designed for in the first place and is a much better alternative to having tags generating reams and reams of HTML.

There are several ways in which the presentation can be externalized: one solution is that the custom tag only determines the last modified date of the file. With this in mind, the usage of such a tag on the page could then be as follows, where the bold tags and message have been moved back into the JSP page:

```
<%@ taglib uri="/fileTaglib" prefix="file" %>

  The examples for this book can be downloaded as a ZIP file from
  <a href="examples.zip">here</a>

  (last modified on <b><file:lastModified file="/examples.zip"/></b>).
```

This partially addresses the issue but does leave a problem in that it still assumes that a default format will be used to actually display the date. There are a couple of solutions here. First of all, the tag could use an attribute so that the page author specifies the format in which the date should be output:

```
(last modified on <b><file:lastModified file="/examples.zip"
                                       format="dd-MMM-yyyy"/></b>).
```

This is a good solution but is inefficient if the last modified date of the file is needed and used more than once on the page. An alternative solution here is to have the `lastModified` tag store the raw value of the file in the page context as an attribute, or to introduce a scripting variable (as discussed in Chapter 4) into the page. Scriptlets or expressions can then be used to generate the appropriate content as follows:

```
<file:lastModified file="/examples.zip">
  (last modified on <b><%= lastModified %></b>).
</file:lastModified>
```

Of course, cooperating tags can also be used in this situation, demonstrating how tags can be reused in composition:

```
<file:lastModified file="/examples.zip">
  (last modified on
  <b>
    <attributes:date format="dd-MMM-yyyy" date="<%= lastModified %>"/>
  </b>).
</file:lastModified>
```

Rules of Thumb

As we've seen, there are many different ways in which content and presentation can be separated when building custom tags. As a rule of thumb, use technologies like CSS when mixing content and presentation is inevitable. A good example here is the tag that we saw a short while ago that generated an HTML select list. In this example, we can't get away from the tag generating some HTML.

If the presentation of the generated content is more complex than simple styles can address, consider having the tags only determine the content rather than presenting it. Instead, leave the presentation to the JSP page and let the tags place values into the page context or as scripting variables into the page. This way, the JSP page is free to use the values as it pleases.

Attributes

Attributes are an essential part of custom tags and without them tags would be relegated to performing simple tasks. With attributes playing such an important role, let's look at a couple of good practices associated with using them.

Optional Attributes

Tag attributes can be defined in the TLD as being optional or required. For tags to work properly in this situation, it is important that default values are provided for those attributes that are optional. There are several ways in which this can be implemented.

If we remember the date tag examples that we saw in Chapter 2, one of the implementations had two optional attributes – one called `format` that represented the format in which the date should be displayed to the user, and one called `date` that represented a specific `java.util.Date` instance that should be displayed:

```
package com.wrox.jsptaglibs.date;

import java.text.DateFormat;
import java.text.SimpleDateFormat;
import java.util.Date;
import java.util.Locale;

import javax.servlet.jsp.JspException;
import javax.servlet.jsp.JspTagException;
import javax.servlet.jsp.tagext.TagSupport;

public class DateTag3 extends TagSupport {

  private String format;

  private Date date;

  public int doStartTag() throws JspException {

    DateFormat df;
    Date d;

    if (this.format != null) {
      // use the specified date format
      df = new SimpleDateFormat(format);
    } else {
      // get the locale of the client and create an appropriate date format
      Locale loc = pageContext.getRequest().getLocale();
      df = DateFormat.getDateInstance(DateFormat.MEDIUM, loc);
    }

    // and use a default date (now) if one has not been set
    if (this.date != null) {
      d = this.date;
    } else {
      d = new Date();
    }

    try {
      // and write out the formatted date to the page
      pageContext.getOut().write(df.format(d));
    } catch (java.io.IOException ioe) {
      throw new JspTagException(ioe.getMessage());
    }

    // and skip evaluating the body of the tag (as there shouldn't be one)
    return SKIP_BODY;
  }
```

```
    public void setFormat(String format) {
      this.format = format;
    }

    public void setDate(Date date) {
      this.date = date;
    }
  }
```

As we can see from the tag handler, when the `format` and `date` variables are declared, they are not assigned a value and start life as `null`. If the attributes are not specified on the page, the mutator methods aren't called and therefore the value of the instance variables do not change. Following on from this, the processing in the `doStartTag()` method checks for `null` values and assigns a default if necessary.

This is just one way that default values can be provided, and in this case is appropriate because the default value for the `format` attribute will change depending on the locale of the client, while the value of the `date` attribute will vary upon each and every request. With a number of optional attributes, checking the values this way could eventually lead to a very bloated `doStartTag()` method. A better way to provide defaults for values is to implement an accessor method for the property:

```
    public DateFormat getFormat() {
      if (this.format != null) {
        // use the specified date format
        return = new SimpleDateFormat(format);
      } else {
        // get the locale of the client and create an appropriate date format
        Locale loc = pageContext.getRequest().getLocale();
        return DateFormat.getDateInstance(DateFormat.MEDIUM, loc);
      }
    }

    public Date getDate() {
      if (this.date != null) {
        return this.date;
      } else {
        return new Date();
      }
    }
```

This helps to remove code that isn't directly related to the processing of the tag out of the `doStartTag()` method.

For reasons relating to tag pooling which we'll see later on in the chapter, setting such dynamic values for attributes is not possible in, for example, the constructor of the tag handler. However, if such a dynamic default value isn't required, there are other ways to provide a default value. If we were building a tag to implement a `for` loop, we would probably have an optional attribute to allow the page author to specify the starting index. In the majority of cases, however, the value of the starting index would be zero. Since the mutator method for the attribute is never called, one way to provide a default value is to assign one when the variable is declared:

```
private int from = 0;
```

Another way is to specify it in the default, no arguments constructor:

```
public ForTag() {
  this.from = 0;
}
```

Alternatively, the default value could be supplied externally and customized at deployment time. Unfortunately, in the current version of the JSP specification, there is nowhere in the TLD file (for example a <default> element in the <attribute> stanza) where default values can be specified.

One workaround is to supply such values in a regular `java.util.Properties` file, or even to use initialization parameters in the servlet context, defined in the web application deployment descriptor (`web.xml`). We'll be seeing how this can be achieved when we look at deployment in the next chapter. Either way, specifying default values externally (where appropriate) means that tags don't have to be modified, recompiled, and redeployed.

Attribute Overloading

Throughout the examples in the book, we've seen how tags can have attributes that either take translation-time values or request-time values. What we've not seen is a situation where we can best make use of an attribute that will accept both types of values of varying types. Allowing both types of attributes to be used increases the flexibility of that tag's usage on the page, and in effect widens the interface provided by that tag and makes it easier to use on the page.

Chapter 2 illustrated that we can declare an attribute to take a `boolean` value:

```
public void setAttribute1(boolean attr);
```

Then, in the TLD, we can specify that a request-time expression can be used as the value for it:

```
<rtexprvalue>true</rtexprvalue>
```

In this situation, both of the following are valid:

```
<prefix:tag attribute1="true"/>
```

```
<% boolean b = true; %>
<prefix:tag attribute1="<%= b %>"/>
```

This works because automatic type translation is applied to the static value of `"true"` in the first example, although the important point here is that both examples are passing a Boolean value to the tag handler. As an example of where this automatic translation can't be applied, let's look at the `iterate` tag again where we might want an attribute called `collection` so that the page author can pass through the `java.util.Collection` over which the tag should iterate:

```
package com.wrox.jsptaglibs.iteration;

import java.util.Collection;
import java.util.Iterator;

import javax.servlet.jsp.JspException;
import javax.servlet.jsp.tagext.TagSupport;

public class IteratorTag extends TagSupport {

  private String type;
  private Collection collection;

  private Iterator iterator;

  public int doStartTag() throws JspException {
    // setup the iterator to be used
    iterator = collection.iterator();

    if (iterator.hasNext()) {
      // if there are elements, put the first one into the
      // page under the name provided by the "id" attribute
      pageContext.setAttribute(getId(), iterator.next());

      // and include the body
      return EVAL_BODY_INCLUDE;
    } else {
      // there are no elements so skip the body
      return SKIP_BODY;
    }
  }

  public int doAfterBody() throws JspException {
    if (iterator.hasNext()) {
      // if there are more elements, put the next one into the
      // page under the name provided by the "id" attribute
      pageContext.setAttribute(getId(), iterator.next());

      // and instruct the JSP engine to re-evaluate the body of this tag
      return EVAL_BODY_AGAIN;
    } else {
      // there are no more elements so skip the body
      return SKIP_BODY;
    }
  }

  public void setType(String s) {
    this.type = s;
  }

  public void setCollection(Collection coll) {
    this.collection = coll;
  }
}
```

Assuming that we once again use the Book and BookManager classes from earlier chapters, the tag would have to be used in conjunction with a request-time expression as follows:

```
<%
  Collection books = BookManager.getInstance().getBooksAsCollection();
%>

<iteration:iterate id="book"
                   type="com.wrox.jsptaglibs.common.Book"
                   collection="<%= books %>">
  ... body content to be iterated over ...
</iteration:iterate>
```

As we've seen, there is nothing wrong in doing this and it's something that we've had to do time and time again in many of the examples in the previous chapters. However, what if the collection is already available, not as a scripting variable, but as an attribute in the page context? One way to make use of this pre-existing collection is to simply extract it from the page context and pass it to the tag:

```
<%
  Collection books = (Collection)pageContext.findAttribute("myBooks");
%>

<iteration:iterate id="book"
                   type="com.wrox.jsptglibs.common.Book"
                   collection="<%= books %>">
  ... body content to be iterated over ...
</iteration:iterate>
```

Again, this works but it is a little messy. A cleaner way would be to simply pass the tag the name of the attribute and let it look up the collection itself:

```
<iteration:iterate id="book"
                   type="com.wrox.jsptaglibs.common.Book"
                   collection="myBooks">
  ... body content to be iterated over ...
</iteration:iterate>
```

This is an example of where automatic type conversion doesn't work. After all, there's no way that the string "myBooks" can be automatically converted to a java.util.Collection instance, and there's nothing behind the scenes to automatically grab the appropriate object out of the page context. This is made apparent by the following error message that is shown when this is attempted with Tomcat:

Unable to convert string 'myBooks' to class java.util.Collection for attribute collection

In an attempt to provide such functionality, let's consider a solution that, at first glance, seems to provide us with a workaround. As the JSP page is trying to find the correct method to call, an easy way around this problem is to simply overload the mutator method:

```
public void setCollection(Collection collectionReference) { ... }
public void setCollection(String collectionReference) { ... }
```

However, the mutator methods that are used to set the values of attributes on custom tags must follow the JavaBeans specification. This means that they must be named appropriately, although another subtle point made in the JSP specification is that the JavaBeans introspection mechanism can be used to find these mutator methods.

Although it is currently unclear in the JavaBeans specification, this does tend to imply that a property can only have a single pair of accessor and mutator methods. What this means is that our overloaded mutator methods break the specification and are therefore something that may not work.

> **Providing multiple implementations of the mutator methods does currently work on some vendors' JSP containers but is something that is not standard nor guaranteed to work in the future. For this reason, and for compliance with the specification, you should not do this in your own tag handlers.**

In the search for another solution, the one thing that `java.lang.String` and `java.util.Collection` have in common is that they both extend `java.lang.Object` and we can use this to our advantage. Instead of defining the mutator method for the `collection` attribute to take a `Collection` as a parameter, we can redefine the tag as follows:

```
package com.wrox.jsptaglibs.iteration;

import java.util.Iterator;
import java.util.Collection;

import javax.servlet.jsp.JspException;
import javax.servlet.jsp.tagext.TagSupport;

public class IteratorTag extends TagSupport {

  private String type;
  private Object collectionReference;

  private Iterator iterator;

  public int doStartTag() throws JspException {
    // setup the iterator to be used
    iterator = getCollection().iterator();

    if (iterator.hasNext()) {
      // if there are elements, put the first one into the
      // page under the name provided by the "id" attribute
      pageContext.setAttribute(getId(), iterator.next());

      // and include the body
      return EVAL_BODY_INCLUDE;
    } else {
      // there are no elements so skip the body
      return SKIP_BODY;
    }
  }
```

```
    public int doAfterBody() throws JspException {
      if (iterator.hasNext()) {
        // if there are more elements, put the next one into the
        // page under the name provided by the "id" attribute
        pageContext.setAttribute(getId(), iterator.next());

        // and instruct the JSP engine to re-evaluate the body of this tag
        return EVAL_BODY_AGAIN;
      } else {
        // there are no more elements so skip the body
        return SKIP_BODY;
      }
    }

    public void setType(String s) {
      this.type = s;
    }

    public void setCollection(Object o) {
      this.collectionReference = o;
    }
```

We've now changed the `setCollection()` method to take an `Object` parameter and following this, we can once again write an accessor method for the attribute that does all of the hard work for us:

```
    public Collection getCollection() {
      if (collectionReference instanceof Collection) {
        return (Collection)collectionReference;
      } else {
        String name = collectionReference.toString();
        return (Collection)pageContext.findAttribute(name);
      }
    }
  }
```

With the tag handler modified we can use it on the page with a request-time expression as before, or a string specifying the name of the attribute to use in the page context. Either way, all that is happening behind the scenes is that the static `String` value is being converted to a `java.lang.Object` – a special automatic type conversion.

Handling Exceptions

One thing that we've not looked at in great detail so far is how best to handle exceptions. When writing Java code, we can, and often must, wrap up blocks of code that could throw an exception inside a `try-catch` block. If an exception is thrown inside the `try` block, the code inside the `catch` block is subsequently executed. Following this, and regardless of whether an exception occurred, the `finally` block is executed. This is a great mechanism and one that we should still use within the tag handlers that we write. After all, if an exception happens within a tag, we should still make an effort to recover. If this isn't possible, throwing a `JspTagException` is a good way to signal to the JSP container that a tag-related exception has occurred.

However, the way that tags are used on the page presents an interesting question on how exceptions can best be handled. Let's revisit how a tag handler is used on the page by looking at the code that is generated when a JSP page is translated into a servlet. For clarity, this example shows a simple tag – one that doesn't implement the IterationTag or BodyTag interfaces:

```
... start of page ...

SomeTag t = ... get tag handler instance from pool ...
t.setPageContext(pageContext);
t.setParent(null);

// set attributes through mutator methods
t.setAttribute1(...);
t.setAttributeN(...);

try {
  if (t.doStartTag() != javax.servlet.jsp.tagext.Tag.SKIP_BODY) {
    ... body content would be here ...
  }

  if (t.doEndTag() == javax.servlet.jsp.tagext.Tag.SKIP_PAGE) {
    return;
  }
} finally {
  ... return tag handler instance back to pool ...
}

... end of page ...
```

As this prototypical example illustrates, most of the tag handler-related code, including the evaluation of the tag's body content, is wrapped up inside a try-catch block. This means that although we can put individual try-catch blocks inside the methods of a tag handler, the JSP container ultimately has control over what happens if an exception is thrown.

In this example, an exception that is thrown from the doStartTag() method would cause the evaluation of the body content and the doEndTag() method to be skipped, before the code in the finally block is executed. At least in this situation we could place some code in the doStartTag() method to catch and handle the exception.

However, an exception that is thrown from the body content of the tag is completely out of our hands because the tag has no way of knowing about it or catching it. This is not good, especially if an expensive resource such as a file or a connection is currently open because we have no way of knowing about the exception and, therefore, cannot close the resource. Fortunately there is now a solution as of JSP 1.2.

The TryCatchFinally Interface

New for the JSP 1.2 specification is an interface called TryCatchFinally. It is separate from the Tag, IterationTag, and BodyTag interfaces and therefore can be implemented by any tag handler that we write, regardless of its type:

```
package javax.servlet.jsp.tagext;

import javax.servlet.jsp.*;

public interface TryCatchFinally {

  void doCatch(Throwable t) throws Throwable;

  void doFinally();
}
```

The `TryCatchFinally` interface has two methods called `doCatch()` and `doFinally()` in which we can place functionality that might typically be written into `catch` and `finally` blocks. For example, in the `doCatch()` method we might choose to rollback a transaction, while the `doFinally()` method might be used for closing a file or a connection to a remote resource. In essence, tags should implement this interface if they would like more control over exception handling.

To see how this interface affects the tag lifecycle, let's once again look at an activity diagram that summarizes this:

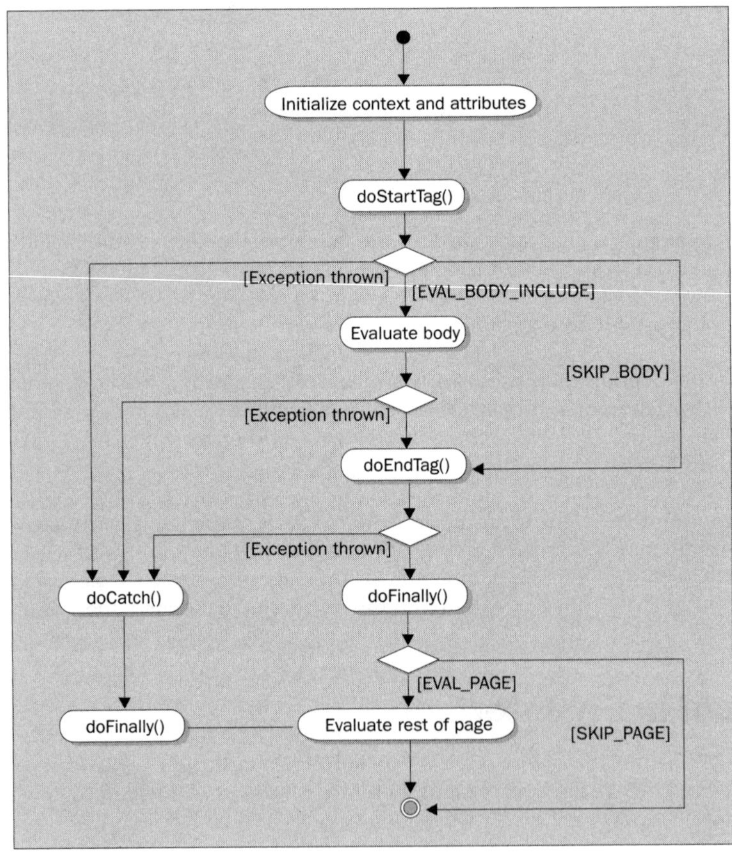

As we can see, implementing this interface introduces some additional steps into the lifecycle. On an implementation level, the code that gets generated during the translation process for a JSP page is now slightly different:

```
... start of page ...

SomeTag t = ... get tag handler instance from pool ...
t.setPageContext(pageContext);
t.setParent(null);

// set attributes through mutator methods
t.setAttribute1(...);
t.setAttributeN(...);

try {
  if (t.doStartTag() != javax.servlet.jsp.tagext.Tag.SKIP_BODY) {
    ... body content would be here ...
  }

  if (t.doEndTag() == javax.servlet.jsp.tagext.Tag.SKIP_PAGE) {
    return;
  }
} catch (Throwable throwable) {
  t.doCatch(throwable);
} finally {
  t.doFinally();
  ... return tag handler instance back to pool ...
}

... end of page ...
```

As this shows, the code that gets generated during the translation process now includes a `catch` block and the relevant calls to the `doCatch()` and `doFinally()` methods. Let's look at these two methods in more detail.

The doCatch() Method

In this example, the JSP specification guarantees that the `doCatch()` method will be called if an exception is thrown in the `doStartTag()` method, the tag's body content, or the `doEndTag()` method. Additionally, and if the tag handler implements the `IterationTag` or `BodyTag` interfaces, the `doCatch()` method will get executed if an exception is thrown within the `doAfterBody()` and `doInitBody()` methods respectively.

In this example, something to notice is that the `doCatch()` method will not be called if an exception is thrown during execution of the mutator methods for the tag's page context, parent, and attributes because they are outside the `try-catch-finally` block. Although the mutators can be included inside the `try` block, it is not guaranteed and therefore it is often best to leave any complex processing of attributes until the `doStartTag()` method rather than when the attribute values are set.

If the exception should be propagated further up the calling stack, it is recommended that the `doCatch()` method handles the exception as required, and then rethrows it, or throws a new exception.

The doFinally() Method

As the `finally` block always gets called regardless of whether an exception was thrown, the `doFinally()` method on the tag handler will always get called too.

Although tag handlers are generally small components, there is still much that can go wrong, especially when dealing with things such as remote objects. Implementing this interface is a way to build tags that are better equipped to deal with such problems, and therefore, it will make your tag libraries more robust and resilient to failure.

The Tag Lifecycle Revisited

Now that we've seen the `TryCatchFinally` interface, we are now in a position to look at how to build tags that work correctly with the tag lifecycle.

Tag Handler Reuse and Pooling

Something that we touched upon briefly in the Chapter 8 is that the JSP specification allows JSP container vendors to pool tag handler instances. This can actually be performed in several slightly different ways.

Tag Handler Pooling

The first of these is that the JSP container can maintain a pool of tag handler instances, much like a pool of database connections. When a tag handler is required on a page, an instance is retrieved from the pool rather than a fresh instance being created on the page. The handler is then returned to the pool when the page has finished with it. By doing this the JSP container reduces the overheads associated with instantiating tag handlers for every occurrence of the tag in the page and therefore an improvement in performance is seen.

Tag Handler Reuse

The second way that tags can be pooled, or rather reused, is on a single page. Consider the following JSP fragment:

```
<prefix:tag/>
<prefix:tag/>
```

A JSP container implementing such a strategy (often referred to as **aggressive reuse**) would only create a single instance of the tag handler to service both occurrences of the tag as follows:

```
... start of page ...

SomeTag t = new SomeTag();
t.setPageContext(pageContext);
t.setParent(null);

try {
```

```
    // first occurrence of <prefix:tag/>
    if (t.doStartTag() != javax.servlet.jsp.tagext.Tag.SKIP_BODY) {
      ... body content would be here ...
    }

    if (t.doEndTag() == javax.servlet.jsp.tagext.Tag.SKIP_PAGE) {
      return;
    }

    // second occurrence of <prefix:tag/>
    if (t.doStartTag() != javax.servlet.jsp.tagext.Tag.SKIP_BODY) {
      ... body content would be here ...
    }

    if (t.doEndTag() == javax.servlet.jsp.tagext.Tag.SKIP_PAGE) {
      return;
    }
  } finally {
    t.release()
  }

  ... end of page ...
```

This also provides performance improvements as the overheads associated with instantiating tag handlers are again reduced. In addition to this, notice how the `setPageContext()` and `setParent()` methods are not re-executed for the second occurrence.

Combined Pooling and Reuse

These two methods for improving performance aren't mutually exclusive and it is possible for a JSP container to combine the two strategies. Here, a tag instance would be retrieved from the pool and reused on the page many times before being returned to the pool.

Rules for Reusing Tag Handler Instances

Although this sounds straightforward, the JSP specification actually only permits the reuse of tag handler instances under a strict condition. Regardless of which strategy is used by the JSP container, tag handler instances can only be reused between occurrences if the set of attributes that the tags use are the same; however, their values can be different.

*This is referred to as the **AttSet** (set of attributes) in the JSP specification.*

In other words, the same tag handler instance could be used to service the following two custom tags:

```
<prefix:tag attribute1="123" attribute2="abc"/>
<prefix:tag attribute1="123" attribute2="def"/>
```

In this example, an initial tag handler is created to service the first occurrence of the tag as usual:

```
... start of page ...

SomeTag t = new SomeTag();
t.setPageContext(pageContext);
t.setParent(null);

try {
  // first occurrence of <prefix:tag attribute1 attribute2/>
  t.setAttribute1("123");
  t.setAttribute2("abc");

  if (t.doStartTag() != javax.servlet.jsp.tagext.Tag.SKIP_BODY) {
    ... body content would be here ...
  }

  if (t.doEndTag() == javax.servlet.jsp.tagext.Tag.SKIP_PAGE) {
    return;
  }
```

Following this, the same instance would be reused for the second occurrence:

```
  // second occurrence of <prefix:tag attribute1 attribute2/>
  t.setAttribute2("def");

  if (t.doStartTag() != javax.servlet.jsp.tagext.Tag.SKIP_BODY) {
    ... body content would be here ...
  }

  if (t.doEndTag() == javax.servlet.jsp.tagext.Tag.SKIP_PAGE) {
    return;
  }
} finally {
  t.release()
}

... end of page ...
```

Reuse can happen because the same set of attributes is used, but notice here that only the mutator for `attribute2` is called because it now has a different value. Although the container could re-execute the `setAttribute1()` method, it is not obliged to and not doing so is another way that performance can be improved. This strategy is used in some of the current implementations of JSP containers and has an important implication in that tag attributes should be persistent between invocations. In other words, once an attribute has been set, its value should not be altered because it might not be reset when the tag is reused.

Since reuse only happens when tags have the same set of attributes, two different tag handler instances would have to be used to service the following:

```
<prefix:tag attribute1="123" attribute2="abc"/>
<prefix:tag attribute1="123"/>
```

The reason behind this is that there is no simple way to reset the value of attribute2 back to its initial, default value upon which the tag handler might be dependent.

The release() Method

All of these strategies improve performance but have always raised some questions within the JSP community over how the tag lifecycle is affected when reusing tag handler instances – especially concerning the release() method. Let's again take a look at the code that is generated for a simple tag:

```
... start of page ...

SomeTag t = new SomeTag();
t.setPageContext(pageContext);
t.setParent(null);

// set attributes through mutator methods
t.setAttribute1(...);
t.setAttributeN(...);

try {
  if (t.doStartTag() != javax.servlet.jsp.tagext.Tag.SKIP_BODY) {
    ... body content would be here ...
  }

  if (t.doEndTag() == javax.servlet.jsp.tagext.Tag.SKIP_PAGE) {
    return;
  }
} finally {
  t.release()
}

... end of page ...
```

This example is taken from Tomcat 4.0 that, in its current form, doesn't use pooling to improve performance. When a tag is encountered in the page, the corresponding tag handler is instantiated, processing occurs and then the release() method is executed.

A common misconception is that the release() method is called after every occurrence of the tag – after the invocation of its doStartTag() and doEndTag() methods. This is not the case, however, as the release() method is called when the JSP container has finished with the tag handler instance. In the example that we just looked at, Tomcat doesn't use tag pooling and hence once the processing of that tag has finished, the tag handler is no longer required and the release() method is called. An analogy here is the destroy() method of a servlet, called when the servlet is taken out of service.

When tag handler instances are pooled, the JSP container obtains an existing tag handler from the pool instead of creating a new instance. The tag is processed, and following this it is returned back to the pool. Once returned to the pool the same tag handler may be reused to service many more tags on the same, or different pages. Eventually, the JSP container will determine that a tag handler instance is no longer required. This could be because the load on the web site has decreased, or simply because the JSP container has been instructed to shut down. When this happens and a tag handler is no longer required, the JSP container calls the release() method.

The JSP specification states that "the page compiler guarantees that the `release()` method will be invoked on the tag handler before the handler is released to the GC". However, what isn't specified is exactly when it will be called. If tag handlers are reused on the page, an instance would be created and several invocations of the `doStartTag()` and `doEndTag()` methods might be made before the container has finished with the tag. Here, the `release()` method could be called immediately after the last `doEndTag()` invocation or even at the end of the page.

This brings us on to some more questions about when the state associated with a tag handler should be reset.

Resetting Pre-Invocation State

When writing tags, state is often stored as instance variables that are associated with only the current invocation. For example, the `for` loop tag that we built in Chapter 5 used an instance variable (called `index`) as the counter for the loop. Since we now know that the `release()` method isn't called between invocations of custom tags, where is the best place to reset the `index`?

If a tag handler instance is reused, the values of the attributes could be the same, in which case the JSP container isn't obliged to re-execute the mutator methods. Therefore, resetting state in the attribute mutator methods isn't a good idea and leaves us with a couple of possibilities.

First of all, state can be reset in the `doStartTag()` method. No matter whether a tag handler is used for the first time or reused, the `doStartTag()` method is always executed as this starts the processing associated with the tag. This is a good solution for resetting the counter variable in the `for` loop tag.

However, it may be the case that a file is opened in the `doStartTag()` method, a reference to which is stored as an instance variable in the tag handler. In this situation, we should also remember to close the file at the end of the tag. As the discussion of the `TryCatchFinally` interface highlighted, it is possible that the `doEndTag()` method is never called for a particular tag. For this reason, and because we know that `release()` is guaranteed not to be called between invocations, the best place in which to close the file is the `doFinally()` method. Once the file has been closed, the `doStartTag()` method is then free to open up another file on the next invocation.

Resetting Long-Lived State

Now that we know that the `release()` method is called when the JSP container has finished with the tag handler, this provides the perfect place in which to free up long-lived, expensive resources.

A good example here is the `useRemoteBean` tag from the previous chapter. To look up a remote object, a `javax.naming.Context` instance must be created. This can be a fairly expensive operation and therefore, instead of creating it during each execution of the `doStartTag()` method, it would be more efficient to create it once and hang onto it for the lifetime of the tag. The `release()` method could then be used to close the context, or simply to set the reference to `null` to help the garbage collector.

One final thing to mention about implementing a `release()` method is to always make sure that `super.release()` is called. This way, any state held by the superclass can also be cleared.

Performance Guidelines

When wrapping up reusable functionality on a JSP page, an often asked question is whether tags are slower than using just a regular JavaBean. Back in Chapter 8, we came to the conclusion that tag handlers are almost JavaBeans anyway. The key difference between JavaBeans and custom tags is that tags are container-managed components that are (conceptually) short-lived and perform a specific action on the page. For this reason, it may be the case that a new tag handler instance will be created for each occurrence of the tag and during any snapshot in time of the server there may be hundreds of tag handlers in memory.

Fortunately, and as we've just discussed, the JSP specification allows vendors to pool tag instances. This is a great way of reducing the overheads associated with using custom tags and is another reason why you might choose vendor A's web server over vendor B's.

With this in mind, there are still some further enhancements that can improve the performance of a web application that makes extensive use of custom tags. We've already seen how the `release()` method can be used to free long-lived resources and caching such resources is a great start.

In addition to this, every attribute on a tag requires that a mutator method be implemented. A simple way to improve performance is to keep the number of attributes to a minimum, which means that there are fewer methods to call, but there is also an interesting side effect. Since tags are more likely to use the same set of attributes, it is more likely that tag handlers will be pooled and subsequently reused when used in those containers that support this feature.

Summary

This chapter has opened up the discussion on some of the more theoretical facets of custom tag design and development. First of all, we looked at what makes a good tag library and saw how regular component-based development and OO design principles are equally applicable to the design of custom tags and tag libraries. Following on from this, we then took a look at how the audience of a tag library can determine the granularity of the design, and how the naming conventions can also play an important role.

We then turned our focus to a more hands-on view of tag development by looking at how content and presentation can be successfully separated for a more maintainable, reusable tag library. Attributes are an important part of custom tags, so next up was a look at some practices for taking advantage of optional attributes, and also how attributes can be overloaded.

Finally, we revisited the tag lifecycle and took a detailed look at some of the specifics around tag pooling, reuse, and the resetting of state. The `TryCatchFinally` interface was also introduced as a way to build more resilient tags where the `doCatch()` and `doFinally()` methods provide a tag handler with more control over handling any exceptions that might occur during processing of the tag or its body content.

Now that we've looked at some of the topics relating to designing good tag libraries, let's take a more detailed look at some of the issues around deploying them.

LONDON

10

Validation and Deployment

Up to this point, we have looked at many different topics associated with developing tag libraries. These have primarily belonged to two areas: designing tags, and knowing in what situations custom tags are a better proposition than JavaBeans. To present a fully rounded discussion of tag libraries, the final topic we will look at is deployment.

Apart from looking at the practicalities of deployment, we will also delve into some of the other issues around the deployment and use of tag libraries, including:

- Validation to help present the page author with useful error messages
- An in-depth look at the tag library descriptor (TLD) file
- Manual and automatic deployment of tag libraries
- Tag library documentation
- Tag troubleshooting and some common "gotchas"

These are all as equally important as deploying a tag library because ultimately, for a tag library to be successful, it must also be useful and easy to use. Let's start the discussion by looking at how we can make tags easy to use, especially when they are not being used as designed.

Validation

Custom tags are very flexible components that can be used on the page in many different ways. Tags can be used in isolation, they can cooperate, be nested, and so on. When designing tags, we have a good idea of how our tags should be used on the page. For example, returning SKIP_BODY from the doStartTag() method of a tag handler indicates that the body content of the tag will be skipped and therefore implies that the body content will be empty. Although this is the case, there are still several ways in which that tag could be used on the page including, for example, with the presence of body content that will simply be ignored at request time.

As developers we have a clear vision of how a tag is to be used, but we have limited control over the way a page author uses it. A tag that ignores the body content for no apparent reason is not page author friendly – especially if inadequate documentation has been provided along with the tag library – since any HTML text the page author puts in will simply disappear from the resultant output. For this reason, many of the current JSP containers perform some rudimentary validation at translation time and in fact, such validation is required by the JSP specification.

Validating Tag Syntax

The most obvious type of validation that occurs on the page is that the custom tag's syntax is being checked. This involves checking whether they have a start tag and an end tag, and whether attributes, if used, are quoted properly. In addition to this, the container also checks whether the tag can actually be found within the specified tag library using the prefix used to qualify the tag.

This is the most basic form of validation and is run against all custom tags that are used on the page. In addition to this, it is possible to specify constraints in the tag library descriptor file on a tag-by-tag basis. At a minimum, all of the constraints specified in the TLD must be met for the tag to be valid. Let's look at these constraints.

Validating Body Content

One of the constraints that can be specified in the TLD file is the body content of a tag. As we know, there are three types of body content that can be declared – empty, JSP, and tagdependent:

```
<tag>
  ...
  <body-content>[empty | JSP | tagdependent ]</body-content>
  ...
</tag>
```

tagdependent body content means that the meaning of the content is specific to the tag and will probably not be meaningful to the JSP container and so the container doesn't validate it. In the case of JSP, a tag's body content isn't validated per se, although the JSP container will check that it does comply with the JSP specification.

Out of the three body content types, `empty` is perhaps the most interesting in terms of validation since it involves a different type of validation. When a tag's body content is set to `empty`, having content between the start and end tags generates an error at translation time and will result in output such as the following:

Body is supposed to be empty for prefix:tag

Using the `<body-content/>` element of the TLD file is a good way of ensuring that tags without body are used in the way in which they were designed.

Validating Attributes

Another check that is made at translation time determines whether all of the mandatory attributes for a tag have been supplied. Once again, this constraint can be specified in the TLD file, this time using the optional `<required/>` element within the `<attribute/>` stanza:

```
<attribute>
  ...
  <required>[ true | false ]</required>
  ...
</attribute>
```

Setting this value to `true` for one or more attributes will cause an error such as the following when the tag is used without supplying values for all of them:

According to the TLD attribute id is mandatory for tag iterate

Having required attributes is, again, another good way to ensure that a custom tag is used as expected and that all of the required information is supplied. However, more advanced validation, such as checking that the tags and their attributes have been used in the way that they were intended to be used, can't currently be specified in the TLD. Let's take a look at this with an example.

Imagine that we have a tag called `back` that simply renders a hyperlink pointing to the previous page. To provide flexibility, we decide that it would be good to allow page authors to present either a textual label or an image for the hyperlink:

Implementing such a tag is straightforward, and we just have two attributes – one for the label and one for the image source:

```
package com.wrox.jsptaglibs.navigation;

import java.io.IOException;

import javax.servlet.http.HttpServletRequest;
import javax.servlet.jsp.JspException;
import javax.servlet.jsp.JspTagException;
import javax.servlet.jsp.tagext.TagSupport;

public class BackTag extends TagSupport {

  private String label;
  private String src;

  public int doStartTag() throws JspException {

    StringBuffer buf = new StringBuffer();
    HttpServletRequest request;
    request = (HttpServletRequest)pageContext.getRequest();
    String referer = request.getHeader("referer");

    // build up the hyperlink
    buf.append("<a href=\"");
    buf.append(referer);
    buf.append("\">");

    if (label != null) {
      buf.append(label);
    } else {
      buf.append("<img border=\"0\" src=\"");
      buf.append(src);
      buf.append("\">");
    }
    buf.append("</a>");

    try {
      // and write out the HTML fragment to the page
      pageContext.getOut().write(buf.toString());
    } catch (IOException ioe) {
      throw new JspTagException(ioe.getMessage());
    }
    // and skip evaluating the body of the tag (as there shouldn't be one)
    return SKIP_BODY;
  }

  public void setLabel(String label) {
    this.label = label;
  }

  public void setSrc(String src) {
    this.src = src;
  }
}
```

Following this is the TLD file:

```
<?xml version="1.0" encoding="ISO-8859-1" ?>
<!DOCTYPE taglib
  PUBLIC "-//Sun Microsystems, Inc.//DTD JSP Tag Library 1.2//EN"
  "http://java.sun.com/dtd/web-jsptaglibrary_1_2.dtd">

<taglib>

  <tlib-version>1.0</tlib-version>
  <jsp-version>1.2</jsp-version>
  <short-name>navigation</short-name>
  <description>
    Navigation examples for the Deployment chapter.
  </description>

  <tag>
    <name>back</name>
    <tag-class>com.wrox.jsptaglibs.navigation.BackTag</tag-class>
    <body-content>empty</body-content>
    <description>
      Inserts a back link into the page.
    </description>
```

Since the page author will be able to use either a label or an image, both of the attributes have been marked as not required:

```
    <attribute>
      <name>label</name>
      <required>false</required>
      <rtexprvalue>false</rtexprvalue>
    </attribute>

    <attribute>
      <name>src</name>
      <required>false</required>
      <rtexprvalue>false</rtexprvalue>
    </attribute>
  </tag>
</taglib>
```

The following is an example usage of the tag in a JSP page; in this case, we've specified the `label` attribute:

```
...
  <%@ taglib uri="/navigationTaglib" prefix="navigation" %>

  <body>

    <h1>Page Not Found (404)</h1>

    Sorry, the page that you are looking for could not be found,
```

```
    please use the link below to return to the previous page.

    <center>
      <navigation:back label="Back to previous page"/>
    </center>

  </body>
```

As both the attributes have been specified as optional, it is possible that both could be omitted. Although an error is generated at translation time when mandatory attributes are not specified, in this situation there is no error. Because of the way that the tag handler is written, all we get is a hyperlink without an image:

From the perspective of somebody using the tag, it is not clear what has happened, as the tag does seem to be doing something. Ideally, we would like to show a message indicating that the tag has been used incorrectly and that one of the two attributes must be supplied.

Validating Attributes in the Tag Handler

One solution here is to include such validation within the tag handler itself:

```
package com.wrox.jsptaglibs.navigation;

import java.io.IOException;

import javax.servlet.http.HttpServletRequest;
import javax.servlet.jsp.JspException;
import javax.servlet.jsp.JspTagException;
import javax.servlet.jsp.tagext.TagSupport;

public class BackTagWithValidation extends TagSupport {

  private String label;

  private String src;

  public int doStartTag() throws JspException {
```

```
        // check the correct combination of attributes has been used
        if (label == null && src == null) {
          throw new JspTagException(
            "One of the attributes label or src must be supplied.");
        } else if (label != null && src != null) {
          throw new JspTagException(
            "Only one of the attributes label or src must be supplied.");
        }
        ...
      }
    ...
    }
```

Here, we have included a small block of validation in the `doStartTag()` method, before the processing of the tag begins. If neither or both of the attributes have been supplied, we just throw a `JspTagException` with an appropriate message, which in turn gets picked up by the JSP container:

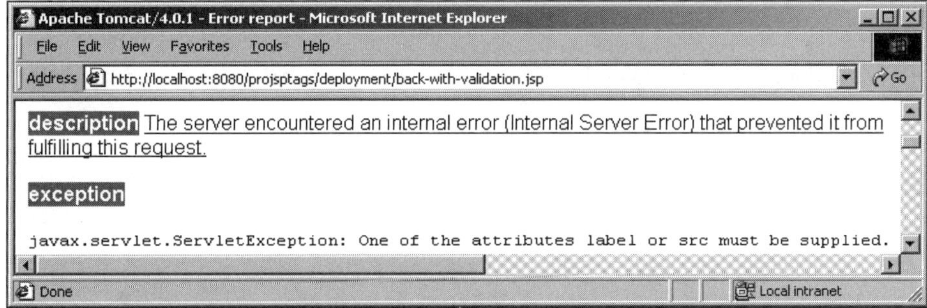

We now have a mechanism to indicate to the page author that something has gone wrong, and that they must supply one of the attributes. This makes the tag easier for people to use correctly. This is undoubtedly helpful, but there are a couple of drawbacks that are worth mentioning.

The first of these is that the page author gets to see a rather nasty stack trace, where the name of the tag isn't actually included. Of course, this may vary between the implementations of JSP containers, but it is a potential problem. Although the fully qualified tag handler class may be included in the stack trace, the page author will only be referencing the tags by the name specified in the TLD, and the prefix defined on the page. If there is no correlation between these and the fully qualified class name, such a stack trace may do more harm than good.

The other problem with implementing validation of tag attributes within the tag handler is that this code only gets executed at request time. While this may not be a problem for most people, if such validation code is only executed at request time, the JSP compiler has no way of knowing whether the tags are actually used correctly on the page. The page will translate without errors at deployment time, but then fall apart when it is actually requested from a browser.

Having validation logic in the tag handler may also not be appropriate in most cases because that code will get executed during every invocation of the tag. This additional performance hit, although small, is unnecessary because, in most cases, determining whether the tag is being used correctly only needs to happen once – when the page is modified. There is, however, one situation where validating attributes at request time is necessary. When request time expressions are used as the values for attributes, their values are not available at translation time and hence they cannot be tested. For this reason, testing the attributes upon each invocation of the tag is a good option. For regular, static attributes though, there is another mechanism that can be used to perform validation.

Many vendor implementations of a JSP container now allow compilation (or translation) of JSP pages at deployment time to stop the initial first hit of compilation from being passed on to the first user to visit the site. Putting checks in place in this stage of the overall site development is ideal, as this stage occurs once after every change to the site pages thus minimizing the performance hit of runtime checking. For this reason, the JSP specification includes a couple of mechanisms for validating tags at translation time.

The TagExtraInfo Class

The `TagExtraInfo` class is part of the `javax.servlet.jsp.tagext` package and, as already seen in Chapter 4, gives more flexibility in specifying information about any scripting variables that a tag will introduce into the page. Something that we've not seen yet is that the `TagExtraInfo` class can have the ability to perform simple validation of a tag's attributes:

```
package javax.servlet.jsp.tagext;

public abstract class TagExtraInfo {

  public boolean isValid(TagData data) {
    return true;
  }

  ...

}
```

The method that we are interested in here is called `isValid()`, which is called at translation time to determine whether the attributes for a tag are valid.

Validating Attributes with a TagExtraInfo Class

Let's see how this works in practice by writing a TEI class for the `back` tag:

```
package com.wrox.jsptaglibs.navigation;

import javax.servlet.jsp.tagext.TagData;
import javax.servlet.jsp.tagext.TagExtraInfo;

public class BackTagExtraInfo extends TagExtraInfo {

  public boolean isValid(TagData data) {

    String label = data.getAttributeString("label");
```

```
    String src = data.getAttributeString("src");

    // validate that the correct combination of attributes has been used
    if (label == null && src == null) {
      return false;
    } else if (label != null && src != null) {
      return false;
    } else {
      return true;
    }
  }
}
```

Here, all we've done is used the same validation logic from the `doStartTag()` method and wrapped it up inside the `isValid()` method. As when declaring scripting variables, we must use the `TagData` parameter to be able to get the values of the attributes. To make use of this TEI class, we must specify its fully qualified class name in the TLD in the same way as before:

```
<?xml version="1.0" encoding="ISO-8859-1" ?>
<!DOCTYPE taglib
  PUBLIC "-//Sun Microsystems, Inc.//DTD JSP Tag Library 1.2//EN"
  "http://java.sun.com/dtd/web-jsptaglibrary_1_2.dtd">

<taglib>

  <tlib-version>1.0</tlib-version>
  <jsp-version>1.2</jsp-version>
  <short-name>navigation</short-name>
  <description>
    Navigation examples for the Deployment chapter.
  </description>

  <tag>
    <name>back</name>
    <tag-class>com.wrox.jsptaglibs.navigation.BackTag</tag-class>
    <tei-class>com.wrox.jsptaglibs.navigation.BackTagExtraInfo</tei-class>
    <body-content>empty</body-content>
    <description>
      Inserts a back link into the page.
    </description>

    <attribute>
      <name>label</name>
      <required>false</required>
      <rtexprvalue>false</rtexprvalue>
    </attribute>

    <attribute>
      <name>src</name>
      <required>false</required>
      <rtexprvalue>false</rtexprvalue>
    </attribute>
  </tag>
</taglib>
```

Wrapping up this sort of validation logic is a good way of externalizing the validation rules for a tag. In addition to checking the presence of attributes as illustrated here, it is also possible to check the values of attributes. For example, you might want to check a specific attribute falls into a certain range or takes one of a possible set of values. As the TEI class is used at translation time, this does mean that the attributes with values evaluated from request time expressions cannot be tested. Checking for the presence of these types of attributes, however, can be done in two ways.

Firstly, the `getAttributes()` method on the `TagData` class returns an `Enumeration` of the names of all specified attributes:

```
Enumeration attributes = data.getAttributes();
```

Checking that an attribute exists is then a matter of running over the enumeration trying to find it. Alternatively there's the `getAttribute()` method, again on the `TagData` class:

```
Object value = data.getAttribute("name");
```

As with the `getAttributeString()` method, the `getAttribute()` method returns the value of the specified attribute, which is of type `Object`. With request time expressions, the actual value of the attribute cannot be known and therefore the value `REQUEST_TIME_VALUE` is returned to indicate that the attribute has been specified although its value isn't yet known. On the other hand, if the attribute hasn't been specified in the page, calling the `getAttribute()` method would simply return `null`. To check the values of request-time expressions, validation must be performed in the tag handler as we've already seen.

When all of the validation has been performed, returning a value of `false` signals to the JSP container that the tag usage isn't valid and an error, like the following, will be generated on the page:

Attributes are invalid according to TagInfo

Although some fairly complex validation can be performed in a very simple way, once again (and depending on the JSP container) it is possible that the information provided in the error message is not sufficient to easily determine where the error is and what is causing it.

Using a TEI class means that validation is performed at translation time, which in turn means that JSP pages can be validated during compilation. The `TagExtraInfo` class was introduced in JSP 1.1 and is still a good mechanism to use for validation, especially if you have to implement a TEI class to declare any scripting variables that a tag introduces into the page. For JSP 1.2, however, a new mechanism was introduced.

Validating Tag Structure and Usage

The validations that we've implemented so far have only focused upon validating how attributes are used, and this is just a small part of checking whether the tag has been used correctly on the page. This is very useful, but equally useful is the ability to determine whether a tag is being used correctly on the page, this time in terms of its structure on the page. For example, it may be that a tag can only ever be used if it is nested within another tag, or perhaps the ordering of tags is important on the page. A new feature in JSP 1.2 is the `TagLibraryValidator` class – a much more powerful and flexible way to perform validation.

During the translation process, and before the actual Java code is generated, the JSP page is transformed into an XML representation of the page. This, the **XML view**, provides another way that the JSP page can be validated.

The actual DTD for the XML view can be found at http://java.sun.com/dtd/jspxml.dtd, *while the equivalent XML schema can be found at* http://java.sun.com/dtd/jspxml.xsd.

What happens behind the scenes is that all of the JSP elements are converted into an XML-compliant representation. For example, scriptlets are represented using the `<jsp:scriptlet>` element and the actual content (for example HTML) is simply wrapped up inside `<jsp:text>` elements. The XML view that is generated by Tomcat for the previous example is as follows:

```
<?xml version="1.0" encoding="UTF-8"?>
<jsp:root version="1.2"
          xmlns:jsp="http:\\java.sun.com\JSP\Page"
          xmlns:navigation="/navigationWithValidatorTaglib">
    <jsp:text><![CDATA[
<html>

  <head>
    <title>Professional JSP Tag Libraries</title>
  </head>

  ]]></jsp:text>
    <jsp:text><![CDATA[

  <body>

    <h1>Page Not Found (404)</h1>

    Sorry, the page that you are looking for could not be found,
    please use the link below to return to the previous page.

    <center>
      ]]></jsp:text>
    <navigation:back label="Back to previous page"/>
    <jsp:text><![CDATA[

    </center>

  </body>

</html>]]></jsp:text>
</jsp:root>
```

As this shows, the content has been wrapped up inside `<jsp:text>` tags, while the custom tags are left as they were used on the page because they are XML-compliant already. While the XML view is not necessarily of interest to most page authors (it is very verbose), page-authoring tools can take advantage of a pure XML representation to help build and validate the pages that are generated.

The TagLibraryValidator Class

The `TagLibraryValidator` class (from the `javax.servlet.jsp.tagext` package) is itself fairly straightforward. The majority of the time, we will be interested in just a single method – `validate()`:

```
package javax.servlet.jsp.tagext;

import java.util.Map;

abstract public class TagLibraryValidator {

  private Map initParameters;

  public void setInitParameters(Map map) {
    initParameters = map;
  }

  public Map getInitParameters() {
    return initParameters;
  }

  public ValidationMessage[] validate(String prefix,
                                       String uri,
                                       PageData page) {

    return null;
  }

  public void release() {
    initParameters = null;
  }
}
```

As its name suggests, the `TagLibraryValidator` class (TLV) is used as a validator at the tag library level. What this means is that rather than validating an individual tag at translation time, it can validate an entire page. One of the parameters that is passed to the `validate()` method is of type `PageData` which is effectively a reference to the XML view of the page to be validated. It has one method called `getInputStream()` that can be used to access the document.

Because a TLV validates at the tag library level, it is associated with a particular tag library through the TLD file. Behind the scenes, whenever that tag library is imported into a page with the `taglib` directive, an instance of the TLV is used to validate the page. With the TLV associated with a tag library, we probably only want to validate the usage of those tags that the tag library contains. For this reason, the other parameters passed through to the `validate()` method are the `prefix` that the library uses on the page (remember, this can change from page to page) and also, the `uri` with which the tag library has been imported.

The ValidationMessage Class

Rather than throw exceptions to signal to the JSP container that something is wrong with the page, the `validate()` method simply returns an array of `ValidationMessage` instances – wrappers for an `id` and a `message`:

```
package javax.servlet.jsp.tagext;

public class ValidationMessage {

  private String id;
  private String message;

  public ValidationMessage(String id, String message) {
    this.id = id;
    this.message = message;
  }

  public String getId() {
    return id;
  }

  public String getMessage(){
    return message;
  }
}
```

The `message` is a simple `java.lang.String` value representing the message that should be shown to the page author describing the error. The `id`, on the other hand, is a useful (albeit currently optional) feature of the JSP specification that can be used to help page authors identify the exact whereabouts of the error.

During translation, and when the XML view of the page is being created, the JSP container can keep track of the location that each XML element corresponds to in the original, raw JSP page. For example, it would know that a particular scriptlet or custom tag came from row 10, column 1 in the original JSP source. During this process, the JSP container could internally maintain such information and assign each element in the XML tree a unique identifier. The JSP specification says that such unique identifiers can be inserted into the XML view of the document by giving each element an additional `jsp:id` attribute.

When we started looking at how to build custom tag attributes in Chapter 2, we saw that there are some restrictions on the strings that can be used for tag prefixes and attribute names because the JSP container creates, and is permitted to manipulate, the XML view of a JSP page. If we were to use these restricted prefixes and names there is a chance that we could clash with the JSP container, potentially causing it to fail to execute the JSP page.

If the JSP container supports this feature, setting the `id` property in the `ValidationMessage` instance means that the container will be able to provide much more detail as to the whereabouts of the error.

Unfortunately, and at the time of writing, current JSP implementations do not support this useful feature but as the cost of using it is low, it is worth including in any TLV classes that you write.

Validating Attributes with a TagLibraryValidator Class

Now that we've covered the basics, let's see how this works in practice by implementing a TLV for the `back` tag that wraps up the same validation logic. First of all we extend the `TagLibraryValidator` class. To perform the validation, we'll be directly using the XML view of the page and therefore must remember to import the relevant XML classes.

> *Although the examples shown here directly manipulate the XML view in memory using the Document Object Model (DOM), there are many other options available including use of the Simple API for XML (SAX), XPath, XSLT, and so on. More information about using XML with Java can be found in Professional Java XML from Wrox Press (ISBN 1-861004-01-X) while information about using XML in conjunction with JSP can be found in Professional JSP 2nd Edition from Wrox Press (1-861004-95-8).*

This example makes use of several XML-related classes (those imported from `javax.xml.parsers`, `org.w3c.dom`, and `org.xml.sax`) and therefore, a requirement to run and compile such classes is an XML library. One such library, Xerces, is included within the distribution for Tomcat. Xerces is an open source implementation of the XML library for Java specifications. To make use of it within a web application, simply copy `xerces.jar` from `%TOMCAT_HOME%\common\lib` into the `WEB-INF\lib` directory of your web application:

```
package com.wrox.jsptaglibs.navigation;

import java.io.IOException;
import java.util.List;
import java.util.ArrayList;

import javax.servlet.jsp.tagext.PageData;
import javax.servlet.jsp.tagext.ValidationMessage;
import javax.servlet.jsp.tagext.TagLibraryValidator;

import javax.xml.parsers.DocumentBuilder;
import javax.xml.parsers.DocumentBuilderFactory;
import javax.xml.parsers.ParserConfigurationException;

import org.w3c.dom.Node;
import org.w3c.dom.NodeList;
import org.w3c.dom.Document;
import org.w3c.dom.NamedNodeMap;

import org.xml.sax.SAXException;

public class NavigationTagLibraryValidator extends TagLibraryValidator {
```

Next we have an instance variable and a default, no arguments constructor that is used to set up a `DocumentBuilder`. This is part of the `javax.xml.parsers` package and is just an abstraction for getting a reference to an XML parser – the object required to parse an XML document into an in-memory representation. Part of the JSP specification states that, like tags, TLVs can be reused to improve performance. Rather than create an XML parser each time, we simply create it once and store it as an instance variable for use later on:

```
  private DocumentBuilder builder;

  public NavigationTagLibraryValidator() {
    try {
      // create a factory and builder - an abstraction for an XML parser
      DocumentBuilderFactory factory = DocumentBuilderFactory.newInstance();
      this.builder = factory.newDocumentBuilder();
    } catch (ParserConfigurationException pce) {
      pce.printStackTrace();
    }
  }
```

Next is the `validate()` method:

```
  public ValidationMessage[] validate(
    String prefix, String uri, PageData page) {

    List messages = new ArrayList();
```

XML documents are essentially just trees of hierarchical information and here, the algorithm behind validating the page is to get the root element and validate it – checking whether it represents a `back` tag and has the appropriate number of attributes:

```
    try {
      // starting with the root node, recursively validate each node
      // in the XML view of the JSP page
      Document doc = builder.parse(page.getInputStream());
      Node node = doc.getDocumentElement();

      validateNode(prefix, node, messages);
    } catch (IOException ioe) {
      ioe.printStackTrace();
    } catch (SAXException saxe) {
      saxe.printStackTrace();
    }

    // and return the errors (if any)
    return (ValidationMessage[])messages.toArray(
      new ValidationMessage[] {});
  }
```

Historically there have been no standards associated with parsing XML documents using the Document Object Model (DOM). Therefore, many DOM parsers instead choose to throw a `SAXException`*, first of all for consistency, and secondly because they may use SAX behind the scenes.*

Most of the work is performed in the following recursive method that performs the actual validation of the specified node. First of all it checks whether the name of the node matches, bearing in mind that the tag library prefix has been specified as a parameter because it can change from page to page:

```
private void validateNode(String prefix, Node node, List messages) {

  // first of all, check whether this node represents the "back" tag
  if (node.getNodeName().equals(prefix + ":" + "back")) {
```

If the current node does match, we need to check that it has attributes. It is an error for the `back` tag to be used without one of the `label` and `src` attributes and therefore a `ValidationMessage` instance is created and added to the current list. Because there are no attributes, there cannot possibly be one called `jsp:id`. This implies that the container doesn't support this feature and therefore, `null` is passed as the `id` to the `ValidationMessage` constructor:

```
    // have the attributes been used correctly?
    if (!node.hasAttributes()) {
      // the tag doesn't have any attributes so raise an error
      ValidationMessage vm = new ValidationMessage(null,
        "One of the attributes label or src must be supplied.");
      messages.add(vm);
```

If there are attributes, the next step is to determine which of `label` and `src` has been supplied. If neither has been supplied, we simply create a `ValidationMessage` instance. This time, we can look for the `jsp:id` attribute and use it when constructing the message. If it doesn't exist, the container doesn't support the feature and again, an `id` of `null` can be used to create the message:

```
    } else {
      // check that only one of label and src has been used
      NamedNodeMap attributes = node.getAttributes();
      Node label = attributes.getNamedItem("label");
      Node src = attributes.getNamedItem("src");

      // check that both attributes haven't been provided
      if (label != null && src != null) {

        // look for the optional jsp:id attribute that the container
        // may have put on the tag - this helps identify where in
        // the JSP the error has occurred
        String jspId = null;
        Node jspIdAttribute = attributes.getNamedItem("jsp:id");
        if (jspIdAttribute != null) {
          jspId = jspIdAttribute.getNodeValue();
        }

        // wrap up the error message and add to the current list
        ValidationMessage vm = new ValidationMessage(jspId,
          "Only one of the attributes label or src must be supplied.");
        messages.add(vm);
      }
    }
  }
```

Once the current node has been validated, we can recursively call this method to validate each of its child nodes in turn:

```
      // and recursively check all of the child nodes
      if (node.hasChildNodes()) {
        NodeList children = node.getChildNodes();

        for (int i = 0; i < children.getLength(); i++) {
          validateNode(prefix, children.item(i), messages);
        }
      }
    }

  }
```

Associating a TLV with a tag library is achieved through the <validator> stanza as illustrated in the following TLD file:

```
<?xml version="1.0" encoding="ISO-8859-1" ?>
<!DOCTYPE taglib
  PUBLIC "-//Sun Microsystems, Inc.//DTD JSP Tag Library 1.2//EN"
  "http://java.sun.com/dtd/web-jsptaglibrary_1_2.dtd">

<taglib>

  <tlib-version>1.0</tlib-version>
  <jsp-version>1.2</jsp-version>
  <short-name>navigationWithValidator</short-name>
  <description>
    Navigation examples for the Deployment chapter.
  </description>

  <validator>
    <validator-class>
      com.wrox.jsptaglibs.navigation.NavigationTagLibraryValidator
    </validator-class>
  </validator>

  <tag>
    <name>back</name>
    <tag-class>com.wrox.jsptaglibs.navigation.BackTag</tag-class>
    <body-content>empty</body-content>
    <description>
      Inserts a back link into the page.
    </description>

    <attribute>
      <name>label</name>
      <required>false</required>
      <rtexprvalue>false</rtexprvalue>
    </attribute>

    <attribute>
```

```
            <name>src</name>
            <required>false</required>
            <rtexprvalue>false</rtexprvalue>
        </attribute>
    </tag>

</taglib>
```

If we were to use the same JSP page as before but this time specify both of the attributes for the `back` tag, Tomcat generates the following error:

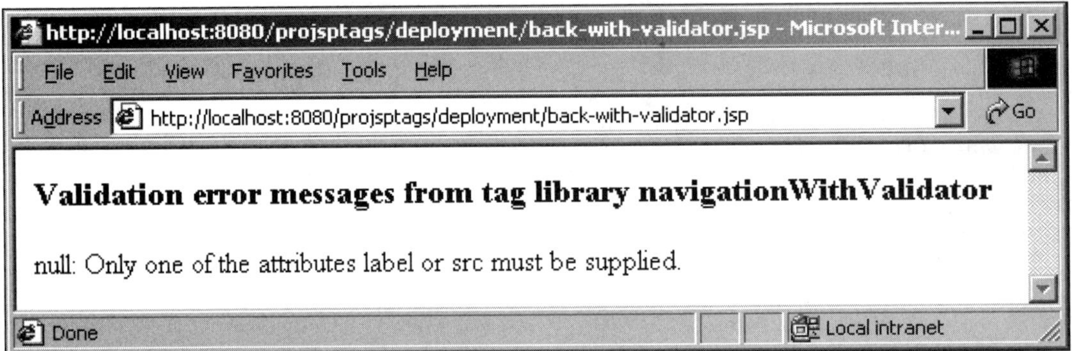

Because Tomcat doesn't yet support the optional `jsp:id` functionality, we are still none the wiser as to the exact location of the error. However, we no longer have a nasty track trace to deal with and the validation messages can be enhanced to give more detail. For example, the message could show the name of the tag, how the tag is being used, or even an indication of the surrounding page elements. This is in fact a fairly complex task and since the content is wrapped up inside JSP-specific XML tags, some manipulation is required to usefully extract the surrounding contextual information.

Although TLVs are typically much more verbose and complex than TEIs, one of the benefits of using them is that all of the errors on a page are shown to the page author at once, giving them a chance to fix all of the errors rather than fixing one and redeploying, only to find another. Let's see this in action along with how the XML view can be used to ensure that tags are nested correctly – something that is much more suited to the flexibility offered by the `TagLibraryValidator`.

Validating Structure with a TagLibraryValidator Class

For this example, we'll use the logic tags that we developed in Chapter 7:

```
<logic:if value="<%= book %>">

  <logic:undefined>
    Sorry, no book was found.
  </logic:undefined>

  <logic:default>
    <h2>
      <%= book.getTitle() %>
```

```
      </h2>
      ... information about the chosen book here ...
    </logic:default>

  </logic:if>
```

For the page to work properly, the `undefined` and `default` tags must be nested (directly or indirectly) underneath an enclosing `if` tag. Once again we extend `TagLibraryValidator` and setup an XML parser for use later on:

```
package com.wrox.jsptaglibs.logic;

import java.io.IOException;
import java.util.ArrayList;
import java.util.List;

import javax.servlet.jsp.tagext.PageData;
import javax.servlet.jsp.tagext.TagLibraryValidator;
import javax.servlet.jsp.tagext.ValidationMessage;

import javax.xml.parsers.DocumentBuilder;
import javax.xml.parsers.DocumentBuilderFactory;
import javax.xml.parsers.ParserConfigurationException;

import org.w3c.dom.Document;
import org.w3c.dom.NamedNodeMap;
import org.w3c.dom.Node;
import org.w3c.dom.NodeList;

import org.xml.sax.SAXException;

public class LogicTagLibraryValidator extends TagLibraryValidator {

  private DocumentBuilder builder;

  public LogicTagLibraryValidator() {
    try {
      // create a factory and builder - an abstraction for an XML parser
      DocumentBuilderFactory factory = DocumentBuilderFactory.newInstance();
      this.builder = factory.newDocumentBuilder();
    } catch (ParserConfigurationException pce) {
      pce.printStackTrace();
    }
  }
```

Next is the `validate()` method. As before, we just get the root element of the XML view and ask that it be validated:

```
  public ValidationMessage[] validate(
    String prefix, String uri, PageData page) {

    List messages = new ArrayList();
```

```
    try {
      // starting with the root node, recursively validate each node
      // in the XML view of the JSP page
      Document doc = builder.parse(page.getInputStream());
      Node node = doc.getDocumentElement();

      validateNode(prefix, node, messages);
    } catch (IOException ioe) {
      ioe.printStackTrace();
    } catch (SAXException saxe) {
      saxe.printStackTrace();
    }

    // and return the errors (if any)
    return (ValidationMessage[])messages.toArray(
      new ValidationMessage[] {});
  }
```

Once again, this is where all of the hard work is done. If we find an `undefined` or `default` tag, we then go on to determine whether it has a parent called `if` by delegating the task to a private `hasParent()` method. If a parent `if` tag couldn't be found, again we create an appropriate message:

```
  private void validateNode(String prefix, Node node, List messages) {
    // first of all, check whether this node represents the
    // "undefined" or "default" tags
    if (node.getNodeName().equals(prefix + ":" + "undefined") ||
        node.getNodeName().equals(prefix + ":" + "default")) {

      // has this node got a parent called "if"?
      if (!hasParent(node, prefix, "if")) {

        String jspId = null;

        if (node.hasAttributes()) {
          NamedNodeMap attributes = node.getAttributes();

          // look for the optional jsp:id attribute that the container
          // may have put on the tag - this helps identify where in
          // the JSP the error has occurred
          Node jspIdAttribute = attributes.getNamedItem("jsp:id");
          if (jspIdAttribute != null) {
            jspId = jspIdAttribute.getNodeValue();
          }
        }

        // the tag is nested incorrectly so raise an error
        ValidationMessage vm = new ValidationMessage(jspId,
          "The " + node.getNodeName() + " tag must be nested within a "
          + prefix + ":if tag.");
        messages.add(vm);
      }
    }
```

In the same way as last time, we then go on to validate all of the child nodes:

```
      // and recursively check all of the child nodes
      if (node.hasChildNodes()) {
        NodeList children = node.getChildNodes();

        for (int i = 0; i < children.getLength(); i++) {
          validateNode(prefix, children.item(i), messages);
        }
      }
    }
```

The `hasParent()` method simply gets the immediate parent node and performs some simple checks. If the parent node is `null` then we've reached the top of the XML document, therefore a parent `if` tag couldn't be found and we return `false`. If the parent node is called `if` (again, taking into account the prefix) we return `true`, otherwise we simply call the `hasParent()` method recursively to navigate up the tree and check the next immediate parent:

```
    private boolean hasParent(Node node, String prefix, String parentName) {
      Node parentNode = node.getParentNode();

      if (parentNode == null) {
        return false;
      } else if (parentNode.getNodeName().equals(prefix + ":" + parentName)) {
        return true;
      } else {
        return hasParent(parentNode, prefix, parentName);
      }
    }
  }
```

With the TLV written, the next step is to associate it with a tag library, ready for use on the page. If we were to try to use the `undefined` and `default` tags without an enclosing `if` tag, we would get the following error message from Tomcat:

Rules of Thumb

To wrap up the discussion of validation, let's look at some rules of thumb and identify the situations when it is best to use each mechanism.

First of all we looked at writing validation inside the tag handler. This is a good approach and is the only way that the values of attributes with request-time expressions can be checked. Because this code is executed upon every invocation of the tag, there is a small performance hit but tags that check their values will be more robust than those that don't – especially when those values are derived from user input.

The other paradigm for validating tags is at translation time, and this is especially useful when pre-compiling JSP pages before or during deployment. As the values of request-time expressions are not known at this time, translation-time validation cannot be used to check the values of such attributes. However, it can check the presence of attributes.

There are two mechanisms available for translation-time validation – the `TagExtraInfo` class and the `TagLibraryValidator` class. The former is a very simple way of validating on a tag-by-tag basis, whereas the latter is a much more powerful, flexible mechanism that can be used to validate the XML view of an entire page from the perspective of a tag library.

This means that a TLV can also be used to validate structure and how tags are used on the page. Although the JSP specification indicates that validation for JSP 1.2-compliant tag libraries should be implemented using TLVs rather than TEIs, for simple validation you may want to stick to using TEI classes as they are much simpler. TLVs have a clear benefit in that they can validate the structure of the page but for checking attributes the additional work doesn't really pay off unless you use a third party TLV. Whichever mechanism you use, making tags more robust and generating page author friendly error messages is important in making them easy to use and reliable.

Now that we've looked at how tags can be used and misused on the page, let's take a more in-depth look at the descriptor used when deploying tag libraries.

Tag Library Descriptor

In the examples that we've seen throughout the book, we've seen many TLD files in which information about tags and tag libraries has been specified. The elements of the TLD that we've seen up until now are those that you'll mainly use on a day-to-day basis, but there are others that you may occasionally need to use.

While the majority of the TLD file is geared towards being used by JSP containers, there are some optional elements that are focused towards use by page authoring tools and IDEs. For example, if a tag library were packaged for use in a page authoring tool, such elements would provide added information for the tools so that they can present property sheets to the user with more details about the tag library. Let's take a look at the complete TLD definition.

The XML Header

As we've seen, the header for a TLD file is as follows:

```
<?xml version="1.0" encoding="ISO-8859-1" ?>
<!DOCTYPE taglib
  PUBLIC "-//Sun Microsystems, Inc.//DTD JSP Tag Library 1.2//EN"
  "http://java.sun.com/dtd/web-jsptaglibrary_1_2.dtd">
```

As usual, this means that the file complies with the specified DTD, available from the Sun web site.

The taglib Element

The root of the TLD file is the `<taglib>` element, under which can be the following elements:

Element Name	Requied	Description
`tlib-version`	Yes	The version of the tag library
`jsp-version`	Yes	The version of JSP on which this tag library depends
`short-name`	Yes	A simple name that could be used by page authoring tools as, for example, a default prefix for the tag library
`uri`	No	A URI uniquely identifying this tag library
`display-name`	No	Another short name, this time intended to be displayed by tools
`small-icon`	No	A small icon (16x16 pixel JPEG or GIF) used by tools, for example, in a toolbar
`large-icon`	No	A large icon (32x32 pixel JPEG or GIF) used by tools, for example, in a toolbar
`description`	No	A short description of the tag library
`validator`	No	Defines a validator class for this tag library
`listener`	No	Defines web application event listeners for this tag library – there may be more than one
`tag`	Yes	Defines tags for this tag library – there may be more than one

In JSP 1.1, the elements allowed in this section of the TLD were `<tlibversion>`, `<jspversion>`, `<shortname>`, `<uri>`, and `<info>` (which is now `<description>`).

The validator Element

As we've seen in this chapter, the `<validator>` element allows a single optional `TagLibraryValidator` to be associated with a tag library. Underneath the `<validator>` element are the following elements:

Element Name	Required	Description
`validator-class`	Yes	The fully qualified class name of the TLV implementation to be used
`init-param`	No	Initialization parameters for the TLV – there may be more than one
`description`	No	A short description of the TLV

The init-param Element

An initialization parameter for a TLV is simply a name-value pair and therefore requires that following elements are nested beneath it:

Element Name	Required	Description
`param-name`	Yes	The name of the parameter
`param-value`	Yes	The value of the parameter
`description`	No	A short description of the parameter

The listener Element

Web application event listeners are part of the Java Servlets 2.3 specification and allow objects to be set up that listen for specific events that occur during the lifetime of a web application. For example, a listener could be set up to listen for attributes placed into the HTTP session, when sessions are created or destroyed, and even when the web application itself (the `ServletContext`) is created and destroyed. An example of a simple session listener is as follows:

```
package com.wrox.jsptaglibs.listener;

import javax.servlet.http.HttpSessionEvent;
import javax.servlet.http.HttpSessionListener;

public class SessionListener implements HttpSessionListener {

  public void sessionCreated(HttpSessionEvent e) {
    System.out.println("A session has been created with the ID "
      + e.getSession().getId());
  }
```

```
    public void sessionDestroyed(HttpSessionEvent e) {
      System.out.println("A session has been destroyed with the ID "
        + e.getSession().getId());
    }
  }
```

A tag library might be interested in listening to such events so that, for example, it can create or destroy the appropriate resources when a new user session is created or destroyed.

Listeners that are associated with a tag library are loaded by the web application in the normal way and once in memory, the web application doesn't regard listeners loaded through a web application or through a tag library any differently.

There is only one element used underneath the `<listener>` element as follows:

Element Name	Required	Description
`listener-class`	Yes	The fully qualified class name of the listener to be registered

The tag Element

Next is the core of the TLD file – the `<tag>` element that allows us to define the tags within the tag library:

Element Name	Required	Description
`name`	Yes	The name of the tag, as used on the page
`tag-class`	Yes	The fully qualified class name of the tag handler
`tei-class`	No	The fully qualified class name of a `TagExtraInfo` implementation
`body-content`	No	The body content type – one of `empty`, `JSP`, or `tagdependent`
`display-name`	No	A short name intended to be displayed by tools
`small-icon`	No	A small icon (16x16 pixel JPEG or GIF) used by tools, for example, in a toolbar
`large-icon`	No	A large icon (32x32 pixel JPEG or GIF) used by tools, for example, in a toolbar
`description`	No	A short description of the tag
`variable`	No	Defines information about scripting variables that this tag introduces into the page – there may be more than one

Table continued on following page

Element Name	Required	Description
attribute	No	Defines information about this tag's attributes – there may be more than one
example	No	An additional descriptive element for illustrating example usage of the tag

In JSP 1.1, the elements allowed in this section of the TLD were <name>, <tagclass>, <teiclass>,< bodycontent>, <info> (which is now <description>) and<attribute>.

The variable Element

A scripting variable is defined with the following sub-elements:

Element Name	Required	Description
name-given	No	The name of the scripting variable
name-from-attribute	No	The name of the attribute that represents the name of the scripting variable
variable-class	No	The fully qualified class name (type) of the variable – the default is java.lang.String
declare	No	Whether a new variable is declared or not – the default is true
scope	No	The scope in which the scripting variable should be defined – one of AT_BEGIN, NESTED or AT_END – the default is NESTED
description	No	A short description of the variable

As we saw when we looked at scripting variables in Chapter 4, although both <name-given> and <name-from-attribute> elements are not required, at least one of them must be specified. This is because a scripting variable can take on a name supplied in the TLD file, or the name supplied as the value of an attribute, but not both.

The attribute Element

An attribute is defined with the following sub-elements:

Element Name	Required	Description
name	Yes	The name of the attribute
required	No	Whether this attribute is mandatory – the default is false
rtexprvalue	No	Whether the value of the attribute can be specified by a request-time expression – the default is false

Element Name	Required	Description
`type`	No	The fully qualified class name of the attribute type – the default is `java.lang.String`
`description`	No	A short description of the attribute

Deploying Tag Libraries

With the tags written and described, the last step is to actually deploy the tag library. Although we've seen how tag libraries can be registered with the web application deployment descriptor, this is not the end of the story. There are in fact several ways we can deploy a tag library. To start off, let's recap on what we've seen up until now.

Unpackaged Tag Libraries

All the example tags in this book have been deployed in the unpackaged state. In other words, the compiled class files have simply been placed underneath the `WEB-INF\classes` directory and this is how they have been made available to the web application.

With the class files in place, a TLD file can be written for a tag library and placed anywhere underneath the `WEB-INF` directory. A convention suggested by the JSP specification is that all TLDs are placed within the `WEB-INF\tlds` directory. Grouping them together makes finding them much easier. There are now two ways in which the tag library can be used.

Referencing a TLD Directly

The first of these methods is to explicitly specify the location of the TLD relative to the root of the web application using the `taglib` directive on the JSP page. For example, if the TLD for the `navigation` tag library was located at `WEB-INF\tlds\navigation.tld`, the tag library that the TLD defines could be imported and used directly on a JSP page as follows:

```
<%@ taglib uri="/WEB-INF/tlds/navigation.tld" prefix="navigation" %>
```

Although we've not seen this in use in the book, it is often a useful way of quickly getting a tag library up and running, and is particularly useful in the early stages of development. The problem here is that the location of the tag library may change or, as we'll see shortly, the tag library is packaged up. In both these situations, all pages that directly reference the TLD file will need to change.

Referencing a TLD With a Symbolic URI

Instead of directly referencing the physical TLD file, a symbolic reference can be defined and used on the page. This is the method by which all of the examples in the book have been deployed and simply involves defining a mapping between a physical TLD file and a symbolic URI in the web application deployment descriptor. For example, adding the following section to the `web.xml` file defines a mapping between the navigation TLD and the URI `/navigationTaglib`:

```
<?xml version="1.0" encoding="ISO-8859-1"?>

<!DOCTYPE web-app
    PUBLIC "-//Sun Microsystems, Inc.//DTD Web Application 2.3//EN"
    "http://java.sun.com/dtd/web-app_2_3.dtd">

<web-app>
  ...

  <taglib>
    <taglib-uri>/navigationTaglib</taglib-uri>
    <taglib-location>/WEB-INF/tlds/navigation.tld</taglib-location>
  </taglib>

  ...
</web-app>
```

The `<taglib-uri>` can really be anything that we choose, but should be an absolute or a relative URI. On the page, as we've seen, the tag library can be imported as follows:

```
<%@ taglib uri="/navigationTaglib" prefix="navigation" %>
```

Using a symbolic reference provides a degree of flexibility that allows tag libraries to be swapped in and out behind the scenes and is currently the mechanism that most people use for the deployment of custom tags. Additionally, the pages do not have to be changed if tag libraries are packaged up into JAR files, as we'll see shortly.

Having the tag handlers and supporting classes in the `WEB-INF\classes` directory is very useful for development purposes as classes can be modified and recompiled in situ. However, for production deployment purposes, it is easier, more efficient, and less error prone to package up the classes into a JAR file.

Semi-Packaged Tag Libraries

A common way in which tag libraries are distributed is by providing a JAR file containing all of the tag handlers and supporting classes and a separate TLD file. To deploy the tag library, the JAR file simply needs to be placed into the `WEB-INF\lib` directory, while the TLD just needs to be placed anywhere underneath the `WEB-INF` directory. Again, placing it in `WEB-INF\tlds` is a good recommendation. One this has been done, the TLD can either be directly referenced, or a symbolic link can be defined in the `web.xml` file.

However, this process is still prone to errors during the deployment process. A better way is to completely package up a tag library.

Prepackaged Tag Libraries

Although introduced in JSP 1.1, many JSP containers have only just recently started to properly support prepackaged tag libraries. A prepackaged tag library is a JAR file containing all of the tag handlers and supporting classes, along with the appropriate TLD files that describe the tag library or libraries.

To package up a tag library, the first step is to generate a regular JAR file containing the class files, nested in a directory structure representing the Java packages. Following this, the TLD file is placed within the META-INF directory of the JAR file. A restriction of the JSP 1.1 specification is that a JAR file must only contain a single tag library descriptor file called taglib.tld, located within the META-INF directory. However, this restriction has been dropped and it is now possible to have multiple TLD files, although they must still have a .tld extension and be located in the META-INF directory. To deploy a prepackaged tag library, all we need to do is drop the JAR file into the WEB-INF\lib directory of a web application and restart the server.

The one thing that we must remember to do is to make use of the optional <uri> element in the TLD file. Where before we were defining a mapping between a TLD and a symbolic URI, dropping the JAR file into the WEB-INF\lib directory will automatically set this up for us – providing that we specify a URI in the first place. For example, the TLD for the navigation tag library could specify the following URI:

```
<?xml version="1.0" encoding="ISO-8859-1" ?>
<!DOCTYPE taglib
  PUBLIC "-//Sun Microsystems, Inc.//DTD JSP Tag Library 1.2//EN"
  "http://java.sun.com/dtd/web-jsptaglibrary_1_2.dtd">

<taglib>

  <tlib-version>1.0</tlib-version>
  <jsp-version>1.2</jsp-version>
  <short-name>navigation</short-name>
  <uri>/navigationTaglib</uri>
  <description>
    Navigation examples for the Deployment chapter.
  </description>

  ... tags omitted for brevity ...

</taglib>
```

When deployed, we will be able to reference the tag library in the same way as before:

```
<%@ taglib uri="/navigationTaglib" prefix="navigation" %>
```

This is a great mechanism and one that makes distribution of tag libraries very straightforward. All you need to do is e-mail somebody the JAR file and ask them to place it into the WEB-INF\lib directory of their web application, after which all of the tag libraries contained within it will be automatically deployed.

Dependencies

When packaging up a tag library, there may be dependencies on other classes. Dependent classes are fairly straightforward to handle in that they either need to be bundled up with the tag library in a JAR file, placed in the WEB-INF\classes directory, or preferably, and in the case of third party libraries, a JAR file containing them can be dropped into the WEB-INF\lib directory. This way, they can be easily made distributed and made available to the web application.

Customizing a Tag Library at Deployment Time

There may be times when some features of a tag library should be externally configurable. For example, specifying the names and locations of servers, or logins and passwords for services that the tags will make use of. Currently, there is no ideal place in the TLD file where such information can be stored although there are a couple of workarounds until this is put in place.

Using a Properties File

The first of these workarounds is to supply such configuration information in a regular `java.util.Properties` file, placed somewhere underneath the `WEB-INF` directory. To load a properties file from this location, all that is needed are the following lines of code:

```
URL url = pageContext.getServletContext()
                         .getResource("/WEB-INF/myTagLib.properties");
Properties props = new Properties();
props.load(url.openStream());
```

And properties can be accessed as follows:

```
props.getProperty("myPropertyName");
```

Alternatively, and to escape the potential problems associated with a proliferation of properties files, other resources such as a database, JNDI, or LDAP could also be used.

Using Servlet Context Initialization Parameters

An alternative solution is to use the initialization parameters in the servlet context. These are defined in the web application deployment descriptor (`web.xml`) and take the following form:

```
<web-app>

  ...

  <context-param>
    <param-name>myPropertyName</param-name>
    <param-value>myPropertyValue</param-value>
  </context-param>

  ...

</web-app>
```

To access this value from a tag handler, all that is needed is the following line of code:

```
pageContext.getServletContext().getInitParameter("myPropertyName");
```

Whichever mechanism is used, externalizing such information rather than bundling it with the tag library (in a JAR file) means that tag libraries are much easier to customize, and don't need to be modified and subsequently redeployed.

Documenting Tag Libraries

One of the final topics that we should look at in the context of deploying tag libraries is that of documentation. When building Java classes, a good way to document what is going on is by placing Javadoc comments in the code. The Javadoc compiler can then be run over the code and documentation is automatically generated – provided that the comments are there to start with.

However, custom tags are generally built for a different audience, and also for a different purpose. While the developers that maintain the tags will find Javadoc comments useful for finding their way around the tag handlers, such comments are pretty much useless for those page authors that work on the page from a presentation perspective. First of all, page authors probably aren't going to be provided with the tag handler source code and Javadocs. In addition to this, the way that a tag can be used requires a different type of documentation. Here, we need supplementary documentation addressing the usage of the tag from a JSP perspective, not the inner workings of the tag handler source code.

There are several ways in which tag libraries can be documented; some good examples can be found in the Jakarta Taglibs project (http:\\jakarta.apache.org\taglibs\). At a minimum, the sort of information that is useful to page authors includes:

- The name of the tag library and a short description of its purpose
- The names and descriptions of the tags in the library
- The attributes that a tag can take, including whether they are required and what values are accepted
- The scripting variables that a tag may introduce
- How the tag should be used on the page (for example, if it should be nested)
- A comprehensive example of how the tag can be used on the page will undoubtedly help authors using it for the first time

There are many ways in which such documentation can be generated, including text files, Microsoft Word documents, PDF files, and HTML pages. As we've seen, a simple way of capturing all of this information is to use the optional attributes of the TLD file, for example `<description>`. This forms a good starting point and will hopefully mean that the information contained within it will stay current when the tag library evolves over time.

As with Javadoc, a good way generating the documentation for a page author is to do so automatically. Although TLD files have a `.tld` extension, they are just regular XML files, and as such can be used as the source for a number of things including XSLT transformations and direct manipulation.

Troubleshooting and Gotchas

At the end of the day, and however well documented your tag libraries are, something will undoubtedly go wrong. To wrap up the chapter, let's briefly look at some of the problems that most people come across sooner or later during the deployment of their tags.

Incorrect Prefixes and Names

When developing custom tags, you'll often find yourself changing the names of tags, and also moving them between tag libraries. In this situation it is easy to use the incorrect prefix on a tag. In the following JSP page taken from earlier in the chapter, the prefix for the `back` tag has been incorrectly specified:

```
<html>
  <head>
    <title>Professional JSP Tag Libraries</title>
  </head>

  <%@ taglib uri="/navigationTaglib" prefix="navigation" %>

  <body>

    <h1>Page Not Found (404)</h1>

    Sorry, the page that you are looking for could not be found,
    please use the link below to return to the previous page.

    <center>
      <navigationTaglib:back label="Back to previous page"/>
    </center>
  </body>
</html>
```

Often, the JSP page will not compile and a stack trace will be presented. In this case, however, requesting this page provides the following results, with the hyperlink no longer present:

At first glance, it is not apparent what is happening here although it does seem as if the tag is not working as it should. A look at the generated source tells the true story:

```
<html>
  <head>
    <title>Professional JSP Tag Libraries</title>
```

```
    </head>

    <body>
      <h1>Page Not Found (404)</h1>

      Sorry, the page that you are looking for could not be found,
      please use the link below to return to the previous page.

      <center>
        <navigationTaglib:back label="Back to previous page"/>
      </center>
    </body>
  </html>
```

Because the JSP engine didn't recognize the tag `<navigationTaglib:back>`, it has simply left it to be included in the generated content because, after all, it might be XML that has been generated legitimately for the client. Unfortunately for us though, the browser has chosen not to render it and therefore gives the impression that something has gone wrong with the processing of the tag. This same behavior happens when the `taglib` directive is missed off the page too.

Conversely, specifying the correct prefix with an incorrect tag name does highlight itself with an error like the following:

No such tag backTag in the tag library imported with prefix navigation

As we can see, the behavior associated with specifying incorrect prefixes and names is different.

Not Using Packages for Tag Handlers

Another common problem is not using packages for tag handler classes. Although it is possible to compile the tag handler and write the TLD for an unpackaged tag handler, problems often occur when the tag is used on the page.

Behind the scenes, JSP containers translate the JSP page into an equivalent servlet. This servlet is often packaged up into a vendor-specific package, for example, Tomcat uses the package `org.apache.jsp`. When tags are used in the page, they are usually specified in the generated Java code using the fully qualified class name of the tag handler:

```
com.wrox.jsptaglibs.navigation.BackTag t = new
                                  com.wrox.jsptaglibs.navigation.BackTag();
```

In this situation, the servlet can easily locate the class and use it. However, the code that is generated for a tag handler that isn't used within a Java package might be as follows:

```
BackTag t = new BackTag();
```

As no package name is referenced, the servlet will try to find the class within the same package as the generated servlet – in the case of Tomcat, `org.apache.jsp`. Rather than highlighting that something is wrong with the tag handler, most JSP containers will just throw out a compilation error on the generated servlet. The moral of the story here is that you should always use a package for tag handlers.

Testing on Multiple JSP Containers

A final gotcha that is very easy to fall into is not testing your tags on different containers. There are two reasons to do this. The first reason is to check that your tags function correctly on another implementation of the JSP specification, therefore checking that you are not relying on any vendor-specific features. This is really more applicable if you are developing a tag library for distribution rather than for a bespoke project, but applicable nonetheless.

The second reason for testing your tags on different containers is because not all containers choose to pool tag instances. If we think about the `for` tag again, such a tag might have a counter, implemented as an instance variable that gets initialized to zero when the tag handler is created. The tag will then be used and in those containers that don't pool tags, the tag handler instance won't be used again. On the next invocation, a new tag handler instance will be created.

However, if a container chooses to pool tags, this type of per-invocation state needs to be reset each time. If the counter wasn't reset in the `doStartTag()` method, it would simply continue to be incremented until the tag was taken out of the pool – not something that you would expect to see. Pooling of tag handlers can have an interesting, unexpected effect on how tags behave and it's for this reason that you should try to test on different containers.

Summary

The deployment of tags is an important and often neglected part of the development process. This chapter wraps up our look at how to develop tags by looking at some of the many topics around deployment.

We started with a look at how validation plays an important role in making tags robust and easy to use. At the end of the day, page authors will probably try to use the tags that you deploy in all sorts of ways that you hadn't expected. Helping them use your tags correctly will make web applications more robust and a good way to do this is by implementing validation logic for the attributes and usage of the tags. This can be performed at request time or translation time by a number of different mechanisms.

Following this we took a more detailed look at the tag library descriptor file format. While many of the elements are not essential to the day-to-day development of tags, there are times when supplying the optional information can be beneficial.

Next we looked at some of the different ways in which tag libraries can be deployed, including a look at how they can be packaged up and automatically deployed. To wrap up this section, we briefly looked at how dependent classes can be deployed, and how tag libraries can be customized at deployment time through the use of properties files or initialization parameters in the web application deployment descriptor.

To complete the chapter, we moved on to look at some of the common gotchas that can happen when deploying tag libraries. Most of the time, incorrectly using a tag or doing something wrong will result in a nasty stack trace in your browser. Occasionally, however, the results are unexpected and the source of the problem can be hard to track down.

This concludes our detailed look at how tag libraries can be developed and deployed. The next chapter brings many of the topics that we've learnt about together in the form of a case study.

LONDON

11

Case Study

The preceding chapters have covered a lot of material, from developing simple tags to those that control their body content, and from designing tags to deploying them. We've seen many examples of how tags can be used on the page in isolation, but not how they can be used together.

In this chapter, we'll look at how tags and tag libraries can be used in conjunction with one another to build up a small web application that will make use of the following tag libraries – `cookie`, `domain`, `html`, `iteration`, `logic`, `menu`, `paging`, and `request`.

Some of these tag libraries we have seen in previous chapters, some are variations on a theme, while we'll also be introducing some that are new. The aim of the case study is to produce a web application that is easy to build, understand, and maintain and, of course, that consists of components that can be reused in other applications in the future. In addition to this, one final goal of the case study is to have as little Java code on the page as possible for the benefit of page authors unfamiliar with Java. This is, as we'll see, something that is achievable.

Setting the Scene

Many of the examples that we've looked at in this book have focused on web pages that present a list of books to the user or generate menus. A common theme throughout most of the examples has been an online bookstore and we will continue this theme in this case study.

The web application that we will build will allow users to browse through an online catalog of currently available books. The previous chapters have shown how we can present the user with a list of books and we're going to use this as a starting point to build a small, but functional, web site.

The web site is basically made up of two parts. The first of these allows the user to look at a list of books in a specific category, while the second allows them to drill down into further details about a specific book. Let's take a look at each of these features in turn before moving on to look at how such functionality can be built using JSP and custom tags.

Viewing a Category

When somebody visits the site, they'll be presented with an HTML page (using a frameset), which contains a header, a left navigation bar, and the content. The left hand frame contains a menu and from here, the user can choose to look at a particular category of books. Clicking a link loads the list into the main part of the page where the title and unique ID (ISBN) of each book is displayed:

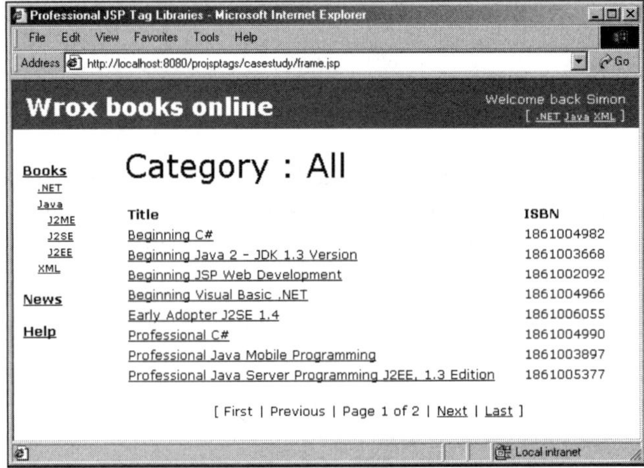

As a category may contain a large number of books, the list is constrained to only show a fixed number. The user can page through the list using the links at the bottom of the page.

Viewing a Book

Clicking on a book title allows the user to find further details of a specific book including a short description, the author(s), price, and so on:

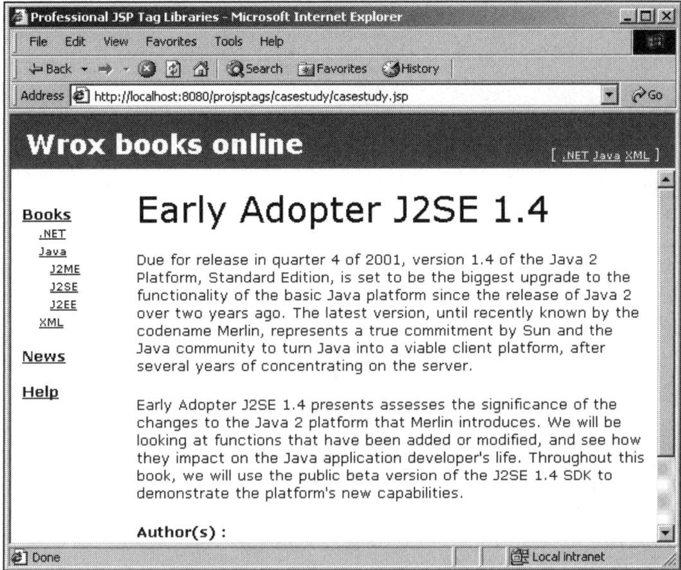

These two pages are the extent of the case study and although small, there is a fair amount of work involved.

Representing the Business Objects

Before we move on to look at how the web application is built, let's quickly recap on the domain – the set of business objects that represent the key concepts in the application. The domain for this application is very straightforward, consisting of only **books** and **categories**.

The Book Class

The representation of a book that we're using for the purposes of this example includes a unique ID (the ISBN), a title, a short description, the price, and a collection of authors:

```
package com.wrox.jsptaglibs.casestudy.common;

import java.io.Serializable;
import java.util.ArrayList;
import java.util.Collection;

public class Book implements Serializable {

  private String isbn;
  private String title;
  private String description = "";
  private float price;
  private Collection authors = new ArrayList();

  public Book() {}
```

```
  public Book(String isbn, String title) {
    this.isbn = isbn;
    this.title = title;
  }

  public String getIsbn() {
    return this.isbn;
  }

  public void setIsbn(String isbn) {
    this.isbn = isbn;
  }

  public String getTitle() {
    return this.title;
  }

  public void setTitle(String title) {
    this.title = title;
  }

  public String getDescription() {
    return this.description;
  }

  public void setDescription(String description) {
    this.description = description;
  }

  public float getPrice() {
    return this.price;
  }

  public void setPrice(float price) {
    this.price = price;
  }

  public void addAuthor(String author) {
    authors.add(author);
  }

  public Collection getAuthors() {
    return this.authors;
  }
}
```

The Category Class

Likewise, a category is fairly simple and consists of a name, a description, and a collection of `Book` instances that are in the category:

```
package com.wrox.jsptaglibs.casestudy.common;

import java.io.Serializable;
import java.util.ArrayList;
import java.util.Collection;
import java.util.List;

public class Category implements Serializable {

  private String name;
  private String description = "";
  private List books = new ArrayList();

  public Category() {}

  public Category(String name) {
    this.name = name;
  }

  public String getName() {
    return this.name;
  }

  public void setName(String name) {
    this.name = name;
  }

  public String getDescription() {
    return this.description;
  }

  public void setDescription(String description) {
    this.description = description;
  }

  public void add(Book book) {
    books.add(book);
  }

  public Collection getBooks() {
    return books;
  }
}
```

Accessing Books and Categories

In a production system, the information about books and categories (the business objects) would more than likely be stored in a persistent data store such as a relational database. For the purpose of this case study, this information has been hard-coded into Java classes.

The BookManager Class

The `BookManager` class is as follows, with most of the data omitted for brevity:

```
package com.wrox.jsptaglibs.casestudy.common;

import java.util.Collection;
import java.util.HashMap;

public class BookManager {

  private static BookManager instance = new BookManager();

  private HashMap books = new HashMap();

  private BookManager() {
    Book book;

    book = new Book("1861002092", "Beginning JSP Web Development");
    books.put(book.getIsbn(), book);
    // more books added here
  }

  public static BookManager getInstance() {
    return instance;
  }

  public Book getBook(String isbn) {
    return (Book)books.get(isbn);
  }

  public Book[] getBooksAsArray() {
    return (Book[])books.values().toArray(new Book[0]);
  }

  public Collection getBooksAsCollection() {
    return books.values();
  }
}
```

This singleton class is a container for a number of `Book` instances, with the important methods being `getBook()`, `getBooksAsArray()`, and `getBooksAsCollection()` that allow us to look up books in different ways.

The CategoryManager Class

The singleton `CategoryManager` class is very similar to the `BookManager` class and maintains a collection of populated `Category` instances:

```
package com.wrox.jsptaglibs.casestudy.common;

import java.util.HashMap;

public class CategoryManager {
```

```
    private static CategoryManager instance = new CategoryManager();

    private HashMap categories = new HashMap();

    private CategoryManager() {
      Category category;

      category = new Category("J2SE");
      category.setDescription("This is where you'll find books about the "
                            + "core Java platform, including topics such "
                            + "as networking, IO and Swing.");
      category.add(BookManager.getInstance().getBook("1861003668"));
      category.add(BookManager.getInstance().getBook("1861006055"));
      categories.put(category.getName(), category);

      // more categories added here
    }

    public static CategoryManager getInstance() {
      return instance;
    }

    public Category getCategory(String name) {
      return (Category)categories.get(name);
    }
  }
```

The important method here is `getCategory()` that allows us to look up a specific, named category. Now that we have the business objects implemented, let's move on to see how the user interface is built.

Building the Frameset

The first part of the web site is to define the frameset that we'll be using (in this case `casestudy.jsp`). There are three frames – `headerFrame`, `leftNavFrame`, and `contentFrame`. The HTML for this is as follows:

```
<html>
  <head>
    <title>Professional JSP Tag Libraries</title>
  </head>

  <frameset rows="48,*">

    <frame src="header.jsp" name="headerFrame"
      scrolling="no" frameborder="0" noresize>

    <frameset cols="100,*">
      <frame src="leftnav.jsp" name="leftNavFrame"
        scrolling="no" frameborder="0" noresize>
      <frame src="category.jsp?name=All" name="contentFrame"
        scrolling="auto" frameborder="0">
```

```
        </frameset>

      </frameset>
    </html>
```

Each of the frames in the frameset points to a different JSP page so let's take a look at these in turn.

The Left Hand Menu

The `leftNavFrame` contains most of the navigation for the site by allowing the user to choose a category of books that they are interested in knowing more about. In addition to this are a couple of links to other parts of the site – News and Help:

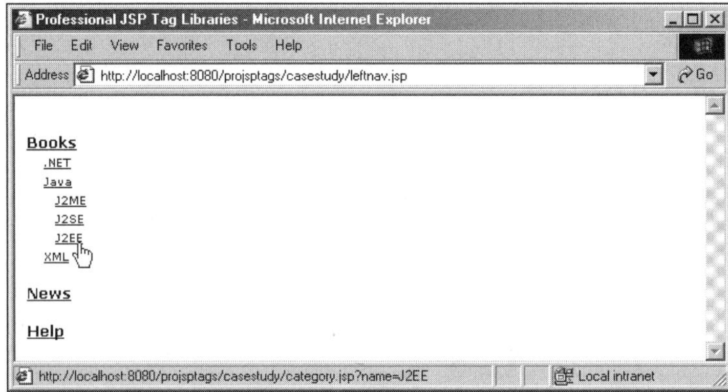

Building the Menu Structure

There are many ways in which a list of hyperlinks could be built, but rather than have a static list we've opted for a hierarchy that is generated dynamically. Back in Chapter 7, we introduced the `menu` tag library that allowed us to build a list of hyperlinks very easily. Although we didn't take advantage of it at that time, we did note that the supporting classes (`Menu`, `MenuItem`, and `MenuEntry`) allow us to build tree structures that can be arbitrarily deep.

In a production system, such menu structures might be stored in the database. For the purpose of the case study, however, we will maintain the menu structure for the web site in a singleton Java class called `MenuManager` in the same way that we did for the examples in Chapter 7:

```
package com.wrox.jsptaglibs.casestudy.menu;

import java.util.HashMap;

public class MenuManager {

  private static MenuManager instance = new MenuManager();

  private HashMap menus = new HashMap();
```

```
  private MenuManager() {
    Menu root = new Menu("/", "home.jsp");
    Menu books = new Menu("Books", "category.jsp?name=All");

    Menu java = new Menu("Java", "category.jsp?name=Java");
    java.add(new MenuItem("J2ME", "category.jsp?name=J2ME"));
    java.add(new MenuItem("J2SE", "category.jsp?name=J2SE"));
    java.add(new MenuItem("J2EE", "category.jsp?name=J2EE"));

    books.add(new MenuItem(".NET", "category.jsp?name=.NET"));
    books.add(java);
    books.add(new MenuItem("XML", "category.jsp?name=XML"));
    root.add(books);

    root.add(new MenuItem("News", "news.jsp"));
    MenuItem menuitem = new MenuItem("Help", "help.jsp");
    menuitem.setTarget("_blank");
    root.add(menuitem);

    menus.put("main", root);
  }

  public static MenuManager getInstance() {
    return instance;
  }

  public Menu getMenu(String name) {
    return (Menu)menus.get(name);
  }
}
```

Here, the constructor creates a menu structure in memory and, once built, the menu is called `main` and is added to the collection of menus that this class maintains. To get a reference to this menu, clients can simply use the `getMenu()` method by specifying the name of the menu that they would like to use.

Rendering the Menu

Now that we have the menu structure represented and easily accessible, the next step is to generate the JSP page that will render it. Since we are now taking advantage of the fact that we can nest menus and menu items, we must revisit the `menu` tag library and make some changes.

The first problem that we have is that we no longer have a simple collection of `MenuItem` instances to iterate over on the page. Instead, we have a potentially complex structure. In addition to this, many web sites render the different levels of the menu in different ways. For example, and as shown in the previous screenshot, the main items are displayed in a different font and the hyperlinks are indented depending on how deep they are in the tree.

Custom tags can perform iteration on the page, but iterating over (or walking through) such a complex tree structure is a fairly tricky task especially because the depth isn't known. One solution to this would be to simply assume that the maximum depth of such a structure is an arbitrary number of levels, and then simply keep drilling down into the structure until we reach that level. However, this is slightly inflexible since it does potentially place restrictions on how the tag can be used in the future. A better solution is to flatten the menu structure into a simple list of items that need to be displayed on the page. Upon flattening the menu, we can assign each element a number that corresponds to the level that it relates to in the tree – zero for the root, one for its children, two for their subsequent children, and so on. In this example, "/" is the root (level 0), Books is level 1, and Java is level 2.

Once we have this flat collection, iterating over it with a custom tag is trivial. This solves the iteration problem although it doesn't address how we can render each level of the tree differently. One solution here is to write some conditional code in a scriptlet of the form: "if the current level is 1, show the hyperlink in bold". However, we must resist this temptation and instead use the ability that tags have to evaluate their body content. To see how this all works, let us first look at the JSP page and then each of the tags in turn.

The Page

Despite the initial complexity of rendering a nested hierarchy of elements, the page here is fairly short, readable, and easy to understand. We start with the usual header and the `taglib` directive:

```
<html>
  <head>
    <title>Professional JSP Tag Libraries</title>
  </head>

  <%@ taglib uri="/casestudyMenuTaglib" prefix="menu" %>

  <body>
```

Following this is the `getMenu` tag. In a real system there may be many different menus for different parts of the site. The `getMenu` tag is a simple, convenient way of finding a named menu and it inserts the resulting `Menu` object into the page context under the name specified by the `id` attribute:

```
    <menu:getMenu id="menu" name="main"/>
```

Next is the `showMenu` tag that, behind the scenes, is slightly different to the one shown in Chapter 7 because it flattens the menu structure before iterating over it. As the menu has already been introduced into the page context, we simply specify the name and let the `showMenu` tag look up the `Menu` reference itself:

```
    <menu:showMenu name="menu">
```

The functionality provided by the `getMenu` tag could have been incorporated into the `showMenu` tag. However, we've chosen to keep them separate so that the way menus are found can be swapped in and out independently of how they are rendered on the page. This ultimately makes the `showMenu` tag much more reusable without change.

Nested within the showMenu tags are one or more showLevel tags that provide conditional logic for rendering the current menu entry. The body content will only be evaluated if the supplied level attribute matches the level of the current menu entry. Here we are saying that level 1 menu entries get rendered in bold while level 2 and 3 entries get indented and displayed with a smaller font. Further nested is the showMenuEntry tag that generates the hyperlink in a similar way to the showMenuItem tag in Chapter 7:

```
      <menu:showLevel level="1">
        <br/>
        <b><menu:showMenuEntry target="contentFrame"/></b>
        <br/>
      </menu:showLevel>

      <menu:showLevel level="2">
          
        <font size="-2"><menu:showMenuEntry target="contentFrame"/></font>
        <br/>
      </menu:showLevel>

      <menu:showLevel level="3">
            
        <font size="-2"><menu:showMenuEntry target="contentFrame"/></font>
        <br/>
      </menu:showLevel>

    </menu:showMenu>
  </body>
</html>
```

Now that we've seen how the menu is built up on the page, let's look at how the tags themselves are built.

The getMenu Tag

The first of the menu tags, getMenu, is very straightforward. We define a single attribute called name that it uses to look up the menu. Once found, the resulting Menu reference is put into the PageContext under the name specified by the id attribute:

```
package com.wrox.jsptaglibs.casestudy.menu;

import javax.servlet.jsp.JspException;
import javax.servlet.jsp.tagext.TagSupport;

public class GetMenuTag extends TagSupport {

  private String name;

  public int doStartTag() throws JspException {

    // find the named Menu and put it into the page context
    pageContext.setAttribute(getId(),
      MenuManager.getInstance().getMenu(name));

    return SKIP_BODY;
```

```
  }

  public void setName(String name) {
    this.name = name;
  }
}
```

The showMenu Tag

Next is the showMenu tag that performs the iteration on the page. The first thing that it must do is flatten the menu structure underneath the supplied menu attribute. Each element in the menu structure is of type Menu or MenuItem, both of which extend MenuEntry. When flattening the structure, we additionally need to keep track of the level in the tree that the menu entry came from. Rather than add an attribute to the MenuEntry class, we'll create a simple wrapper for this information called FlatMenuEntry:

```
class FlatMenuEntry {

  private MenuEntry menuEntry;

  private int level = 0;

  FlatMenuEntry(MenuEntry menuEntry, int level) {
    this.menuEntry = menuEntry;
    this.level = level;
  }

  MenuEntry getMenuEntry() {
    return this.menuEntry;
  }

  int getLevel() {
    return this.level;
  }
}
```

The tag itself is just a regular tag that implements the IterationTag interface. However, it has an attribute called name whose value is set to “menu”, and some additional state that will be used by the nested tags:

```
package com.wrox.jsptaglibs.casestudy.menu;

import java.util.ArrayList;
import java.util.Collection;
import java.util.Iterator;
import java.util.List;

import javax.servlet.jsp.JspException;
import javax.servlet.jsp.tagext.TagSupport;

public class ShowMenuTag extends TagSupport {

  private String name;
```

```
private Iterator iterator;

private MenuEntry currentMenuEntry;

private int currentLevel = 0;
```

Before the iteration can take place, the menu structure must be flattened. With the wrapper class written, flattening the menu is simply a matter of taking each entry in the tree and flattening everything beneath it. This can be easily achieved with a recursive method as follows:

```
private Collection flatten(Menu menu, int level) {
  MenuEntry menuEntry;
  Iterator it;

  // add the specified Menu itself as the first element in the list
  List flatMenu = new ArrayList();
  flatMenu.add(new FlatMenuEntry(menu, level));

  // and now flatten the children (going one more level down)
  level++;
  it = menu.menuEntries();
  while (it.hasNext()) {
    menuEntry = (MenuEntry)it.next();

    if (menuEntry instanceof MenuItem) {
      // simply add the MenuItem into the list
      flatMenu.add(new FlatMenuEntry(menuEntry, level));
    } else {
      // we've found another Menu so flatten it further
      flatMenu.addAll(flatten((Menu)menuEntry, level));
    }
  }

  return flatMenu;
}
```

With this in place, the tag lifecycle methods are now very similar to many others that we've seen. The only real difference here is that we're maintaining some additional state (`currentMenuEntry` and `currentLevel`) during each loop of the iteration:

```
public int doStartTag() throws JspException {
  // find the Menu object ...
  Menu menu = (Menu)pageContext.findAttribute(name);

  // ... flatten the menu structure from a tree into a simple list
  // and setup the iterator to be used
  iterator = flatten(menu, 0).iterator();

  if (iterator.hasNext()) {
    FlatMenuEntry fme = (FlatMenuEntry)iterator.next();

    // store the current state so that it can be used by child tags
    this.currentMenuEntry = fme.getMenuEntry();
```

```
            this.currentLevel = fme.getLevel();

            // and include the body
            return EVAL_BODY_INCLUDE;
          } else {
            // there are no menu items so skip the body
            return SKIP_BODY;
          }
        }

        public int doAfterBody() throws JspException {
          if (iterator.hasNext()) {
            FlatMenuEntry fme = (FlatMenuEntry)iterator.next();

            // store the current state so that it can be used by child tags
            this.currentMenuEntry = fme.getMenuEntry();
            this.currentLevel = fme.getLevel();

            // and instruct the JSP engine to re-evaluate the body of this tag
            return EVAL_BODY_AGAIN;
          } else {
            // there are no more menu items so skip the body
            return SKIP_BODY;
          }
        }
```

Finally, we have the mutator method for the attribute and the accessor methods for the additional state that nested tags will be making use of:

```
        public void setName(String name) {
          this.name = name;
        }

        public MenuEntry getCurrentMenuEntry() {
          return this.currentMenuEntry;
        }

        public int getCurrentLevel() {
          return currentLevel;
        }
      }
```

The reason behind providing accessor methods for the state rather than using the page context is that ideally we don't want this information available on the page itself. After all, having access to information in a JSP page makes it much easier to write scriptlets instead of using tags. As there is a definite structure to the way that the tags are used on the page, we can simplify the way that they are used by having the nested tags cooperate implicitly with their parent behind the scenes.

The showLevel Tag

The `showLevel` tag is used to conditionally determine how the current menu entry should be rendered. The logic behind this is simple and the body content of the tag is only evaluated if the value of the supplied `level` attribute is the same as the "current level":

```
package com.wrox.jsptaglibs.casestudy.menu;

import javax.servlet.jsp.JspException;
import javax.servlet.jsp.tagext.TagSupport;

public class ShowLevelTag extends TagSupport {

  private int level;

  public int doStartTag() throws JspException {

    // find the parent showMenu tag
    ShowMenuTag t = (ShowMenuTag)findAncestorWithClass(this,
                                                        ShowMenuTag.class);

    // if the specified level matches the level of the current MenuEntry,
    // evaluate the body content
    if (level == t.getCurrentLevel()) {
      return EVAL_BODY_INCLUDE;
    } else {
      return SKIP_BODY;
    }
  }

  public void setLevel(int level) {
    this.level = level;
  }
}
```

Notice here that this tag searches for its parent `showMenu` tag and asks it for the current level. A side effect of not making state available to the page is that it "persuades" people to use the tag library, and additionally, to use it how it was designed. Exposing information about the current menu entry means that scriptlets can be written to render the menu instead of the tags.

The showMenuEntry Tag

Last but not least is the tag that actually generates the HTML hyperlink – `showMenuEntry`. As we're using frames we should also render the `target` attribute of the anchor tag. Because the `target` property might already be defined on a `MenuItem` (for example the Help menu item), we make sure that we don't override this value:

```
package com.wrox.jsptaglibs.casestudy.menu;

import java.io.IOException;

import javax.servlet.jsp.JspException;
import javax.servlet.jsp.JspTagException;
import javax.servlet.jsp.tagext.TagSupport;

public class ShowMenuEntryTag extends TagSupport {

  private String target;
public int doStartTag() throws JspException {
```

```
    // find the parent ShowMenuTag
    ShowMenuTag t = (ShowMenuTag)findAncestorWithClass(this,
                                                      ShowMenuTag.class);

    // and ask it for the current menu entry
    MenuEntry menuEntry = t.getCurrentMenuEntry();

    try {
      // now build up the hyperlink
      StringBuffer buf = new StringBuffer();

      buf.append("<a href=\"");
      buf.append(menuEntry.getUrl());
      buf.append("\"");

      // including the optional target, although we should use
      // the target defined on the MenuItem if possible
      String targetToUse = target;

      if (menuEntry instanceof MenuItem) {
        MenuItem item = (MenuItem)menuEntry;

        if (item.getTarget() != null) {
          targetToUse = item.getTarget();
        }
      }

      if (targetToUse != null) {
        buf.append(" target=\"");
        buf.append(targetToUse);
        buf.append("\"");
      }

      // finish off the HTML and write it to the page
      buf.append(">");
      buf.append(menuEntry.getName());
      buf.append("</a>");

      pageContext.getOut().write(buf.toString());
    } catch (IOException ioe) {
      throw new JspTagException(ioe.getMessage());
    }

    return SKIP_BODY;
  }

  public void setTarget(String target) {
    this.target = target;
  }
}
```

Once again, this tag searches for its parent `showMenu` tag and asks it for information about the current element, in this case by getting a reference to the current `MenuEntry` instance.

The Tag Library Descriptor

For completeness, the TLD file for this tag library is as follows:

```
<?xml version="1.0" encoding="ISO-8859-1" ?>
<!DOCTYPE taglib
  PUBLIC "-//Sun Microsystems, Inc.//DTD JSP Tag Library 1.2//EN"
  "http://java.sun.com/dtd/web-jsptaglibrary_1_2.dtd">

<taglib>

  <tlib-version>1.0</tlib-version>
  <jsp-version>1.2</jsp-version>
  <short-name>menu</short-name>
  <description>
    Menu examples for the Case Study chapter.
  </description>

  <tag>
    <name>getMenu</name>
    <tag-class>com.wrox.jsptaglibs.casestudy.menu.GetMenuTag</tag-class>
    <body-content>empty</body-content>
    <description>
      A convenient way of locating a specific,
      named menu and placing it into the page context.
    </description>

    <attribute>
      <name>id</name>
      <required>true</required>
      <rtexprvalue>false</rtexprvalue>
    </attribute>

    <attribute>
      <name>name</name>
      <required>true</required>
      <rtexprvalue>false</rtexprvalue>
    </attribute>
  </tag>

  <tag>
    <name>showMenu</name>
    <tag-class>com.wrox.jsptaglibs.casestudy.menu.ShowMenuTag</tag-class>
    <body-content>JSP</body-content>
    <description>
      Provides iteration over a menu structure named in the page context.
    </description>

    <attribute>
      <name>name</name>
      <required>true</required>
      <rtexprvalue>false</rtexprvalue>
    </attribute>
  </tag>
```

```
  <tag>
    <name>showLevel</name>
    <tag-class>com.wrox.jsptaglibs.casestudy.menu.ShowLevelTag</tag-class>
    <body-content>JSP</body-content>
    <description>
      Conditionally evaluates the body content
      if the current level matches the specified level.
    </description>

    <attribute>
      <name>level</name>
      <required>true</required>
      <rtexprvalue>false</rtexprvalue>
    </attribute>
  </tag>

  <tag>
    <name>showMenuEntry</name>
    <tag-class>
      com.wrox.jsptaglibs.casestudy.menu.ShowMenuEntryTag
    </tag-class>
    <body-content>JSP</body-content>
    <description>
      Generates a hyperlink for a menu entry.
    </description>

    <attribute>
      <name>target</name>
      <required>false</required>
      <rtexprvalue>false</rtexprvalue>
    </attribute>
  </tag>

</taglib>
```

The Header

The next part of the site to look at is the header, which consists of a static title, and also the top-level categories from the left hand frame. In addition to this, there is an optional message to welcome back users who have previously registered:

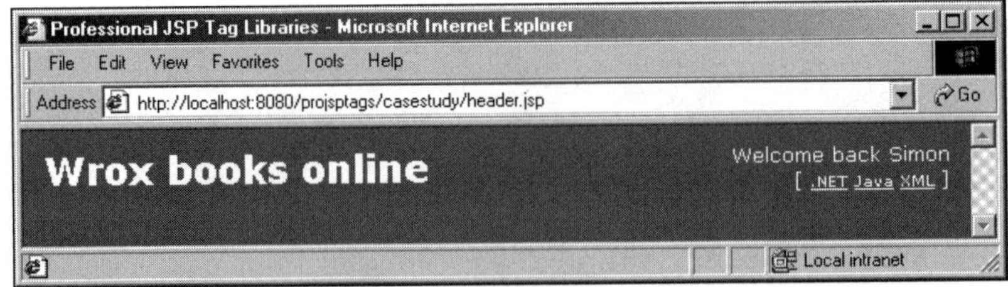

The JSP page itself is fairly simple and, as usual, begins with the opening HTML tags and the `taglib` directives:

```
<html>
  <head>
    <title>Professional JSP Tag Libraries</title>
  </head>

  <%@ taglib uri="/casestudyCookieTaglib" prefix="cookie" %>
  <%@ taglib uri="/casestudyMenuTaglib" prefix="menu" %>
```

Next is the body of the page containing a table in which the content is laid out.

```
  <body bgcolor="#CC0033" topmargin="8">

    <table width="100%">
      <tr>
        <td><h2>Wrox books online</h2></td>
```

A feature of many web sites is the ability for users to register their details so that the site can present them with personalized content. Although the functionality to register users is not part of the case study, assuming that it uses cookies means that this is a good opportunity to use the `cookie` tag library that we developed in Chapter 3 to present a "welcome back" message:

```
        <td align="right" valign="top">
          <cookie:exists name="visitorName">
            Welcome back <cookie:value name="visitorName"/>
          </cookie:exists>

          <br/>
```

The other interesting part of the header is that the top-level entries from the menu are also displayed here too. The tag library being used is the same as in the left hand frame, but we have the flexibility to only show those menu entries that are at level 2 in the menu structure. This is a great example of how a tag library can be reused to produce different results depending on how it is used on the page:

```
          [
          <menu:getMenu id="menu" name="main"/>
          <menu:showMenu name="menu">
            <menu:showLevel level="2">
              <font size="-2">
                <menu:showMenuEntry target="contentFrame"/>
              </font>
            </menu:showLevel>
          </menu:showMenu>
          ]

        </td>
      </tr>
    </table>
  </body>
</html>
```

The Category Page

Now we come on to the first of the two core pages in the site – the page that displays a category. As illustrated in the following screenshot, the JSP page takes a single parameter called `name` representing the category that should be displayed:

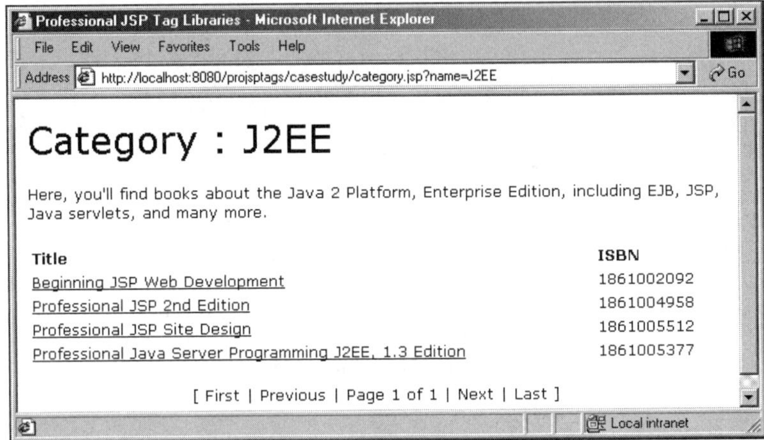

Despite its simple appearance there is a large amount of work going on behind the scenes. Before we look at the tags, let's get an overview of how the page works and see how everything fits together.

First of all there are the opening HTML tags and `taglib` directives:

```
<html>
  <head>
    <title>Professional JSP Tag Libraries</title>
  </head>

  <%@ taglib uri="/casestudyDomainTaglib" prefix="domain" %>
  <%@ taglib uri="/casestudyHTMLTaglib" prefix="html" %>
  <%@ taglib uri="/casestudyLogicTaglib" prefix="logic" %>
  <%@ taglib uri="/casestudyPagingTaglib" prefix="paging" %>
  <%@ taglib uri="/casestudyRequestTaglib" prefix="request" %>

  <body>
```

To show information about a category, the page must first of all determine which category should be displayed. This is achieved by requesting the page with a parameter called `name`. Although parameters are easily extracted from the `request` object by calling the `getParameter()` method, doing so introduces some Java code into the page which is something that we are trying to avoid. Instead, we can use a custom tag:

```
    <request:parameter id="name" name="name"/>
```

The `parameter` tag simply looks for the parameter specified by the `name` attribute and makes the value of it available as a scripting variable under the name specified by the `id` attribute. An alternative to placing the value of the parameter into the page as a scripting variable is to only place the resulting value into the page context. However, as this is a tag that could be reused on many different pages, introducing a scripting variable allows the page author to use it in a number of situations.

Now that we have found out which category is to be displayed, the next step is to get a reference to the `Category` instance representing it. The `CategoryManager` class has a `getCategory()` method which allows us to find a specific, named category, and this would be easy to wrap up in a scriptlet. However, instead we've chosen to use a tag called `category` to do this for us. It looks up the `Category` instance with the name specified by the `name` attribute and makes it available as a scripting variable. Again, the tag introduces a scripting variable because we don't know how page authors might want to use it in the future:

```
<domain:category id="category" name="<%= name %>"/>
```

Following this is a tag that looks up the list of books from a category, with the resulting collection of `Book` instances being introduced into the page. Rather than force the page author to look up a category before using this tag, the `category` attribute represents the name of the category instead of a physical `Category` instance:

```
<domain:books id="books" category="<%= name %>"/>
```

The next step is to display the information about the chosen category and the list of books that it contains. As highlighted before, it is possible for such a page to be called with an incorrect or missing parameter – either accidentally or by somebody trying to break the site. If this were the case, the `category` tag would fail to find the named `Category` instance and we therefore wouldn't be able to display any information.

Depending on how the page was written, a best-case scenario would be that the page simply didn't display anything, and in a worse case scenario, the user would probably be presented with something like a `NullPointerException`. For this reason we should check whether a category was found and tailor the output as appropriate.

Once again, the `logic` tag library built in Chapter 7 can be used to provide this conditional functionality. First of all is the `if` tag that sets up the block of conditional processing. The `value` attribute allows us to specify the value that we would like to test:

```
<logic:if value="<%= category %>">
```

Then, nested beneath this are the tags that form the conditions and like an `if` block, the body content is only evaluated for the first condition that matches. The `undefined` tag checks for an undefined (for example `null`) value and evaluates its body content if this is the case. Effectively this is the same as a scriptlet that checks for the condition `category == null`:

```
  <logic:undefined>
    Sorry, no category was found.
  </logic:undefined>
```

The other condition that is used here is `default`. It acts as a catchall in the same way that an `else` block does. In this case the body content is evaluated if the category is not undefined. This is the normal route through the page and it is here that the details of the category are displayed:

```
      <logic:default>
```

First of all there is some top-level information about the category – its name and description:

```
        <h1>Category :
          <jsp:getProperty name="category" property="name"/>
        </h1>

        <p>
          <jsp:getProperty name="category" property="description"/>
        </p>
```

Next is an HTML table that displays the books in the category. A common feature of many web sites is the ability to display information in pages to reduce the size of the response that is sent back to the user. A good example here is a search engine only displaying ten or so results per page. This is the purpose of the `page` tag:

```
        <table width="100%">
          <paging:page page="pageNumber" size="8"
                       id="book"
                       type="com.wrox.jsptaglibs.casestudy.common.Book"
                       collection="books">
```

Further nested is the `header` tag allowing a header to be output before the rows in the HTML table:

```
            <paging:header>
              <tr>
                <td>
                  <b>Title</b>
                </td>
                <td>
                  <b>ISBN</b>
                </td>
              </tr>
            </paging:header>
```

Then there's the body of the table that contains the data. Here we're showing the title of the book and the ISBN. The `html` tag library is used to construct a hyperlink allowing the user to drill down for more information:

```
            <paging:body>
              <tr>
                <td>
                  <html:a href="book.jsp"
                          label="<%= book.getTitle() %>">
                    <html:param name="isbn" value="<%= book.getIsbn() %>"/>
                  </html:a>
                </td>
```

```
            <td>
              <jsp:getProperty name="book" property="isbn"/>
            </td>
          </tr>
        </paging:body>
```

The last part of the table is a footer that contains links to allow the user to scroll backwards and forwards to other pages of information. Some more tags in the `page` tag library generate these links:

```
        <paging:footer>
          <tr align="center">
            <td colspan="2">
              <br/>
              [
                <paging:firstPage label="First"/> |
                <paging:previousPage label="Previous"/> |
                Page <paging:pageNumber/> of <paging:pageCount/> |
                <paging:nextPage label="Next"/> |
                <paging:lastPage label="Last"/>
              ]
            </td>
          </tr>
        </paging:footer>
```

Finally we have the appropriate closing tags:

```
          </paging:page>
        </table>
      </logic:default>

    </logic:if>
  </body>
</html>
```

With our look at how the page works complete, let's now go into more detail by looking specifically at how the `request`, `domain`, `paging`, and `html` tag libraries work.

The request Tag Library

The `request` tag library in this case study consists of a single tag called `parameter`. As we've seen, this is used to extract request parameters and make them available in the page as scripting variables. Essentially this is just a convenient way of performing `request.getParameter()` on the page without using Java code. Another benefit is that, as an enhancement, it could handle converting strings into other types such as numbers and Boolean values:

```
package com.wrox.jsptaglibs.casestudy.request;

import javax.servlet.jsp.JspException;
import javax.servlet.jsp.PageContext;
import javax.servlet.jsp.tagext.TagSupport;

public class GetParameterTag extends TagSupport {
```

```
   private String name;

   public int doStartTag() throws JspException {

      // get the named parameter and put it into the page context
      String value = pageContext.getRequest().getParameter(name);
      pageContext.setAttribute(getId(), value, PageContext.REQUEST_SCOPE);

      return SKIP_BODY;
   }

   public void setName(String name) {
      this.name = name;
   }
}
```

As request parameters are generally only used during the request, the resulting value is inserted into the page context under request scope. Should the value be required for longer than this, an enhancement to the tag would be to specify the scope on the page in the same way as the `<jsp:useBean/>` tag.

The Tag Library Descriptor

The TLD for this tag library is straightforward.

```
<?xml version="1.0" encoding="ISO-8859-1" ?>
<!DOCTYPE taglib
  PUBLIC "-//Sun Microsystems, Inc.//DTD JSP Tag Library 1.2//EN"
  "http://java.sun.com/dtd/web-jsptaglibrary_1_2.dtd">

<taglib>

  <tlib-version>1.0</tlib-version>
  <jsp-version>1.2</jsp-version>
  <short-name>request</short-name>
  <description>
    Request examples for the Case Study chapter.
  </description>

  <tag>
    <name>parameter</name>
    <tag-class>
      com.wrox.jsptaglibs.casestudy.request.GetParameterTag
    </tag-class>
    <body-content>empty</body-content>
    <description>
      Gets a parameter from the request and makes
      it available as a variable.
    </description>

    <variable>
      <name-from-attribute>id</name-from-attribute>
      <variable-class>java.lang.String</variable-class>
      <declare>true</declare>
      <scope>AT_BEGIN</scope>
```

```
    </variable>

    <attribute>
      <name>id</name>
      <required>true</required>
      <rtexprvalue>false</rtexprvalue>
    </attribute>

    <attribute>
      <name>name</name>
      <required>true</required>
      <rtexprvalue>false</rtexprvalue>
    </attribute>
  </tag>

</taglib>
```

The domain Tag Library

The next tag library that is used on the page is the `domain` tag library. This is tied in with the business objects that we've developed to support the application and is a convenient way of accessing these objects from a JSP page. The tags are acting as view helpers in that they help us retrieve data (the model) for the JSP page (the view) to display.

The category Tag

First of all is the `category` tag that looks up a named category and introduces it into the page:

```
package com.wrox.jsptaglibs.casestudy.domain;

import javax.servlet.jsp.JspException;
import javax.servlet.jsp.tagext.TagSupport;

import com.wrox.jsptaglibs.casestudy.common.CategoryManager;

public class CategoryTag extends TagSupport {

  private String name;

  public int doStartTag() throws JspException {

    Category cat = CategoryManager.getInstance().getCategory(name);

    // look up the category and put it in the page context
    if (cat != null) {
      pageContext.setAttribute(getId(), cat);
    }

    // and include the body
    return EVAL_BODY_INCLUDE;
  }

  public void setName(String name) {
```

```
    this.name = name;
  }
}
```

The books Tag

Next is the books tag that looks up a collection of books from a named category. The category attribute is optional and, if omitted, the default behavior is to get a collection of all the books:

```
package com.wrox.jsptaglibs.casestudy.domain;

import javax.servlet.jsp.JspException;
import javax.servlet.jsp.tagext.TagSupport;

import com.wrox.jsptaglibs.casestudy.common.BookManager;
import com.wrox.jsptaglibs.casestudy.common.Category;
import com.wrox.jsptaglibs.casestudy.common.CategoryManager;

public class BooksTag extends TagSupport {

  private String category;

  public int doStartTag() throws JspException {

    if (category != null) {
      // get all of the books for the specified category
      Category cat = CategoryManager.getInstance().getCategory(category);
      pageContext.setAttribute(getId(), cat.getBooks());
    } else {
      // or all books if a category wasn't specified
      pageContext.setAttribute(getId(),
        BookManager.getInstance().getBooksAsCollection());
    }

    // and include the body
    return EVAL_BODY_INCLUDE;
  }

  public void setCategory(String category) {
    this.category = category;
  }
}
```

The Tag Library Descriptor

The TLD for this library is as follows:

```
<?xml version="1.0" encoding="ISO-8859-1" ?>
<!DOCTYPE taglib
  PUBLIC "-//Sun Microsystems, Inc.//DTD JSP Tag Library 1.2//EN"
  "http://java.sun.com/dtd/web-jsptaglibrary_1_2.dtd">

<taglib>
```

```
  <tlib-version>1.0</tlib-version>
  <jsp-version>1.2</jsp-version>
  <short-name>domain</short-name>
  <description>
    Domain examples for the Case Study chapter.
  </description>

  <tag>
    <name>books</name>
    <tag-class>
      com.wrox.jsptaglibs.casestudy.domain.BooksTag
    </tag-class>
    <body-content>JSP</body-content>
    <description>
      Finds the books in the specified category.
    </description>

    <variable>
      <name-from-attribute>id</name-from-attribute>
      <variable-class>java.util.Collection</variable-class>
      <declare>true</declare>
      <scope>AT_BEGIN</scope>
    </variable>

    <attribute>
      <name>id</name>
      <required>true</required>
      <rtexprvalue>false</rtexprvalue>
    </attribute>

    <attribute>
      <name>category</name>
      <required>false</required>
      <rtexprvalue>true</rtexprvalue>
    </attribute>
  </tag>

  <tag>
    <name>category</name>
    <tag-class>
      com.wrox.jsptaglibs.casestudy.domain.CategoryTag
    </tag-class>
    <body-content>JSP</body-content>
    <description>
      Finds the category with the specified name.
    </description>

    <variable>
      <name-from-attribute>id</name-from-attribute>
      <variable-class>
        com.wrox.jsptaglibs.casestudy.common.Category
      </variable-class>
      <declare>true</declare>
      <scope>AT_BEGIN</scope>
    </variable>
```

```
    <attribute>
      <name>id</name>
      <required>true</required>
      <rtexprvalue>false</rtexprvalue>
    </attribute>

    <attribute>
      <name>name</name>
      <required>true</required>
      <rtexprvalue>true</rtexprvalue>
    </attribute>
  </tag>

</taglib>
```

The paging Tag Library

The `paging` tag library is the largest and most complex used in the case study because of the flexibility that it provides. The core functionality provided by this tag library is the ability to easily create pages of information through which the user can scroll. For example, imagine that we have a large collection of items. Instead of displaying all of the elements in the collection on a single page, it is often better to present the information in smaller, more manageable pieces, page by page. As we'll see shortly, such functionality is possible to implement with JSP and custom tags, and provides the page author with a fair amount of flexibility in how they can use it.

The page Tag

This is the main tag and is the outermost parent of all the other tags in the library. Where the `iterate` tag we've seen in previous chapters provides iteration over all of the objects in a collection, the `page` tag only provides iteration over those elements that are to be shown in the current page. Although both tags perform slightly different tasks, their usage on the page is similar:

```
<paging:page page="pageNumber" size="8"
             id="book"
             type="com.wrox.jsptaglibs.casestudy.common.Book"
             collection="books">
  ... content to be iterated over ...
</paging:page>
```

The `id`, `type`, and `collection` attributes are the same as used on the `iterate` tag but `page` and `size` are new. The `size` attribute allows the page author to specify how many items should be displayed per page. This is optional and defaults to 10. The `page` attribute is used to specify the number of the page that should be displayed. However, rather than allowing the page number to be hard-coded into the page, the value of this attribute is actually the name of a request parameter that specifies the number of the page that should be displayed. Using the `page` tag (as just shown) means that the page on which it is used can be requested as follows:

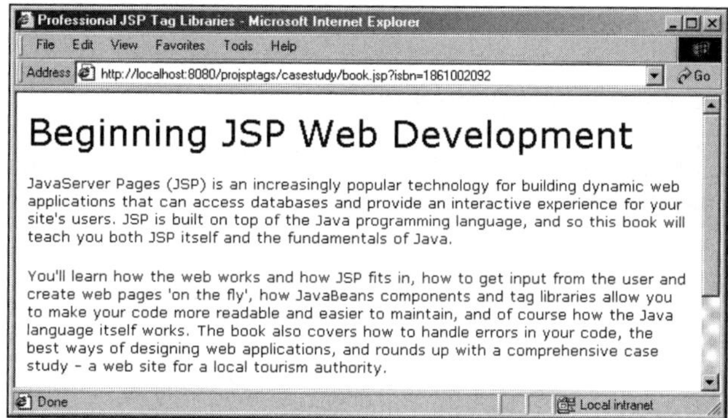

Let's see how this works by looking at how the tag is built. First of all are the attributes and their corresponding mutator methods:

```
package com.wrox.jsptaglibs.casestudy.paging;

import java.util.Collection;

import javax.servlet.jsp.JspException;
import javax.servlet.jsp.tagext.TagSupport;

public class PageTag extends TagSupport {

  private Object collectionReference;
  private String page;
  private int size = 10;
  private String type;

  public void setCollection(Object collectionReference) {
    this.collectionReference = collectionReference;
  }

  public void setPage(String page) {
    this.page = page;
  }

  public void setSize(int i) {
    this.size = i;
  }

  public void setType(String s) {
    this.type = s;
  }
```

Next are some instance variables that are used during the processing of the tag. Here we have `index` and `indexOnPage` that are used as counter variables:

```
  private int indexOnPage;
  private int index;
```

Next is objects that is used to reference the objects that the tag is iterating over:

```
private Object[] objects;
```

Finally there's pageNumber and pageCount representing the current page number and the number of pages that will be displayable given the collection and the size of each page:

```
private int pageNumber;
private int pageCount;
```

With the attributes and instance variables declared, we'll additionally write some accessor methods for use internally and by nested tags. First of all is the getCollection() method that works out whether the value specified for the collection attribute was a reference to a java.util.Collection or the name of an attribute in the page context. This method is primarily for use within the tag and as we saw in Chapter 9, it is an example of "attribute overloading":

```
public Collection getCollection() {
  if (collectionReference instanceof Collection) {
    return (Collection)collectionReference;
  } else {
    String name = collectionReference.toString();
    return (Collection)pageContext.findAttribute(name);
  }
}
```

The other accessors are really to support the tags that will be nested inside this one on the page:

```
public String getPage() {
  return this.page;
}

public int getPageNumber() {
  return this.pageNumber;
}

public int getPageCount() {
  return this.pageCount;
}
```

The purpose of this tag is to provide iteration on the page and for this reason the majority of the code in the tag handler will be fairly typical and straightforward. The only real difference between this and other iteration tags is that it doesn't iterate from the start of the collection to the end. This is illustrated in the doStartTag() method, which determines the extent of the iteration and sets up the values of the instance variables before commencing:

```
public int doStartTag() throws JspException {

  // what are we iterating over?
  objects = getCollection().toArray();

  // how many pages are there?
```

```
    if (objects.length == 0) {
      pageCount = 1;
    } else {
      // work out the number of whole pages
      pageCount = objects.length/size;

      // and add one more if we don't have a whole number of pages
      if (objects.length % size > 0) {
        pageCount++;
      }
    }

    // where are we starting from?
    try {
      pageNumber =
        Integer.parseInt(pageContext.getRequest().getParameter(page));
    } catch (NumberFormatException nfe) {
      // the parameter wasn't specified, or was specified incorrectly so
      // assume that we are looking at the first page
      pageNumber = 1;
    }

    // is the page number in range?
    if (pageNumber < 1) {
      pageNumber = 1;
    } else if (pageNumber > pageCount) {
      pageNumber = pageCount;
    }

    // now we've worked out the page number, what is the starting point
    // in the collection?
    index = (pageNumber-1) * size;
    indexOnPage = 0;

    if (index < objects.length) {
      // put the indexes and the current element into the page
      pageContext.setAttribute("index", new Integer(index+1));
      pageContext.setAttribute("indexOnPage", new Integer(indexOnPage+1));
      pageContext.setAttribute(getId(), objects[index]);
    }

    // and include the body
    return EVAL_BODY_INCLUDE;
  }
```

During each iteration, the values of the `index` and `indexOnPage` variables are introduced into the page in addition to the current element in the collection as they might be required for generating numbered lists. Remember, the person developing the page might not be familiar with zero-based indices, so keep this in mind whenever introducing these sorts of values into the page.

The `doAfterBody()` method is much more like those that we have seen before in that it instructs the body content to be re-evaluated if there are more elements in the collection to be displayed on the current page:

```
public int doAfterBody() throws JspException {
  // increment the counter
  index++;
  indexOnPage++;

  if ((indexOnPage < size) && (index < objects.length)) {
    // put the indexes and the current element into the page
    pageContext.setAttribute("index", new Integer(index+1));
    pageContext.setAttribute("indexOnPage", new Integer(indexOnPage+1));
    pageContext.setAttribute(getId(), objects[index]);

    // and instruct the JSP engine to re-evaluate the body of this tag
    return EVAL_BODY_AGAIN;
  } else {
    // there are no more elements so skip the body
    return SKIP_BODY;
  }
}
```

Finally we have some methods on the tag handler that determine which part of the page should be rendered at any point in time. We'll see where these are used shortly but basically they are the conditions under which the header, body, and footer should be shown:

```
  public boolean showHeader() {
    return indexOnPage == 0;
  }

  public boolean showBody() {
    return index < objects.length;
  }

  public boolean showFooter() {
    return (indexOnPage >= (size-1)) ||
      (index >= (objects.length-1));
  }
}
```

Because the page tag is introducing each element of the collection into the page, a TEI class is required as follows:

```
package com.wrox.jsptaglibs.casestudy.paging;

import javax.servlet.jsp.tagext.TagData;
import javax.servlet.jsp.tagext.TagExtraInfo;
import javax.servlet.jsp.tagext.VariableInfo;

public class PageTagExtraInfo extends TagExtraInfo {

  public VariableInfo[] getVariableInfo(TagData data) {
    return new VariableInfo[] {
      new VariableInfo("index", "java.lang.Integer",
        true, VariableInfo.NESTED),
      new VariableInfo("indexOnPage", "java.lang.Integer",
```

```
          true, VariableInfo.NESTED),
        new VariableInfo(data.getId(), data.getAttributeString("type"),
          true, VariableInfo.NESTED)
      };
    }
  }
```

The header Tag

Nested inside the page tag can be a header tag. The body content of this tag can be used to display header information and is only included once per page. Again, custom tags are about making the JSP page more readable and maintainable, while at the same time reducing the effort required on the part of the page author. The header tag is simply a convenient way of wrapping up conditional logic of the form, "if we're on the first row, show the header". If this is the case, the body content is evaluated; otherwise it is ignored. This is where the page tag's showHeader() method is used:

```
package com.wrox.jsptaglibs.casestudy.paging;

import javax.servlet.jsp.JspException;
import javax.servlet.jsp.tagext.TagSupport;

public class HeaderTag extends TagSupport {

  public int doStartTag() throws JspException {

    PageTag t = (PageTag)findAncestorWithClass(this, PageTag.class);

    if (t.showHeader()) {
      return EVAL_BODY_INCLUDE;
    } else {
      return SKIP_BODY;
    }
  }
}
```

The body Tag

The body tag is very similar to the header tag and it's inside here that the content to be displayed in the page can be written:

```
package com.wrox.jsptaglibs.casestudy.paging;

import javax.servlet.jsp.JspException;
import javax.servlet.jsp.tagext.TagSupport;

public class BodyTag extends TagSupport {

  public int doStartTag() throws JspException {

    PageTag t = (PageTag)findAncestorWithClass(this, PageTag.class);

    // if the body of the page can be shown, evaluate the
    // body content of this tag
```

```
      if (t.showBody()) {
        return EVAL_BODY_INCLUDE;
      } else {
        return SKIP_BODY;
      }
    }
  }
```

The footer Tag

Last but not least is the `footer` tag, whose body content gets evaluated when the last row is reached:

```
  package com.wrox.jsptaglibs.casestudy.paging;

  import javax.servlet.jsp.JspException;
  import javax.servlet.jsp.tagext.TagSupport;

  public class FooterTag extends TagSupport {

    public int doStartTag() throws JspException {

      PageTag t = (PageTag)findAncestorWithClass(this, PageTag.class);

      if (t.showFooter()) {
        return EVAL_BODY_INCLUDE;
      } else {
        return SKIP_BODY;
      }
    }
  }
```

The pageNumber Tag

A useful feature when presenting pages to the user is to tell them which page number they are currently looking at. Of course, this information could have been introduced into the page but for convenience and to reduce the potential for Java code on the page, we've decided to make it available as a tag that simply outputs this value. Once again, this tag must be used within a `page` tag:

```
  package com.wrox.jsptaglibs.casestudy.paging;

  import java.io.IOException;

  import javax.servlet.jsp.JspException;
  import javax.servlet.jsp.JspTagException;
  import javax.servlet.jsp.tagext.TagSupport;

  public class PageNumberTag extends TagSupport {

    public int doStartTag() throws JspException {

      // get the parent Page tag and ask it which page we're looking at
      PageTag t = (PageTag)findAncestorWithClass(this, PageTag.class);
```

```
    try {
      pageContext.getOut().print(t.getPageNumber());
    } catch (IOException ioe) {
      throw new JspTagException(ioe.getMessage());
    }

    return SKIP_BODY;
  }
}
```

Notice here how there is no formatting or presentation logic embedded into the tag. This is best left to the JSP page, where it belongs.

The pageCount Tag

Another useful feature is the ability for the user to know the number of pages:

```
package com.wrox.jsptaglibs.casestudy.paging;

import java.io.IOException;

import javax.servlet.jsp.JspException;
import javax.servlet.jsp.JspTagException;
import javax.servlet.jsp.tagext.TagSupport;

public class PageCountTag extends TagSupport {

  public int doStartTag() throws JspException {

    // find the parent and ask it how many pages there are
    PageTag t = (PageTag)findAncestorWithClass(this, PageTag.class);

    try {
      pageContext.getOut().print(t.getPageCount());
    } catch (IOException ioe) {
      throw new JspTagException(ioe.getMessage());
    }

    return SKIP_BODY;
  }
}
```

The firstPage Tag

The final set of tags in the tag library is for generating hyperlinks so that the user can scroll from one page to another. All that these tags need to do is generate the appropriate hyperlink and through some clever use of the HTTP request we have most of the information that we need.

As the functionality required to generate these links is very similar regardless of which page the user is scrolling to, this is a good opportunity to take advantage of inheritance in the tags. Here we have an abstract class that contains all of the functionality required to build the links along with an abstract method called `getPageNumber()`. Concrete classes must implement this to indicate which page the hyperlink should jump to:

```
package com.wrox.jsptaglibs.casestudy.paging;

import java.io.IOException;

import javax.servlet.http.HttpServletRequest;
import javax.servlet.jsp.JspException;
import javax.servlet.jsp.JspTagException;
import javax.servlet.jsp.tagext.TagSupport;

public abstract class ScrollToPageTag extends TagSupport {

  private String label;
  private String src;

  public int doStartTag() throws JspException {

    PageTag t = (PageTag)findAncestorWithClass(this, PageTag.class);

    HttpServletRequest request;
    request = (HttpServletRequest)pageContext.getRequest();

    // to generate the link, we need to build up the same URL as the one
    // used to request this page, making sure that we strip off the
    // parameter that was used to specify the page number (if there was one)
    StringBuffer buf = request.getRequestURL();
    String query = request.getQueryString();
    buf.append("?");

    if (query != null) {
      int index = query.indexOf(t.getPage() + "=");

      if (index > -1) {
        // the page number parameter was specified, so remove it
        buf.append(query.substring(0, index));
      } else {
        buf.append(query);
        buf.append("&");
      }
    }

    // now figure out which page is to be displayed and add the new
    // parameter back on to the reconstructed URL
    int newPageNumber = getPageNumber();

    buf.append(t.getPage());
    buf.append("=");
    buf.append(newPageNumber);

    // now we can generate the hyperlink (if the page is in range)
    String href = buf.toString();
    buf = new StringBuffer();

    if (newPageNumber < 1 || newPageNumber > t.getPageCount() ||
        newPageNumber == t.getPageNumber()) {
```

```
      if (label != null) {
        buf.append(label);
      } else {
        buf.append("<img border=\"0\" src=\"");
        buf.append(src);
        buf.append("\">");
      }
    } else {
      buf.append("<a href=\"");
      buf.append(href);
      buf.append("\">");

      if (label != null) {
        buf.append(label);
      } else {
        buf.append("<img border=\"0\" src=\"");
        buf.append(src);
        buf.append("\">");
      }

      buf.append("</a>");
    }

    try {
      // write out the HTML fragment to the page
      pageContext.getOut().write(buf.toString());
    } catch (IOException ioe) {
      throw new JspTagException(ioe.getMessage());
    }

    // and skip evaluating the body of the tag (as there shouldn't be one)
    return SKIP_BODY;
  }

  public void setLabel(String label) {
    this.label = label;
  }

  public void setSrc(String src) {
    this.src = src;
  }

  protected abstract int getPageNumber();
}
```

With the superclass built, writing the `firstPage` tag takes almost no time at all:

```
package com.wrox.jsptaglibs.casestudy.paging;

public class FirstPageTag extends ScrollToPageTag {

  protected int getPageNumber() {
    return 1;
  }
}
```

The previousPage Tag

The `previousPage` tag involves slightly more work in that it must know which page is currently being displayed:

```
package com.wrox.jsptaglibs.casestudy.paging;

public class PreviousPageTag extends ScrollToPageTag {

  protected int getPageNumber() {
    PageTag t = (PageTag)findAncestorWithClass(this, PageTag.class);

    return t.getPageNumber() - 1;
  }
}
```

The nextPage Tag

Likewise with the `nextPage` tag:

```
package com.wrox.jsptaglibs.casestudy.paging;

public class NextPageTag extends ScrollToPageTag {

  protected int getPageNumber() {
    PageTag t = (PageTag)findAncestorWithClass(this, PageTag.class);

    return t.getPageNumber() + 1;
  }
}
```

The lastPage Tag

Finally is the `lastPage` tag:

```
package com.wrox.jsptaglibs.casestudy.paging;

public class LastPageTag extends ScrollToPageTag {

  protected int getPageNumber() {
    PageTag t = (PageTag)findAncestorWithClass(this, PageTag.class);

    return t.getPageCount();
  }
}
```

The Tag Library Descriptor

Here is the TLD for the page tag library:

```
<?xml version="1.0" encoding="ISO-8859-1" ?>
<!DOCTYPE taglib
  PUBLIC "-//Sun Microsystems, Inc.//DTD JSP Tag Library 1.2//EN"
  "http://java.sun.com/dtd/web-jsptaglibrary_1_2.dtd">

<taglib>

  <tlib-version>1.0</tlib-version>
  <jsp-version>1.2</jsp-version>
  <short-name>paging</short-name>
  <description>
    Paging examples for the Case Study chapter.
  </description>
```

First of all is the page tag with its TEI class and many attributes:

```
  <tag>
    <name>page</name>
    <tag-class>com.wrox.jsptaglibs.casestudy.paging.PageTag</tag-class>
    <tei-class>
      com.wrox.jsptaglibs.casestudy.paging.PageTagExtraInfo
    </tei-class>
    <body-content>JSP</body-content>
    <description>
      Iterates over a specified array of objects, showing
      pages of information at a time.
    </description>

    <attribute>
      <name>collection</name>
      <required>true</required>
      <rtexprvalue>true</rtexprvalue>
    </attribute>

    <attribute>
      <name>page</name>
      <required>true</required>
      <rtexprvalue>false</rtexprvalue>
    </attribute>

    <attribute>
      <name>size</name>
      <required>false</required>
      <rtexprvalue>false</rtexprvalue>
    </attribute>

    <attribute>
      <name>id</name>
      <required>true</required>
      <rtexprvalue>false</rtexprvalue>
```

```
    </attribute>

    <attribute>
      <name>type</name>
      <required>true</required>
      <rtexprvalue>false</rtexprvalue>
    </attribute>
  </tag>
```

Following this are the tags that represent the different parts of the page – header, body, and footer:

```
  <tag>
    <name>header</name>
    <tag-class>com.wrox.jsptaglibs.casestudy.paging.HeaderTag</tag-class>
    <body-content>JSP</body-content>
    <description>
      A container for the header of the page.
    </description>
  </tag>

  <tag>
    <name>body</name>
    <tag-class>com.wrox.jsptaglibs.casestudy.paging.BodyTag</tag-class>
    <body-content>JSP</body-content>
    <description>
      A container for the body of the page.
    </description>
  </tag>

  <tag>
    <name>footer</name>
    <tag-class>com.wrox.jsptaglibs.casestudy.paging.FooterTag</tag-class>
    <body-content>JSP</body-content>
    <description>
      A container for the footer of the page.
    </description>
  </tag>
```

Then there's pageNumber and pageCount:

```
  <tag>
    <name>pageNumber</name>
    <tag-class>
      com.wrox.jsptaglibs.casestudy.paging.PageNumberTag
    </tag-class>
    <body-content>empty</body-content>
    <description>
      Displays the current page number.
    </description>
  </tag>

  <tag>
    <name>pageCount</name>
```

```
    <tag-class>com.wrox.jsptaglibs.casestudy.paging.PageCountTag</tag-class>
    <body-content>empty</body-content>
    <description>
      Displays the number of pages.
    </description>
  </tag>
```

Finally there are the tags that allow the user to jump to a particular page:

```
  <tag>
    <name>previousPage</name>
    <tag-class>
      com.wrox.jsptaglibs.casestudy.paging.PreviousPageTag
    </tag-class>
    <body-content>empty</body-content>
    <description>
      Inserts a hyperlink into the page allowing the user
      to see the previous page.
    </description>

    <attribute>
      <name>label</name>
      <required>false</required>
      <rtexprvalue>false</rtexprvalue>
    </attribute>

    <attribute>
      <name>src</name>
      <required>false</required>
      <rtexprvalue>false</rtexprvalue>
    </attribute>
  </tag>

  <tag>
    <name>nextPage</name>
    <tag-class>com.wrox.jsptaglibs.casestudy.paging.NextPageTag</tag-class>
    <body-content>empty</body-content>
    <description>
      Inserts a hyperlink into the page allowing the user
      to see the next page.
    </description>

    <attribute>
      <name>label</name>
      <required>false</required>
      <rtexprvalue>false</rtexprvalue>
    </attribute>

    <attribute>
      <name>src</name>
      <required>false</required>
      <rtexprvalue>false</rtexprvalue>
    </attribute>
  </tag>
```

```
<tag>
  <name>firstPage</name>
  <tag-class>com.wrox.jsptaglibs.casestudy.paging.FirstPageTag</tag-class>
  <body-content>empty</body-content>
  <description>
    Inserts a hyperlink into the page allowing the user
    to see the first page.
  </description>

  <attribute>
    <name>label</name>
    <required>false</required>
    <rtexprvalue>false</rtexprvalue>
  </attribute>

  <attribute>
    <name>src</name>
    <required>false</required>
    <rtexprvalue>false</rtexprvalue>
  </attribute>
</tag>

<tag>
  <name>lastPage</name>
  <tag-class>com.wrox.jsptaglibs.casestudy.paging.LastPageTag</tag-class>
  <body-content>empty</body-content>
  <description>
   Inserts a hyperlink into the page allowing the user
   to see the last page.
  </description>

  <attribute>
    <name>label</name>
    <required>false</required>
    <rtexprvalue>false</rtexprvalue>
  </attribute>

  <attribute>
    <name>src</name>
    <required>false</required>
    <rtexprvalue>false</rtexprvalue>
  </attribute>
</tag>

</taglib>
```

The HTML Tag Library

The final tag library that we are interested in contains two tags – `anchor` and `param`. The JSP specification provides the `<jsp:forward/>` tag for easily forwarding on the request to another page. Nested within this tag can be one or more `<jsp:param/>` tags that make it easy to pass parameters to the forwarded page, especially if they contain characters that need to be URL encoded.

URL encoding is the process of transforming ASCII characters into a standard string that all web servers understand. For example, a space character is transformed into the string %20.

The tags in this tag library provide similar functionality by generating a hyperlink, optionally with parameters. Take the following example:

```
<html:a href="myPage.jsp" label="Click here">
  <html:param name="param1" value="value1"/>
  <html:param name="param2" value="value2"/>
</html:a>
```

This might generate something like the following:

```
<a href="myPage.jsp?param1=value1&param2=value2">Click here</a>
```

Let's see how these two tags work.

The anchor Tag

The `anchor` tag is fairly straightforward and unlike many of the other tags waits until the `doEndTag()` before generating its content. As part of its state it maintains a `HashMap` of parameter names and values that are provided by the nested `param` tags. Therefore, the `anchor` tag will have only collected all of the attributes by the time that the end tag has been reached:

```
package com.wrox.jsptaglibs.casestudy.html;

import java.io.IOException;
import java.net.URLEncoder;
import java.util.HashMap;
import java.util.Iterator;

import javax.servlet.jsp.JspException;
import javax.servlet.jsp.JspTagException;
import javax.servlet.jsp.tagext.TagSupport;

public class AnchorTag extends TagSupport {

  private String label;
  private String src;
  private String href;

  private HashMap parameters;

  public int doStartTag() throws JspException {

    parameters = new HashMap();

    // evaluate the body of the tag (all the hard work
    // is done in the doEndTag() method)
    return EVAL_BODY_INCLUDE;
  }
```

```
public int doEndTag() throws JspException {

  // now we can generate the hyperlink
  StringBuffer buf = new StringBuffer();
  buf.append(href);

  if (!parameters.isEmpty()) {
    buf.append("?");

    String key;
    String value;
    Iterator it = parameters.keySet().iterator();
    while (it.hasNext()) {
      key = (String)it.next();
      value = (String)parameters.get(key);

      // remembering to encode the name=value pair
      buf.append(URLEncoder.encode(key));
      buf.append("=");
      buf.append(URLEncoder.encode(value));

      if (it.hasNext()) {
        buf.append("&");
      }
    }
  }

  StringBuffer html = new StringBuffer();
  html.append("<a href=\"");
  html.append(buf.toString());
  html.append("\">");

  if (label != null) {
    html.append(label);
  } else {
    html.append("<img border=\"0\" src=\"");
    html.append(src);
    html.append("\">");
  }

  html.append("</a>");

  try {
    // write out the HTML fragment to the page
    pageContext.getOut().write(html.toString());
  } catch (IOException ioe) {
    throw new JspTagException(ioe.getMessage());
  }

  return EVAL_PAGE;
}

public void setLabel(String label) {
  this.label = label;
```

```
  }

  public void setSrc(String src) {
    this.src = src;
  }

  public void setHref(String href) {
    this.href = href;
  }
```

The one question that we've not answered yet is how the parameters find their way into the `anchor` tag. This is achieved by the nested `param` tags cooperating with their parent `anchor` tag, in this case by using a public method that they can call on the `AnchorTag` class:

```
  public void addParameter(String name, String value) {
    parameters.put(name, value);
  }
}
```

One final point to note about the tag is that the `HashMap` of parameters is reset within the `doStartTag()`. If this isn't done, parameters would continually be added when the tag is used in a container that pools and reuses instances.

The param Tag

The `param` tag is nested within the `anchor` tag and therefore simply needs to call the `addParameter()` method with the values of its `name` and `value` attributes:

```
package com.wrox.jsptaglibs.casestudy.html;

import javax.servlet.jsp.JspException;
import javax.servlet.jsp.tagext.TagSupport;

public class ParamTag extends TagSupport {

  private String name;

  private String value;

  public int doStartTag() throws JspException {

    AnchorTag t = (AnchorTag)findAncestorWithClass(this, AnchorTag.class);
    t.addParameter(name, value);

    // and skip the body content for this empty tag
    return SKIP_BODY;
  }

  public void setName(String name) {
    this.name = name;
  }

  public void setValue(String value) {
```

```
    this.value = value;
  }
}
```

The Tag Library Descriptor

Here's the TLD for the `anchor` and `param` tags:

```
<?xml version="1.0" encoding="ISO-8859-1" ?>
<!DOCTYPE taglib
  PUBLIC "-//Sun Microsystems, Inc.//DTD JSP Tag Library 1.2//EN"
  "http://java.sun.com/dtd/web-jsptaglibrary_1_2.dtd">

<taglib>

  <tlib-version>1.0</tlib-version>
  <jsp-version>1.2</jsp-version>
  <short-name>html</short-name>
  <description>
    HTML examples for the Case Study chapter.
  </description>

  <tag>
    <name>a</name>
    <tag-class>com.wrox.jsptaglibs.casestudy.html.AnchorTag</tag-class>
    <body-content>JSP</body-content>
    <description>
      Inserts a hyperlink into the page.
    </description>

    <attribute>
      <name>href</name>
      <required>true</required>
      <rtexprvalue>true</rtexprvalue>
    </attribute>

    <attribute>
      <name>label</name>
      <required>false</required>
      <rtexprvalue>true</rtexprvalue>
    </attribute>

    <attribute>
      <name>src</name>
      <required>false</required>
      <rtexprvalue>true</rtexprvalue>
    </attribute>
  </tag>

  <tag>
    <name>param</name>
    <tag-class>com.wrox.jsptaglibs.casestudy.html.ParamTag</tag-class>
    <body-content>JSP</body-content>
```

```
      <description>
        Specifies a parameter for a hyperlink.
      </description>

      <attribute>
        <name>name</name>
        <required>true</required>
        <rtexprvalue>true</rtexprvalue>
      </attribute>

      <attribute>
        <name>value</name>
        <required>true</required>
        <rtexprvalue>true</rtexprvalue>
      </attribute>
    </tag>

  </taglib>
```

The Book Page

The final page of the application that we'll look at is the page that displays the details of a specific book to the user. It works in a similar way to the categories page, taking a parameter that specifies the book that the user is interested in:

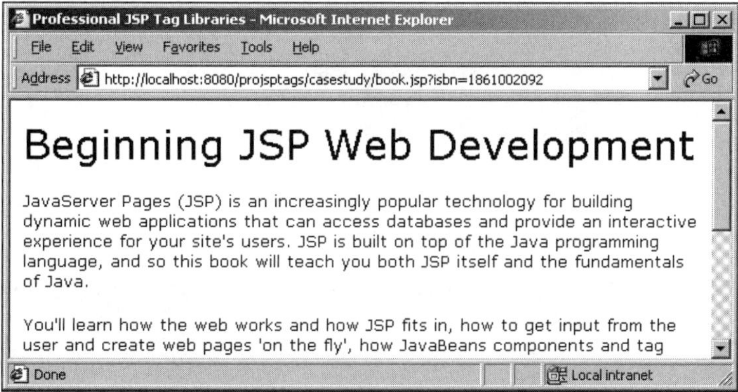

First of all there's the opening HTML tags and `taglib` directives:

```
<html>
  <head>
    <title>Professional JSP Tag Libraries</title>
  </head>

  <%@ taglib uri="/casestudyDomainTaglib" prefix="domain" %>
  <%@ taglib uri="/casestudyIterationTaglib" prefix="iteration" %>
  <%@ taglib uri="/casestudyLogicTaglib" prefix="logic" %>
  <%@ taglib uri="/casestudyRequestTaglib" prefix="request" %>
```

```
    <body>
```

Next we're reusing the `parameter` tag again to extract the value of the `isbn` parameter. The resulting scripting variable is used as the criteria for finding the book that is performed using another tag from the `domain` library that simply adds a `Book` object into the page context:

```
      <request:parameter id="isbn" name="isbn"/>
      <domain:book id="book" isbn="<%= isbn %>"/>
```

Following this we display the information about the book, or an error message if one could not be found:

```
      <logic:if value="<%= book %>">

        <logic:undefined>
          Sorry, no book was found.
        </logic:undefined>

        <logic:default>
          <h1><jsp:getProperty name="book" property="title"/></h1>

          <jsp:getProperty name="book" property="description"/>
```

When displaying the authors, we can again make use of the `iterate` tag instead of resorting to a scriptlet:

```
          <p>
            <b>Author(s) :</b>
              <ul>
                <iteration:iterate id="author" type="java.lang.String"
                                   collection="<%= book.getAuthors() %>">
                  <li><%= author %>
                </iteration:iterate>
              </ul>
          </p>

          <p>
            <b>Price :</b> $<jsp:getProperty name="book" property="price"/>
          </p>
        </logic:default>

      </logic:if>
    </body>
  </html>
```

A Review of the Case Study

Although the case study itself is fairly simple, it does make use of many tags, many tag libraries, and many of the concepts that we've learnt about in the book. To recap, here's a list of what we've made use of:

- Simple tags with and without body content
- Conditionally and programmatically controlling body content evaluation
- Simple tags with attributes
- Cooperation, explicitly through the page context and implicitly through nesting
- Inheritance in building tags
- View helpers and integration with the business objects

In addition to all of this, we've used as little Java code as possible. In fact, the only Java code that we used is wrapped up in request-time expressions to specify the values for some of the tag attributes. Eliminating all of the Java code from a page on one hand is very idealistic but, on the other hand, something that **is** possible. We'll be seeing how in the next chapter.

Reuse and Maintainability

As we've seen, the application makes use of several tag libraries. Each of these are geared towards providing different functionality on the page but one thing that all of them have in common is that they help to allow easier, more maintainable development of JSP pages. No matter how small, any reusable piece of functionality can be wrapped inside a custom tag. This was demonstrated with the `parameter` tag that although small and simple helped prevent the use of Java code on the page.

Such tags are useful on many pages within a web application but, from a higher level, there are many common features of web applications that are also candidates for being turned into a tag library. One such example here is the paging tags that can make displaying pages of information almost as easy as presenting all of it.

Additions and Enhancements

Although the tags in this case study have been many and varied in nature, there is still much more that can be done. Here are some examples of possible additions and enhancements.

Sorting Functionality

When presenting lists of information to the user, it is often required that the information is sorted in a particular way. An addition to the `iteration` and `paging` tag libraries would be the ability to specify how the collection should be sorted. This could be achieved by specifying the name of a property belonging to each element in the collection (such as `title` on `Book` instances), or even by specifying the name of a `java.util.Comparator`.

A further extension is that a tag library could be built that generates links that allow the user to sort the information in different ways. As an example of how this might be useful, adding this functionality would allow the user to be able to sort the list of books by title or ISBN.

A Tabbed Control

Traditional GUI applications often use many tabs in a single window to group related information. This paradigm has also been adopted by many web sites and is a good candidate for a tag library. Here, tags could be built that generate the tab control along with hyperlinks to take the user to different tabs. Each tab could be a separate JSP page and would represent a specific view of the underlying data. For example, the book page could have tabs showing different information about the book – one for the overall information, one for a detailed summary, one for errata, and so on.

Banner Ads

Banner ads – clickable adverts that usually reside at the top of the page – are something that is present on most commercial web sites. Rather than coding these into the JSP page, custom tags could be used to specify which ad should be used. Alternatively, the information could be stored in a database and the custom tag could include the logic to randomly select one, or (using cookies) select one that the user hasn't yet seen.

Identifying Candidates for Tag Libraries

As a final note, wherever a JSP task pops up that would normally be achieved using Java code, step back and ask yourself whether it is possible to achieve with custom tags instead. Then, when you've come up with a solution, try to think about how the tag or tag library could be reused on other pages and, if possible, other applications. Two good examples of this in the case study are the request `parameter` tag and the HTML `anchor` tag. They may be small but they'll help to save time and effort in the long run – exactly what custom tags are for.

Summary

This chapter has presented a case study showing how many of the topics that we've learnt about can be taken and combined into a powerful collection of tag libraries. While building the application, we have seen some existing tag libraries; some that are variations and some that are completely new. Although the web application is fairly simple, the functionality behind it isn't.

Such an application would have been fairly easy to write using Java scriptlets but doing so would have been more difficult to maintain and harder to extend in the future. Using custom tags has given us a collection of reusable components from which we can build further pages and web applications in the future. In addition to this, the system is more maintainable because all of the complex logic is wrapped inside custom tags and not exposed on the page. A side effect of all of this is that the pages are shorter, cleaner, and easier to understand for people that might not be as proficient in Java as we are.

Looking at this case study has presented an insight to examples of tag libraries that are possible to build, and examples of the functionality that it is possible to wrap up. However large or small your web applications, having a set of reusable tag libraries will provide you with many of the benefits that we have discussed including a higher quality solution and a quicker time to market. But what if it is not possible to build them yourself? Here, an answer might be third party tag libraries, the subject of the final chapter.

LONDON

12

Third Party Tag Libraries

Equipped with the knowledge presented in the previous chapters you should now be in a position to build collections of tags to address the majority of the needs for the JSP-based applications that you build in the future. However, it is not always convenient or appropriate to build your own tag libraries. Perhaps time or cost are an issue or you simply don't want the ongoing maintenance overhead that building your own libraries would require.

This chapter takes a look at some of the popular third party tag libraries that are now available, including:

- Those that are part of the Struts Framework
- Jakarta Taglibs
- JSP Standard Tag Library (JSTL)

Taking a comprehensive look at each of these tag libraries in any depth is no small task and has been the subject of several books to date. For this reason we'll take a different perspective and concentrate on what they provide to the JSP developer, rather than how they work.

One of the important points about the JSTL is that it allows us to easily build tags that integrate with the unique features that it provides. Therefore, to wrap up the chapter we'll also look at how some of these features of the JSTL can be integrated with the tags that we build ourselves. Let's start the discussion by looking at why we might consider third party tag libraries.

Why Third Party Tag Libraries?

We've already hinted at why you might want to consider using a third party tag library, but probably the most important reasons are those of time, effort, cost, and quality. After all, it's often more cost effective to "buy, not build" and this is especially true when considering the open source projects such as Struts and Jakarta Taglibs. In addition to this, the major third party tag libraries would have been subjected to immense testing, debugging, and documentation which helps to ensure a high level of quality and greater confidence in building your solution to time and to budget.

So, now that we've looked at why you might want to choose a third party tag library, let's look at some of the criteria that you might use to help decide which one to go for.

Choosing a Third Party Tag Library

Apart from cost, there are several things to watch out for when choosing a third party tag library:

- **JSP Version**
  The first to consider, is whether the tag library supports the JSP version that you are using. After all, a tag library relying on JSP 1.2 features isn't going to work on a version 1.1-only compliant server. Even then, since compliant containers implement features in different ways behind the scenes, it is still worth checking that the third party tag library that you choose will work on both your development platform and also your production platform if they are different.

- **Wide Support**
  Technicalities aside, one of the other criteria that may be important is whether the tag library has wide support. This is not mandatory, but is something that is worth bearing in mind when thinking about upgrade paths and maintenance issues – particularly for commercial tag libraries.

- **Standards**
  A final criterion in choosing a third party tag library, as we'll see when we look at the JSP Standard Tag Library (JSTL), is whether it represents or implements a standard of some description. If such standards exist, it might be more beneficial in the long term to adopt those standards for the sake of future maintenance and upgrade paths. In addition to this is portability between servers as choosing a vendor-specific tag library can tie you into using that vendor's server and therefore restrict your deployment options in the future.

Struts

Struts, a part of the Jakarta project, is a complete open source framework for building JSP and servlet applications based around the Model 2 architecture. There are really two parts to the Struts – the core components that comprise the Model 2 framework and the tag libraries that are designed to help build clean, maintainable JSP pages. Before we can look at the tag libraries we must first understand how the core part of the framework operates.

Installing Struts

Currently, Struts is available in three distributions – binary, library, and source. The binary distribution contains the entire Struts Framework precompiled, along with some web applications; some of these are examples, one is for the documentation, and finally, one that can be used as a starting point for our own applications. This is a fairly large download, and for this reason, the library distribution is also available and simply contains just the Struts Framework without the example web applications.

Finally, the source distribution is useful if you would like to take a closer look at how the internals of Struts work. All of these can be downloaded from the Jakarta web site at http://jakarta.apache.org/builds/jakarta-struts/release/.

With the binary and library distributions, once downloaded, take the four TLD files (`struts-form.tld`, `struts-html.tld`, `struts-logic.tld`, and `struts-template.tld`) and place them in the `WEB-INF` directory of your web application. Next, the following mappings need to be defined in the `WEB-INF/web.xml` file of your web application. These are the recommended mappings, but of course you are free to use symbolic URIs:

```
<taglib>
  <taglib-uri>/WEB-INF/struts-bean.tld</taglib-uri>
  <taglib-location>/WEB-INF/struts-bean.tld</taglib-location>
</taglib>

<taglib>
  <taglib-uri>/WEB-INF/struts-html.tld</taglib-uri>
  <taglib-location>/WEB-INF/struts-html.tld</taglib-location>
</taglib>

<taglib>
  <taglib-uri>/WEB-INF/struts-logic.tld</taglib-uri>
  <taglib-location>/WEB-INF/struts-logic.tld</taglib-location>
</taglib>

<taglib>
  <taglib-uri>/WEB-INF/struts-template.tld</taglib-uri>
  <taglib-location>/WEB-INF/struts-template.tld</taglib-location>
</taglib>
```

Finally, copy `struts.jar` into the `WEB-INF/lib` directory of your web application as this contains the tag handlers.

If you are planning to use the entire Struts Framework, there are some additional steps that are required to configure the various components in the framework. Further information on these steps, including any web server specific instructions can be found at http://jakarta.apache.org/struts/userGuide/installation.html.

The Core Components

The Model 2 architecture is based upon the classic **MVC** (**model-view-controller**) architecture whereby the components that make up the application are loosely coupled. The model represents the information on which the application is operating; the controller manipulates this information (the model) and the view displays information from the model. The following diagram shows how this architecture works in a web application environment:

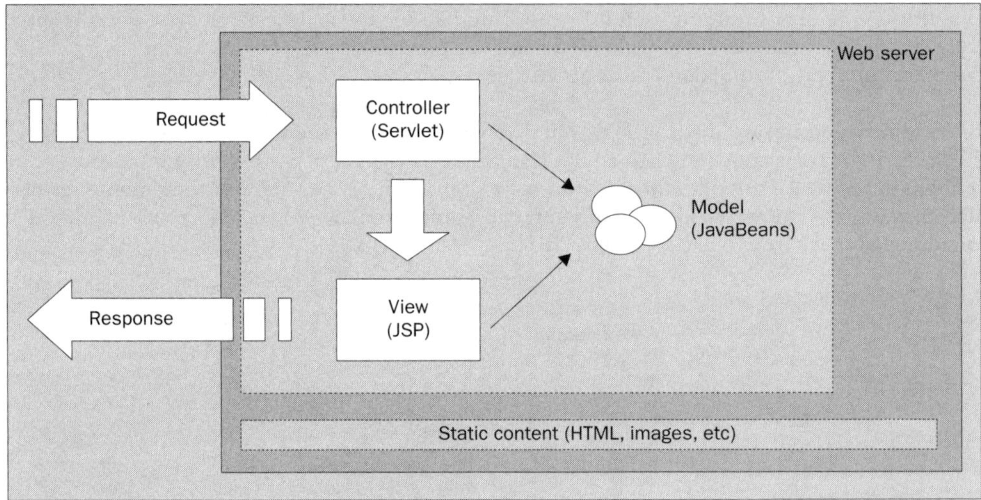

Requests (for example, from web browsers) are accepted by the controller component that is typically implemented as a Java servlet. Following this, the model (typically JavaBeans) is manipulated before the request is forwarded on to a view (typically a JSP page) so that the model can be rendered.

A more in-depth look at web application design, including a look at the Model 2 architecture can be found in the book Professional Java Servlets 2.3 from Wrox Press (ISBN 1-861005-61-X).

Building this type of a framework can be fairly time consuming and Struts was developed to mitigate the work involved in creating sites based on this model. It builds upon the concepts provided by MVC and this is illustrated in the following diagram:

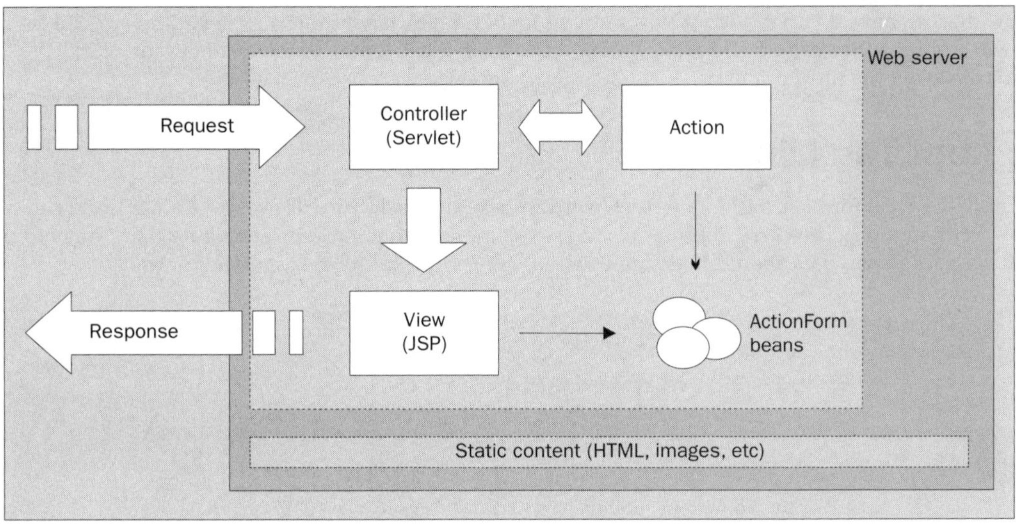

Essentially, the way that the request is serviced is the same as in a regular Model 2 architecture. The controller is implemented by a servlet called `ActionServlet`, provided as part of the Struts Framework. However, instead of manipulating the model, the controller delegates this task to specialized `Action` classes. The model is implemented using JavaBeans that are all subclasses of `ActionForm`, again provided by the framework.

To use an example, imagine that we need to build an HTML form for receiving user-specific information. Using Struts, we would first build the HTML form containing the text fields and controls (for example, checkboxes and drop-down lists) with which the user interacts. The next step is to write an `ActionForm` bean representing the information that is to be captured by the HTML form. This, a regular Java class, would simply contain properties corresponding to the fields and controls used on the HTML form along with the appropriate JavaBean style accessors and mutators.

Next, when the form is submitted, an `Action` class wrapping up the functionality would be executed. This might include validating the information that the user entered and persisting it away to a database. Finally, the action is registered through an XML configuration file and the application is ready to run.

When a user accesses the page containing the HTML form, they fill it in and submit it. This request is intercepted by the `ActionServlet`, which finds the appropriate `ActionForm` and `Action` classes for the request, through the configuration files. An instance of the `ActionForm` bean is then created and its properties are set using the values entered in the form. Following this, the work of servicing the request is delegated to an instance of the specialized `Action` class and finally, the request is forwarded onto a view component such as a JSP page.

Struts is a very flexible, powerful framework and this brief overview of the core components only scratches the surface.

> *As we are only interested in Struts from a JSP tag library perspective, further information can be found at* http://jakarta.apache.org/struts/.

Now that we have a very basic understanding of what the Struts Framework is and how it can be used to service requests, we can now look at the tag libraries that are a part of the Struts Framework. We'll start with probably the most important – the `html` tag library.

The html Tag Library

Building HTML forms is fairly straightforward, so you may ask, why do we need a tag library to help us out? Writing a page involves defining a `<form>` element with an `action` attribute that points to the URL that the form data should be submitted to. A fairly typical form is shown below:

```
<html>
  <head>
    <title>Professional JSP Tag Libraries</title>
  </head>

  <body>
    <h1>Wrox books online</h1>
    <h3>Enter your username and password to logon.</h3>

    <form action="process-logon.jsp">
```

Following this are the input fields in the form, each with a type, a name, and various other optional attributes:

```
      Username : <input type="text" name="username" size="32">
      <br/>
      Password : <input type="password" name="password" size="16">
```

Finally, the button used to submit the form:

```
      <br/><br/>
      <input type="submit" value="Submit">

    </form>
  </body>
</html>
```

This example generates the following page that might be used to log on to a web site:

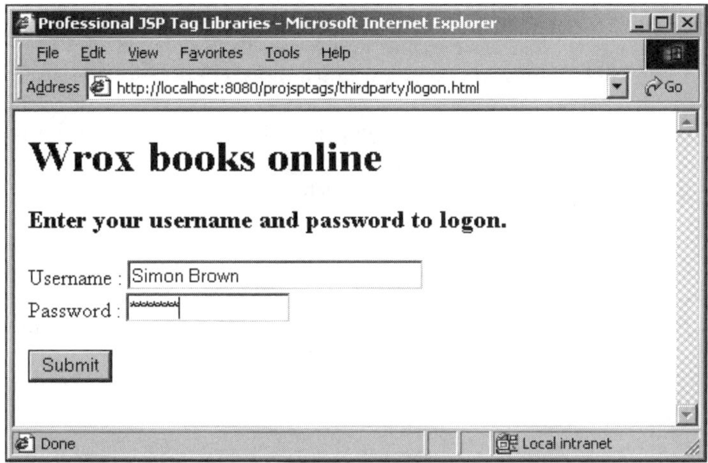

The HTML used above is simple and we've not had to introduce any Java code into the process. Submitting the form would send the information entered by the user to the specified JSP page or servlet. This, in turn, might perform some validation and of course check that the credentials entered match a valid user that is stored, for example, in a database. If successful, the user might subsequently be presented with a "welcome back" page indicating that they've logged into the site. However, what happens if the user has entered an incorrect username or password?

In this case we'd probably want to send them back to the logon page and ask them to try again. This is where it starts to get interesting, as sending them back to the same logon page isn't going to mean much to them.

Ideally we would like to display an error message and pre-populate the username text field with the value that they entered last time. This is useful for two reasons. First of all, the user can visually check that they did enter the correct username and secondly, blanking out information due to a validation error and forcing it to be typed back in again can be extremely annoying, especially on long forms. As it stands, the HTML form isn't capable of performing this type of functionality and we'd have to resort to some clever coding within the JSP page.

Perhaps, for example, we could keep the values entered by the user in the HTTP session or they could be passed through as parameters when the logon page is sent back to the user. Either way, the page containing the HTML form must contain logic to display the appropriate error messages and pre-populate the form fields with the values that were entered. This can quickly result in unmaintainable JSP pages.

A solution here is a custom tag library that does all of the hard work behind the scenes and helps build and render HTML forms. For example, a JavaBean containing the information from the form could be stored in the session context. Custom tags could then be built that mimic the standard HTML form tags. When these tags are encountered on the page, the tag handler could check for the bean in the session context, and if present, pull out the information and generate the HTML control pre-populated.

With the knowledge gained from the preceding chapters, such a tag would be fairly straightforward to build. All it needs to do is accept an attribute specifying the name of the field, use this to find the appropriate piece of information, and generate the HTML:

```
Username : <html:text name="username"/>
```

One of the key points about HTML tags is that they are very flexible, allowing page authors to specify characteristics such as the font, size, style, color, and so on. In fact, JavaScript event handlers can also be added to most of the HTML form controls for lightweight, client-side validation.

While building a custom tag is easy, in doing so the page author loses much of this flexibility because the tag is now responsible for generating the HTML. One way around this is to additionally mimic the full set of attributes for each and every HTML tag that you wish to build – not a small task by any means.

Fortunately, these issues have been addressed by the Struts team in the form of the `html` tag library – a comprehensive collection of tags specifically designed to help build HTML forms. One point to mention here is that, while the Struts core components can be used without the `html` tag library (they simply help us build views), the `html` tag library is intended to be used in conjunction with the core components.

So what does the `html` tag library look like? Here's the same page, written this time using the Struts Framework's `html` tags:

```
<html>
  <head>
    <title>Professional JSP Tag Libraries</title>
  </head>

  <%@ taglib uri="/WEB-INF/struts-html.tld" prefix="html" %>

  <body>

    <h1>Wrox books online</h1>

    <h3>Enter your username and password to logon.</h3>
    <html:form action="logon.do">

      Username : <html:text property="username" size="32"/>
      <br/>
      Password : <html:password property="password" size="16"/>

    <br/><br/>
    <html:submit property="submit" value="Submit"/>

  </html:form>

  </body>
</html>
```

As you can see, the JSP page does look fairly similar to the pure HTML version that we saw previously except that custom tags are now being used to render the HTML form controls. Behind the scenes, the `action` attribute of the `<html:form/>` tag is used to look up the action that is executed when this form is submitted. In doing so, it also generates the appropriate `action` (URL) attribute of the generated HTML `<form>` tag. In addition to looking up the action, the tag also tries to find, or failing that create, an instance of the `ActionForm` bean that corresponds to this form – the JavaBean into which the data from the form will be stored.

The other custom tags on the page (and in fact the other tags that mimic the HTML form controls in the library) make use of a `property` attribute, and this is simply a way of matching up and referencing a particular property of the JavaBean. If the bean exists, the tags can pre-populate the controls. In this case, the JavaBean behind the scenes would need properties called `username` and `password` respectively. In addition to this, the framework to set the values on the JavaBean when the form is submitted also uses these property names.

The `html` tag library also offers a comprehensive collection of tags for helping to build HTML forms and HTML pages in general. Here's a table summarizing the tags:

Tag name	Purpose
`base`	Generates an HTML base element, for anchoring the current page and making all relative links in the page specific to it
`Button`	Generates an HTML button, generally used for submitting HTML forms
`cancel`	Generates a cancel button
`checkbox`	Generates a checkbox field in a form
`file`	Generates a file select control (generally a field with a button containing an ellipsis)
`form`	Generates the opening and closing HTML form tags
`hidden`	Generates a hidden HTML form field
`html`	Generates the opening and closing HTML elements of a page
`image`	Generates a form field of type `image`, generally used as graphical submit buttons
`img`	Generates an `<img>` tag
`link`	Generates a hyperlink
`multibox`	As checkbox, but a useful variation when dealing with large numbers of check boxes behind the scenes
`option`	Generates an option within a select list (see below)
`options`	Generates one or more options within a select list (see below)
`password`	Generates a password input field
`radio`	Generates a radio button
`reset`	Generates a form reset button
`select`	Generates the opening and closing select tags for a drop-down list containing options

Table continued on following page

Tag name	Purpose
submit	Generates a submit button
text	Generates a regular text input field
textarea	Generates a text area input field

As you can see, this list is quite comprehensive and even more so when you consider that the tags shown here also mimic the majority of the attributes available on their HTML counterparts, allowing the page author to specify characteristics such as the size, CSS style, and so on. In addition to these are the attributes on the tags used for writing the corresponding event handlers that allow client-side JavaScript to be executed when events such as a key press or a mouse click happen on the field.

A great deal of work has gone into producing this tag library to make it useful, easy to use, and also to make it feel more natural and flexible for those people who will be building the JSP pages. This is an important point because it will reduce the obstacles while migrating from regular HTML to the Struts html tag library.

Also provided by the html tag library are tags to render any errors that may have been generated during the processing of the Action class when the form is submitted. For example, the Action class could check that the username had been specified in the form and raise an error if it hadn't. The errors tag is a simple way of presenting these errors back to the user without resorting to Java code and scriptlets:

```
<font color="red"><html:errors/></font>
```

The essence behind the html tag library is that it can use and interrogate the Struts Framework and generate fragments of HTML to present to the user. These tags aim to reduce the effort required on the part of the page author while providing functionality that helps increase the user's experience with the site.

The bean Tag Library

The next tag library to look at is the bean library. Many of the pages that we've seen have either made use of attributes within the page context, or made use of scripting variables within the page. This is nothing new and the standard <jsp:useBean/> tag provides this functionality for free.

However powerful, this tag is not very flexible and can only be used to reference or create new JavaBeans in a page. The Struts bean tag library takes this one step further by providing an enhanced set of functionality associated with using JavaBeans in and on the page.

The key difference that the tags in this library (and in fact the html library too) have is that they can access individually named and indexed properties on JavaBeans more easily. With the standard tags and those that we've developed in the book, simple references to JavaBeans can be made by supplying the name of an object that is currently bound into one of the scopes request, page, session, or application.

For example, if we think back to the Book and Category classes from the previous chapters, we might choose to iterate over a collection called books that has been bound into the page context:

```
<iteration:iterate id="books"
                   type="com.wrox.jsptaglibs.common.Book"
                   collection="books">

  ... content to be iterated over ...

</iteration:iterate>
```

This assumes, of course, that a collection called books is currently available as an attribute that can be looked up through the page context. If instead we had a reference to a Category instance, we would first have to get the collection of books, possibly using a small scriptlet:

```
<%
  Category category = (Category)PageContext.findAttribute("category");
  pageContext.setAttribute("books", category.getBooks());
%>
```

In Struts, however, there is support for accessing any property of a named JavaBean through a pair of attributes called name and property. This means that instead of just specifying the name of a JavaBean, the Struts tags support the ability to reference **properties.** For example, a tag might have the following combination of attributes:

```
name="book" property="title"
```

Using these attributes on one of the Struts tags would find the book object in the page context and then use its title property. However, this doesn't stop here and through a simple syntax for the property attribute, Struts tags additionally support **nested properties**. If we were to assume that the Book object had an author property of type Author that subsequently had a string property called name, the following could be used to reference the name of a book's corresponding author:

```
name="book" property="author.name"
```

Behind the scenes, the tag would look up the book bean in the page context and call the getAuthor() method, on which it would then call the getName() method. In addition to this, the Struts tags are also able to reference **indexed properties.** If we assume that the Book class maintains a collection of Author objects, we can specify a particular author with the following:

```
name="book" property="author[0]"
```

Once again, behind the scenes, this is simply equivalent to calling the appropriate accessor methods which in this case would be book.getAuthor(0) – a method to get the first author from an array or collection. Of course, the properties and accessors do have to be in place but the real power here is that the Struts tags provide a very simple way of exposing the information contained within complex data structures to the page.

So, with these principles in mind let's take a look at some of the tags that the bean tag library has to offer.

Creating and Copying Attributes

The first tag we will look at is define, a powerful alternative to the standard <jsp:useBean/> tag. Whereas the standard tag can only create or look up JavaBeans, the define tag also provides the ability to create new objects, but supplements this with the functionality to create new objects based upon a copy or a property of an existing bean.

For example, the define tag can be used to create an attribute based upon the name and scope property of an existing attribute. If we imagine that there is a bean called category already bound into the page context, we can create a new bean called books that points to the collection of Book instances for that category:

```
<bean:define id="books" name="category" property="books"/>
```

In essence, this is a shortcut for calling the getBooks() method on the category object, and subsequently placing the resulting reference into the PageContext under the name books. This is a very powerful feature and is useful for reducing Java code in the JSP page, but remember the powerful syntax of the property attribute can also be used to extract further named properties from a Java object:

```
<bean:define id="author" name="category" property="books[0].author"/>
```

The define tag is really a useful way of removing scriptlets that create new objects and place them into the page context. It is much like the standard <jsp:useBean/> tag although it has the ability to copy existing objects and reference nested and indexed properties.

Copying Information

Another example of a very useful tag in the bean library is called parameter, which allows values from request parameters to be copied into named, request-scoped objects of type java.lang.String:

```
<bean:parameter id="categoryName" name="categoryName"/>
```

Along a similar line, the cookie tag extracts the value of a cookie and makes it available as a named object of type java.lang.String:

```
<bean:cookie id="visitorName" name="visitorName"/>
```

Finally, the header tag is used to copy information out of the HTTP header into a named object of type java.lang.String:

```
<bean:header id="referer" name="referer"/>
```

Here, tags provide a good solution to the problems of retrieving information that is not easily available without resorting to Java code on the page.

Resource Bundles and I18N

The final tag that we'll look at in the bean library is called message. As we saw in Chapter 8, in Java it is possible to define **resource bundles**: classes or properties files that contain localized content such as text that will appear on the user interface. For example, you might define two bundles: one containing the text for the English version of the application and one for the French. With the explosion of the Web, the ability to generate user interfaces in more than just a single language is becoming more and more important, primarily from a user perspective, but also from a business and marketing perspective.

Resource bundles are a mechanism for separating out the localized content that would be displayed on a user interface from the code that is responsible for generating that user interface. Writing a ResourceBundle as a properties file is straightforward, the entries of which consist of a key and a value:

```
logon.title=Timesheet Application Logon
username.label=Username
password.label=Password
```

As the example in Chapter 8 demonstrated, making use of resource bundles does require some Java code and the Struts message tag has been created to wrap this process. Behind the scenes, the tag looks up the resource bundle that is appropriate to the current user along with the value associated with the key attribute, then renders the text back into the page:

```
<bean:message key="logon.title"/>
```

As web sites are applications that can easily be distributed around the world, internationalizing your applications mean that you can reach a far wider audience than ever before. For this reason, and as a recommendation, it is worth considering internationalizing your applications, especially since now it is easy to do, thanks to the message tag.

The logic Tag Library

The next tag library to look at is called logic. This, as you might expect, contains various tags that help provide conditional functionality on the page in a similar way to the tags that we developed in Chapter 7. Let's take a look at some of the tags.

Comparing Values

The conditional tags that are provided with the Struts Framework are fairly powerful as they support a wide range of conditional operations. Rather than using an if tag containing nested conditions (as we did in Chapter 7), the Struts condition tags take a different approach in that they can be used on their own, without an enclosing parent like if. In other words, all of the tags take the following form:

```
<%@ taglib uri="/WEB-INF/struts-logic.tld" prefix="logic" %>

<logic:tagName [header | cookie | parameter | name | property] value>
  ... body content to be rendered if the condition is true ...
</logic:tagName>
```

Here, the `value` attribute is used to supply the value that should be tested against, while the other attributes are used to specify the value/variable that should be tested, from a bean, property, cookie, or header. There are various ways in which the values can be tested, and this is communicated by the name of the tag, a complete list of which is as follows:

Tag	Purpose
`equal`	Checks for equality
`notEqual`	Checks for inequality
`greaterEqual`	Tests whether the variable is greater than or equal to the value
`lessEqual`	Tests whether the variable is less than or equal to the value
`greaterThan`	Tests whether the variable is greater than the value
`lessThan`	Tests whether the variable is less than the value

Let's see a couple of examples of the conditional tags and the power they have over working on data that isn't necessarily part of the page context.

If a `Book` instance in an online store was already available in the page context, the following fragment might be used to compare the `price` property with a defined threshold value to highlight a good deal:

```
<logic:lessThan name="book" property="price" value="10">
  Buy now, great value!
</logic:lessThan>
```

Once again, we're using the `name` and `property` attributes of the tag to specify a JavaBean and the specific property that should be tested. Another example of how the tags might be used is to check the value of a specific request parameter, without first placing it into the page context with the `parameter` tag from the `bean` library:

```
<logic:equal parameter="loggedIn" value="false">
  You are not currently logged in.
</logic:equal>
```

Something that is worth noting with the Struts conditional tags is that they mainly deal with string comparisons rather than comparisons between objects. Since a large part of the Struts Framework is geared towards building HTML forms, and the values associated with these forms are strings, this is not too much of a problem.

Another issue shown up by the example that we've just looked at is that the `equal` tag will throw a `JSPException` if the page is not requested with a parameter called `loggedIn`. Solving this is easy, thanks to some more tags provided by the logic library – `present` and `notPresent`.

Testing for the Presence of Values

The `present` and `notPresent` tags check for the presence of a particular value. Once again, this is not constrained to attributes in the page context because these tags can check request parameters, cookies, and values in the HTTP header:

```
<logic:tagName [header | cookie | parameter | name | property]>
  ... body content to be rendered if the condition is true ...
</logic:tagName>
```

Using the tags is simple, they are just wrapped around the content that should be displayed if the condition is `true`. The following example might be used to check the value of a request parameter called `isbn`, ensuring that it has been specified:

```
<logic:present parameter="isbn">
  ... lookup the book ...
</logic:present>

<logic:notPresent parameter="isbn">
  You must select a book!
</logic:notPresent>
```

Collection Utilities

Alongside the condition tags is an `iterate` tag, similar to the one that we developed back in Chapter 5, but much more powerful because of the way properties can be specified. The example that follows shows how the `property` attribute can be used to select the collection that is iterated over:

```
<%@ taglib uri="/WEB-INF/struts-bean.tld" prefix="bean" %>
<%@ taglib uri="/WEB-INF/struts-logic.tld" prefix="logic" %>

... find category and add to page scope ...

<logic:iterate id="book" type="com.wrox.jsptaglibs.common.Book"
  name="category" property="books">

  <p>
    <b><bean:write name="book" property="title"/></b>
    <br/>
    ISBN : <bean:write name="book" property="isbn"/>
  <p/>

</logic:iterate>
```

Here, and in a similar way to the `iterate` tag that we built in Chapter 5, the `id` attribute is the name of the page-scoped attribute that will be used to reference each element in the collection and `type` is the fully qualified class name of each element. The other two attributes, `name` and `property`, identify the collection that should be iterated over. In this example, we're using the `books` property of a page-scoped bean called `category`.

Using the `property` attribute means that we don't have to look up the collection of books and place it into the page context before using the `iterate` tag. Of course, doing so is easy with the `bean` library, although it's no longer necessary in this example.

The final tag library provided by Struts is called `template`.

The template Tag Library

Often pages in a web site have a fixed layout, for example they might have a header section, a menu of navigation links on the left, and a central content section. Without using HTML frames, one way to layout these elements is to use the HTML `<table>` tag as follows:

```
<html>
  <head>
    <title>Professional JSP Tag Libraries</title>
  </head>

  <body>

    <table width="100%">
      <tr>
        <td colspan="2">
          ... header section here ...
        </td>
      </tr>

      <tr>
        <td width="100">
          ... navigation here ...
        </td>

        <td width="540">
          ... content here ...
        </td>
      </tr>
    </table>
  </body>
</html>
```

Once a layout has been decided, a page like this could be given to a team and each page developer could then fill in the blanks. However, if we suddenly decide that we'd like to change the layout in some way, perhaps by making the left navigation menu larger, we'd have to open up every page and change the table dimensions manually.

The Struts `template` tag library provides a way of abstracting this information from the pages through a template that all the other pages in the site make use of. Defining a template is straightforward and involves the use of the `get` tag:

```
<html>

  <head>
    <title>Professional JSP Tag Libraries</title>
```

```
    </head>

    <%@ taglib uri="/WEB-INF/struts-template.tld" prefix="template" %>

    <body>
      <table width="100%">
        <tr>
          <td colspan="2">
            <template:get name="header"/>
          </td>
        </tr>

        <tr>
          <td width="100">
            <template:get name="navigation"/>
          </td>

          <td width="540">
            <template:get name="content"/>
          </td>
        </tr>
      </table>
    </body>
  </html>
```

A template defines the structure of the page, indicating where all of the different components are to be positioned. In this case, we have three areas: `header`, `navigation`, and `content`, although we're not specifying the actual content. Instead, we must now create an "instance" of the page:

```
<%@ taglib uri="/WEB-INF/struts-template.tld" prefix="template" %>

<template:insert template="template.jsp">
  <template:put name="header" content="header.html"/>
  <template:put name="navigation" content="navigation.jsp"/>
  <template:put name="content" content="content.jsp"/>
</template:insert>
```

Here, the `insert` tag is used to say that the result of using the template previously defined in `template.jsp`, above, will be inserted into the page. Specifying the physical content for the three areas in the template is achieved using the `put` tag. We simply provide URLs of the real content at request-time. The contents of these URLs are included into the page through the template and delivered to the user.

For completeness, here are the other pages, starting with `header.html`:

```
<h1>This is the header</h1>
```

Next is `navigation.jsp`:

```
  This is the navigation...
```

Finally, the `content.jsp`:

```
<p>
  This is the content...
</p>
```

The following screenshot shows the result of using these pages in conjunction with the template:

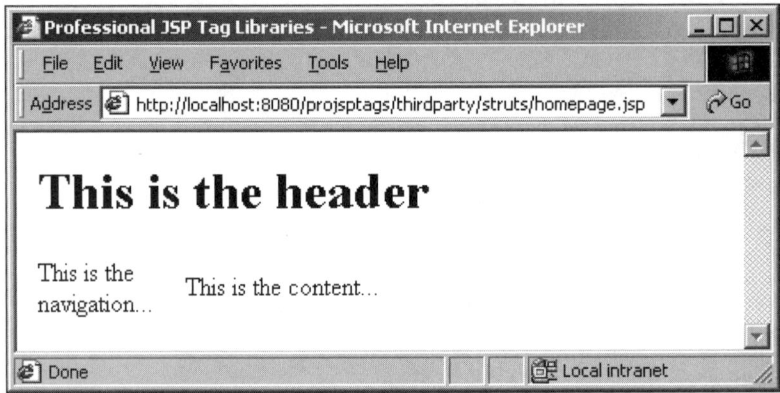

Although simple, this is an extremely powerful tag library and it has the potential to greatly decrease the burden of maintaining the web sites that are based around a defined structure. After all, changing the layout is a simple matter of changing the template. It also shows another very powerful use of custom tags.

Many of the tags that we've seen perform some sort of action on the page and while this is still true of the tags in the `template` library, they provide something extra – the ability to separate the content and the presentation at a much higher level than we've seen before.

A Summary of the Struts Tag Libraries

Although we've only had a brief look at the tags that are provided as part of Struts, one of the things that they all have in common is, once again, that they try to reduce the effort required on the part of the page author and increase the maintainability of web applications by moving Java code out of the page and into reusable components. This is especially apparent with the `html` tag library where the tags themselves have access to and integrate well with the core Struts components.

From this perspective, Struts provides a rich toolset for building Model 2 applications that contain a great deal of user input in the way of HTML forms. It is a very popular framework, and certainly one to consider if you are building such applications. However, there may be times when you don't need such a rich framework. In this situation it is still possible to use parts of the `bean`, `logic`, and `template` tag libraries without the rest of the framework and reap the benefits of using these powerful, flexible tag libraries.

Jakarta Taglibs

Jakarta Taglibs is again part of the Jakarta Project. Unlike Struts, Jakarta Taglibs is a collection of tag libraries, instead of a complete framework to build applications. Here, the aim is to provide an open source repository for useful, production-quality custom tag libraries.

Currently, there are over twenty tag libraries that have been accepted into the project, and undoubtedly as you are reading this there are more in the pipeline. As at the time of writing, here is a list of the current tag libraries:

Tag library	Description
`Application`	Tags that can be used to access information contained within the application context of a web application.
`Benchmark`	Tags that help perform basic benchmarking of JSP pages.
`BSF`	Tags that form a wrapper around the Beans Scripting Framework – an architecture for incorporating scripting language support. Further information on BSF can be found at http://alphaworks.ibm.com/tech/bsf/.
`DateTime`	Tags that help with date, time, and time zone-related functions. For example, displaying the date in a localized manner.
`DBTags`	Tags that help with accessing SQL databases from within a JSP page.
`I18N`	Tags that help construct internationalized web applications.
`Input`	Tags that help generate HTML forms – similar to those in Struts.
`IO`	Tags that allow you to perform requests to external services (such as HTTP, SOAP, FTP, and so on) from within a JSP page.
`JMS`	Tags that send and receive messages from within JSP.
`JNDI`	Tags that can use JNDI for accessing and binding objects.
`Log`	Tags that wrap up the functionality provided by another Jakarta project – log4j, an open source logging API for Java.
`Mailer`	Tags that send e-mail from within a JSP page.
`Page`	Tags that can be used to access information contained within the page context of a web application.
`Random`	Tags that generate random numbers and strings.
`Regexp`	Tags that perform regular expressions-related functions.
`Request`	Tags that access all information about HTTP requests for a JSP page.

Table continued on following page

Tag library	Description
Response	Tags that can be used to access information contained within the HTTP response of a page.
Scrape	Tags that can scrape content from web pages for redisplaying elsewhere.
Session	Tags that can be used to access information contained within the session context of a web application.
Standard	The reference implementation of the JSP Standard Tag Library (JSTL).
String	Tags that provide utilities around strings.
Utility	Some example tags demonstrating custom tag coding techniques.
XSL	Tags that perform XSL transformations.
Xtags	Tags that allow XML documents to be accessed and processed using XPath references.

More information about the Jakarta Taglibs project along with detailed documentation and source code for each of the tag libraries can be found at http://jakarta.apache.org/taglibs/.

Installing Jakarta Taglibs

Currently, all of the tag libraries that make up the Jakarta Taglibs project are downloadable as a single archive. In a pre-compiled binary format they can be downloaded from http://jakarta.apache.org/taglibs/binarydist.html, and if you are interested in how the tags work behind the scenes, the source for the entire Taglibs project can be downloaded from http://jakarta.apache.org/taglibs/sourcedist.html.

With the binary distribution, once downloaded, extract the files to a temporary directory and find the tag library (for example `benchmark`) that you are interested in. To use the tag library, simply copy the JAR file containing the tag handler classes (for example `benchmark.jar`) into the `WEB-INF\lib` directory of your web application, and copy the TLD (for example `benchmark.tld`) somewhere under the `WEB-INF` directory. Finally you can define a mapping between the TLD and a symbolic URI, although, as we saw in Chapter 10, this is not required to get the tags up and running. Using the tag library is then simply a matter of importing the tag library into the JSP page and using the tags.

Let's take a look at a few of the tag libraries currently available.

The Benchmark Tag Library

One of the arguments against using custom tags is that they are typically slower in terms of performance than using scriptlets on their own. As we've seen, if this is the case, the benefits of increased maintainability, reusability, and a long-term reduction in effort easily outweigh these deficiencies. Now, with the `benchmark` tag library, you can very easily run some rough benchmarks over the page for comparison purposes. Although it's not a full-fledged benchmarking package, it is more than ideal for quickly looking at how long it takes fragments of a JSP page to execute. As illustrated by the following JSP code snippet, the tag library is very simple to use:

```
<benchmark:duration>
  ... content to be benchmarked here ...
</benchmark:duration>
```

The output from these tags simply shows the number of milliseconds that it takes to evaluate the body content. This is a good use of tag libraries and although you wouldn't want to keep them in for deployment, this library shows how tags can be a useful aid during the development and testing stages of a project.

The Log Tag Library

The `Log` tag library is another good example of how tags can be useful in the development stages of a project although you might want to keep these tags in when deploying to a production environment too. There are now many tools that support remote debugging on JSP source code, but if you don't have access to these, an alternative is to simply use log statements.

When writing JSP pages, typically you would do something like the following to output debugging information into the server console:

```
<%
  System.out.println("Value of x is now " + x);
%>
```

The `log4j` logging framework is also part of the Jakarta Project and provides a very flexible way to perform logging. Some of its key features include being able to log to different **categories**, a way of organizing messages, and **appenders,** classes that perform the actual logging to the console, a database, messaging through JMS, and so on.

Further information about log4j can be found at http://jakarta.apache.org/log4j/.

Owing to its ease of use and flexibility, the log4j framework is incredibly popular. Although using the framework is easy, using it from a JSP page does introduce Java code into the page and hence the `Log` tag library was created. Effectively it provides a tag-based wrapper around the log4j framework and allows a very easy way to perform logging from JSP pages.

There are five levels of logging available in log4j (debug, info, warn, error, and fatal), each of which has a corresponding tag. For example, logging a debug message could be achieved using the following; the attributes `category` and `message` are optional:

```
<log:debug category="myCategoryName" message="Finished building HTML form"/>
```

```
<log:debug category="myCategoryName">
  The value of x is now <%= x %>
</log:debug>
```

Again, this is a great use of custom tags and shows another important use for custom tags as wrappers for functionality that is already available through a predefined Java interface rather than re-implementing the interface.

The Scrape Tag Library

The final tag library that we'll look at is called `Scrape`. Screen scraping has been around for a while now and is a technique for extracting information from the old text-based user interfaces. Essentially, it's a way of integrating with legacy systems.

For the past few years, the adoption of XML as a mechanism for integrating enterprises has grown rapidly, with web services taking this integration to a new level. Accessing such information is now straightforward with tag libraries such as `IO`, also from Jakarta Taglibs. There are, however, times when you may need to include information that is not currently available through an XML feed or a web service. For example, the information that you need to display is only available on the web, as a web page.

For this reason the `Scrape` tag library was created to provide an easy way to scrape information from web pages for redisplay elsewhere. The tags themselves are very easy to use, as illustrated by the following example:

```
<scrp:page url="http://www.somedomain.com/exchangeRates.jsp">
   <scrp:scrape id="qt" begin="<table>" end="</table>" anchors="true"/>
</scrp:page>
```

Here, the `page` tag is used to specify the page (URL) that should be scraped, while the nested `scrape` tag indicates which part of the resulting page should be grabbed. In this example, everything between (and including) the HTML `table` tags (the anchors) will be grabbed.

Once again, this is an innovative use of custom tags and is a good workaround when information is not available as a nicely packaged bundle. Using tags as a data retrieval mechanism is a not only a good way of keeping the page clean from Java code, but it also means that only the tags need to be modified if the source of the data does change in the future.

A Summary of the Jakarta Taglibs Project

The Jakarta Taglibs project is a huge resource for tags and tag libraries, although it is also very useful for learning more about tags themselves and their potential. After all, all you have to do is download the source code and dive straight in. In addition to this is a tutorial, links to other sites, and the `taglib-user` and `taglib-dev` mailing lists for users and tag developers respectively.

Finally, if you can't find what you're looking for you could always write the tag library and submit it to the Jakarta Taglibs project for everybody else to make use of. Further details on the process behind this can be found at http://jakarta.apache.org/taglibs/addtaglib.html.

JSP Standard Tag Library

The third party tag library that we'll be looking at now is the JSP Standard Tag Library (JSTL), although calling it a third party tag library is not strictly correct; the JSTL effort is a part of the Java Community Process (JSR-052) and is working towards a common set of custom tags that can be used on all JSP-compliant containers.

Currently there are many ways of writing tags that perform common tasks such as iteration, conditional processing, and so on. In addition to this, there are currently many pre-built versions of such tags available for use on the Internet. Since such tasks are common across many applications, the expert group behind the JSTL has been defining a standard set of such tags. This has several benefits.

First of all, it reduces the need for a developer to build a custom version of these common types of tags, which means more time concentrating on the application in hand. As part of their value-added features, many web server vendors now supply a set of tags for exactly this purpose. While this is great, by using them there is a chance that you will get tied into that specific server, or have to learn how to use a different set of tags when you switch vendors. In these situations, another benefit of the JSTL is that because they will run on any JSP-compliant server, a standard set of tags means that you only have to learn how to use them once.

Although it is a project under the remit of the Java Community Process, a reference implementation of the standard (currently only compatible with JSP 1.2-compliant servers) is being hosted by the Jakarta Taglibs project. At the time of writing, the JSTL is still in an early access phase and the expert group is still working upon them. The reference implementation can be downloaded from the Jakarta Taglibs project, but they may change before the final release. For this reason, rather than looking at each and every tag, we'll once again present an overview that provides a flavor of what will hopefully be in the final release.

> *More up-to-date information about the JSP Standard Tag Library can be found at http://jakarta.apache.org/taglibs/doc/standard-doc/intro.html, while information about JSR-052 can be found at http://www.jcp.org/jsr/detail/52.jsp. More in-depth information, including many examples on how to use the JSTL can also be found in Early Adopter JSP Standard Tag Library, from Wrox Press (ISBN 1-861006-24-1).*

Installing JSTL

In its current EA form, and like the other tag libraries that we've looked at, the JSTL can be downloaded in either a binary (pre-compiled) or sourcecode distribution, from http://jakarta.apache.org/builds/jakarta-taglibs/releases/standard/ and http://jakarta.apache.org/builds/jakarta-taglibs/nightly/src/ respectively.

Once downloaded, simply copy the three JAR files (`standard.jar`, `jstl.jar`, and `js.jar`) into the `WEB-INF/lib` directory of your web application. The TLD files for the tag libraries have been included in these JAR files and as such, it is not necessary to define any mappings within the `WEB-INF/web.xml` file.

> *In addition to this, the JSTL can be downloaded as part of the new Java Web Services Developer Pack that is currently in early access and available from http://java.sun.com/webservices/downloads/webservicespack.html. This also includes Tomcat 4.0, ant (the open source build tool), and many of the web services-related Java APIs for XML. Also, a web services tutorial using these technologies is available.*

Let's start our tour with a look at JSTL's support for an expression language.

Support for an Expression Language

One of the most important features of the JSTL is that it contains support for an expression language. When using JavaBeans or their properties in conjunction with custom tags, we either have to resort to request-time expressions, or make use of the powerful functionality that the Struts tags provide. As an example, let's look at the conditional tag that we developed in Chapter 7:

```
<logic:if value="<%= myObject %>">
  ... conditional tags ...
</logic:if>
```

When the `if` tag is used on the page, specifying the object to be tested must be done through a request-time expression. After all, we're effectively passing an object reference to the tag handler. In Chapter 9 we looked at attribute overloading where we can supply an object reference or the name of an existing bean that has been bound into one of the scopes – `request`, `page`, `session`, or `application`. The tag handler has to then work out whether it has been passed an object reference or the name of an object that it has to go and look up.

This is a good solution for increasing the flexibility of a tag but it does require some effort on the part of the tag developer. It also reduces the use of request-time expressions on the page that, due to their syntax, are often a source of many errors. In addition to this, it could be difficult to track down what is going wrong if a name has been supplied instead of an actual reference.

As we've seen, the Struts tags help to remedy this problem by providing a powerful set of tags that are able to create scoped beans based upon information from request parameters, cookies, HTTP headers, and of course other bean properties.

The downside to this is that the Struts tags use different attributes to identify where the information should come from. For example, the `equal` tag has several attributes to be used if testing data from the request, a cookie, the header, or a bean. More attributes means more variations of the tags and therefore, from a tag development point of view, more maintenance.

A solution to this is an expression language that can be used for providing values for any attribute on a tag. While such support will probably be part of a future JSP specification, for now it is provided by the JSTL. For this reason, the JSTL currently supports four different expression languages in its current EA release in an effort to obtain feedback from the JSP community about which one should be taken forward as the default. As of at the time of writing, the expression languages included are as follows:

- Simplest Possible Expression Language (SPEL), further information on which can be found at http://jakarta.apache.org/taglibs/doc/standard-doc/spel/spel.html
- ECMAScript (the standardized JavaScript), further information on which can be found at http://jakarta.apache.org/taglibs/doc/standard-doc/EcmaScriptEL.html
- JPath (based upon features from XPath)
- JXPath (can apply XPath expressions to objects)

So what do expressions look like?

Expressions as Values for Tag Attributes

Let's look at some simple expressions to familiarize ourselves with the language. Although ECMAScript is currently the default language, we'll make use of SPEL in our examples, purely for the simplicity that it provides.

To start with, let's see how it is possible to access properties on named, scoped beans. Like the simple syntax available for referencing properties in the Struts tags, SPEL uses a similar syntax:

```
$category.books
```

If we assume that an object called `category` is bound into the page, this expression can be used to get the value of the `books` property. One point to notice here is that the expression starts with a dollar (`$`) symbol. One of the problems associated with using an expression language is differentiating static strings from those that should be evaluated. For this reason, most of the expression languages available in JSTL make use of a special symbol (usually a dollar character) to say, "this is an expression that needs to be evaluated."

In addition to looking up named objects, it is also possible (in SPEL) to retrieve information from a specific scope. In the next example, the names of the variables we are interested in are preceded by the scope in which they can be found:

```
$param:myParameter
$session:category
```

Like Struts, expressions also allow us to reference named properties, nested properties, and indexed properties. However, the real power of an expression language is its capability to perform operations and evaluations. The following example shows how an expression might be written to test the value of a named, scoped object:

```
$session:loggedIn != 'true'
```

This is really just the start of what the expression languages can offer. SPEL is the smallest and simplest expression language, but also the one that is most aligned to the features of JSP. The others have much more power and therefore are also much more complicated. For example, JXPath can apply XPath expressions to regular object graphs (as opposed to XML documents), using them to retrieve a single object. Also, it can use XPath filters to select one or more objects.

If you've done any JavaScript programming, ECMAScript will probably be the most familiar to you and provides a great deal of functionality. Using an expression language feels a little strange to start with but you'll soon get used to it. Now that we've seen some of the expressions that can be used, let's look at some of the tags provided by the JSTL.

The JSTL Tag Libraries

JSTL consists of many different tags and for this reason JSTL could be called a collection of tag libraries. The list of tag libraries is as follows:

- **Core**
  Provides the core JSTL tags that perform iteration, conditional processing, and expression language support:

```
<%@ taglib uri="http://java.sun.com/jstl/ea/core" prefix="c" %>
<%@ taglib uri="http://java.sun.com/jstl/ea/core-rt" prefix="c" %>
```

- **Formatting**
  Provides tags that support I18N and localized formatting and parsing:

```
<%@ taglib uri="http://java.sun.com/jstl/ea/fmt" prefix="fmt" %>
<%@ taglib uri="http://java.sun.com/jstl/ea/fmt-rt" prefix="fmt" %>
```

- **SQL**
  Provides tags that allow direct database access from within JSP pages:

```
<%@ taglib uri="http://java.sun.com/jstl/ea/sql" prefix="sql" %>
<%@ taglib uri="http://java.sun.com/jstl/ea/sql-rt" prefix="sql" %>
```

- **XML Processing**
  Provides tags that allow parsing and XSL transformation of XML documents:

```
<%@ taglib uri="http://java.sun.com/jstl/ea/xml" prefix="x" %>
<%@ taglib uri="http://java.sun.com/jstl/ea/xml-rt" prefix="x" %>
```

The above are the recommended `taglib` directives that may be used to import the tags into a JSP page. In the current release, the tags are packaged up into a JAR file that can simply be dropped into the `WEB-INF\lib` directory of a web application. As we saw in Chapter 10, the TLD files can also be placed into the JAR file (as with `standard.jar`) for automatic deployment of the tag libraries and this is the case with the JSTL libraries too.

One other point to mention about the JSTL tag libraries is that there are actually two versions of the majority of the tags – one that takes advantage of the new expression language and one that doesn't, making use of request-time expressions instead. This is useful if you want the flexibility provided by the standard tags but don't want to use the expression language support yet, perhaps because of the additional performance overhead or its immaturity. To access these tag libraries, simply append `-rt` to the end of the taglib `uri` as shown by the second versions of the `taglib` directives above.

The core Tag Library

The `core` tag library, as its name suggests, contains all of the tags that form the core part of the standard. This, as we'll see shortly, includes tags whose main purpose is to support the expression language as well as tags that perform iteration and conditional processing.

In addition to these are tags related to using web-related resources. This includes a tag called `import` allowing URL-based resources to be included into the page. Unlike the standard `<jsp:include/>` tag, however, the `import` tag allows resources to be included from outside of the web application, and from sources other than HTTP such as, for example, FTP.

The fmt Tag Library

The `fmt` tag library provides I18N formatting facilities, including those provided by the Struts `<bean:message/>` tag. There is much more to this library too, including the ability to format and parse dates and numbers in a locale-specific way, display localized exceptions, and so on.

The sql Tag Library

The `sql` tag library, as you might expect, provides access to SQL databases. While for reasons of maintainability, reusability, security, and so on it can be argued that a JSP page isn't the best place to have database logic, the `sql` tag library, like `DBTags` from the Jakarta Taglibs project, allows page authors to query and update SQL databases. Together with the tags in the core library, the `sql` library is a useful way of writing small applications or prototypes quickly and without introducing any Java code into the page.

The x Tag Library

The final tag library that is included as part of the current JSTL release contains tags that are useful for performing XML parsing and transformation. These tags are included as a part of the JSTL because the XML information, be it from web services, web sites, or enterprise applications on your network, is becoming increasingly popular. With this in mind, many JSP-based applications now have to present information from these different data sources and having tags to make the job easier is certainly a good thing.

Now that we've taken a brief look at the tag libraries that make up the JSTL, let's look at some of the core tags in more detail.

Expression Language Support Tags

The first set of tags we will look at are those that directly support the use of an expression language. These are part of the `core` tag library and, as such, can be imported onto the page with the following `taglib` directive:

```
<%@ taglib uri="http://java.sun.com/jstl/ea/core" prefix="c" %>
```

The expr Tag

Request-time expressions are a useful way of supplying object references and results of expressions to custom tag attributes, but of course they are also designed to output these results back into the page. For example, displaying the value of a property could be performed using the following request-time expression:

```
<%= book.getAuthor().getEmailAddress() %>
```

The JSTL provides a similar tag called `expr` that can be used to output the result of evaluating an expression into the page:

```
<c:expr value="$book.author.emailAddress"/>
```

As request-time expressions are often used to output information back to the page, the `expr` tag is of immense benefit, reducing the need for Java code on the page dramatically. A nice feature of the `expr` tag is that it is possible to supply a default value to be used just in case the expression can't be evaluated. An expression might fail evaluation for several reasons, including a misspelling or the object that it refers to cannot be found:

```
<c:expr value="$book.author.emailAddress" default="Unknown"/>
```

Trying to reference an object that doesn't exist in a request-time expression will probably present the user with a nasty `NullPointerException` and working around this problem would require some conditional processing such as the following:

```
<%= book.getAuthor() != null && book.getAuthor().getEmailAddress() != null
  ? book.getAuthor().getEmailAddress() : "Unknown" %>
```

As we can see, the power of expressions and the supporting tags allows us to reduce the amount of Java code in a page. A final feature of this and many other tags in the library is the ability to omit an attribute and supply its value as the tag's body content. In this case, the `expr` tag allows us to supply the default value through the body content:

```
<c:expr value="$book.author.emailAddress">
  <c:expr value="$book.publisher.emailAddress" default="Unknown"/>
</c:expr>
```

In this example, if the author or the author's e-mail address isn't available, the default behavior is to simply use that of the publisher. This is a nice feature and is useful in those circumstances where the value can't be provided very easily, for example if it was the value of another expression or another tag.

The set Tag

Like the other tags that we've seen that allow objects to be created and stored in the available scopes, the `set` tag performs this same function with the exception that it can make use of expressions:

```
<c:set var="books" scope="session" value="$category.books"/>
```

> **Notice here that an attribute called `var` is used to specify the name of the variable. Typically, and with the examples in the book, an attribute called `id` was used. A different name was chosen on purpose to highlight the fact that the JSTL tags don't actually introduce scripting variables into the page.**

Once again, the `value` attribute can be omitted and specified within the body content of the tag.

The declare Tag

The final tag that provides support for the expression language is the `declare` tag. Since scripting variables don't get introduced into the page, it means that request-time expressions cannot be used alongside the JSTL. As a side effect, this also means that many of the current (non-JSTL) tag libraries that make use of attributes capable of dealing with request-time expressions also can't be used alongside JSTL.

Fortunately, the `declare` tag solves this problem by making a scoped object available as a scripting variable. For example, the following could be used to create a scripting variable in the page called `books` from the existing scoped object of the same name:

```
<c:declare id="books" type="java.util.Collection"/>
```

Another option, rather than using the `declare` tag, is for our own tags to integrate with the expression language. We'll be seeing this shortly. For now, though, let's move on to look at how iteration has been supported in the JSTL.

The forEach Tag

As we've seen, there are many ways to build tags that perform iteration. We could use the `IterationTag` interface, the `BodyTag` interface, call the tag `iterate`, `loop`, `while`, and so on. Part of the JSTL is to provide a standard tag that can be used on any JSP-compliant server to perform iteration on a page – a very common task in most JSP-based applications.

In the JSTL, this standard tag is called `forEach` and is also included as part of the core tag library. As you might expect, it is very powerful yet very simple to use. Let's look at an example of how it might be used on the page, before taking a look at some of the flexibility that it offers:

```
<%@ taglib uri="http://java.sun.com/jstl/ea/core" prefix="c" %>

... find category and add to page scope ...

<c:forEach var="book" items="$category.books">

  <p>
    <b><c:expr value="$book.title"/></b>
    <br/>
    ISBN : <c:expr value="$book.isbn"/>
  </p>

</c:forEach>
```

The `forEach` tag is very easy to use and in this example uses only two attributes. The first of these (`var`) is the name under which each object will be created, while the second (`items`) specifies the collection over which the tag will iterate. As you can see, the JSP source is very clean and displaying the properties of each book is achieved with the `expr` tag once again.

This example only demonstrates a small amount of the flexibility that is on offer. First of all, the `forEach` tag can iterate over arrays (primitives and objects), instances of `java.util.Collection` (lists, sets, maps, and so on), `java.sql.ResultSet`, `javax.sql.RowSet`, and additionally a string made up of comma-separated values.

The `forEach` tag can also perform an arbitrary number of iterations by specifying the `begin` and `end` attributes instead of `items`:

```
<c:forEach var="i" begin="1" end="10">
  <c:expr value="$i"/>
</c:forEach>
```

The final feature to look at is that of the iteration status.

Iteration Status

The forEach tag has another optional attribute (called status) that can be used to expose the status of the current iteration. This is an interesting twist and instead of making properties such as index and count available separately, they've been bundled up into a JavaBean. A benefit of this is that only one object needs to be bound into the page scope instead of several, therefore providing an improvement in performance because fewer setAttribute() calls are being made on the PageContext.

As an example, the following JSP fragment shows how it is possible to get the current position (count) in the iteration:

```
<%@ taglib uri="http://java.sun.com/jstl/ea/core" prefix="c" %>

... find category and add to page scope ...

<c:forEach var="book" items="$category.books" status="status">

  <p>
    <c:expr value="$status.count"/>
    <b><c:expr value="$book.title"/></b>
    <br/>
    ISBN : <c:expr value="$book.isbn"/>
  </p>

</c:forEach>
```

In this example, we're asking the forEach tag to make available the current status of the iteration through a scoped object called status. From here, we can access the current (one-based) position of the iteration using the count property. Additional properties that can be accessed here include flags indicating whether the current item is the first or last item in the iteration (first and last respectively) and as the var attribute is optional on the forEach tag, there is also a property to retrieve the current item called current.

Although we've not looked at the entire feature set of the forEach tag, it is clear to see why having such a powerful tag available on all JSP containers is useful. After all, implementing all of this functionality is no small task, especially when we consider the ability to iterate over pretty much any type of collection while still taking advantage of the expression language support.

The final set of tags that we'll look at provides a standard way of performing conditional processing on the page.

Conditional Tags

Currently there are two types of conditional tags available that are designed to support the two most common ways in which conditional logic is used – if and choose.

The if Tag

The if tag provides a way of performing simple conditional tests, evaluating its body content if the condition is true. For example, the following could be used to test whether the current user is logged in or not:

```
<%@ taglib uri="http://java.sun.com/jstl/ea/core" prefix="c" %>
...
<c:if test="$session:loggedIn == 'false'">
  You are not currently logged in.
</c:if>
```

If the test evaluates to true, the body content gets evaluated. The major difference here between this and the other conditional tags that we've seen is that the tag itself is taking advantage of the expression language support. Rather than having tags called equal, notEqual, and so on, the test is being performed by the expression language.

The if tag is very simple for doing one-shot tests. If more flexibility over the processing is required, for example you have some mutually exclusive conditions, then the choose tag is more appropriate.

The choose Tag

The choose tag is much more like the tag that we developed back in Chapter 7 and allows if-then-else (or rather, choose-when-otherwise) blocks to be implemented on the page. Again, let's look at an example:

```
<%@ taglib uri="http://java.sun.com/jstl/ea/core" prefix="c" %>

<c:choose>

  <c:when test="$session:loggedIn == 'false'">
    You are not currently logged in.
  </c:when>

  <c:otherwise>
    Click <a href="logout.jsp">here</a> to logout.
  </c:otherwise>

</c:choose>
```

Here, the when and otherwise tags must be used within an enclosing choose tag. As with the logic tags that we developed in Chapter 7, only the body content associated with the first test that evaluates to true is rendered. Once again, the expression language is used to provide the test, and there may be one or more when tags nested within a choose tag.

A Summary of the Core JSTL Tags

Although the JSTL is currently in early access, the functionality that it provides page authors is both very powerful and very flexible. The key feature of the JSTL is undoubtedly the support for expression languages and this is something that many people in the JSP community are keeping an eye on with interest, since it provides new, powerful ways in which more maintainable, clearer JSP pages can be written.

The tags that make up the core part of the JSTL provide a way to integrate with the expression language support, but additionally provide a great set of useful tags that address a wide range of common needs when writing JSP-based applications. A lot of time has been spent looking at not only the features that people need from a standard tag library, but also the semantics of how those tags should be used. The current implementation demonstrates this by providing a rich, fully featured set of tags while at the same time making them easy to use and understand.

With the expression support being such a key feature of the JSTL, the final topic that we're going to look at is how we can build our own tags to use the expression language.

Integrating Expression Language Support

So we've looked at the expression language and we've also looked at the functionality that the standard tags provide. As it stands, the JSTL is still evolving and undoubtedly is not yet all things to all people. The support for an expression language is very powerful and fortunately it is possible to build our own tags that take advantage of this. There may be several reasons why we would want to do this.

First of all, the tags provided by the JSTL might not provide exactly the functionality that we need and in this case we can extend or enhance the functionality that they provide. Alternatively, of course, we could build a new tag to use in conjunction with the JSTL. An example here might be the `paging` tag library or the domain-specific tag library that we saw in the last chapter.

As we've learnt from our brief look at the `core` tags, JSTL tags don't introduce scripting variables into the page; instead they keep them stored away in the page context. This is beneficial in that it reduces the temptation to put Java code into the page, but also makes it harder to integrate them with the tags that we write ourselves as we must manually extract the bean from the `PageContext` and declare it as a scripting variable. The `declare` tag does a good job of bridging the gap between these two paradigms, but it would be better if we could just make use of the same types of expressions ourselves.

Fortunately this is possible and fairly straightforward to do.

Evaluating Expressions

Taking advantage of the expression language support is simply a matter of using the `ExpressionEvaluatorManager` class from the `org.apache.taglibs.standard.lang.support` package. The method that we are interested here is as follows:

```
public static Object evaluate(String attributeName,
                              String expression,
                              Class expectedType,
                              Tag tag,
                              PageContext pageContext)
    throws ExpressionException, JspException;
```

This method allows us to evaluate an arbitrary expression and get the resulting object back as a reference. The `attributeName` is the name of the attribute that we would like to evaluate and is just used for reporting errors and helping the page author figure out what has gone wrong. The next parameter, `expression`, is the expression itself, followed by the `expectedType` which is a `java.lang.Class` reference corresponding to the expected type (class) of the object to which the expression evaluates. Finally, `tag` and `PageContext` are internally used by the evaluator so that it has access to the same contextual information as the tag that requested the attribute to be evaluated.

The `evaluate` method declares that it throws two types of exceptions – `ExpressionException` (from the `javax.servlet.jsp.jstl.core` package) and `JspException`. An `ExpressionException` is thrown if the expression couldn't be evaluated for any reason. For example, perhaps the expression was invalid or perhaps the object that it referred to just didn't exist. These types of errors can be caught and shouldn't affect other expressions on the page from being evaluated. For example, the `expr` tag shows the default value if an expression cannot be evaluated. A `JspException`, on the other hand, tends to imply something more serious has happened such as a fatal IO exception or a problem with the evaluator itself.

Now that we know how our tags can evaluate expressions, before we move on to building such a tag, let's look at how twin tags can be supported.

Supporting Twin Tags

The JSTL as it currently stands supports two versions of the majority of the tags – one set that supports the expression language and one that uses regular request-time expressions. This is useful for several reasons and it means that the standard tags can be used by anybody that doesn't want to use the expression language. Another reason is that a future version of the JSP specification might be able to natively support an expression language. This means that we'll no longer need to explicitly evaluate expressions with the `ExpressionEvaluatorManager` as the JSP container will do this for us. If this does happen, the versions of the tags that provide support for the expression language themselves can be discarded, leaving only their request-time expression counterparts.

For the moment, though, supporting twin tags is worthwhile and as the example below demonstrates, it is very easy to do.

Building a Twin Tag

As the JSTL already contains tags that iterate and perform conditional logic, let's revisit the `book` tag from the case study. Although it's a simple tag that doesn't provide much functionality, it is useful in illustrating how a tag can be built to support the expression language.

The method for supporting twin tags recommended by the JSTL expert group is that instead of writing two separate tag handlers, we write three classes. The first of these is an abstract base class and the other two are concrete implementations – one that uses request-time expressions and one that supports the expression language by using the expression language support.

The BookTag Class

To start with, let's build the abstract base class:

```
package com.wrox.jsptaglibs.domain;

import javax.servlet.jsp.JspException;
import javax.servlet.jsp.tagext.TagSupport;

import com.wrox.jsptaglibs.common.BookManager;

public abstract class BookTag extends TagSupport {

  protected String isbn;

  public int doStartTag() throws JspException {

    if (isbn != null) {
      // look up the book and put it in the page context
      pageContext.setAttribute(getId(),
                               BookManager.getInstance().getBook(isbn));
    }
    return SKIP_BODY;
  }
}
```

Essentially, there's nothing new here and as we've seen when we've used inheritance earlier, the base class implements the functionality provided by the tag. What is different here is that the mutator method for the tag attribute is not implemented. Instead, only the instance variable used to store its value is. We'll see why this is, shortly.

The BookTagRT Class

Next we'll build the regular version of the tag that supports RT expressions. Since the functionality has been implemented in the superclass, the `BookTagRT` only provides an implementation for the mutator method for its attribute:

```
package com.wrox.jsptaglibs.domain;

import javax.servlet.jsp.JspException;
import javax.servlet.jsp.tagext.TagSupport;

public class BookTagRT extends BookTag {

  public void setIsbn(String isbn) {
    this.isbn = isbn;
  }
}
```

The BookTagEL Class

Finally we have the implementation that supports the expression language:

```
package com.wrox.jsptaglibs.domain;

import javax.servlet.jsp.JspException;
import javax.servlet.jsp.tagext.TagSupport;
```

```
import org.apache.taglibs.standard.lang.support.ExpressionEvaluatorManager;

public class BookTagEL extends BookTag {

  private String isbnEL;

  public int doStartTag() throws JspException {

    this.isbn = (String)ExpressionEvaluatorManager.evaluate(
      "isbn", isbnEL, String.class, this, pageContext);

    return super.doStartTag();
  }

  public void setIsbn(String isbnEL) {
    this.isbnEL = isbnEL;
  }
}
```

Once again, this is pretty straightforward and this time the tag implements its own mutator method which saves the value of the expression in an instance variable. The tag then overrides the `doStartTag()` method to evaluate the expression, and then delegate all processing back to the superclass.

The reason for implementing different mutator methods, and not having them defined on the superclass, is that the parameter could potentially be different. For example, a request-time tag could take a reference to a `java.util.Collection`, but the expression language version would always take a string.

The Tag Library Descriptor Files

The final step is to write the TLD files. Rather than have a single TLD containing both tags, we've opted to use one for the request-time expression tags, and one for the expression language tags. This way, page authors only import the one that they are interested in using.

First of all is the regular TLD:

```
<?xml version="1.0" encoding="ISO-8859-1" ?>
<!DOCTYPE taglib
  PUBLIC "-//Sun Microsystems, Inc.//DTD JSP Tag Library 1.2//EN"
  "http://java.sun.com/dtd/web-jsptaglibrary_1_2.dtd">

<taglib>

  <tlib-version>1.0</tlib-version>
  <jsp-version>1.2</jsp-version>
  <short-name>domain</short-name>
  <description>
    Examples for the Third Party Tag Libraries chapter.
  </description>

  <tag>
    <name>book</name>
    <tag-class>com.wrox.jsptaglibs.domain.BookTagRT</tag-class>
    <body-content>empty</body-content>
```

```
    <description>
      Finds the book with the specified ISBN.
    </description>

    <variable>
      <name-from-attribute>id</name-from-attribute>
      <variable-class>com.wrox.jsptaglibs.common.Book</variable-class>
      <declare>true</declare>
      <scope>AT_END</scope>
    </variable>

    <attribute>
      <name>id</name>
      <required>true</required>
      <rtexprvalue>false</rtexprvalue>
    </attribute>

    <attribute>
      <name>isbn</name>
      <required>true</required>
      <rtexprvalue>true</rtexprvalue>
    </attribute>
  </tag>

</taglib>
```

Notice here that the value of the `<tag-class>` element corresponds to `BookTagRT` and that the `<rtexprvalue>` element of the `isbn` attribute is set to `true`, meaning that the tag can take request-time expressions.

Next is the expression language version:

```
<?xml version="1.0" encoding="ISO-8859-1" ?>
<!DOCTYPE taglib
  PUBLIC "-//Sun Microsystems, Inc.//DTD JSP Tag Library 1.2//EN"
  "http://java.sun.com/dtd/web-jsptaglibrary_1_2.dtd">

<taglib>

  <tlib-version>1.0</tlib-version>
  <jsp-version>1.2</jsp-version>
  <short-name>domain</short-name>
  <description>
    Examples for the Third Party Tag Libraries chapter.
  </description>

  <tag>
    <name>book</name>
    <tag-class>com.wrox.jsptaglibs.domain.BookTagEL</tag-class>
    <body-content>empty</body-content>
    <description>
      Finds the book with the specified ISBN.
    </description>
```

```
    <variable>
      <name-from-attribute>id</name-from-attribute>
      <variable-class>com.wrox.jsptaglibs.common.Book</variable-class>
      <declare>true</declare>
      <scope>AT_END</scope>
    </variable>

    <attribute>
      <name>id</name>
      <required>true</required>
      <rtexprvalue>false</rtexprvalue>
    </attribute>

    <attribute>
      <name>isbn</name>
      <required>true</required>
      <rtexprvalue>false</rtexprvalue>
    </attribute>
  </tag>

</taglib>
```

This time, the `<tag-class/>` element refers to the `BookTagEL` class, while the `<rtexprvalue/>` for the `isbn` attribute is now set to `false`.

Using the Tags

For completeness, let's see how the tags can be used on the page. First of all is the request-time expression tag:

```
<html>

  <head>
    <title>Professional JSP Tag Libraries</title>
  </head>

  <%@ taglib uri="/domainTaglib-rt" prefix="domain" %>

  <body>

    <domain:book id="book" isbn='<%= request.getParameter("isbn") %>'/>

    <h1><jsp:getProperty name="book" property="title"/></h1>

    <jsp:getProperty name="book" property="description"/>

  </body>

</html>
```

This page simply imports the RT version of the tag library and uses a request-time expression to obtain the request parameter, `isbn`. The EL version on the other hand uses a SPEL expression to extract the parameter from the request:

```
<html>

  <head>
    <title>Professional JSP Tag Libraries</title>
  </head>

  <%@ taglib uri="http://java.sun.com/jstl/ea/core" prefix="c" %>
  <%@ taglib uri="/domainTaglib-el" prefix="domain" %>

  <body>
    <c:expressionLanguage
      evaluator="org.apache.taglibs.standard.lang.spel.Evaluator">

      <domain:book id="book" isbn="$param:isbn"/>

      <h1><jsp:getProperty name="book" property="title"/></h1>

      <jsp:getProperty name="book" property="description"/>

    </c:expressionLanguage>
  </body>

</html>
```

Both the pages generate identical results, but one uses Java code and one doesn't. As this demonstrates, making use of the expression language support within our own tags is very straightforward and just involves making use of the `ExpressionEvaluatorManager` class.

Although we've not looked at this feature, the current implementation of the JSTL allows the page author to select which expression language they wish to use on the page. It is envisaged that this functionality will be removed, but an important point about integrating with the expression language support is that tags can be written independently of the language that is being used on the page. This feature will ultimately enhance the portability of the tags that we write.

A Summary of JSTL

As we've said before, the JSTL is still evolving and with each release it keeps adding more features and becomes more refined. The inclusion of an expression language is an important step forward for the JSP community and one that is mostly welcomed by developers. However, it brings some controversies because of some potential drawbacks in making an expression language available for use in JSP pages.

The first of these potential problems is performance because instead of passing references of Java objects to tags with a request-time expression, the expressions that are used on the page are parsed and evaluated. In reality, however, this is not so much of an issue as there is more and more work being put into this area. A greater potential problem, however, is purely the power of the expression languages, although this does depend on how much functionality that they expose to the page author.

All of the examples that we've seen have made use of SPEL, a very small language that is very easy to use yet offers most of the functionality that many people may need. ECMAScript, on the other hand, is a full-fledged programming language and providing such capabilities on the page could lead to some potential problems.

For example, although custom tags strive towards removing Java code from the page, to make it more readable, maintainable, and reusable, it is still possible to create nasty expressions with the expression language. Before when we had request-time expressions as the values for attributes, we could potentially have very long and complex expressions in a language that we're not quite familiar with. Having large expressions on the page could in turn reduce the readability and also the maintainability as fragments of business logic start becoming embedded into the attributes of custom tags. However, this is really a worst-case scenario, but whichever expression language is chosen, one of the important things that we must remember is to be pragmatic while using it, keeping the principles of good design in mind.

Although an early access, the reference implementation currently provides a rich, full-featured set of custom tags that perform many of the common tasks associated with JSP-based development. With the ability for us to extend the existing tags and create our own tags that support the expression language, the JSTL is going to be a great addition to any JSP developer's toolkit.

Summary

This chapter has rounded off our look at JSP tag libraries by looking at some of the popular third party tag libraries that are currently available. Presenting a complete guide to all of the tags and features available is a massive task and for this reason, we looked at some of the key features to try and get a flavor of what is on offer.

The three tag libraries (or rather frameworks) are all very different and provide their own unique selling points. Struts is a complete open source framework for building web applications based upon the Model 2 architecture and for this reason, half of the framework is geared towards this, while the other half is geared to reducing the effort required to build the JSP pages themselves. The tag libraries that ship with Struts are very powerful and easy to use.

Jakarta Taglibs, on the other hand, is a repository purely for open source tag libraries. Currently there are over twenty different tag libraries, providing functionality from accessing page-scoped variables to database access, page scraping, and XML transformations.

Last but not the least is the JSP Standard Tag Library (JSTL), an effort that is currently underway by the JSR-052 expert group. It too provides a number of different tag libraries, although the aim here is to provide a standard set of tags that page authors can learn to use in any JSP-compliant container. In addition to a set of standard tags is the support for an expression language that is one of the most important additions to the JSP space to date.

Although seemingly small, custom tags are an interesting part of the JSP specification and, as the JSTL have started to demonstrate, they have the potential to change the way that JSP pages are developed in the future. With the knowledge gained from this book, you should be well on your way to build tags that help people write more readable, maintainable JSP pages with less effort, while at the same time building up a library of useful and reusable components.

Tag API Reference

This appendix contains a reference guide to the JSP 1.2 classes that form the tag extension API.

javax.servlet.jsp.tagext

The `javax.servlet.jsp.tagext` package is the package containing all of the classes that are related to the tag extension API. Several of these are for use only by JSP containers or development tools and are of limited interest to us as tag developers, however they have been included here for completeness.

javax.servlet.jsp.tagext Interfaces

There are four interfaces in this package, three that represent the different types of tag handler and an additional interface for managing exception handling.

BodyTag

```
public interface BodyTag
  extends IterationTag
```

This interface is implemented by tag handlers that need more programmatic control over the evaluation of the body content, in addition to the ability to be able to manipulate it.

```
public static final int EVAL_BODY_TAG
```

This was a valid return code for the doStartTag() and doAfterBody() methods. It has now been deprecated in favor of EVAL_BODY_BUFFERED and EVAL_BODY_AGAIN respectively.

```
public static final int EVAL_BODY_BUFFERED
```

This is a valid return code from the doStartTag() method to instruct a new BodyContent instance to be created.

```
public void setBodyContent(BodyContent b)
```

Sets a reference to the BodyContent object for this tag.

```
public void doInitBody() throws JspException
```

This method is provided so that tag handlers can perform some one-off initialization of the BodyContent before the actual content of the tag is evaluated.

IterationTag

```
public interface IterationTag
  extends Tag
```

This interface should be implemented by those tags wishing to programmatically re-evaluate their body content.

```
public static final int EVAL_BODY_AGAIN
```

This constant represents one of the valid return codes for the doAfterBody() method.

```
public int doAfterBody() throws JspException
```

The doAfterBody() method is called by the JSP container after evaluation of a tag's body content has been performed. As with the doStartTag() and doEndTag() methods, this can throw a JspException should anything go wrong. Valid return codes for this method are SKIP_BODY and EVAL_BODY_AGAIN.

Tag

```
public interface Tag
```

This is the interface that every tag handler must implement at a minimum.

```
public static final int SKIP_BODY
public static final int EVAL_BODY_INCLUDE
```

These constants represent the values that may be returned from the doStartTag() method.

```
public static final int SKIP_PAGE
public static final int EVAL_PAGE
```

These constants, on the other hand, represent the values that may be returned from the doEndTag() method.

```
public void setPageContext(PageContext pc)
```

This is called by the JSP container to pass the tag handler a reference to the JSP PageContext for the page on which the tag is being used.

```
public void setParent(Tag t)
```

This is also called by the JSP container to pass the tag handler a reference to its closest enclosing tag handler. The reference passed in may be null if the tag is not nested.

```
public Tag getParent()
```

Gets a reference to the tag's closest enclosing tag handler.

```
public int doStartTag() throws JspException
```

The doStartTag() method is called when the starting, or opening, tag is encountered on the page. Should anything go wrong, this method can throw a JspException. Valid return codes for this method are SKIP_BODY and EVAL_BODY_INCLUDE.

```
public int doEndTag() throws JspException
```

The doEndTag() method is called when the ending, or closing, tag is encountered on the page and again it can throw a JspException. This method is called regardless of how the tag is used on the page, but subject to the rules of the tag lifecycle. Valid return codes for this method are SKIP_PAGE and EVAL_PAGE.

```
public void release()
```

This method is called by the JSP container to tell the tag to release long-term state. It is guaranteed to be called before garbage collection although if tag handler instances are reused, the tag handler instance could be used to service other requests before this happens. This method is not intended to be used for resetting per-invocation state such as tag attributes.

TryCatchFinally

```
public interface TryCatchFinally
```

This is an interface providing tag handlers with more control over how tags handle exceptions and clean up resources. This interface can be implemented by any tag handler.

```
public void doCatch(Throwable t) throws Throwable
```

This method is called by the JSP container when an exception is caught during the processing of the tag, or during evaluation of its body content.

```
public void doFinally()
```

This method is guaranteed to be called (after the `doEndTag()` method if no exception is thrown) by the JSP container and is useful for freeing up resources.

javax.servlet.jsp.tagext Classes

There are several classes in this package that provide default implementations of the interfaces detailed above, namely `TagSupport` and `BodyTagSupport`. The others are ancillary classes that are used for additional features of custom tags, such as introducing variables into the page and validation, or for representing information about a specific tag instance and its attributes.

BodyContent

```
public abstract class BodyContent
  extends JspWriter
```

This is a specialized `JspWriter` (from the `javax.servlet.jsp` package) that is used in conjunction with the `BodyTag` interface. A `BodyContent` object is effectively a temporary scratchpad in which the tag handler can manipulate content before handing it back to the page.

```
protected BodyContent(JspWriter e)
```

Creates a new instance with the specified `JspWriter` as its parent, enclosing writer.

```
public void flush() throws java.io.IOException
```

Since a `BodyContent` object is only a temporary working area, the `flush()` method has been re-implemented here to simply throw an exception.

```
public void clearBody()
```

Clears the body content associated with this instance.

```
public abstract java.io.Reader getReader()
```

Gets the value of the body content as a `Reader`.

```
public abstract String getString()
```

Gets the value of the body content as a string.

```
public abstract void writeOut(java.io.Writer out) throws java.io.IOException
```

This method can be used to write the contents of this instance to another `Writer`, for example another `JspWriter`.

```
public JspWriter getEnclosingWriter()
```

Gets a reference to the enclosing `JspWriter`. Since `BodyContent` extends `JspWriter`, this could be another `BodyContent` instance if body tags have been nested.

BodyTagSupport

```
public class BodyTagSupport
  extends TagSupport
  implements BodyTag
```

This class is a default implementation of the `BodyTag` interface.

```
protected BodyContent bodyContent
```

An instance variable in which to store this tag's `BodyContent` object.

```
public BodyTagSupport()
```

Creates a new instance.

```
public int doStartTag() throws JspException
```

Called when the starting tag is encountered, the default implementation here returning `EVAL_BODY_BUFFERED`.

```
public int doEndTag() throws JspException
```

Called when the ending tag is encountered, the default implementation here returning `EVAL_PAGE`.

```
public void setBodyContent(BodyContent b)
```

Called by the JSP container to set this tag's `BodyContent` instance.

```
public void doInitBody() throws JspException
```

Called to allow some initialization before evaluation of the body content begins, after the `doStartTag()` method has been called and only if it returns `EVAL_BODY_BUFFERED`.

```
public int doAfterBody() throws JspException
```

Called after evaluation of the body content to determine whether it should be re-evaluated. The default implementation here returns `EVAL_PAGE`.

```
public void release()
```

Called to release state before garbage collection.

```
public BodyContent getBodyContent()
```

Gets a reference to the tag's `BodyContent` instance.

```
public JspWriter getPreviousOut()
```

Gets a reference to the previous, or enclosing, `JspWriter`.

PageData

```
public abstract class PageData
```

This class corresponds to the XML view of a JSP page.

```
public abstract java.io.InputStream getInputStream()
```

Gets an `InputStream` from which, with an XML parser, the XML view can be parsed, manipulated and validated.

TagAttributeInfo

```
public class TagAttributeInfo
```

This class is used internally by the JSP container to represent a single attribute that a tag has. It is used at translation time and contains information included in the TLD file.

```
public static final String ID
```

This is a constant used to represent the name of the commonly used `id` attribute.

```
public TagAttributeInfo(String name,
                        boolean required,
                        String type,
                        boolean reqTime)
```

Creates an instance with the specified properties.

```
public String getName()
public String getTypeName()
public boolean canBeRequestTime()
public boolean isRequired()
```

All of these methods are accessors for the properties associated with a `TagAttributeInfo` instance.

```
public static TagAttributeInfo getIdAttribute(TagAttributeInfo[] a)
```

This is a static convenience method which, given an array of `TagAttributeInfo` objects, finds the one representing the `id` attribute.

```
public String toString()
```

An implementation of the `toString()` method for debugging purposes.

TagExtraInfo

```
public abstract class TagExtraInfo
```

This class is used to provide additional information about a tag in terms of the variables that it would like to introduce into the page, and the conditions under which this tag is considered valid on the page.

```
public VariableInfo[] getVariableInfo(TagData data)
```

This method is called by the JSP container at translation time to get information on the variables that the tag will be introducing into the page.

```
public boolean isValid(TagData data)
```

Again, this method is called by the JSP container at translation time to determine whether the tag is valid.

```
public final void setTagInfo(TagInfo tagInfo)
```

Called by the JSP container to pass some basic information about the tag to the `TagExtraInfo` class.

```
public final TagInfo getTagInfo()
```

Retrieves the basic information about the tag.

TagInfo

```
public class TagInfo
```

This class is really for internal use by the JSP container and represents all of the information specified in the `tag` stanza of the TLD file. This class is used at translation time.

```
public static final String BODY_CONTENT_JSP
public static final String BODY_CONTENT_TAG_DEPENDENT
public static final String BODY_CONTENT_EMPTY
```

These constants represent the three types of body content – `JSP`, `tagdependent` and `empty`.

```
public TagInfo(String tagName,
               String tagClassName,
               String bodycontent,
               String infoString,
               TagLibraryInfo taglib,
               TagExtraInfo tagExtraInfo,
               TagAttributeInfo[] attributeInfo)
```

The constructor for representing JSP 1.1 tags. This is maintained for backwards compatibility.

```
public TagInfo(String tagName,
               String tagClassName,
               String bodycontent,
               String infoString,
               TagLibraryInfo taglib,
               TagExtraInfo tagExtraInfo,
               TagAttributeInfo[] attributeInfo,
               String displayName,
               String smallIcon,
               String largeIcon,
               TagVariableInfo[] tvi)
```

The constructor for representing JSP 1.2 tags, where variables can be declared in the TLD.

```
public String getTagName()
public TagAttributeInfo[] getAttributes()
public VariableInfo[] getVariableInfo(TagData data)
public boolean isValid(TagData data)
public void setTagExtraInfo(TagExtraInfo tei)
public TagExtraInfo getTagExtraInfo()
public String getTagClassName()
public String getBodyContent()
public String getInfoString()
public void setTagLibrary(TagLibraryInfo tl)
public TagLibraryInfo getTagLibrary()
public String getDisplayName()
public String getSmallIcon()
public String getLargeIcon()
public TagVariableInfo[] getTagVariableInfos()
```

All of these methods are simply accessors for the properties associated with the `TagInfo` class.

```
public String toString()
```

An implementation of the `toString()` method for debugging purposes.

TagLibraryInfo

```
public abstract class TagLibraryInfo
```

This class is again used internally by the JSP container, this time to represent the information associated with the tag library as a whole. It maintains a collection of `TagInfo` instances corresponding to the tags in the tag library. Again, this class is used at translation time.

```
protected String prefix
protected String uri
protected TagInfo[] tags
protected String tlibversion
protected String jspversion
protected String shortname
protected String urn
protected String info
```

These are simply instance variables used to store the information associated with the tag library.

```
protected TagLibraryInfo(String prefix,
                         String uri)
```

Creates a new instance, passing the `prefix` and `uri` that are used on the page.

```
public String getURI()
public String getPrefixString()
public String getShortName()
public String getReliableURN()
public String getInfoString()
public String getRequiredVersion()
```

All of these methods are accessors associated with the properties in the `TagLibraryInfo` class.

```
public TagInfo[] getTags()
public TagInfo getTag(String shortname)
```

These methods are used to get information about tags in the tag library.

TagSupport

```
public class TagSupport
  implements IterationTag, java.io.Serializable
```

A default implementation of the `IterationTag` interface. Most tag handlers will directly subclass this class.

```
protected String id
```

An instance variable for maintaining an `id` property – commonly used on custom tags.

```
protected PageContext pageContext
```

An instance variable to store a reference to the JSP `PageContext`.

```
public TagSupport()
```

Creates a new instance.

```
public static final Tag findAncestorWithClass(Tag from,
                                               Class klass)
```

A static helper method to find an enclosing (parent) tag handler of a particular type. It's a convenience for calling `getParent()` and checking with the `instanceof` operator.

```
public int doStartTag() throws JspException
```

Called when the starting tag is encountered, the default implementation here returning `SKIP_BODY`.

```
public int doEndTag() throws JspException
```

Called when the ending tag is encountered, the default implementation here returning `EVAL_PAGE`.

```
public int doAfterBody() throws JspException
```

Called after the body content has been evaluated to determine whether it should be re-evaluated. The default implementation here returns `SKIP_BODY`.

```
public void release()
```

Called to release state before garbage collection.

```
public void setParent(Tag t)
```

Called by the JSP container to set a reference to this tag's closest, enclosing tag.

```
public Tag getParent()
```

Returns the closest, enclosing tag.

```
public void setId(String id)
```

A simple mutator method that sets the value of the `id` property.

```
public String getId()
```

An accessor for the `id` property.

```
public void setPageContext(PageContext pageContext)
```

Called by the JSP container to set a reference to the JSP `PageContext`.

```
public void setValue(String k, Object o)
```

Allows a name-value pair to be associated with the tag handler instance.

```
public Object getValue(String k)
```

Retrieves the value of a name-value pair associated with the tag handler.

```
public void removeValue(String k)
```

Removes a name-value pair associated with the tag handler.

```
public java.util.Enumeration getValues()
```

Returns an `Enumeration` over the name-value pairs associated with a tag handler.

TagData

```
public class TagData
  implements Cloneable
```

This class contains a translation-time representation of a tag's attributes and is used in conjunction with the `TagExtraInfo` class.

```
public static final Object REQUEST_TIME_VALUE
```

A special value used by this class to indicate that the value for an attribute hasn't yet been determined because it is the result of a request-time expression.

```
public TagData(Object[][] atts)
```

Creates a new `TagData` instance with the attribute names and values in a two-dimensional array.

```
public TagData(java.util.Hashtable attrs)
```

Creates a new `TagData` instance with the attribute names and values in a `HashTable`.

```
public String getId()
```

A convenience method for getting the value of the `id` attribute.

```
public void setAttribute(String attName,
                         Object value)
```

Sets the value of an attribute.

```
public String getAttributeString(String attName)
```

Gets the value of a named attribute as a string.

```
public java.util.Enumeration getAttributes()
```

Returns an `Enumeration` over the attributes.

TagLibraryValidator

```
public abstract class TagLibraryValidator
```

This class is used to build powerful, flexible classes that are capable of validating the usage of a tag on the page, or simply validating the page itself.

```
public void setInitParameters(java.util.Map map)
```

Called by the JSP container to pass through any initialization parameters specified for this validator class in the TLD file.

```
public java.util.Map getInitParameters()
```

Returns a `Map` of the initialization parameters.

```
public ValidationMessage[] validate(String prefix,
                                    String uri,
                                    PageData page)
```

Called by the JSP container to instruct the validator to validate the page. As a validator is associated with a tag library (through a TLD file), the container passes through to this method the `prefix` and `uri` that the tag library is being used with on the page. The `page` parameter is a reference to the XML view of the page.

```
public void release()
```

Called when the validator is no longer required, much like the `release()` method on a tag handler.

TagVariableInfo

```
public class TagVariableInfo
```

This class is effectively a JSP 1.2 version of the `VariableInfo` class that is used to represent information about the scripting variables that a tag introduces into the page. It is used at translation time and is created from the information provided in the TLD file. The main difference between this and the `VariableInfo` class is the `nameFromAttribute` and `nameGiven` properties.

```
public TagVariableInfo(String nameGiven,
                       String nameFromAttribute,
                       String className,
                       boolean declare,
                       int scope)
```

Creates a new instance with the specified properties.

```
public String getNameGiven()
public String getNameFromAttribute()
public String getClassName()
public boolean getDeclare()
public int getScope()
```

All of these methods are simply accessors.

ValidationMessage

```
public class ValidationMessage
```

This class is used to represent the error messages that will be sent back to the page author should validation with a `TagLibraryValidator` class fail for any reason.

```
public ValidationMessage(String id,
                         String message)
```

Creates a new instance with the specified `id` and message. The `id` property is an optional identifier (provided by the container) that can be used to help the page author identify the exact location of the error.

```
public String getId()
```

An instance variable for storing the `id` property.

```
public String getMessage()
```

An instance variable for the `message` property.

VariableInfo

```
public class VariableInfo
```

This class is used in conjunction with the `TagExtraInfo` class for representing the characteristics of the variables that a tag will be introducing into the page.

```
public static final int NESTED
public static final int AT_BEGIN
public static final int AT_END
```

These constants represent the various scopes that a scripting variable can have with respect to the tag that introduced it.

```
public VariableInfo(String varName,
                    String className,
                    boolean declare,
                    int scope)
```

Creates a new instance representing a variable to be introduced.

```
public String getVarName()
public String getClassName()
public boolean getDeclare()
public int getScope()
```

The following methods are primarily used by the JSP container and get the properties of the variable.

javax.servlet.jsp

There is one class in this package that is directly relevant to building custom tags – `JspTagException`.

javax.servlet.jsp Exceptions

JspTagException

```
public class JspTagException
  extends JspException
```

This is a subclass of `JspException` that can be used to signal, or differentiate, that an error has occurred with a custom tag rather than the JSP page itself.

```
public JspTagException()
```

This constructor simply creates a new `JspTagException` instance.

```
public JspTagException(String msg)
```

This constructor on the other hand creates an exception with the specified message and is much more useful for maintenance and determining the cause of an error.

LONDON

Installing Tomcat 4.0

In this appendix we'll discuss the basics of how to install and configure Tomcat 4.0, the latest version of the open-source JSP and Servlet Reference Implementation. Tomcat 4.0 is the main web container that is used in this book.

Installing Tomcat 4.0

While there are many Servlet and JSP engines available (as of this writing, Sun's 'Industry Momentum' page at http://java.sun.com/products/jsp/industry.html lists nearly 40), we have chosen to focus our attention on Tomcat 4.0. Tomcat is produced by the Apache Software Foundation's Jakarta project, and is freely available at http://jakarta.apache.org/tomcat/.

Since Tomcat is primarily used by programmers, its opensource development model is of particular benefit as it brings the developers and users close together. If you find a bug, you can fix it and submit a patch; if you need a new feature, you can write it yourself, or suggest it to the development team. Tomcat is also the reference implementation of the JSP and Servlet specifications, version 4.0 supporting the latest Servlet 2.3 and JSP 1.2 versions. (Version 3.2.1 is the current version of the Servlet 2.2/JSP 1.1 reference implementation.) Many of the principal developers are employed by Sun Microsystems, who are investing considerable manpower into ensuring that Tomcat 4.0 provides a high-quality, robust web container with excellent performance.

A Word on Naming

The naming of Tomcat 4.0 components can be a little confusing, with the names **Tomcat**, **Catalina**, and **Jasper** all flying around. So, to avoid any problems with terminology:

- **Catalina** is a Servlet container – that is, an environment within which Java Servlets can be hosted.
- **Jasper** is the JSP component of Tomcat – in fact, it's just a Servlet that understands how to process requests for JSP pages.
- **Tomcat** comprises Catalina, plus Jasper, plus various extra bits and pieces including batch files for starting and stopping the server, some example web applications, and `mod_webapp`.
- **mod_webapp** is the component that will allow you to connect Tomcat to the Apache web server. Catalina includes a web server of its own, but you may also wish to connect it to an external web server to take advantage of Apache's extra speed when serving static content, or to allow you to run JSP or Servlet-based applications alongside applications using other server-side technologies such as PHP. As of this writing `mod_webapp` is in alpha-testing, but expect it to become stable soon. In time, connectors for other major web servers should also appear.

Basic Tomcat Installation

These steps describe installing Tomcat 4.0 on a Windows 2000 system, but the steps are pretty generic; the main differences between platforms will be the way in which environment variables are set.

- You will need to install the Java 2 Standard Edition software development kit, if you have not already done so; JDK 1.3 can be downloaded from http://java.sun.com/j2se/1.3/.
- Download a suitable Tomcat 4.0 binary release from http://jakarta.apache.org/tomcat/ – the file will be called something like `jakarta-tomcat-4.0-xx.zip`. (Other archive formats are available which may be more suitable if you are on a Unix-type platform.). Alternatively, it is by far the easiest option on Windows to install the executable version that then needs only double-clicking to install.
- Unzip the file you downloaded into a suitable directory. On a Windows machine, unzipping into `C:\` will create a directory named `C:\jakarta-tomcat-4.0-xx` containing the Tomcat 4.0 files.
- Create `CATALINA_HOME` and `JAVA_HOME` environment variables pointing to the directories where you installed the Tomcat and Java 2 SDK files – typical values are `C:\jakarta-tomcat-4.0-xx` for `CATALINA_HOME` and `C:\jdk1.3` for `JAVA_HOME`.

  Under Windows 2000, environment variables are set using the System control panel. On the Advanced tab, click on the Environment Variables... button. In the resulting dialog box, add `CATALINA_HOME` and `JAVA_HOME` as system variables:

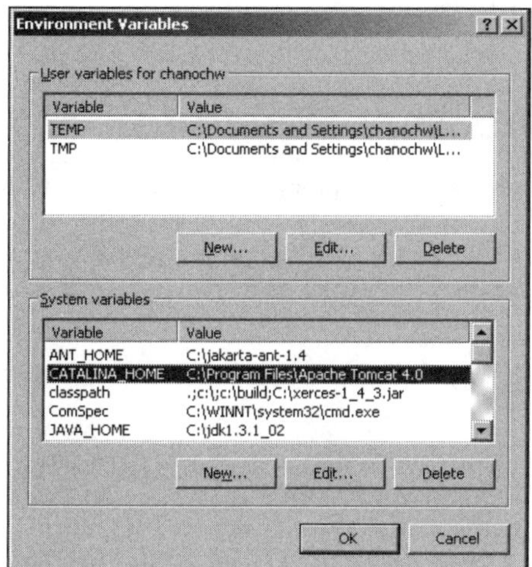

These environment variables allow Tomcat to locate both its own files (using `CATALINA_HOME`), and the Java 2 SDK components it needs, notably the Java compiler (using `JAVA_HOME`).

If you are using Windows 98, environment variables are set by editing the `C:\autoexec.bat` file. Add the following lines:

```
set CATALINA_HOME=C:\jakarta-tomcat-4.0-xx
set JAVA_HOME=C:\jdk1.3
```

Under Windows 98 you will also need to increase the environment space available, by right-clicking on your DOS prompt window, selecting **Properties**, going to the **Memory** tab, and setting the initial environment to 4096 bytes.

- Start Tomcat by running the `startup.bat` batch file (`startup.sh` on Unix-type systems), which can be found in the `%CATALINA_HOME%\bin` directory (in other words, the `bin` directory inside the directory where Tomcat is installed).

  Tomcat will start up and print some status messages:

```
Catalina
Starting service Tomcat-Standalone
Apache Tomcat/4.0.1
Starting service Tomcat-Apache
Apache Tomcat/4.0.1
```

- We now have Tomcat 4.0 up and running, using its internal web server (on port 8080). Point your web browser at http://localhost:8080/; you should see the default Tomcat home page.

  Spend some time exploring the examples and documentation provided with Tomcat.

To shut down Tomcat, run the `shutdown.bat` batch file (`shutdown.sh` on Unix-type systems), again from the `%CATALINA_HOME%\bin` directory.

The Tomcat 4.0 Directory Structure

Looking inside our Tomcat installation directory we find a few text files, and various directories:

- `bin` contains Windows batch files and Unix shell scripts for starting and stopping Tomcat, and for other purposes, together with the `bootstrap.jar` JAR file needed for the first stage of starting Tomcat.
- `classes` is not created by default, but if it exists any `.class` files it contains will be visible to all web applications.
- `common` contains Java code needed by all parts of Tomcat: `.jar` files (Java library files) in the `common\lib` directory, and `.class` files in `common\classes`. Notable among the `.jar` files is `servlet.jar`, which contains the classes defined by the Servlet 2.3 and JSP 1.2 specifications. You will need to have `servlet.jar` listed in your `CLASSPATH` environment variable when compiling classes (for example, Servlets) that use these APIs.
- `conf` contains Tomcat's configuration files, notably `server.xml` (used to configure the server – which hostname and port number to use, which web applications to deploy, etc.) and the server-wide `web.xml`.

> **Note that settings in the server-wide `web.xml` file (located in `%CATALINA_HOME%\conf`) apply to the whole server, but that this behavior is not mandated by the Servlet specification. Applications making use of it will not be portable to other servlet containers.**

- `jasper` contains `.jar` files containing parts of the JSP engine.
- `lib` is populated with various `.jar` files (library files) required by web applications, including parts of the JSP engine. You can add your own `.jar` files here and they will be visible to all web applications.
- `logs` is where Tomcat places its log files. Logging is configured in `server.xml`.
- `server` contains the files comprising Catalina, and other required libraries: `.jar` files in `server\lib`, and `.class` files in `server\classes`.
- `src` contains the source code for Tomcat, along with the documentation (interspersed with the source code).
- `webapps` is the location where Tomcat looks for web applications to deploy. Any `.war` file placed here, or any expanded web application directory structure stored within the directory, will automatically be deployed when Tomcat starts up.

  The URL path under which the application is deployed will correspond to the name of the `.war` file or directory; for example, if you place a `myapplication.war` file or a `myapplication` directory within `webapps`, Tomcat will automatically deploy it as http://localhost:8080/myapplication/.

The automatic deployment settings may not suit your application, in which case you may prefer to store the application outside the webapps directory and configure it as desired using server.xml.

- work is used by Tomcat to store temporary files, notably the .java source files and compiled .class files created when processing JSPs.

Note that this directory structure has changed slightly since the Tomcat 4.0 Beta 1 release.

Tomcat 4.0 Configuration

The Tomcat documentation has improved considerably compared to early versions and should be your first stop if you need to configure Tomcat in any way. However, there are a few steps that are sufficiently common that we cover them here.

Deploying a Web Application

There are two ways to tell Tomcat to deploy a web application:

- As mentioned above, you can deploy an application simply by placing a .war file or an expanded web application directory structure in the %CATALINA_HOME%\webapps directory.
- However, the default settings may not be suitable for your application, in which case it will be necessary to edit %CATALINA_HOME%\conf\server.xml and add a <Context> element for your application.

The default server.xml file is well commented, and you should read these to familiarize yourself with the contents of this file. Various additional elements, not shown or described here but included in the default server.xml, provide for logging and other similar functionality, and define authentication realms. The default server.xml also includes commented-out sections illustrating how to set up a secure (HTTPS) connector, and to set up database-driven authentication realms. It also includes elements that work together with the mod_webapp Apache module.

The outline structure of server.xml is as follows:

```
<Server>
  <Service>
    <Connector/>
    <Engine>
      <Host>
        <Context/>
      </Host>
    </Engine>
  </Service>
</Server>
```

At the top level is a <Server> element, representing the entire Java Virtual Machine. It may contain one or more <Service> elements:

```
<Server port="8005" shutdown="SHUTDOWN" debug="0">
```

A <Service> element represents a collection of one or more <Connector> elements that share a single 'container' (and therefore the web applications visible within that container). Normally, that container is an <Engine> element:

```
<Service name="Tomcat-Standalone">
```

A <Connector> represents an endpoint by which requests are received and responses are returned, passing them on to the associated <Container> (normally an <Engine>) for processing. This <Connector> element creates a non-secure HTTP/1.1 connector, listening on port 8080:

```
<Connector className="org.apache.catalina.connector.http.HttpConnector"
           port="8080" minProcessors="5" maxProcessors="75"
           acceptCount="10" debug="0"/>
```

An <Engine> element represents the Catalina object that processes every request, passing them on to the appropriate <Host>:

```
<Engine name="Standalone" defaultHost="localhost" debug="0">
```

The <Host> element is used to define the default virtual host:

```
<Host name="localhost" debug="0" appBase="webapps">
```

A <Context> element is used to define an individual web application:

```
<Context path="/examples" docBase="examples" debug="0"
         reloadable="true">
</Context>
```

The attributes of the <Context> element are:

- path determines the URL prefix where the application will be deployed. In the example above, the application will be found at http://localhost:8080/examples/.
- docBase specifies the whereabouts of the .war file or expanded web application directory structure for the application. Since a relative file path is specified here, Tomcat will look in its webapps directory (this was configured in the <Host> element, above) but an absolute file path can also be used.
- debug specifies the level of debugging information that will be produced for this application.
- reloadable intimates whether the container should check for changes to files that would require it to reload the application. When deploying your application in a production environment, setting its value to "false" will improve performance, as Tomcat will not have to perform these checks.

```
      </Host>

    </Engine>

  </Service>

  <!-- Snip details of service for the mod_webapp connector -->

</Server>
```

The Manager Application

Tomcat 4.0's default configuration includes a web application that allows web applications to be deployed, undeployed, and reloaded while Tomcat is running. This application is installed by default in the /manager web application, and contains four commands:

- http://localhost:8080/manager/list lists all web applications currently deployed in this virtual host.
- http://localhost:8080/manager/install?path=/myapp&war=mywar deploys the web application specified by the war request parameter, at the context path given by the path parameter.
- http://localhost:8080/manager/reload?path=/myapp reloads all the Java classes in the specified web application. This works even if automatic class reloading is disabled.
- http://localhost:8080/manager/remove?path=/myapp shuts down and undeploys the specified web application.

When specifying a web application to the 'deploy' command, the value of the war request path must have one of these forms:

- file:/absolute/directory/path – the absolute path to the directory containing the unpacked web application.
- jar:file:/absolute/path/to/mywar.war!/ – a URL specifying the absolute path to the .war file.
- jar:http://host:port/path/to/mywar.war!/ – a URL specifying the location of the HTTP-accessible .war file.
- http://localhost:8080/manager/sessions?path=/myapp lists sessions for the specified web application.
- http://localhost:8080/manager/start?path=/myapp starts the specified web application.
- http://localhost:8080/manager/stop?path=/myapp stops the specified web application.

Before you can use the manager application you need to set up a user in tomcat-users.xml with the role manager:

```
<tomcat-users>
  <user name="tomcat"  password="tomcat" roles="tomcat" />
  <user name="role1"   password="tomcat" roles="role1"  />
  <user name="both"    password="tomcat" roles="tomcat,role1" />
  <user name="admin"   password="adminpassword" roles="manager" />
</tomcat-users>
```

With this addition, the manager application works just fine:

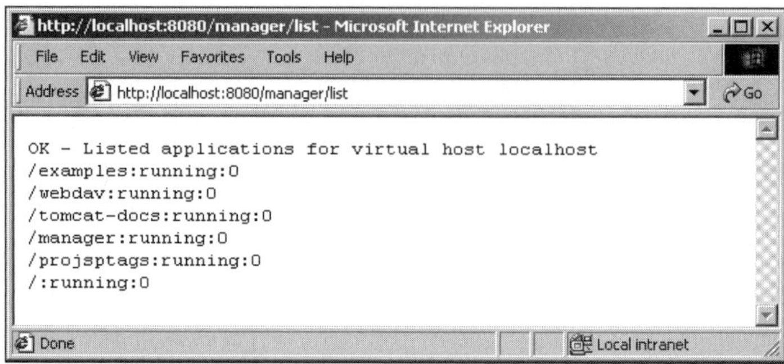

Getting Help

If you need help with Tomcat 4.0, and this appendix and the documentation just haven't helped, your first port of call should be the Tomcat web site, http://jakarta.apache.org/tomcat/. There are two mailing lists dedicated to Tomcat issues:

- tomcat-user, for Tomcat's users – this is where you can ask questions on configuring and using Tomcat. The Tomcat developers should be on hand to help out as necessary.
- tomcat-dev, which is where the developers themselves lurk. If you decide to get stuck in with contributing to improving Tomcat itself, this is where the action is.

LONDON

Index

A Guide to the Index

The index is arranged hierarchically, in alphabetical order, with symbols preceding the letter A. Most second-level entries and many third-level entries also occur as first-level entries. This is to ensure that users will find the information they require however they choose to search for it.

A

B

C

D

E

F

G

J

K

N

O

P

Q

R

S

T

U

V

W

Notes

Notes

Notes

Registration Code: 6217CQ91C85FI001

Wrox writes books for you. Any suggestions, or ideas about how you want information given in your ideal book will be studied by our team. Your comments are always valued at Wrox.

Free phone in USA 800-USE-WROX
Fax (312) 893 8001

UK Tel.: (0121) 687 4100 Fax: (0121) 687 4101

Professional JSP Tag Libraries – Registration Card

Name ______________________

Address ______________________

____

____

____

City ____________ State/Region ____________

Country ____________ Postcode/Zip ____________

E-Mail ______________________

Occupation ______________________

How did you hear about this book?

- ❒ Book review (name) ____________
- ❒ Advertisement (name) ____________
- ❒ Recommendation ____________
- ❒ Catalog ____________
- ❒ Other ____________

Where did you buy this book?

- ❒ Bookstore (name) ____________ City ____________
- ❒ Computer store (name) ____________
- ❒ Mail order ____________
- ❒ Other ____________

What influenced you in the purchase of this book?

❒ Cover Design ❒ Contents ❒ Other (please specify):

____

How did you rate the overall content of this book?

❒ Excellent ❒ Good ❒ Average ❒ Poor

What did you find most useful about this book? ____________

____

____

What did you find least useful about this book? ____________

____

____

Please add any additional comments. ____________

____

____

What other subjects will you buy a computer book on soon?

____

What is the best computer book you have used this year?

Note: This information will only be used to keep you updated about new Wrox Press titles and will not be used for any other purpose or passed to any other third party.

Note: If you post the bounce back card below in the UK, please send it to:

Wrox Press Limited, Arden House, 1102 Warwick Road,
Acocks Green, Birmingham B27 6HB. UK.

Computer Book Publishers

NO POSTAGE
NECESSARY
IF MAILED
IN THE
UNITED STATES

BUSINESS REPLY MAIL

FIRST CLASS MAIL PERMIT#64 CHICAGO, IL

POSTAGE WILL BE PAID BY ADDRESSEE

WROX PRESS INC.,
29 S. LA SALLE ST.,
SUITE 520
CHICAGO IL 60603-USA